Adventure Guide™ *to*

The
Georgia &
Carolina Coasts
2nd Edition

Blair Howard, Norman Renouf & Kathy Renouf

HUNTER

HUNTER PUBLISHING, INC.
130 Campus Drive, Edison NJ 08818
(732) 225 1900, (800) 255 0343, fax (732) 417 0482

IN CANADA
Ulysses Travel Publications
4176 Saint-Denis
Montreal, Québec H2W 2M5 Canada
☎ 514-843-9882, Ext. 2232 / Fax 514-843-9448

IN EUROPE
Windsor Books International
The Boundary, Wheatley Road, Garsington
Oxford, OX44 9EJ England
☎ 01865-361122; fax 01865-361133

ISBN 1-55650-890-5

© 2000 Hunter Publishing, Inc.

Maps by Lissa K. Dailey, © 2000 Hunter Publishing, Inc.
Cover photo: *Edisto Island, SC. Beachfront homes at sunset.*
Eric Horan/Index Stock

For complete information about the hundreds of other travel guides
offered by Hunter Publishing, visit our Web site at:
www.hunterpublishing.com

4 3 2

Contents

Maps

Coastal Areas of Georgia & The Carolinas

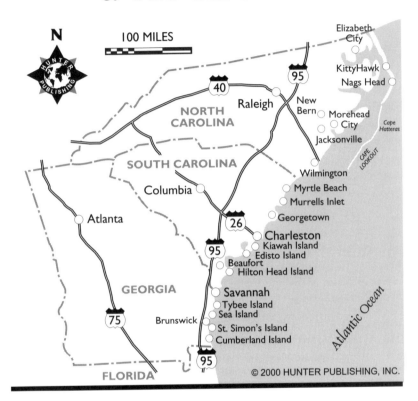

100 MILES

© 2000 HUNTER PUBLISHING, INC.

Introduction

Geography

This book focuses on the narrow strip of land that stretches southward from Virginia Beach, Virginia almost to Jacksonville, Florida: the Low Country and the Barrier Islands that protect it, along with the coastal communities and the great Okefenokee Swamp just to the west. There are more adventures in this region than you can imagine. The tri-state coastal strip represents a world almost unknown to outsiders, except for the resort areas of Savannah, Charleston and

Wilmington. You can still find a deserted beach, wander alone through miles of seemingly virgin forest, sail a small boat on a deserted creek, cast a line into waters that team with fish of every variety, and pick up sand dollars at almost every step. If you love the great outdoors, you'll love the coasts of Georgia and the Carolinas.

The Low Country

Bordered on the west by sandhill ridges and on the east by the barrier islands and the Atlantic Ocean, the Low Country extends from Georgetown South Carolina to St. Marys, Georgia. For more than 200 years, the diversity of flora and fauna found in this region has attracted naturalists, among them such notables as John James Audubon, William Bartram, Mark Catesby and Alexander Wilson.

The Low Country is a flatland of salt marshes, meandering creeks, inlets, coves and peninsulas. Moss-laden live oaks cast friendly shade, and the melodious call of the oyster catcher or the cry of a great blue heron echoes over the calm waters of the salt marsh creeks, creating a sense of serenity found almost nowhere else. It's a tidal land, often ravaged by stormy weather, where the usually gentle tides fill and drain the ponds, flats, and backwaters among acres of lush marsh grass.

The wind blows constantly and rustles the palm fronds and the tendrils of Spanish moss that seem to hang from every branch. The silence of the great outdoors is occasionally broken by the lonely cry of a wheeling gull.

Wildlife

 In the forests, the mammal community includes black bears, American alligators, white-tailed deer, foxes and raccoons.

The animal with highest profile, and the one you are most likely to see, is the black bear. Except in the Great Smoky Mountains National Park, the black bear is a timid creature. Protected only in the state parks, it keeps to itself, though it sometimes strays into populated areas where it forages for food.

White-tailed deer can be found in many forested coastal areas, but are most plentiful in the Croatan and Francis Marion National Forests. You're most likely to see them in the early morning or late afternoon on the edge of the woodlands or in the bordering fields.

The variety of birds that make a home in the Low Country is growing as species are pushed out of their natural habitats farther north. During the winter months, thousands of waterfowl mallards, pintails, teal and many other species of ducks migrate to the area, joining resident wood ducks on the coastal waterways and refuges. In the spring and fall, songbirds and shorebirds visit on their long flights to and from nesting grounds in the north. In the summertime, magnolias blossom, Spanish moss thickens, the oaks take on new vitality, and the resurrection fern seems reborn with each rain. There's always action here: alligators trying to avoid the heat of the noonday sun dig deep swampy dens; the deer in the woodlands graze the afternoon hours away; in the evening, the loggerhead turtles struggle up the beach from the depths of the ocean to lay their eggs, then, worn out from their exertions, struggle back through the sand to the deep waters of the Atlantic.

Climate

 The tri-state region falls into two distinct climatic zones. North Carolina is in the temperate zone, while South Carolina and Georgia are decidedly subtropical. This means you can count on good weather along the coast virtually year- round. The winters can be very cold on the Outer Banks, but January and February can be quite pleasant just a few miles south. Summers are hot and steamy almost everywhere. The beaches are crowded, the seas dotted with boats of all shapes and sizes, and the trails, even some of the more remote ones, are often bustling.

Major Cities

There are three major metropolitan areas along the tri-state coastline: Wilmington, North Carolina; Charleston, South Carolina; and Savannah, Georgia. They are packed with opportunities for urban adventure: sightseeing, fine dining, shopping, walking, and day tripping into the beautiful countryside.

Getting Around

 Getting around in the coastal region of the three states is relatively easy. Two major routes I-95 and US Highway 17 traverse the entire area. I-95 provides the quickest and most direct route north and south, while Highway 17, often called the Ocean Highway, offers a more leisurely, certainly more scenic, route through the coastal towns and villages. While I-95 is the fastest route from one place to another, Highway 17 is the most direct route to all the historic sites, seaside resorts, barrier islands, and outdoor retreats.

Your drive southward on I-95 begins inland on the North Carolina/ Virginia border at Roanoke Rapids. From there it angles eastward until it reaches the coast at Charleston, South Carolina, and then follows the coastline through Georgia into Florida.

Highway 17 takes you much closer to the coastline. It crosses from Virginia into North Carolina near Elizabeth City, continues due south to New Bern on the edge of the Croatan National Forest, and then hugs the shoreline through Wilmington and Myrtle Beach all the way into Charleston. It breaks westward, skirting St. Helena and Port Royal sounds, and then turns southeast again into Savannah. From there it parallels I-95 all the way to Florida and beyond.

Airports

Key airports serving the area are Raleigh/Durham, North Carolina; Charleston and Myrtle Beach, South Carolina; Savannah, Georgia; and Jacksonville, Florida. Scheduled service is also provided to a number of smaller, regional airports, including Kitty Hawk, Beaufort, Hatteras, Mount Olive and South Brunswick in North Carolina; Florence in South Carolina; and Brunswick in Georgia.

Buslines

Service into all three major cities and most of the smaller ones is provided by **Greyhound/Trailways Buslines**, ☎ 800-231-2222.

Railroad

Amtrak provides service north and south, paralleling I-95 to Myrtle Beach, Charleston, Savannah, and Jacksonville in Florida. ☎ 800-USA-RAIL.

RV & Trailer Rentals

Cruise America has a fleet of trailers and RVs that range in size from 15-36 ft. In the low season, you can rent a 23-ft RV to sleep five people for as little as $800 per week, including insurance. A 31-ft top-of-the-line luxury motorhome to sleep six will cost you about $1,200 per week. You'll be required to leave a refundable deposit, depending upon the rental package you choose, of either $100 or $500. Cruise America (☎ 800-327-7778) has branches in most major cities throughout the country.

Maps

A detailed map is essential for adventuring, especially if you're a hiker. As far as this book is concerned, only two sources offer maps that fully meet our needs. Forget the popular road atlases. They are fine if you intend to travel only the main highways. But adventuring means leaving the beaten path. Go to a bookstore and purchase *Delorme's North Carolina Atlas*, a highly detailed, topographical atlas, 88 pages, size 15½ x 11, $16.95. Many hiking trails, most of the smallest forest roads, canoe trails and some fishing locations are shown, along with the locations of state parks, National Parks, historic sites and areas of interest. If you can't get it at your local bookstore, you can contact Delorme Mapping direct (PO Box 298, Freeport ME 04032, ☎ 207- 865-4171).

The second type of map we recommend is the **"quad" map**, available only from the National Forest Service. These highly detailed, sectional maps show even greater detail than the Delorme atlases, but the size isn't as handy and they don't give any consumer information. Hikers, however, will find that the quad maps soon become a necessity.

Quad maps can be purchased from any National Forest Service Supervisor's Office.

Safety

■ Personal Security

Personal security in the cities, as well as in the great outdoors, is a matter of common sense. Stay alert at all times. If you need directions, go to a gas station or convenience store. Carrying mace, pepper spray, or a personal siren is a good idea. Firearms are prohibited in most national and state parks, but are permitted, provided you have the proper licenses, in the National Forests.

Carjacking is a growing problem in Wilmington, Charleston and Savannah. Keep your vehicle doors locked at all times, especially at stoplights. Never pick up hitchhikers. At rest stops and welcome centers, keep a sharp lookout for suspicious characters; stay inside your car until they are gone. It's a good idea to keep a cellular phone handy. Emergency 911 service is available almost everywhere.

Be careful inside public restrooms. Don't leave purses, pocketbooks, bags or any other tempting articles beside the washbasins.

It's a good idea to invest in traveler's checks.

Leave jewelry at home.

■ Animals

Wild animals should not be a problem, if you keep your distance and don't try to feed them. Only the **black bear** and the **alligator** are really dangerous.

To see a bear, even at a distance, is a rare delight. To see one close-up and angry is something else. The cubs are delightful little creatures. Playful, full of fun and curiosity, they will often wander close. Beware. Wherever there's a cub you can be sure mama bear is nearby with ears cocked, ready to defend her young with her life.

Don't give wild animals the opportunity to feed themselves; a scrounging bear is a clever and resourceful creature. Somehow they can identify a brightly colored backpack, and will not hesitate to raid it. Hang packs and food containers from a high branch, at least six feet off the ground. Make sure that the branch will not support the weight of even a small bear. Small animals will also invade your pack or food supply if they can reach it.

Always remember the forests are their homes, not yours. You are a visitor. Treat all wild animals with respect.

Alligators are not picky eaters and will attack almost anything that moves: turtles, snakes, raccoons, fish, deer, other alligators and, of course, humans. They appear lazy and sluggish, but they are alert and can move like lightning on land or in water. The jaws of a full-grown alligator are extremely strong and can easily crush the shell of a large turtle. Males can grow to 11-12 ft and specimens in excess of 17 ft are not unknown. A running alligator reaches speeds over 20 mph.

■ Insects

Insects can be a problem. The forests, swamps and wetlands along the east coast are home to all sorts of winged and creepy, crawly, stinging creatures. They are naturally attracted to the flowers and foliage of the forests, rivers and lakes. Unfortunately, they will also be attracted to you. Check with your doctor or pharmacist for any allergy medication or insect repellent you may need.

Mosquito concentrations are heaviest in the summer months, especially during the evening hours and the farther south you go. Wear a lightweight, long-sleeved shirt or blouse and pants and insect repellent.

Other venomous insects you're likely to encounter are the **fire ant**, the **honeybee**, the **yellow jacket** and the **hornet**. Only in cases where there's an allergy will professional treatment be required; calamine lotion will usually help ease the pain.

More annoying than dangerous are the **deerflies** that live in the forests, **chiggers**, the nasty little red bugs that inhabit the dense bushy areas in the summertime, and ticks.

Insect-Borne Diseases

Unfortunately, **ticks** are becoming a fact of life almost everywhere, but especially so in the woodlands, forests, wetlands and swamps of the coastal plain. Diseases are carried by some and can be inflicted upon humans.

Lyme disease is rapidly becoming a problem in the Smokies, and Rocky Mountain spotted fever has been around for a long time. Both are carried by ticks, and can have a devastating effect upon those that contract them. Anyone venturing into heavily wooded areas needs to be extremely careful.

Rocky Mountain spotted fever is the result of toxins from the bite of the American dog tick found in vast numbers throughout the area. Rocky Mountain spotted fever can be fatal if not treated quickly.

Lyme disease is a tick-borne viral infection for which there is no cure or vaccination. It need not be fatal. A program of antibiotics will keep the disease in check until the immune system can build up antibodies to cope with it.

The symptoms of lyme disease are similar to many other illnesses: low-grade fever, fatigue, head and body pain. The tick bite itself may at first go unnoticed, but, within a month of being bitten, a red rash may appear around the bite. Sometimes the rash is a solid red, sometimes it has a brighter outer edge with little or no color in the middle. Although the rash can vary in size, it usually is about four inches in diameter.

A blood test will usually confirm the disease by detecting antibodies in the immune system, but it can take as long as two months before those antibodies begin to appear.

Precautions

- You're most likely to get bitten in wooded areas where the deer tick lives. That's not the only source: your pet, good friend that he is, can carry the tick to you. Decrease the chances of this happening by using a tick spray, dip, powder or collar to keep them off your pet.

- Wear proper clothing when venturing out into the forests or woodlands – long-sleeved shirts, long pants and a hat. Use repellents and tuck your pants into high socks to keep ticks from crawling under your clothes.

- Keep shoes and boots tightly laced.

- Wear light-colored clothing; it will be easier to spot ticks before they can crawl into an open neck or button hole.

- Wear collared shirts to help stop ticks from crawling onto your neck.

- Check your clothing after an outing. The deer tick is small, often no bigger than a large pinhead, and can be difficult to see.

- If you find a tick attached to your skin, don't try any of the old home remedies for removing it. The application of a lighted cigarette may cause it to regurgitate fluid back into your body, thus causing infection. Use fine-jawed tweezers to grip the tick as gently as possible next to your skin. Do not squeeze the tick's body; you will inject its fluids into the bite.

- There are many good repellents on the market, but the strongest, and therefore the most effective, contain an agent called DEET. It is suggested that you use only repellents with a DEET content of less than 20%; the chemical in stronger concentrations can cause itching and burning.

- Best of all are the proprietary brands of skin softeners, such as Avon's Skin-So-Soft, a product that was used extensively against all sorts of flying bugs and pests during the Gulf War. It smells nice and won't cause burning or itching.

■ Spiders

There are a great many spiders that make their homes in the coastal regions, and some of them bite. There are, however, only two venomous spiders you'll need to watch out for: the **brown recluse** and the **black widow**. Most spider venoms are not harmful to humans, but these two are exceptions, and the brown recluse is the deadliest of all North American spiders. The venom produced by the brown recluse is necrotic. It produces a local swelling and death of tissues around the area where the poison was injected.

The black widow's venom contains neurotoxins that affect the transmission of nerve impulses. The black widow lives in old wooden buildings, on dead logs, wooden benches and picnic tables. It is easily recognized by its jet black color, large bulbous body and distinctive red hourglass-shaped mark on its underside.

The brown recluse makes its home in out-of-the-way nooks and crannies: dusty places, in the roofs of old buildings, garages, shelters, and outhouses. It's slightly smaller than the black widow, but has the same characteristic long legs. Its color varies from a light fawn to a dark chocolate brown.

If you are bitten by either spider you should go immediately to the nearest emergency room for treatment. Many National Park and Forest Ranger Stations can offer immediate first aid, but expert treatment is essential.

■ Snakes

Most members of the pit viper family you should be aware of and stay away from: the **copperhead**, **water moccasin**, **cottonmouth**, Eeastern diamondback rattlesnake and the **timber rattlesnake**. The copperhead, diamondback and timber rattlesnake are fairly common and found throughout most of the forests. The cottonmouth can be found almost everywhere but, like the water moccasin, it often frequents swamps, riverbanks and lake shores. Farther south, you may run across the **coral snake**; watch out for it.

Avoiding Snakebites

- Watch where you step.
- Never put your hands into nooks and crannies or other rocky places. Never go barefoot.
- Sleep up off the ground.
- If you or someone in your party is bitten, administer first aid (do not apply a tourniquet) and transport the victim immediately to the nearest hospital. If you are by yourself, go immediately for help, but try to avoid exerting yourself.

■ Boating

Of all outdoor pastimes, boating seems to be the one in which the most accidents occur. Obey all boating regulations, speed limits and motor restrictions when on the water, especially when traveling around other boats.

- Always handle and store boat fuel and oil properly.
- Never drink and drive. The laws that apply on the road also apply on the water. More than 50% of all boating fatalities are alcohol-related.
- Always wear a life jacket. Four out of five deaths on the water are caused by drowning. Federal law now requires that every boat carry one personal flotation device per passenger. It takes only one unexpected wave from the wake of another boat or a waterlogged branch to throw you into the water. A bang on the head or the sudden shock of cold water can render you helpless.
- Clear water weeds from boats, motors and trailers immediately after returning to the ramp so that you won't spread them to other lakes and rivers.

■ Diving & Snorkeling

It's taken for granted that experienced divers will know of the dangers of diving. Those diving or snorkeling for the first time, however, should be aware that the "deep" is at its most dangerous when diving alone. Always dive with a companion.

- Use **dive flags** when snorkeling or diving.

- Check local **weather** conditions before you dive; it's also a good idea to check with local dive operators.

- **Sharks** are sometimes present off the coasts. Smaller ones may come inshore to a depth as shallow as two feet. It is rare, but it does happen, that swimmers are attacked. Never go into the water if you have an open cut or scrape. Sharks can detect blood from a great distance.

- **Jellyfish** are transparent and difficult to see. They inhabit the inshore waters everywhere; most are harmless. There are, however, some that are not, especially the Portuguese Man-o-War, which is prevalent in the Atlantic. Avoid all jellyfish if you can.

- **Sea urchins** are the spiky little black balls that lie on the sandy ocean floor or in the nooks and crannies among the rocks. Step on one with bare feet at your peril. The spines are brittle, often barbed, and will give you a very nasty sting. Fortunately, urchins are easily seen.

Treatment for Stings

If you do happen to get stung by a jellyfish or urchin you can treat the sting with vinegar to neutralize the stinging cells, then visit the local drug store to get something for the pain. Emergency treatment at a hospital might be necessary for a sting by a Portuguese Man-o-War.

■ The Outdoors

Streams & Creeks

The coastal plain is the land of a thousand beautiful streams, creeks and rivers. Unfortunately, they can be dangerous. After a rainfall, water levels rise quickly and once-shallow streams turn into impassable torrents. There's always someone who thinks he can make it across, whatever the state of the water. Water-worn rocks are smooth and slippery, often overgrown with a fine layer of moss or algae, slimey and treacherous. One false step and you're in the water. If you don't receive a nasty crack on the head, arm, hip or knee, you'll get wet, or you could be swept away in a torrent of whitewater.

The following tips will help keep you out of trouble:

- Always test the water before attempting to cross.

- If you can, use a rope. Loop members of a party together and cross one at a time.

- Stay away from large rocks in the middle of rushing waters; the water around them is often deep and the currents strong.

- Try to step only on dry rock, and be careful of green rocks; dry or not, they can be extremely slippery.

- If someone does take a plunge, especially in winter, dry them quickly and have them change into dry clothing. Many mountain streams and creeks are icy cold, even during the summer months, and hypothermia can be deadly.

Forest Fire

Forest fire is a big problem. Each year, thousands of acres of woodland are lost to fires. Some are the result of arson, some of lightning strikes, but most are caused by careless adventurers. A campfire left smoldering, or a carelessly tossed match or cigarette, can do an untold amount of damage. Make sure fires are completely out. Dowse them with water and then cover them with dirt. It's better not to smoke in the forest, but if you must, use a cigarette lighter and carry your butts out with you.

Thunderstorms

Lightning is something everyone should be concerned with in the forest. If you find yourself caught in a storm in open country, keep moving; don't stand still. Static electricity can build in your body with disastrous results. Remove exposed metal objects from your body. Never shelter under a large tree, and never in a metal-roofed building.

■ Hiking

Although hiking is always a delightful experience, it can be hazardous. The wilderness areas are often vast, forested regions where it's not unusual for hikers to get lost, especially in winter. The victim may be a child that has wandered from a campsite, or simply lagged and strayed from the path. Almost always, the situation could have been avoided if the hiker or the child's parents had adhered to the basics of woodland safety.

If you're new to hiking, you've a lot to learn. There are a number of excellent books to be found in the shops and at your local library that will teach you the ins and outs of hiking. Several come to mind, including *The New Complete Walker III*, by Colin Fletcher; *Backpacking, One Step at a Time*, by Harvey Manning; and *Walk Softly in the Wilderness*, by John Hart. In the meantime, here are some basic rules and hints that even the most experienced hiker would do well to remember.

- **Maps**. Never leave home without one. Maps of the better known hiking trails are available at ranger stations in the National Forests, state parks, bookstores and gift shops. Better yet are the topographical "quad" maps used by geologists and forest rangers. If you can read a road map, you can read a topographical map.

- **Stay on the trail**. The well-maintained trails are clearly marked. Even so, it's easy to take a wrong turn onto a smaller trail, and then onto something that's barely a trail and can lead to real trouble. Stray but a yard or two from the main trail and you'll find it tough to find your way back without the aid of a map and compass. Always plot your progress as you go, take notes, and know your exact position on the map. If you do get lost, don't panic. Stay where you are and don't wander into the woods. Conserve energy and food. If you feel you must move on, stay on the trail and travel by compass in one direction only.

- **Compass**. It goes without saying that a compass will come in handy. If you should happen to stray from the trail, you might have to go five or six miles before you stumble onto another one if you manage to walk a straight line. Maintain a sense of direction at all times.

- **File a hiking plan** with someone you know or at a ranger station just in case you do get lost. Don't forget to call and let them know you've arrived at your destination; if not, they'll be out looking for you.

- **First Aid Kit**. Keep it simple – bandages, elastic wraps, butterfly closures, adhesive tape, aspirin, antihistamines for bee stings, and bug repellent.

- **Knife**. Take along a good hunting knife; either a fixed or folding blade is fine. Buck makes some great outdoor knives, as do Schrade and Case. They are better than

Swiss Army knives with all their bits and pieces. A heavy knife with a strong, sharp blade is all you'll need.

- **Flashlight**. Not needed if you're on a day hike, right? Wrong. Make one wrong turn, and a four-hour hike can quickly turn into an all-night experience. The woodland grows dark much more quickly than does open terrain and the trails become difficult to see, let alone follow. A walk in the dark through unknown territory can be a terrifying experience.

- **Batteries**. Never assume that batteries are good. Always carry at least one spare set.

- **Wet Weather Gear**. You don't necessarily need a full set of rain gear, especially if you're only going on a short hike. A large three- or four-ply garbage bag will do in an emergency and takes up very little space. It might look strange, but it's better to stay dry than to be soaked to the skin, and suffer even further when the rain stops and the sun turns your wet clothing into something a medieval torturer would have been proud to own. For extended hikes, take a poncho or a lightweight rain suit. In the winter, dress appropriately.

- **Matches**. You'll need waterproof matches in addition to your cigarette lighter. Lighter flints can get wet and refuse to work. A small fire can save your life.

- **Hats**. Always wear a hat. It will keep bugs out of your hair and your body heat in. Up to 35% of body heat can be lost through a bare head. During winter a good warm hat could save your life.

- **Snacks**. Rarely regarded as an essential, an extra snack or two can do wonders for your disposition. A candy bar will give you extra energy. Take more than you think you'll need; you won't be sorry.

- **Water**. It's always a good idea to carry plenty of water. Many wilderness streams look pure and inviting, and they may be. Some, however, can be polluted. It's best not to take chances.

- **Camp Stove**. Not essential unless you're staying overnight. You should avoid lighting fires if you can. Forest fires are a potential danger, often destroying thousands of acres at a time.

■ **Waterfalls**. Beautiful, but deceptive, they seem to have a magnetic attraction for all who visit the wilderness. You may want to get a better look. They can be deadly to those who step out of bounds. The rocks are smooth, worn by millions of years of fast water, covered in algae or moss, and thus extremely slippery. One wrong or careless step can send you plummeting to the rocks below.

■ Plants

There are many poisonous plants indigenous to the coastal plain. At least a dozen of them, including some species of mushrooms, are deadly if ingested; a great many more will cause nasty skin rashes. Especially deadly are the **jimson weed** – which can cause coma and even death – and most members of the **nightshade** family.

Poison oak and **poison ivy**, along with several other varieties of poisonous creepers, proliferate throughout the forests. They can cause a nasty, inflamed rash. Some people are more sensitive to the stinging plants than others; some have no reaction. If you're venturing into the woodlands, learn to identify them. Their most distinctive feature is a characteristic three-leaf arrangement.

To avoid problems, assume that everything is poisonous. Don't put anything into your mouth; not even if you're sure you know what it is. Don't touch plants you can't identify. Don't pick flowers.

Even the most experienced adventurer may fall victim to curiosity or misidentification. A victim of poisoning should quickly drink two or three glasses of water to dilute the poison, then vomiting should be induced – syrup of ipecac works well – and transported to the nearest emergency room with a sample of the poisonous plant.

■ Sunburn

Carry a good sunscreen. Check with your pharmacist to ensure the proper SPF (sun protection factor) for your skin type.

History

 This section of the East Coast has always been popular with adventurers. Giovanni da Verrazano was the first European to explore the tri-state coastline in 1524. A Florentine in the employ of France, he was impressed by the wealth of natural resources he found. Meanwhile, Spain had been maintaining a presence farther south since 1513 and, on hearing of Verrazano's successes, redoubled its efforts to claim all of the New World. In 1525, Spanish explorers ventured northward along the coast to Cape Fear. Hernando de Soto, traveling from his base in Florida, also struck northward, arriving in western North Carolina in 1540. Spain's earliest efforts at colonization, though extensive, were not successful. The settlement established at Cape Fear in 1525 failed and it wasn't until they had managed to establish a strong foothold at St. Augustine in Florida that annexation became practical. It was only a matter of time before the conquistadors began to spread Spanish interests north, south and west. By late 1526, moving northward along the coast from one island to another, they had established forts and missions up to what is now known as Parris Island; they called it Santa Elena.

Unfortunately, the lines of communication were too long. Santa Elena was more than 200 miles from the Spanish base at St. Augustine, and the fort, under almost constant Indian attack, was abandoned in 1586. Slowly, the other northern coastal outposts followed suit until only Santa Catalina de Guale on what is now St. Catherine's Island in Georgia remained. It too was abandoned when British adventurers arrived in 1683.

The British were aggressive from the beginning in their intentions to annex the tri-state region. Their first efforts at colonization began in North Carolina – at that time part of Virginia – but were unsuccessful. Following the establishment of Jamestown in Virginia, settlers began to move southward. Charleston, South Carolina was settled first. From there, Scottish and Welsh pioneers pushed the borders of the new colony outward, first to Cape Fear, North Carolina, where they established the plantations that would supply provisions to the British Navy, and then into Georgia where they built a fort at Darien.

■ Pillaging in the New World

Britain's colonies in the New World, after the first disastrous years at Jamestown, were successful and profitable. Great houses and plantations were established and soon a steady flow of valuable staples began arriving in British home ports: tobacco, sea island cotton, hemp, rice and indigo. The new prosperity brought more settlers from England and the colony continued to grow. But the rich cargoes going from the New World to Europe were attractive to adventurers of a different kind. Throughout the 17th and early 18th centuries, pirates, corsairs, brigands, ne'r-do-wells and privateers, all drawn by the promise of easy pickings and quick riches, flocked to the seas off the East Coast by the thousands. Men like Edward Teach (Blackbeard), "Calico Jack" Rackham, Henry Morgan, Captain Kid, Major Stede Bonnet, and even nefarious female buccaneers Anne Bonney (Calico Jack's mistress) and Mary Reed, scoured the ocean in search of vulnerable merchant ships. Only slightly better were the so-called privateers, the likes of Francis Drake and John Hawkins, whose expeditions were financed by cartels of private investors – often kings and queens. The privateers usually raped, pillaged and plundered in the name of whichever sovereign happened to be on the throne at the time. While most made their dubious livings on the high seas, when the action was slow they came ashore to pillage coastal communities too weak to defend themselves. Sir Francis Drake laid waste to St. Augustine as early as 1586.

■ The Demise of Buccaneering

The end of buccaneering came early in the 18th century. For years the coast of North Carolina had been a hotbed of piracy. Blackbeard made his headquarters in Pamlico Sound, while Major Stede Bonnet made his at Cape Fear. Bonnet, a wealthy French landowner from Barbados, turned to piracy simply for the adventure. He took to the high seas in a 10-gun sloop, the *Revenge*, in 1717 and began raiding merchant ships off the Virginia coast. His career was short. He was hanged in November 1718.

Blackbeard also met his end on November 21, 1718, when a British warship under the command of Robert Maynard cornered him off the coast of Virginia and engaged his crew in a fierce battle that raged for several hours. During the fray Blackbeard received more than 25 sword and pistol wounds, but he fought until he dropped dead on his own quarter deck. His head was severed from his body and carried to Hampton, Virginia, where it was mounted on a pole and raised at the entrance to the harbor.

Captain John Rackham, called "Calico Jack" for the patterned trousers he wore, was a pirate captain from 1718 to 1720. During this short time he plundered many ships. He and his men were captured and brought to trial at St. Jago de la Vega, Jamaica. Among Rackham's crew were his mistress, Anne Bonney, and Mary Read. They are the only female pirates on record. Rackham, along with Read, was hanged in Port Royal on November 17, 1720. It was the end of an era.

The pirates were gone, but the legends remained. Even today, the stories of buried treasure on the barrier islands from Kitty Hawk, North Carolina to Cumberland Island off southern Georgia make interesting reading, but the riches remain undiscovered.

■ Fall & Rise of the South

By the outbreak of the Civil War at Fort Sumter in Charleston, South Carolina, the islands and coastal plain were dominated by great cotton and rice plantations, the product of grand dreams and slavery. The Union blockade of the Confederate coastline was one of the most significant successes of the war. Many of the islands were occupied by Union forces, and slowly the great plantations declined. By 1865 the tri-state coastline had become a wasteland.

After the war, with the advent of Reconstruction, it was the ports that helped revive Southern fortunes. Then the fishing and farming industries began to flourish once more until, by the turn of the century, the South had risen again. Wealthy industrialists from the North and Midwest bought vast tracts of land and even some of the barrier islands along the coastal plain to use as private hunting and fishing retreats. Following World War I, yet another kind of industry came to the region – tourism.

The Georgia & Carolina Coasts Today

Today, the entire area is one long chain of tourist attractions: historic sites, towns and cities, old forts, resorts, beaches and magificent plantations and, in the sea, the remains of a thousand shipwrecks. The narrow strip of land that borders the Atlantic is a vacation seashore. In North Carolina, the Outer Banks are a haven for lovers of the great outdoors – *the* place to go camping, play golf and tennis, go beachcombing, birdwatching, scuba and wreck diving, honeymooning, or simply lounging. In South Carolina, one resort runs into the next, virtually uninterrupted all the way to Savannah. From Savannah southward, the Golden Isles form a chain of white dunes, rolling hammocks of seagrass and oats, marshes and old-growth trees hung with moss, all of which provide a home to more than 300 species of shore and marine wildlife. The area has some of the most popular vacation retreats on the eastern seaboard.

How To Use This Book

Each geographical region is described with a detailed report of attractions and adventures, camping, hotels, dining, and information services to be found within each area. The listings for restaurants, campgrounds and accommodations are not always recommendations. In some instances they are short descriptions of the facilities – an indication of what's available.

■ Hotel Reservation Terms

When it comes to making reservations, hotel employees talk a different language than the rest of us. Some of the terms used may mean something different than what you might expect. The following may make things a little clearer.

- **Oceanview** means exactly what it implies, a view of the ocean, not a room on the oceanfront. Your room may be at the top of a hill and the ocean a tiny blue speck in the distance. When making your reservation, be sure to ask exactly what they mean by the term.

- **Oceanfront** means the room or property faces directly onto the ocean, and is usually located on the ocean side of the street.

- The terms **forestside**, **courtside**, **streetside**, and **poolside** are self-explanatory.

- An **efficiency** is minimally equipped to prepare and serve meals. The minimum includes, but is not limited to, a stove, refrigerator, sink, and appropriate cooking and serving utensils.

- **American Plan (AP)** means with three meals.

- **Modified American Plan (MAP)** means with two meals, usually breakfast and dinner.

- **European Plan (EP)** means without meals.

Adventures

The Nature of Adventure

Adventure means different things to different people. To some it means whale watching off the icy coast of Antarctica, a safari through the jungles of the Amazon, hiking snow-covered trails in Alaska, or diving among sharks on the Great Barrier Reef in Australia. To others it means a day of shopping in a suburban mall, fine dining, or simply lounging in the sunshine beside the pool at a luxury hotel. These activities are all available along the coasts of Georgia and the Carolinas. True, the snows are not as frequent or the drifts as deep as in Nome, but the ocean is just as inviting as in Florida or California, and the jungles of the National Forests and wildlife refuges can hold as many adventures as those in Central America. You won't be disappointed.

Adventure for most people does mean an excursion into the great outdoors: hiking, fishing, scuba diving, snorkeling, boating or horseback riding. A large portion of this book is devoted to that type of experience. But here on the mid-Atlantic coast, adventure can mean much more than outdoor recreation. This is an area rich in history and culture, home to some of the most delightful and intriguing towns and cities in the nation. Adventure here can also mean sightseeing. It can mean driving the backcountry roads in search of an exciting new experience. It can mean shopping: antique stores, gift shops and craft fairs that abound throughout the region, not to mention some of the finest shopping malls in the southeastern United States. And, for the gourmet adventurer, it can also mean fine dining and luxury hotels.

While this book is a guide to the more conventional outdoor adventures, it's also a guide for those who would rather spend their time in relative comfort, within the bounds of civilization, close to the shops, stores, restaurants and attractions that have made places like Hilton Head, Charleston, and Savannah famous.

■ Antiquing & Craft Hunting

The antique business is popular throughout the tri-state region. You'll find shops and stores on every street in every small town, and on almost every backcountry road. If antiquing means adventure to you, then you will be thrilled. Check the newspapers in each area for auctions, sales, and shops.

Like antiques, country crafts are a very big business. The old skills have been passed from generation to generation, and everything from handmade country furniture to tiny wooden, glass and fabric gifts is available at reasonable prices. Goodies can be bought anywhere and everywhere: craft festivals, roadside stores, flea markets and even garage sales.

■ Boating

 Boating is perhaps the most popular outdoor sport in the area. You'll find many opportunities – along with the locations of public access boat ramps and docks – listed within each geographic section.

Boating is allowed on most of the larger lakes, and to a lesser extent on smaller lakes where motor restrictions may apply.

■ Birdwatching

 More than 150 species of wild birds make their homes in the woods, forests, and hammocks along the East Coast. Bird lovers can expect to see red-tailed hawks, ospreys (fish hawks), pelicans, ruffed grouse, wild turkey, five types of owl, vultures, ravens, blue herons, a wide variety of warblers, seven species of woodpeckers, a variety of gulls and other sea birds. If you're lucky, you may see such rare birds as the eastern screech owl, the endangered red-cockaded woodpecker, the hooded warbler, golden eagle, peregrine falcon or even a bald eagle.

Birding is best in the early morning. Find a spot and remain still and quiet. Be sure to take a good field guide, binoculars and a notebook. The optimal months are April and May, and September and October; May is best of all.

■ Camping

Camping is very much a part of the East Coast experience, and a number of options are available.

First, there are the commercial campgrounds. These vary in size, quality of service, and amenities from one operator to another. Then there are the state and National Park campgrounds. While most of them may not have the level of luxury of large commercial operations, some offer facilities and recreational opportunities that rival those in private campgrounds, including some extra opportunities that the commercial grounds don't have: group camping, youth camping and primitive camping.

Commercial Campgrounds

Profit is the motivating force at commercial campgrounds. Large or small, they are in business to make money, and that's good for the camper. Competition – and there's a lot of it – means the commercial campgrounds are constantly striving to improve facilities, services and recreational opportunities. Commercial campgrounds are usually clean, tidy and well cared for. Security in the smaller campgrounds often leaves a lot to be desired, but it's taken much more seriously at the larger establishments where gates are manned 24 hours a day and on-site personnel patrol the grounds.

Most of the larger campgrounds are self-sufficient, offering amenities ranging from laundromats to full-service shops and stores, to marinas and restaurants. Some do not allow tents, catering only to campers with RVs or trailers. Many have rental units available: RVs, trailers, cabins, etc. Many more offer rental bicycles, boats, paddle boats, and canoes. Larger campgrounds will have staff on hand to look after your needs around the clock; smaller ones might have staff available only for check-in during the daylight hours. Most will have a list of rules and regulations that restrict pets, alcohol, and noise and activities after dark.

KOA Kabins

These are rustic wooden cabins at most commercial KOA campgrounds that provide some of the comforts of home and all the fun of camping out. Each Kabin sleeps at least four, has an outdoor grill and picnic table, and campers have full use of the campground's amenities and services: hot showers, flush toilets, laundry, convenience store and recreational facilities.

National Forest Campgrounds

There are many campgrounds located in the National Forests on the East Coast. Facilities at most are rarely as extensive as they are at their sister state park units. Some are downright basic – no hookups, hand-pumped water, and so on. If you're one of those die-hard primitive campers that likes to get down and dirty, you'll find yourself at home in the National Parks.

Most of the campgrounds are fairly small, but they are well kept, clean, and often far from the busy highways and noisy commercial attractions. If you don't mind roughing it a little, the National Forest campgrounds offer great value for money. Be sure to take what you need; service outlets can be many miles away from your campground.

State Park Campgrounds

Dozens of state parks and forests are scattered along the coastal plain. Many offer a range of facilities and recreational opportunities that rival those of their privately owned competitors; almost all host camping opportunities that the commercial establishments don't – primitive camping, hiking trails, and lakes for fishing and boating. As you might expect, although many state parks are near major cites, camping is almost always a wilderness experience.

Fees vary from park to park, depending on the available facilities, but you'll always find them reasonable – often less than half the price of a comparable commercial campground.

While most state park grounds don't offer full-service hookups (which include sewer), they do offer water and electricity for tents, trailers and RV campers, and a dumping station somewhere on the property. Restrooms and bathhouses have hot showers and flush toilets, and all state park facilities are handicapped-accessible.

Group camping and youth camping are offered at most state parks in designated areas. Youth facilities are for use by non-profit organizations, while group facilities are for family reunions and gatherings of friends. Facilities in group camping areas vary throughout the park system, from full-service group cabins to limited accommodations.

Primitive camping is also available at most state parks. Overnight backpacking and canoeing into these areas is strictly for the physically fit, experienced outdoor enthusiast.

For campers who like a roof overhead, many state parks offer a variety of rustic cottages and cabins that sleep four to six persons. These locations are identified in the individual park listings. Some of the cabins feature the rustic appeal of the original Civilian Conservation Corps construction; others are more contemporary, with a full range of modern amenities.

Vacation cabins are a little more luxurious than the camping cabins. Usually, they provide all the comforts of home, including private baths and kitchens. The facilities in these cabins vary from park to park, but typically sleep up to six and may offer fireplaces and/or air conditioning.

Group cabins offer sleeping facilities in groups of units, or in large dormatories. They usually feature fully equipped kitchens, dining rooms, and/or meeting spaces.

Reservations for cabin rentals usually will be accepted up to one year in advance with a deposit equal to a two-night stay. Calls for reservations should be made between 8 AM and 5 PM, Monday through Friday.

Like camping fees, cabin rental fees vary from park to park according to season and the type of facilities offered, and are subject to change.

Accessibility

Most of the campgrounds, state, national and commercial, are easily accessible. Access to some of the more primitive locations within the national and state parks does, however, require lengthy and often strenuous hikes. Campers going primitive must be in good physical shape.

Availability

At times, availability of campsites can be a problem, especially in the spring and early fall. Book your site as far in advance as possible to ensure a berth at your campground of choice.

The high season for camping on the East Coast seems to begin when the first blooms of spring appear and ends when the last leaf has fallen in early November. Die-hard campers can still be found roughing it when the snow is two feet deep in the forests.

The most popular campgrounds stay heavily booked throughout spring, summer and fall. When the schools are out, and on most major holidays, like Easter, Labor Day and Christmas, it's almost impossible to find a berth at any of the larger commercial grounds. And you can bet the choice sites at the state parks, allocated either by reservation or on a first-come, first-served basis, will almost always be occupied.

If you're looking for a cabin, you should choose your location as far in advance as possible, and then book your reservation immediately; many are reserved up to a year in advance.

Costs

Commercial. Costs vary from campground to campground from around $16 per night for a basic site with few frills to a high of $50 for a site with all the amenities, including private deck, table and chairs.

State Parks. Costs at state parks are much more predictable. You'll pay between $8 and $16 per night for your site, depending upon the location and the season. A waterfront site may cost you an extra $2 per night; use of the boat ramp could cost $2-$4 more. Rental cabins at state parks can cost – depending on the location and the season – anywhere from $15-$100 per night.

Camping fees for **senior or disabled** visitors are usually discounted, often as much as 50%.

Primitive camping costs run from zero to about $5 per person per night; $2 for persons under 18.

National Forests. Rates vary from forest to forest. Generally, the lower the fee, the fewer the facilities. Electrical and sewage hookups are practically nonexistent and most National Forest campgrounds do not have hot showers (some don't even have piped water). Most campgrounds have flush toilets and the facilities are generally handicapped-accessible.

National Forest fees range from free to a high of $20. Tent camping for single units with capacity of up to five people starts at around $5 per night. Where group camping is available, the fee for a minimum group of at least 30 people is usually around $25.

Credit Cards

Credit cards are accepted at most commercial and some state park campgrounds throughout the region.

Length Of Stay

Commercial. There are no restrictions at commercial campgrounds. You can visit for as long as you like.

State Parks. Maximum of two weeks.

National Parks. Fourteen days out of any one 30-day period.

Pets

Pets are not permitted in the camping areas at most state parks.

Pets are welcome in National Park campgrounds but must be kept quiet and on a leash.

Pets are welcome at some commercial campgrounds.

It is unlawful in all three states to leave pets in your vehicle, locked or not.

Security

Most of the campgrounds listed in this book maintain good security and have the safety of their guests in mind. Most state parks are gated and locked at night.

Many commercial campgrounds are not gated. They usually have on-site staff working security around the clock. Even so, it pays to be extra careful.

■ Canoeing & Kayaking

 Numerous opportunities for paddling exist here. These range from quiet lakes to wide rivers; fast-running whitewaters to the open sea. Some of the routes pass through state and National Parks, some through the great National Forests. Some are in controlled waters where the levels rise and fall with the opening and closing of a dam. The canoe trails described in this book are in scenic country, some of it considered to be among the most spectacular in the nation.

Canoes and kayaks, along with basic instruction, are available for rent at most whitewater outfitters and at some coastal locations. Many offer vacation packages that include not only rafting or kayaking, but horseback riding, and hayrides, too.

While the coastal areas, lakes, streams and rivers offer hundreds of miles of canoeing possibilities, most of the waters open to canoes are also open to other users, including anglers, motorboaters, and waterskiers. In most areas, the waterways are publicly owned, but in some places the riverbanks belong to private individuals and are not open to public use. Canoe and adventure outposts will equip you for a canoe trip, pick you up at your exit point, and shuttle you back to your car.

■ Diving & Snorkeling

 From Sanderling, North Carolina to Jekyll Island, Georgia, the East Coast offers hundreds, even thousands of opportunities for diving and snorkeling. Unfortunately, due to wind and tides, the waters can become quite murky, and visibility is diminished. Farther from shore, however, the water is clear and the visibility much better. Diving is at its best when the winds are light, usually during the summer and fall.

More than 4,000 shipwrecks lie beneath the waters off the East Coast. Dozens of certified dive operators will take you exploring. They also provide diving instruction, excursions, tours, rental gear and valuable information – technical and geographic.

Snorkeling and diving are important and popular activities on the East Coast. Those who think they're too old, or that diving is not the sport for them, and those who feel that it might be but can't quite pluck up the courage to give it a try, should reconsider – it's never too late, it's easy, and you're missing the experience of a lifetime. Almost every city in the United States has at least one outdoor adventure company that will teach you the sport quickly, usually in comfort at the local YMCA or YWCA, and at reasonable cost. On the coast itself, there are many dive operators that offer instruction packages where you can learn the basics in an afternoon. Even the poorest swimmer can snorkel in shallow waters.

■ Fall & Spring Color

Autumn, when the days are clear and sunny and the nights cool and crisp, irresistibly lures millions of visitors to the parks and forests of the East Coast. The woodland trails are a riot of gold, amber, yellow, copper and red; the reflections on the surface of the lakes turn the world upside down. Even the streets of the big cities and tiny rural communities blaze with the colors of fall.

Spring, like autumn, also brings something special. Each year, from late March through early June, the forests and woodlands burst into new life. The air fills with the scent of dogwood, honeysuckle, foamflowers, trillium, and lady's-slipper.

■ Festivals & Events

A full schedule of festivals and events, interpretive and environmental demonstrations, and volunteer opportunities abound in this area. The state parks within the region are no exception. Many offer a variety of get-togethers, nature programs, organized walks and hikes, and lectures. There's always something going on.

■ Fishing

From Virginia Beach to Saint Simons Island, Georgia, the saltwater fishing along the East Coast is extremely good. The beaches provide a popular platform, but there are literally hundreds of fishing piers and docks scattered along the coast. From some you may fish for free; some will charge you a couple of dollars for a day. As for deep-sea fishing, you can charter boats at numerous locations and head out in search of the big billfish, tuna and shark.

The fishing spots listed in each section of the book have been selected for a good reason. Some are popular and often crowded; some are not so well known and therefore quite peaceful. Some are easily accessible; some are a little off the beaten path. There are, of course, a great many more places to fish along the East Coast, but to find them you'll have to do some exploring.

Fishing Licenses

Freshwater fishing licenses are required for all persons aged 16 and older. They can be obtained at any local bait or tackle shop, and at any State Wildlife Resources Agency Office. It's also a good idea to check for local regulations that may be in effect.

Deep-Sea Fishing

An expensive but exhilarating pastime, deep-sea fishing is a popular sport in these waters. Boat captains from Virginia Beach to Jacksonville stand ready to take you on board and whisk you out to sea, often 20 miles or more, in search of the big one. The big one is no more prolific anywhere than here. Among the species that populate these waters are the mighty tarpon, sharks of every shape and size, including the hammerhead and tiger shark, tuna, blue marlin, dolphin (the fish, not Flipper), barracuda, amberjack, cobia, black sea bass, king mackerel, swordfish and, the most spectacular of all, the sailfish. Charters are available everywhere for a half-day, full day, or you can charter for several days. Rates, depending upon the location and season, run from $250 for a four-hour trip to as much as $600 for a full 12 hours.

Fishing The Coastal Waters

Almost 600 miles of coast, not to mention the shores of the barrier islands that protect them and the many thousands of miles of streams, provide some of the best coastal fishing waters in the United States. Within these waters, anglers can expect to enjoy their sport at its very best. Aside from the excitement of deep-sea charter fishing, you can hit the surf, marsh creeks, salt river inlets and streams almost anywhere along the coast and have a good day. So, what can you expect to catch?

Atlantic Croaker. This smaller member of the drum family is one of the most abundant coastal fish. It takes the hook readily, and it makes a good meal. There are 13 species of drums and croakers found in these coastal waters; all have the ability to makes sounds. It's rare that you'll catch one that doesn't grunt or croak when taken from the water. Croakers are bottom feeders that live on small crustaceans, clams, snails and other little critters they consider delicacies. The adult croaker found in these waters are about nine-15 inches and weigh a few pounds.

Black Drum. This fish is found along the Atlantic coast from Massachusetts to Argentina, but is most abundant in the warmer waters. Like the Atlantic croaker, it's a bottom feeder with small, sharp teeth in the jaws and large, flat teeth on the floor and roof of the mouth for crushing clams, snails, crabs and other hard-bodied, bottom-dwelling animals. The black drum is the largest of the bony fish you're likely to encounter inshore. Their size ranges from 10 to 40 lbs; the largest on record was from the coast of Florida and weighed 146 lbs. Its color is usually an even black with an overall glossy appearance. It has numerous whiskers. It's not a good table fish.

Flounder. Both the summer and southern flounder are abundant in these waters. They are so similar in appearance that most anglers cannot tell them apart. Like most flatfish, both are adept at changing color to match the bottom on which they happen to be. At birth the eyes are positioned on both sides of the head. During early development, one eye migrates from its normal position to join the other on one side of the head. At this time the flounder gives up its upright swimming position and swims with the eyed-side up. Both species have large mouths with a single row of sharp teeth in both jaws. They are bottom feeders, living on small crustaceans and fish.

Kingfish. Three species of kingfish (whiting, as they are known locally) are found in these waters, all closely related: southern, northern and gulf kingfish. When they are young, the three are difficult to distinguish, but older fish can be easily identified. The gulf kingfish is a plain silver-gray, while the other two have dark bars on their sides. The bars on the southern kingfish are usually less distinct than those on the northern kingfish. These are small fish, reaching a maximum length of about 17 inches and rarely weighing more than three lbs. Those you are likely to catch will be smaller, in the range of ½-1½ lbs. Small though they are, they are tough fighters and abundant along the beaches and barrier islands. They are great table fish, with a distinctive flavor. Lightly sprinkle fillets with salt, pepper and garlic powder and poach in white wine and butter.

Red Drum. This fish is found along the Atlantic and Gulf coasts from Massachusetts to Texas. While it does have some commercial standing, it's sought mostly by anglers as a sport fish. Adult fish are most abundant during the summer months in or just beyond the surf line along the beaches, especially on the barrier islands. During the colder months the fish move offshore and are no longer available to surf fishermen. Adult fish are easily identified by the large eyespot – usually one on each side, but sometimes several – located just in front of the tail, and by its lack of whiskers. Specimens of five feet and 75 lbs have been recorded. Those you are likely to catch will be much smaller, around 10-15 lbs; you might get lucky and hook one as big as 40 lbs.

Sheepshead. This species belongs to a large group called porgies. Several species of porgies are found in these waters – the scup, pinfish, spotted tail pinfish, and the white bony porgy. All are usually found close to the shore, and often in schools. The sheephead shares many of the porgy characteristics. It stays close the bottom, feeding on small crustaceans and fish, is laterally compressed, flattened on both sides and has a steep forehead. It is easily identified from its brother species by seven vertical black bars along the length of the body, and is distinguishable from the young black drum by its lack of whiskers. The biggest porgies found in these waters are around 20 lbs, but those you are likely to catch will weigh five-10 lbs. Small crabs are often used for bait. The sheepshead is a delicious table fish.

Spotted Sea Trout. This is the most sought-after sport fish in the southeastern United States. It's a truly estuarine fish, living all of its life in the river inlets, bays, sounds and creeks along the coastline. Its abundance in the small tidal creeks and rivers makes it available to anglers with small boats. The spotted sea trout is a member of the drum family. It is one of three species that can be found in these waters; the silver sea trout and the weakfish are the other two. The three are easily distinguished from other local fish by slender, streamlined bodies, projecting lower teeth, and one to three sharply pointed teeth projecting from the upper jaw. In addition, the spotted sea trout is easily distinguished by the round black spots scattered all over the upper fins and body. All three species are quite good table fish, but the spotted sea trout is the most popular with anglers. Adult fish are one-two ft and can weigh two-five lbs.

Striped Bass. The "striper" is equally at home in salt- or freshwater, leaving the coastal waters and moving upriver to spawn. It rarely strays far from land. These fish can grow to a considerable size; the largest taken in North Carolina weighed 125 lbs. Fish of 100 lbs are rare, but fish weighing 50-60 lbs are not unusual. Distribution along these coastal waters is uneven. They seem to be confined to the major rivers and the estuaries, and are rarely caught from the beaches.

■ Hiking

 Hiking is a major pastime almost everywhere along the East Coast. Literally hundreds of hiking and nature trail systems thread the entire tri-state region. Thousands of miles of foot trails lead through rolling pine forests, beside slow-moving rivers, and along the beaches. There are the hundreds of miles of country lanes and backroads available for backpacking, walking, strolling, and birdwatching, and are all open the year-round for public use. Within each section you'll find popular trails, as well as some of the lesser known ones listed, describing their location, length, entry and exit points, and the degree of difficulty.

■ Horseback Riding

 Horseback riding is available in most state parks and in all of the National Forests. Well-marked equestrian trails take riders through some of the most scenic portions of the coastal plain. Staging areas or corrals and overnight camping for horses and riders are available in many of the parks. Be sure to call ahead when planning your ride or organizing a group event. Contact the National Park Service or the National Forest Service to learn about trail conditions and any special regulations.

The following rules and regulations for equestrians are in effect throughout the National Forests:

- Horse trails are marked with a symbol.

- Unmarked trails or those marked by a sign with a red slash through a horse are reserved for hiking only. Open and gated forest service roads are available for horseback riding, unless they are signed as being closed to this type of use.

- Obey trail and road closures.

- Stay on the trail. Taking shortcuts causes erosion and widens trails.

- Travel in small groups, preferably six or fewer.

- Plan your trip to avoid the spring thaw and extended wet weather.

- Pack it in, and pack it out. In other words, leave no trash in the forest.

- Communicate with other trail users, so your horses can safely pass.

- Hikers and mountain bikers should yield to horses, unless horsemen have a convenient place to pull off.

- When camping, use a highline with tree-saver straps to tether your horse.

- Highline your horse 100 ft away from streams and creeks and away from trails and campsites.

- Pack some grain since grazing is limited.

- Break up and scatter manure.

- Fill in pawed holes when leaving camp.

- Horses are not permitted in developed campgrounds and picnic areas.

■ Photography

Photography is an adventure? For many of us it is. Rarely do we have any idea exactly what we are putting on film, or how it will turn out when we get home.

A photograph can be many things: a simple record of a visit to a particular attraction, a very personal souvenir, even a work of art. These days you don't have to be an expert to obtain consistently good results. Modern automatic-everything cameras – auto-focus, auto exposure, etc. – have brought good photography to almost everyone, not just the pro. And you don't need to spend your life savings on equipment, either. A nice point-and- shoot 35mm for around $60 will do just as good a job in the right hands as will the Nikon 4F that costs thousands of dollars.

Helpful Tips

Here are some tips and simple techniques to help you shoot better photos. They should make your adventures in photography a little more successful, a little more pleasing, and ensure you won't be disappointed when you get your photos back from the lab.

- Film is not expensive. So carry plenty with you and shoot lots of frames.

Adventures

- Also carry a spare set of batteries. There's nothing more annoying than to have your camera quit and then have to search for batteries.

- Don't be afraid to put your film through the airport security machines. Unless it's a very high-speed film, the machine won't hurt it.

- Use a low-speed film. Fine-grain film of 100 speed will produce the best results. The lower the speed of the film, the sharper the image will be. True, a low-speed film is not always the most practical. However, it's the one you should use when possible, especially on bright, sunny days. Use a high-speed film only when low light or a telephoto lens makes it a necessity.

- Shoot at the highest shutter speed you can. This will reduce camera shake. Often, you'll hear people bragging about how they can hand-hold a 200mm lens with the shutter set to 1/30th of a second. The rule is, "the longer the lens, the faster the shutter speed." You should never hand-hold a camera and shoot at a shutter speed slower than the focal length of the lens. For example you would only hand-hold a camera fitted with a 180mm lens when the shutter speed is set to 1/250th of a second or more; never slower. Likewise a 50mm lens could be hand-held with the shutter set to 1/60th of a second, but no slower.

- The best light for photography is in the early morning and late afternoon. The colors are warmer and the shadows deeper. At noon, when the sun is overhead, the lighting is flat and uninteresting.

- Good composition means good photographs. Dull days, and skies without detail mean dull photographs. Such situations call for a little thought before you shoot. A technique called "framing" will eliminate large, detailless areas from your pictures and thus improve them; shoot from beneath tree branches, through doorways and windows, and include odd sections of wall and pieces of furniture in the picture. Walk around the subject until you find something, anything, you can place in the picture that will break up those large, uninteresting areas of sky. Never place a dominant point of interest in the center of your picture; move it up or down just a little, or place it a little to one side. Make sure you have the shot framed properly; beware of cutting the tops off heads and buildings. Finally, make sure there is no trash lying around to spoil an otherwise special picture.

- Never shoot into the sun. For the best effect, the sunlight should be coming from behind one shoulder, but never, unless you're looking for silhouettes, from the front.

- Take notes. Memories can be short when there are lots of images to consider – was that really Christ Church or was it the one on Main St in Brunswick? There's nothing worse than getting a half-dozen rolls of film back from the lab and not remembering what you're looking at.

- Don't miss the opportunity to shoot underwater. Even if you don't intend to go diving, you should take a camera to the beach; the fish in the shallow waters are colorful and abundant. You can purchase one of those neat little underwater cameras that come ready to shoot, then take the whole thing in for processing. Or rent a more sophisticated underwater camera from one of the many dive shops.

Photo Opportunities

The coastal regions of Georgia and the Carolinas, with their lush scenery and unique culture and history, make them a photographer's dream. Here are just some of the many outdoor photo opportunities.

Rooftops and Windows. The historic homes dotting the hills and valleys, the crowded streets of the old cities, and the fine old churches, mansions and plantations provide endless opportunities to be creative. Take a moment to compose your shots. Use a long lens and group sections of several roofs or different colored corners of the cottages together. Try cropping in only small sections of a building – say a shutter or a door – and you'll be able to create some remarkable images.

The **Ribbon of Green** that stretches the entire length of the tri-state coastline encompasses many thousands of acres of reserves, parks and beaches that have been nurtured and protected by the local, state and National Park systems through the years. They offer a wide variety of wildlife, lush landscapes and unforgettable views. Try low angle shots, from ground level across the flower beds, the sun shining through a palmetto fan or Spanish moss, the gnarled and twisted shapes of the live oaks, or closeups of flowers. You'll have no trouble finding subjects for your camera among the rocks, dunes and reserves.

The **Forts and Batteries**. These present opportunities of a slightly different kind. The great stone structures, earthworks and trenches are impressive, and make great pictures, but you can do even better. Once again, a little time taken to compose the shot will make all the difference. Try to isolate sections of the old structures for an avant-garde look: a flight of stone steps or a view of the ocean, beach or city framed by a gun port. Use a long lens across the battlements to draw it all together.

Churches and Graveyards. These, too, offer unique and interesting opportunities. The churches themselves can be the focal point of your efforts. The headstones and tombs in the churchyards, some with the strangest epitaphs, can be used to create interesting shots.

Homes and Gardens. In Charleston, Wilmington, Savannah and a hundred other less well-known coastal towns and villages, the homes and gardens are impeccably groomed, tailored and nurtured. Whether private homes or properties belonging to the state or nation, informal or formal gardens featuring hundreds of species of flora and fauna, they all provide a thousand points of color, light, and opportunities for unique pictures.

Out-of-the-Ordinary. Always be on the lookout for that little something with a difference. After all, art is in the eye of the creator as well as the beholder. Don't be afraid to take pictures in the rain – afternoon showers don't last long and the results as the sun breaks through the clouds can be spectacular. Of course, you'll need to protect your camera from water, but don't let that put you off. Taking pictures of people bustling about crowded streets of Charleston or Savannah in the rain can be fun and productive. Good luck and good shooting.

■ Shell Collecting

 Has there ever been a visitor to a beach who hasn't wandered the water's edge, gazing down at the sand, looking for shells? Unfortunately, the more popular the beach, the less chance you'll have of finding something special. The best time for shelling is just after high tide; the ocean's treasures are still lying on the sand. The best places are those where people rarely go, and there are few of those left.

Types Of Shells

Most common are the tiny **bivalves** – small animals with a shell consisting of two valves (sides), joined together by a hinge. These two valves are opened and closed by powerful muscles, but after the animal has died they often become separated or spread out.

Whelks are members of the gastropod family. These animals have a single large shell, coiled into a helix. Several whelks are fairly common on the coast and barrier islands: the channeled whelk, as its name suggests, has deep grooves at the joints; the lightning whelk has a row of knobs on the shoulder of the body whorl; the whitish knobbed whelk has knobs on the shoulder of the body whorl and an orange mouth.

The **moon shell** is the home of another gastropod – a snail that feeds on clams which they dig out of the sand. Usually white or pale yellow in color, the empty shells can often be found just beneath the surface of the sand, left behind by the receding tide.

Other nice shells you can find are the **glassy lyonsia, coquina shell, blue mussel, Atlantic Bay scallop, eastern oyster, giant Atlantic cockle, northern softshell clam, angel wing, Atlantic surf clam, Atlantic jackknife clam, stiff pen shell** and numerous other small bivalves and gastropods.

Adventures

Georgia Coast

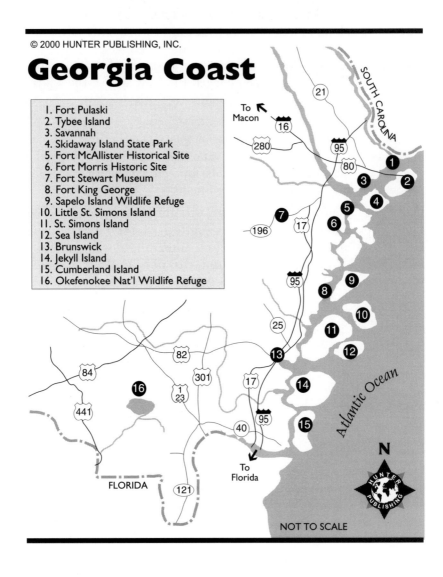

1. Fort Pulaski
2. Tybee Island
3. Savannah
4. Skidaway Island State Park
5. Fort McAllister Historical Site
6. Fort Morris Historic Site
7. Fort Stewart Museum
8. Fort King George
9. Sapelo Island Wildlife Refuge
10. Little St. Simons Island
11. St. Simons Island
12. Sea Island
13. Brunswick
14. Jekyll Island
15. Cumberland Island
16. Okefenokee Nat'l Wildlife Refuge

SOUTH CAROLINA

To Macon

Atlantic Ocean

FLORIDA

To Florida

N

NOT TO SCALE

Georgia

Savannah & Tybee Island

■ History of Savannah

 Savannah was founded upon the philanthropic ideals of British General and colonist **James Oglethorpe**. Born in London on December 22, 1696, son of a wealthy baronet, he was educated at Eton and Oxford, served in the war against the Turks in 1716-1717, and was praised for his services at the siege of Belgrade. Upon returning to England he was elected to Parliament, at the tender age of 26.

A gentleman in every sense of the word, Oglethorpe had a sympathetic attitude toward those less fortunate than himself. He viewed the long-established practice of imprisoning English debtors to be one of his country's great injustices. And, a champion of the cause of religious freedom, he believed that oppressed members of dissenting religious sects should be afforded a place of refuge. Unable to change the system, Oglethorpe determined to remove its victims. To that end, he suggested that a colony populated by the economically less fortunate and the religious non-conformists in Georgia would serve also as a buffer to separate the English settlers in the Carolinas from the Spanish settlers in Florida. His heartfelt and persuasive arguments won a charter for the Georgia Colony in 1732.

On February 12, 1733 Oglethorpe, with more than a hundred settlers, landed at Yamacraw Bluff on the Savannah River to establish America's 13th, and final, colony. By the time he returned to England the next year, Georgia was attracting colonists of German Lutheran, Moravian and Scottish Presbyterian faiths. Oglethorpe returned to Georgia in late 1735. He brought with him the founders of the Methodist movement, brothers John and Charles Wesley, who, subsequently, conducted preaching missions throughout the colonies.

In 1736 Oglethorpe oversaw the construction of Fort Frederica on St. Simons Island as a defense against the Spanish to the south. When war broke out between England and Spain three years later, he led an unsuccessful attack on St. Augustine and finally defeated the Spanish forces at the Battle of Bloody Marsh in 1742. Though Oglethorpe enjoyed general popularity, some colonists opposed his rules prohibiting drinking and slavery. One such adversary, a subordinate, charged him with mismanaging the expeditions to St. Augustine. In 1743, Oglethorpe was recalled to England to stand court martial proceedings, and, while he was vindicated, he never returned to Georgia, remaining in England where he continued his military career. James Edward Oglethorpe died at Cranham Hall in Essex, England, on June 30, 1785.

In 1744 the Port of Savannah was established, greatly augmenting the city's strategic importance. By the outbreak of the American Revolution a bustling commercial center had evolved, with ships coming and going from around the globe. Savannah was captured by the British in 1778 and thus held until the close of hostilities. With that peace came prosperity as the city's port traffic increased steadily with the growth of the plantation-based economy of tobacco and cotton. It was a good time for Savannah.

In 1861, war came again to Savannah, this time in the form of the Civil War. Early on, Savannah was an important supply point for the Confederacy, but the fall of Fort Pulaski in 1862 closed the port to all sea traffic except for a few brave blockade-runners. The city itself fell to General Sherman's troops on December 22, 1864, prompting the General, based at the Green-Meldrim House, to send the following famous message: "To President Lincoln, I beg to present to you as a Christmas gift, the city of Savannah with 140 guns and plenty of ammunition and also about 25,000 bales of cotton."

■ Savannah Today

Today, Savannah, the oldest city in Georgia and just 18 miles from the Atlantic Ocean, is once again a leading port of the Southeast. With its population of 150,000, it is the third largest city in Georgia. As a center of historical interest, Savannah exceeds all other cities in Georgia and is one of the state's leading tourist attractions. It is also considered to be one of the most beautiful cities in the United States. The foresight of James Oglethorpe can be credited with much of what visitors see today. The old city, a marvel of early town planning, remains virtually as he conceptualized it some 260 years ago. In fact, in 1996 a 2½-square-mile area in downtown Savannah, containing 2,358 buildings of architectural and/or historical interest, was designated as a Registered National Landmark, making it one of the largest urban historic landmark districts in the nation. This city plan also is the only city in the United States nominated to UNESCO's World Heritage List.

*The **Historic Savannah Foundation**, ☎ 912-651-2125, 501 Whitaker Street, in Hodgson Hall, since 1955 has been the catalyst for the restoration of Savannah's architectural heritage.*

Savannah was voted "one of the top 10 US Cities to Visit," by *Condé Nast Traveler* and attracts more than 5,000,000 visitors per year. It hosts numerous cultural events, the most important of which take place in the springtime. Be advised, however, that, during that period, available accommodation is scarce. We'd recommend you book well in advance. Among the longstanding traditions is a **St. Patrick's Day Parade**, in its 176th year in 2000, and second in size only to the one held in New York City. That event alone draws 300,000 to 500,000 celebrants. This is followed quickly by the more sedate **Savannah Tour of Homes and Gardens**, which, as of 2000, is in its 65th year.

Savannah's close proximity to the ocean gives rise to another local attraction, the beach resort of **Tybee Island**. Since the late 19th century, Tybee Island has become a popular retreat for Savannahians. As early as 1889, a train ran from Savannah to Tybee and, in the early part of the 20th century, the Central of Georgia Railroad carried as many as 5,000 passengers daily on the one-hour ride for daily or weekend excursions. Progress encroached, however, and the June 1923 opening of the first road running parallel to the tracks sounded the death knell for train service. It ceased just 10 years later. Nevertheless, the legacy has not been entirely lost. The tracks have been converted into a well-used bike path, Rails to Trails, and Tybee Island, still a popular destination, hosts many celebrations. Perhaps the favorite is July 4th, with its huge fireworks show. Just 18 miles from downtown, this is well worth a visit for its attractions, both historical and recreational. Or, for the best of both worlds: stay at Tybee Island, visit the city and enjoy both.

■ Climate

The climate is temperate, with a average temperature of 51 in winter, 66 in spring, 80 in summer, and 66 in the fall. Sunshine is plentiful in all seasons; there are rarely more than two or three days in succession without it. Savannah and the islands can be quite humid in summertime and subject to frequent afternoon thunder showers. Then, of course, there's the hurricane season; only rarely does this present a problem, but once every 10 years or so you can expect a big blow.

■ Getting Here

By Air

 Savannah International Airport is served by most major airlines, including Delta, USAir, and United, with direct service through hubs in Atlanta, Charlotte, Raleigh, Columbia, New York, Dallas, Charleston, Washington, Jacksonville, and other major cities. The taxi fare from the airport to the business district (one way) is $18 for one person, plus $5 for each additional person. The limousine fare is $15 one-way, or $25 round-trip.

By Car

 From the north and south: I-95 is the direct connection north and south from New England to Miami, while Hwy 17, often called the Ocean Highway, offers a more leisurely, picturesque route through the coastal towns and villages north and south from Charleston to Jacksonville.

From the west: I-16 runs east and west to and from Atlanta via Macon.

■ Getting Around

 A word to the wise for those contemplating driving around the city of Savannah: parking can be a real problem. If you are intent upon doing so, then purchase a 48-hour **Visitor Parking Pass** from the Parking Services office, 100 East Bryan Street, at the Bryan Street Garage; at the Visitors Center; or at many of Savannah's hotels and inns. The pass costs only $5 and allows parking, without charge, in metered spaces with time limits of an hour or more; on Broughton Street in time-regulated spaces; in time-regulated spaces on River Street and on its ramps; in city parking garages on State, Montgomery and Bryan Streets; in the city lots at the Savannah Visitors Center and the in Liberty and Montgomery lot.

Cycling is a good way to avoid an almost continuous hunt for a parking place. Bicycles are available for rent from **Savannah Bicycle Rentals**, ☎ 912-447-0800, 200 West Congress Street, in the City Market parking garage. They are open seven days a week, from 10 am to 6, and the prices are reasonable indeed: $6 an hour, $10 a half-day, or $20 a day. What's more, with advance reservations, Savannah Bicycle Rentals will save you time and hassle with a drop-off/pick-up service.

The **Chatham Area Transit (CAT)** offers regular, convenient service on electric-powered buses from downtown hotels, inns and the Visitors Center to the Historic District and other attractions. The fare is a reasonable $1.50 for an all-day pass, or 50¢ per ride.

■ Sightseeing

Historic District

Without doubt, the main attraction in Savannah is the Historic District itself, with its unique layout. Indeed, the plan conceived by Oglethorpe is considered today, more than 250 years later, one of the world's best. Systematically, Oglethorpe laid out a series of 40 wards. The center of each was a square with two lots on the east and west sides designated for important buildings. An additional 40 lots were on the north and south sides. Wards were separated from each other by wide boulevards, six running north to south and seven running east to west. Even Oglethorpe could not have realized that, with the advent of 20th-century traffic, these boulevards would become the main arteries preserving the integrity and peacefulness of the public squares. Thus, visitors find today a city unlike any other. Amidst the magnificent array of architecture – private homes, public buildings and churches – 21 of the original 24 squares have survived. Most bear the name of a prominent Revolutionary or Confederate hero and are adorned with monuments, statues or fountains. Streets, boulevards and squares alike are lined with majestic oak trees dressed in Spanish moss and accentuated by a colorful display of gardenias, camellias, azaleas, palmettos and magnolias.

You may be surprised to learn that Spanish Moss isn't moss at all. A member of the pineapple family, it is a flowering plant that blooms from April to July, has no roots, and lives only in humid areas, where it absorbs water directly from the air.

Savannah
Historic District

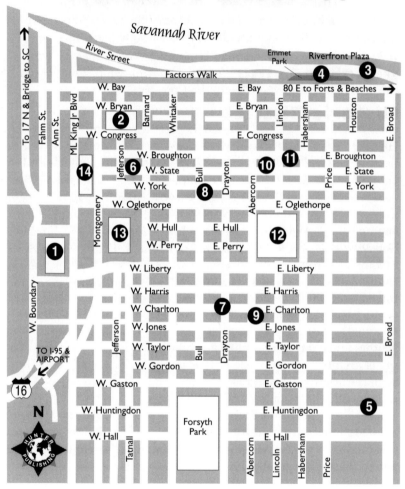

1. Savannah Visitors Center, 1860
2. City Market
3. Ships of the Sea Museum
4. Waving Girl Statue
5. King-Tisdell Cottage
6. Telfair Mansion & Art Museum, 1800s
7. Green-Meldrim House, 1853
8. The Juliette Gordon Low Birthplace, 1820
9. Andrews House, 1849
10. Owens-Thomas House, 1816
11. Davenport House, 1815-1820
12. Colonial Park Cemetery
13. Civic Center
14. County Courthouse

Tours

There are so many places of historical and architectural significance that it is difficult to take everything in. We advise that you take an organized tour to acquaint yourself with Savannah. There are plenty of choices when it comes to tour operators. The following are just a few of the companies that will show you around historic Savannah.

Tours on Tape, ☎ 912-944-0460, Savannah Visitors Center, or ☎ 912-232-0582, 313 Abercorn Street, offers two tapes at $12 each. The first narrates a driving tour of the "Downtown Historic District"; the second narrates "A Drive in the Country."

Old Savannah Tours, ☎ 912-234-8128, 800-517-9007 or e-mail oldsavtour@aol.com, 250 Martin Luther King Boulevard, offers a Historic Loop Tour of the entire Historic District by trolley. These depart from the Savannah Visitors Center between 9 am and 4:30 daily on a 20-25-minute schedule and allow a full day of unlimited on/off boarding privileges at 13 convenient stops. The cost is $20 per person and includes the commentary of a licensed guide and admission to one house museum. Those intrigued by *Midnight in the Garden of Good and Evil*, the bestseller set in Savannah, will undoubtedly want to join up with either the 10 or 2 Book Tour. For $17 per person, including entry to the Bonaventure Cemetery, this specialized tour takes you to all the locations mentioned in that book.

Ragtop Tours, ☎ 912-944-0999, 19 East Perry Street, will show you the sights in style. The name should have given a clue to the means of transport, nostalgically plush Kennedy-era Cadillac and Lincoln convertibles. For a reasonable $40 per couple (additional passengers may tag along at $10 each), you will be treated to a one-hour tour of Savannah, that will be, in a word, unforgettable.

Carriage Tours of Savannah, ☎ 912-236-6756, operates horse carriage tours. These depart Monday through Saturday, between 9 and 3 on the hour, from the City Market and Visitor's Center; between 6 and 9 on the hour from the City Market, Hyatt Hotel and, by reservation, from the Pirate's House Restaurant. The regular fare is $17 for adults.

While undoubtedly requiring a little more effort, the best way to see and understand historic Savannah is at the street level, on foot, and accompanied by a knowledgeable guide. If that is your preference, then the people to talk and walk with **The Savannah Walks Inc.**, ☎ 912-238-WALK (9255), 888 SAV-WALK or 800 729-3420, 123 East Congress Street, Reynold's Square. In the mornings, the choices are the Civil War Walk and the Savannah Stroll. The latter is repeated

Georgia

during the day, when other choices are the Churches & Graveyard Walk, A Walk Through "Midnight," the Southern Belles Walk or the Savannah Gates and Gardens Walk. In the evenings you may take your choice of Ye Olde Pub Walk and the LowCountry Ghosts Walk. Morning and daytime walks depart from Reynold's Square. Evening walks leave from Johnson Square. Fares are $13 for adults, with the exception of the Historic Homes Walk, which costs $19. If more than one tour takes your fancy, special discounts are available for multiple tours. Allow 1½ to two hours for most walks, and, if the skies are threatening, bring an umbrella; tours take place rain or shine, although they may be cancelled in extreme weather. Be aware also that the schedule may vary slightly during the winter and holiday seasons. To ensure the highest standards of quality, the size of each group is limited and reservations are required.

The most unusual method of transport around Savannah is **Savannah Pedicab**, ☎ 912-232-7900, 200 West Congress Street. Sit back, relax and allow yourself to be pedaled around town in a tricycle-powered rickshaw. Rates are $20 for a half-hour and $40 for an hour; a full day will cost you $100; or you can pay by the ride.

Churches

There are numerous churches of many different denominations in Savannah. Most, though, are not open to tourists, and, therefore, can be admired only from the outside. The more important of these are listed here. The **Cathedral of St. John the Baptist**, ☎ 912-233-4709, is found at Lafayette Square, 222 East Harris Street. Its congregation was first organized in the late 1770s, making it the oldest Roman Catholic Church in Georgia. The present structure, which replaced earlier ones, was dedicated in 1876. The **First African Baptist Church**, ☎ 912-233-6597, Franklin Square, 23 Montgomery Street, was founded in 1773. It lays claim to being the oldest continuously active, autonomously developed African-American church on the continent of North America. The congregation of **Temple Mickve Israel**, ☎ 912-233-1547, Monterey Square, 20 East Gordon Street, was organized in July 1733, just five months after Oglethorpe's colonization of Georgia. It is the oldest in the South and the third oldest in the nation. It is, also, the only Gothic synagogue in America, built between 1776 and 1778, and a home to the country's oldest Torah. The adjoining museum, open to the public, boasts more than 1,790 historical books of congregational activities and letters from Presidents Washington, Jefferson and Madison.

Fort Pulaski

Along the way to Tybee Island, on Route 80, is Fort Pulaski, ☎ 912-786-5787. Constructed at the mouth of the Savannah River, the structure is comprised of 25,000,000 bricks, boasts walls 7½ feet thick, and, when it was completed in 1847, was considered to be the ultimate defense fortification of its era. Fifteen years later, a siege by Federal troops during the Civil War put its strength to the test. Sadly, it failed. Artillery bombardment, launched over a period of 30 hours from Tybee Island more than a mile away, ultimately breached the walls. This marked the first time such an attack successfully penetrated a masonry fortification, thus beginning a change in military defensive strategies that would echo around the world. These days, the remarkably well preserved fort is open to the public daily from 9 to 5:15. Audio stations within the fort offer brief historical explanations and Park Rangers are on hand to answer questions. At the Visitor Center, which opens from 8:30 to 5, there is an introductory video, exhibits and a bookstore. Over and above the historical interest, visitors will enjoy the views over the Atlantic Ocean and the salt marshes that cover much of the park's 5,600 acres.

Touring the Fort

As you tour the fort you'll find a series of numbered markers, each at a significant point of interest. To enter the fort you must first cross the outer drawbridge and walk across the demilune to the second drawbridge and the sally port, the only entrance into the main structure.

Stop 1: The Sally Port. The sally port is a structure very similar in design to the medieval castles in Europe. The massive drawbridge is counterbalanced by a series of great counterweights; you can see them in the rooms on either side of the entrance. The great portcullis drops down through a slot as the drawbridge is raised. Finally, the inner doors could be closed, making the fort secure against all outsiders.

Stop 2: The Gorge. The gorge, located along the western, or rear, section of the fort, and is so called because it contains the sally port, the only entrance to the fort. The living quarters are also located in the gorge: the enlisted men occupied the quarters to the north of the sally port, the officers those to the south.

Stop 3: The Barrack Rooms. These rooms, located in the casemates meaning bomb-proof shelter, were lit by oil lamps or candles. Each has a large fireplace with cooking equipment, and the rear walls are pierced by loopholes angled to provide the fort's defenders with a wide field of fire.

Stop 4: The North Magazine. The walls of the magazine are 12-15 ft thick. On the second day of the Federal bombardment, shells exploding near the magazine threatened to blow it up.

Stop 5: The Northwest Bastion. A bastion is a section of a fort or castle that extends beyond the main walls of the structure, usually at its corners, that provides a field of fire in all directions, but especially along the walls to the left and right. Fort Pulaski has two half-bastions, one at the north end of the west wall and one at the south. They are called half-bastions because they extend out in only one direction and give protection only to the west wall. The rectangular openings in the bastion wall are gun ports situated to provide protecting cannon crossfire toward the main drawbridge and the point of the demilune. The openings in the ceiling are smoke vents, and the circular grooves in the floor originally held iron tracks that carried the wheels of the gun carriages.

Stop 6: The Gun Galleries. The bomb-proof gun galleries surround the fort on four sides giving the structure the look of a great cathedral or monastery. The galleries at Fort Pulaski are fine examples of arched casemates. The arches were built over wooden forms. The bricks, each one hand-cut to fit, were carefully placed and then mortared in position. When the mortar was dry, the forms were removed, leaving the beautiful arches you see.

Stop 7: The Water System. There are 10 water cisterns, or storage tanks, within the walls of the fort beneath the brick pavements of the two center casemates of each galley. Each cistern holds 20,000 gallons of fresh water and is filled by a system of pipes that carries rainwater down from the roof.

Stop 8: The Terraplein. The flat surface along the top of the rampart which carries the gun platforms is called the terraplein. The guns mounted on the ramparts had a far greater range than those mounted in the casemates below, because of their elevated position; they were, however, extremely vulnerable to the new rifled guns in the Federal batteries on Tybee Island. The parapet of the terraplein was supposed to provide protection for the guns and their crews; the rifled guns, however, made short work of them, leaving both guns and crews exposed to the enemy.

Stop 9: The Terraplein at the East Angle. From here you will have a fine view of the north shore of Tybee Island. The two Federal batteries containing the three great rifled guns that did most of the damage to the walls of the fort were located just to the north of the present highway bridge. The nine other Federal batteries were located along the shoreline toward the lighthouse for a distance of about two miles.

Stop 10: The Prison. From October 1864 to March 1865, the southeast, the northeast, and a section of the south casemates were used as a military prison.

Stop 11: The Breach. The Federal batteries just to the north of the modern highway bridge were able to batter the walls here at the southeast angle to the extent that they were breached, leaving the interior open to explosive shellfire. These walls were reconstructed by engineers of the 48th New York Volunteers in 1862, after the surrender of the fort.

Stop 12: The Southwest Bastion. The interior of this section of the fort was destroyed by a fire in 1893. The restoration of the bastion was left incomplete in order to show details of the foundation construction.

Stop 13: Headquarters. It was here, on April 11, 1862, that Colonel Olmstead executed the terms for the surrender of the fort. The officers' quarters were destroyed by a lightning fire in 1925. This room was restored in 1935.

Stop 14: The Cistern. This room, too, was destroyed by the fire of 1925. It was left unrestored in order to show details of its construction. The cylindrical brick structure you see below floor level is the top of a water cistern.

Stop 15: The Bottle Collection. In 1935, the men dredging of the mud from the moat found more than 1,000 bottles thrown into the waters by workmen during the construction of the fort, and later by Confederate and Union soldiers. A part of the collection is on display in this room.

Stop 16: The Moat. The moat completely surrounds the fort and, like the European castles of old, was designed to protect the walls from intruders. It varies in width from 30 to 48 ft, and has an average depth of about seven ft. Water enters the moat from the south channel of the Savannah River and is controlled through a series of tide gates. A variety of marine life makes its home in the waters of the moat: turtles, crabs, shrimp, and fish.

Stop 17: The Demilune. The great triangular-shaped structure to the rear of the fort is called the demilune. Most of the work here was completed in 1869, after the Civil War. The structure hides a series of

Georgia

passageways connecting four powder magazines to the gun emplacements.

Stop 18: The Damaged Wall. Here it is still possible to see evidence of the damage done to the walls of the fort by the great rifled guns in the Federal batteries. The breach was repaired in 1862 using red brick that contrasts with the original structure of brown brick. The pockmarks along the entire southeast wall facing Tybee Island are evidence that the walls were struck hundreds of times by a variety of projectiles, many of which are still embedded in the brickwork.

Stop 19: The Cemetery. This small cemetery was established as the fort was being constructed. During the Civil War, soldiers, Union and Confederate, were temporarily buried there. The 8-inch Confederate gun that marks the site was damaged during the Federal bombardment.

Stop 20: The Waving Girl. Florence Martus, the daughter of an ordnance sergeant on Cockspur Island was born in the Officers' Quarters just after the Civil War. As a small child she was fascinated by the great ships that sailed past the fort on their way to destinations all around the world. She would stand and wave a white handkerchief at the departing ships; the sailors waved back. As a teenager, Florence went to live with her brother in a small white cottage on the riverbank about five miles upriver from the fort. From that time on, for more than 44 years, she waved at every ship that passed her home; a tablecloth or sheet by day and a lantern by night; each ship, as it passed, would return her salute with three blasts of the whistle. The legend of the Waving Girl of Savannah is known by sailors all over the world.

Historic Houses

The **Owens-Thomas House**, ☎ 912-233-9743, 124 Abercorn Street, designed and built between 1816 and 1819 by William Jay, is an elegant Regency-style villa considered one of the finest examples of this type of architecture in the US. His client for this project was cotton merchant and banker, Richard Richardson. It was from this house that the Marquis de Lafayette, in 1825, gave a speech to the citizens of Savannah. Presently, the old house is furnished with rare antiques of the construction period, which are complemented by a fine collection of European and Chinese porcelains and numerous artifacts of historical significance. Beyond the main house and across the expanse of exquisite, formal landscaped gardens, is the carriage house. Guided tours are conducted Monday from midday to 5, Tuesday to Saturday from 10 to 5, and Sunday from 2 to 5. The last tour departs at 4:25.

The **Andrew Low House**, ☎ 912-233-6854, 329 Abercorn Street, was built in 1848 under the direction of the wealthy Savannah merchant whose name it bears. This stuccoed brick house is most noted for its carved woodwork, fine plaster cornices, and crystal chandeliers.

 Cookie lovers will be interested to learn that Juliette Gordon Low, founder of the Girl Scout movement in 1912, made her home here.

Among the famous guests who spent time in the old house were General Robert E. Lee and novelist William Makepeace Thackerey. It is literally jam-packed with fine examples of 19th-century furniture and memorabilia. It is open each Monday, Tuesday, Wednesday, Friday and Saturday between 10:30 and 3:30, and on Sunday from noon to 3:30. Guided tours depart at half-hour intervals.

The **Davenport House**, ☎ 912-236-8097, built between 1815 and 1820 by Isaiah Davenport, is among the finest examples of Federal architecture in Savannah. It was saved from demolition, following its condemnation in 1950 by the faithful efforts of the Historic Savannah Foundation. The old building, famous for delicate plaster work, fine wrought iron, and an unusual elliptical stairway, was restored, decorated as it might have been during the early 19th century, and furnished with English and American pieces of the period. Opening hours are Monday-Saturday from 10 to 4 and Sunday from 1 to 4. Tours depart at half-hour intervals.

The **Green-Meldrim House**, ☎ 912-233-3845, 14 West Macon Street, was designed in the early 1850s by John Norris of New York for his client Charles Greene. It stands today as an example of the Gothic Revival architecture typical of the South prior to the Civil War. It had the rather dubious honor of serving as headquarters for General Sherman during his troops' occupation of Savannah in 1864. Though today it functions as the Parish House of St. John's Church, you can take a tour on Tuesday, Thursday and Friday between the hours of 10 and 4 or Saturday between 10 and 1.

The **Juliette Gordon Low Birthplace**, ☎ 912-233-4501 or fax 233-4659, 142 Bull Street, built between 1818 and 1821, was the home of Girl Scout founder Juliette Gordon Low. She was born here on Halloween night of 1860 and died here on January 17, 1927. The home has been restored and refurnished with period furniture (many of which are Low family pieces) to appear as it would have in 1886, the year of Juliette's marriage. Also look for a lovely Victorian garden with original outbuildings. The house and grounds presently serve as

Georgia

a national center for the Girl Scouts of America. Visit Monday, Tuesday, Thursday and Saturday between 10 and 4, and Sunday from 12:30 to 4:30.

The **King-Tisdale Cottage**, ☎ 912-234-8000, 502 East Harris Street, named for Eugene and Sarah King, and Mrs. King's second husband, Robert Tisdale, is a circa 1896 Victorian cottage which has been restored to its original condition. Here you will find Savannah's premier Black heritage museum, with interesting artifacts, memorabilia and exhibits. Be sure, before leaving, to sign up for the Negro Heritage Trail Tour, which takes in 17 sites that figured prominently in Savannah's Black history and departs from the Visitors Center on Martin Luther King Jr. Boulevard. The museum is open Tuesday to Saturday from noon to 5.

Museums

The **Savannah History Museum**, ☎ 912-238-1779, or fax 651-6827, 303 Martin Luther King Jr. Boulevard, is a large museum housed in what was the passenger station of the Central of Georgia Railway. Here, the history of Savannah and eastern Georgia unfold through a mixture of multimedia presentations, animated dioramas and traditional exhibits. Among these are two theaters, one that focuses on Savannah's early history and another that plays out a local 1779 battle of the American Revolution. A model of the *SS Savannah* (the first steamship to cross the Atlantic – from Savannah to Liverpool in 1819), an 1890 locomotive, an extensive collection of military uniforms, a cotton gin, one of Johnny Mercer's Oscars, and (of course) Forrest Gump's famous bench. If you've seen the movie, you will remember Forrest sitting on a bench in Chippewa Square in front of the General Oglethorpe Monument. While the bench was a product of poetic license – nothing more than a movie prop, many residents wanted to place a bench in the square permanently. Purists, favoring historical authenticity, shuddered at the idea. A compromise was reached in 1995, when the bench found a home in the Savannah History Museum, along with Gump's suitcase and box of chocolates – all a gift to Savannah from Paramount Pictures Corporation. Visit the museum daily 9 to 5.

The **Telfair Mansion & Art Museum**, ☎ 912-232-1177, 121 Barnard Street, is an 1818 Regency-style mansion designed and built by English architect William Jay upon a site where once stood the Government House, home to Georgia's royal governors. The house is furnished with fine antiques and period pieces, many of which once belonged to Governor Edward Telfair, and its Octagon Room is said to be the finest of its genre in the United States. Also the oldest art museum in the Southeast, the museum wing displays a permanent collection of art dating from the 18th century through the present. Most notable are collections of important American and European paintings and sculptures, prints, silver, fine furniture and decorative arts.

This home, too, has a Midnight in the Garden of Good and Evil *connection. Sylvia Shaw Judson's statue of the Bird Girl was made famous by the cover of the novel.*

Opening hours are Monday, noon to 5, and Tuesday to Saturday, 10 to 5.

The **Ships of the Sea Maritime Museum**, ☎ 912-232-1511, 41 Martin Luther King Jr. Boulevard, is also housed within a mansion. This one, completed in 1819, was built for merchant William Scarborough, a principal investor in the SS Savannah. For nearly a century, from 1878 to 1972, it housed a public school that enrolled, exclusively, children of African descent. In 1974, it was designated a Historic Landmark, and its restoration was undertaken in 1976 as a Bicentennial project. The building remains among the Historic District's most interesting attractions, and today plays host to collections of early navigational equipment, model ships, ships' figureheads, a number of exhibits that interpret Savannah's seagoing history, all sorts of interesting artifacts and memorabilia, and a shipwright's carpenter shop. Look especially for the collection of ships in bottles, which are exquisitely made, rare, and easily equal in value to their life-sized counterparts. Visit Tuesday through Sunday, 10 to 5 pm.

Tybee Island

Moving on to Tybee Island, you will discover another chapter of fascinating history. At one time or another the island was governed by Spanish, French or Confederate forces and even pirates.

The native Euchee Indians called the island Tybee, meaning "salt."

It was James Oglethorpe who foresaw very early on the island's potential for a lucrative shipping trade. Knowing of the treacherous shoals along the Savannah River, he established the first **Tybee Light**, in effect just a small beacon, in 1734. Presently it stands 154 feet tall, with the lower 60 feet dating from 1773 and the upper 94 feet being built in 1867. Interestingly, the walls taper from a base that is

12 feet thick to only 18 inches at the summit. In 1985 it was officially opened to the public, and supervised tours wind up the 178 steps to the observation deck, 145 feet above the ground, daily.

 The original Fresnel lens, nearly eight feet tall, magnifies the 30,000 candlepower light to such intensity that it is visible 18 miles out at sea!

The lighthouse, like the Tybee Island Museum just across the road, is operated by the **Tybee Island Historical Society,** ☎ 912-786-5801, 30 Medding Drive. The **Tybee Island Museum,** on the site of Fort Scraven, is housed in one of the old coastal batteries that were built in 1898 and features exhibits that trace the history of the island. Both the museum and lighthouse are open in the summer, April through Labor Day, daily, except Tuesday, from 10 to 6. The rest of the year, visit on Monday, Wednesday, Thursday and Friday from noon to 4 and on Saturday and Sunday from 10 to 4.

Private Homes & Gardens

Wandering around Savannah you will have discovered that many of the most interesting properties in the city are privately owned and, tantalizingly, only their silhouettes are visible for viewing. But all that changes for one weekend at the end of March each year during the **Annual Savannah Tour of Homes and Gardens**, operated by the Savannah Tour of Homes and Gardens, ☎ 912-234-8054 or fax 234-2123, 18 Abercorn Street. The year 2000 saw the 65th annual tour. Self-guided walking tours continue throughout the day and in the twilight hours. A complimentary slide preview provides an introduction to each tour, which takes in six to eight sights of varying ages and sizes. In addition, there are a number of other tours, receptions, church services, concerts, teas and even riverboat cruises.

A WORD TO
THE WISE
Tickets often sell out for the Homes and Gardens tour, so order yours early. Another complication is accommodations. To avoid disappointment you must book many months in advance.

Another popular tour is held at the end of April, The Garden Club of Savannah presents an annual **N.O.G.S. Tour of Hidden Gardens**, ☎ 912-238-0248, PO Box 13892, Savannah, GA 31416. In 1999, a $20 ticket allowed access to eight walled gardens and the award-winning Massie School Gardena, plus an invitation to a Simply Southern Tea at the Telfair Museum of Art. The year 2000 marks this tour's 25th anniversary.

Public Parks & Open Spaces

Outdoor lovers will find much to please them in Savannah. **Forsyth Park**, laid out in 1851, is among Savannah's most picturesque, especially in springtime when the azaleas are in bloom. The grounds are spread over 20 acres at the southern end of the Historic District between Whitaker and Drayton. If you are in need of a respite from walking, you can relax and enjoy the tranquility. On the other hand, if you are feeling particularly energetic, a one-mile jogging course awaits you. A lovely old fountain, circa 1858 and similar to the one in the Place de la Concorde in Paris, is the park's signature piece. Other highlights include the Confederate Monument in the extension to the south and a Fragrant Garden for the blind.

The **Colonial Park Cemetery** lies between Habersham and Abercorn Streets, with its northern boundary running along Oglethorpe. From 1750 to 1853 this served as a public burial ground, and is the last resting place for many of Georgia's early citizens. Among the more famous is Button Gwinnett, a signatory to the Declaration of Independence.

The **Trustees Garden Site**, south of Bay Street on East Broad Street, is the original site of a 10-acre experimental garden constructed in 1733 by the colonists and modeled after the Chelsea Botanical Gardens in London. Though myriad cuttings were collected from around the world and much faith was invested in the wine industry and in mulberry trees (essential for silk), unsuitable climatic conditions and soil led to the failure of both. Happily, though, the peach trees and upland cotton that were planted would become major crops for both Georgia and South Carolina. The **Herb House**, now incorporated within the Pirates' House restaurant and shop complex, was built in 1734 as a residence for the gardener of the Trustees Garden. It is considered to be the oldest house in the state of Georgia.

The **City Market**, to the east of Franklin Square and just two blocks from River Street, has long been the commercial and social hub of Savannah. A survivor of numerous calamities over the centuries, including the threat of demolition, this recently restored four-block area includes interesting shops, stores, art galleries, studios, restaurants, taverns and even live entertainment. It is easy to find, easy to shop, and well worth a little time. Who knows what unusual little goodies you'll find?

Georgia

Factors Walk stretches along a river bluff on Bay Street between Martin Luther King Jr. Boulevard and Emmet Park. The name derives from merchants that conducted a trade in cotton and other commodities on this street during the 19th century. Many of their offices have been converted to inns, restaurants and specialty stores, accessed off of the main street by way of attractive pedestrian walkways or small parks.

Those unfamiliar with the area might be deceived by the optical illusion that nothing exists between Bay Street and the river, but something certainly does. A series of steep ramps, paved with cobblestones transported as ballast on ships returning empty-handed from England, lead down to River Street and what, at one time, were warehouses. From Savannah's early days until the demise of its shipping eminence following an epidemic of yellow fever in the early 1800s, **River Street** was the hub for the city's maritime trade, a hive of almost continuous activity. Over the next century, however, the fortunes of the riverfront declined in concert with the river trade until only a host of abandoned warehouses stood sentinel over the waterway. Finally, in the mid-1970s, revitalization came to River Street under the banner of the River Street Urban Renewal Project. Investments of $7,000,000-plus transformed the many abandoned structures into a colorful mix of restaurants, shops and businesses. Today, this once dilapidated area hosts numerous festivals and special events, details of which can be obtained from the **Savannah Waterfront Association**, ☎ 912-234-0295. By day or by night, this may well be the most popular tourist area in Savannah.

■ Adventures

On Water

Fishing

Savannah

 Savannah has plenty of opportunities for fishing if you are so inclined. Greg Davis, and his wife Holly Dixon Davis, both USCG-licensed Captains, run the **Savannah Light Tackle Fishing Company**, ☎ 912-355-3271, fax 352-0419 or www.sltfishing.qpg.com, PO Box 3666, Savannah, Georgia, 31414. You can choose from a number of packages, with prices quoted here being for two. Inshore Fishing packages include a Half-Day (four hours) at $175, Full Day (six-eight hours) at $300 or Redfish Tide (two-three hours) at $150. Offshore Fishing packages include Gulf Stream Fishing (12-14 hours) at $1,200 or Live Bait King Mackerel (six hours) at $600.

A WORD TO
THE WISE

Be advised that if you elect to go Gulf Stream Fishing (a 70-mile trip) the ride can get rough.

Alternatively, you may prefer one of the their other interesting excursions; perhaps, a Trip Through Georgia's Barrier Islands or a Sunrise or Sunset Dolphin Cruise. Prices range between $150 and $400, and, depending on their duration, include snacks, lunch and drinks.

Savannah's first and only fly fishing shop, **Oak Bluff Outfitters**, ☎ 912-691-1115, fax 691-1117, e-mail oakbluff@worldnet.att.net or www.oakbluff.com, a few minutes from downtown at 4501 Habersham Street, specializes in guided fishing and nature trips. Fly-casting and tying lessons, scheduled upon request, as well as group classes, are held at the shop that carries a particularly eclectic array of goods. In addition to a wide range of fly fishing tackle (which you would expect), there are clothes – most notably lines of quality goods from Orvis, Filson and Barbour. There is even a special corner for the ladies. You can be sure that something will take your fancy from among the selections of decoys, Battenkill luggage, sunglasses picture frames, watches, books, etc. If you are a dog lover, check out the luxury dog beds and other canine accessories.

Tybee Island

It goes without saying that many professional fishing guides work the island. We recommend **Tybee Island Charters, Inc.**, ☎ 912-786-4801, owned and operated by USCG-licensed Captains Cecil and Elizabeth Johnson. Their Deep Sea Fishing expeditions sail from the Tybee Island Fisherman's Co-Op at Lazaretto Creek in search of amberjack, barracuda, king and Spanish mackerel, sea bass, shark or triggerfish, with four- , six- or eight-hour adventures costing $300, $400 and $500, respectively. If are looking to reel in dolphin, grouper, snapper and wahoo, an 11-hour trip will cost $600. For the really big catch – marlin, sailfish and tuna, book either a 13-hour or a 15-hour trip into the Gulf Stream, with the prices being $800 and $1,000, respectively. Closer to shore, you can enjoy a spot of Inshore Fishing, for catch bass (redfish), flounder, shark, sheepshead, tarpon or whiting. A four-hour trip costs $200 and a six-hour trip is $300. All of the Island Charters' prices are quoted for two people or, if you don't mind sharing the space, the deep-sea trips accommodate up six people.

Georgia

Rates include bait, tackle, ice and taxes, but exclude the mate's tip and food and drink for yourself.

If fishing isn't your thing, the Captains Johnson also guide a Sightseeing Cruise. Dolphin Watches, Birdwatching Tours, Sharks Teeth and Fossil Digs, Savannah River and Intracoastal Waterway Tours, Hilton Head and Daufuskie Island Tours and Island Hopping Tours can also be arranged. For each the fee, per couple, is $60 per hour, with a two-hour minimum.

Kayaking

Tybee Island

 Kayaking is a bit more novel way to see the area. **Sea Kayak Georgia**, ☎ 912-786-8732, 888-KAYAKGA (529-2542), e-mail SeaKayakGA@aol.com, www.seakayakgeorgia. com, run by Dale Williams, offers a variety of local half-day, day-long and overnight trips. Also available are trips farther afield, along the Georgia Coast, in Florida, through the Okefenokee Swamp, in Coastal Maine and even in Scotland and the British Isles. For newcomers to the sport, there are many instructional courses throughout the year. All instructors are certified by the American Canoe Association, the British Canoe Association, or both, with many having also worked as professional interpretive naturalists.

Cruises

Savannah

 No visit to Savannah would be complete without some investigation of the Savannah River, the city's lifeblood. A most enticing option is a cruise upon either the 325-passenger *Savannah River Queen* or its larger and newer sister, the 600-passenger *Georgia Queen*. Both ships are owned and operated by the **River Street Riverboat Company**, ☎ 912-232-6404, 800-786-6404, fax 234-7881, e-mail sales@savannah-riverboat.com, www.savannah-riverboat.com, 9 East River Street. There are a variety of cruises from which to choose. Throughout the year, on various days and times according to the season and with no reservations required, there is a one-hour Narrated Sightseeing Tour, for a fare of $13.95 per person. During the months March to October, sailing at midday, you can take a 1½-hour Saturday Luncheon Cruise ($22.95) or a Sunday Brunch Cruise ($24.95). Each is narrated and requires a prepaid reservation. Other cruises that might appeal are the Monday Gospel Dinner Cruise, the Moonlight Entertainment Cruise and the Murder Afloat Cruise. And, romantic weekenders will find special delight on the two-hour Dinner Entertainment Cruise. Sailing year-round and departing at 7, this includes a buffet dinner, offers live entertainment for both listening and dancing, and costs $34.95 per person. Prepaid reservations are required.

Tybee Island

You can't buy a beer, except in a restaurant, on a Sunday in Georgia. But if you are 21 years or older, you can set sail on the *Atlantic Star*, ☎ 912-786-STAR (7827), from the Lazaretto Creek Marina and indulge in the thrills of casino gambling. The 90-foot vessel, with a crew of 12 and carrying a maximum of 88 passengers, sets sail on Monday, Wednesday, Thursday, Friday and Saturday at 7 and on Saturday and Sunday at 1 for four-hour cruises. The cost of $9.95 each per person includes an open buffet of snack foods, access to a full-service bar on board, and three hours of gambling time. Hopefully, lady luck will tap your shoulder as you try your hand at one of three blackjack tables (with minimums/maximums of $5 to $100, $10 to $200 and $25 to $500, respectively); shoot craps (with $5 to $300 double odds) or take on one of 21 slot machines (playing at 25¢ to $1). Reservations are a necessity; book several days prior to sailing.

Eco/Cultural Adventures

For a close encounter with any number of aquatic friends, pay a visit to the **Tybee Island Marine Science Center**, ☎ 912-786-5917, 1510 Strand. Here, you can walk right off of the beach to view eight aquariums, a touch tank containing specimens indigenous to the coast of Georgia, and a variety of exhibits. Summer hours are Monday to Saturday from 9 am to 4 pm and Sunday 1 to 4pm. Winter hours are on Monday to Friday from 9 am to 2 pm.

In the Air

Midway Between Savannah & Statesboro

Pressing on to new heights, a hot air balloon adventure may be just the ticket to get you off to a flying start. Andy and Teresa Cayton of **Feather Air of Savannah**, ☎ 912-858-2529, 4326 Wilma Edwards Road, Black Creek, make 45-minute to one-hour flights every Friday, Saturday and Sunday, weather conditions allowing (meaning winds 10 mph or less). Flights, best taken just after sunrise or two hours before sunset, glide peacefully for five to seven miles over the most interesting countryside at an elevation of no more than 1,000 feet, unless otherwise requested. You will be treated to a post-flight champagne reception, then receive a certificate to commemorate your trip and to verify your bravery. To avoid a let-down, make reservations well in advance.

Spas & Fitness Centers

Savannah

Perhaps you are in need of rejuvenation. At 5212 Paulsen Street, there is a luxury day spa that has as its stated mission "to make you look and feel your best." The professional staff at **The Rejuvenation Center**, ☎ 912-355-3972, prides itself on quality and service. The choice of treatments here is comprehensive. These include facials, body treatments, hand and foot treatments, cosmetic services, hair removal, nail services, body massage, hydrotherapy, and a host of packages which offer a combination of the above and can be custom-designed to your specifications. Whether you have 30 minutes and a limited budget, or a full day and healthy resources, there is something at The Rejuvenation Center to suit your need.

■ Where to Stay

Savannah

The **Granite Steps**, ☎ 912-233-5380 or fax 236-3116, 126 East Gaston Street, among the newcomers to town, also happens to be one the smallest and most luxurious. The Italianate-style house, circa 1881, is located in the Historic District, just a couple of blocks from wonderful Forsyth Park and a 10-minute stroll from River Street. The five guestrooms each feature a working fireplace and are outfitted in a mix of historic local furniture, antiques and contemporary accent pieces. Two have a queen-sized bed, a balcony patio and a large shower, and one has a whirlpool tub. The other three are suites, each comprised of a sitting room, a bedroom with king-sized bed, and a marble bathroom – complete with fireplace, large walk-in shower and whirlpool tub. The rates are not inexpensive, $250 a night for a queen-sized room and $350 for a suite.

The **Magnolia Place Inn**, ☎ 912-236-7674, 800-238-7674, Fax 236-1145, e-mail b.b.magnolia@mci2000.com, www.magnoliaplaceinn.com, 503 Whitaker Street, is housed in an 1878 Steamboat Gothic house with sweeping verandas overlooking verdant Forsyth Park. In the main house are 13 guestrooms, each with private bath. Six have double Jacuzzi tubs and 11 have working fireplaces. In an adjoining property there are two suites, each with working fireplace and one with a jumbo Jacuzzi tub. The rooms are named in honor of men who figured prominently in the shaping of Savannah's destiny and rent for between $135 and $250 a night, according to location, size and facilities.

The **Hamilton Turner Inn**, ☎ 912-233-1833, 888-448-8849, www.hamilton-turnerinn.com, 330 Abercorn Street, is located in Lafayette Square at the heart of the Historic District. Originally built for a wealthy jeweler, Samuel P. Hamilton, in 1873, it is among the finest examples of Second French Empire architecture in the United States and was one of the first homes in Savannah to have electricity.

 Literature lovers will be intrigued to know that this home was subsequently owned by Nancy Hillis (the character Mandy in the book Midnight in the Garden of Good and Evil*).*

It has 14 luxury guestrooms and suites, each with private bath, telephone with dataport, television with HBO, and VCR with well-stocked video library. There are whirlpools, fireplaces and balconies overlooking the square in some rooms. Rates vary from $160 to $260 a night.

The **Ballastone Inn**, ☎ 912-236-1484, 800-822-4553, fax 236-4626, 14 East Oglethorpe Avenue, named after the legendary stones that were used as a foundation for much of Savannah, is a four-story mansion in the center of the Historic District. The charming 17-room inn has been awarded AAA Four-Diamond and Mobil Four-Star recognition. Rooms are classified as Standard at $195 to $225, Superior at $255 to $285, or Suite at $315 to $345. Be advised, however, that during the very busy spring months of March, April and May and in October, a $60 supplement is levied on each room/suite.

The **President's Quarters**, ☎ 912-233-1600, 888-592-1812, fax 238-0849, e-mail info@presidentsquarters.com, www.presidentsquarters.com, 225 East President Street, is just three blocks from River Street. These twin 1855 Federal-style townhouses, which once stood on their own block, were originally owned by Andrew Gordon Low of the family of Juliette Gordon Low, founder of the American Girl Scouts. In

1987, the properties were transformed into a sophisticated inn comprised of 19 rooms and suites, each named after an American President that has visited Savannah. Rates range between $137 and $225 per night.

The **Foley House Inn**, ☎ 912-232-6622, 800-647-3708, fax 231-1218, e-mail foleyinn@aol.com, www.foleyinn.com, 14 West Hull Street, is found on Chippewa Square, the site where scenes of *Forrest Gump* were filmed. The house, dating from 1896, was fully restored in 1982 by Inge Svensson Moore, who was born in Denmark, and her husband, Mark, formerly from New York City. The 19 guestrooms – with a mixture of king-sized, queen-sized and double beds – delicately blend traditional décor and modern amenities. Five rooms boast an oversized Jacuzzi tub and most have a gas fireplace. Rates are $165 to $275 per night.

The **Gastonian Gallery Bed & Breakfast**, ☎ 912-238-3294, 800-671-0716, www.gastongallery.com, 211 East Gaston Street, is housed in a charming 19th-century Italianate townhouse in Savannah's Historic District. An interesting collection of guestrooms offers a variety of accommodations, each with private bath – although, in some cases, access may be outside of the room. Rates range from $90 to $225 a night and a two-night minimum stay is required.

The **Hilton Savannah DeSoto**, ☎ 912-232-9000, 800-426-8483, fax 231-1633, www.Savannahdesoto, in the center of the Historic District at 15 East Liberty Street, is named in honor of Hernando DeSoto, the first European recorded as having seen the Savannah River. Today's guests choose from among 246 tastefully decorated guestrooms and three suites. Rates vary considerably, according to season and other considerations, so you should call well in advance of your trip to inquire as to rates and special promotions.

Tybee Island

The **Marsh Hen B&B**, ☎ 912-786-0378, 888-786-0378, www.tybeeisland.com/masrhhen.htm, at 702 Butler Avenue, is just a half-block from the beach. Proprietress Sally Russell has created an easy-going ambiance. The Master Suite, airy and spacious, features an elegant Jacuzzi tub; a second guestroom has a private bathroom. Your choice of a Continental or full breakfast awaits you each morning, a two-night minimum stay is required, and the high-season rates are $150 and $100.

The **17th Street Inn**, ☎ 912-786-0607, fax 786-0602, www.tybeeisland.com/lodging/17thstreetinn, owned and operated by Susie

Morris, is also a short half-block from the beach. It offers a choice of suites furnished with antique iron beds. Value lovers will find it attractive that each room has a fully furnished kitchen, some with eat-in table and chairs. For those who are of a mind to eat outside, three grills await your culinary artistry and tables and chairs are set out on the decks. Summer rates are between $110 and $125 per night

■ Where to Eat

Savannah

The **So' Soleil**, ☎ 912-234-1212, One West Broughton Street, trades in a 19th-century mercantile building within the Historic District under the direction of English chef and owner Ian Winslade, and his wife, Gypsie. Avoiding heavy sauces and extreme seasonings, Ian employs a more subtle approach to cooking. The resulting combination of ingredients, flavorings and textures yields a cuisine that is most accurately described as French-Mediterranean. Open for dinner Monday through Thursday from 6 to 10, Friday and Saturday from 6 to 11 and Sunday from 6 to 9. Lunch is served on Monday through Saturday from 11:30 to 2:30 and Sunday brunch is on offer from 11:30 to 3.

Another modern-minded and eclectic restaurant, the **Sapphire Grill**, ☎ 912-443-9962 or e-mail reservations@sapphiregrill.com, is at 110 West Congress Street near the Savannah City Market. This brainchild of Chef Chris Nason and his partner Geoffrey Batton offers dining in rooms of differing characters on two floors of a Savannah Greybrick building. The first floor, decorated with stainless steel and glass accented with deep sapphire hues, exudes an ambiance of energy. The second floor is subdued, quieter and imbued with romance. The cuisine is imaginative. Open for dinner Monday through Thursday from 6 to 10:30 and Saturday and Sunday from 5:30 to 11. Reservations are recommended.

An altogether more exotic ambiance can be found at the **Casbah Moroccan Restaurant**, ☎ 912-234-6168, www.casbahrestaurant.com, 118 East Broughton Street, between Abercorn and Drayton. Here, beneath an authentic Moroccan ceremonial tent décor and with entertainment by captivating belly dancers, you can experience genuine Moroccan cuisine. It opens for dinner Tuesday to Sunday from 5:30 to 10:30, and reservations are suggested.

Close by, but a continent apart in style is British-owned **Churchill's Pub**, ☎ 912-232-8501, the oldest bar in Savannah. Built in England

Georgia

around 1850, it was relocated to a home in Grand Central Station, New York City, until the 1920s. It was then transported to 9 Drayton Street in Savannah, where, before re-establishing itself as a traditional British pub, it endured stints as a dance club, restaurant, ice cream and soda shop, and country and western saloon. In 1997, it was featured in the movie *Midnight in the Garden of Good and Evil*. The ambiance, like the food, is as convincingly English as you will find this side of the Atlantic. And it is as great a place to stop in for a pint or two of English ale as it is to have a meal. Open Monday to Saturday from 11:30 to 2 and Sunday between 5 and 2, with dinner served until 10.

The **Bistro Savannah - Fresh Market Cuisine**, ☎ 912-233-6266, located in the Historic Market Area at 309 West Congress Street, has earned a reputation for itself as a leading seafood restaurant, although other tastes are accommodated. It opens for dinner Sunday through Thursday from 6 to 10:30 and Friday and Saturday from 5:30 to 11.

The **Shrimp Factory**, ☎ 912-236-4229, fax 233-0011, www. shrimpfactory.com, makes its home within an early 18th-century warehouse that overlooks the harbor. It is found at 313 East River Road, two blocks east of the Hyatt Regency Hotel. Not surprisingly, the specialty is shrimp – served in as many different ways as you can imagine. It is open Monday to Thursday from 11 to 10, Friday and Saturday from 11 to 11 and Sunday from noon to 10. Lunch is served until 4 and dinner from 4 to close.

The **125 River House Seafood & Bakery**, ☎ 912-234-1900, 800-317-1912, fax 234-7007, www.riverhouseseafood.com, 125 West River Street, is just west of the Hyatt Regency Hotel. This establishment has been operating since 1982 in a restored 1850s "King Cotton" warehouse. Next door and also overlooking the river, is the River House Bakery, also affectionately known as the Pecan Pie & Cheese Cake Co. During the 1980s, the River House management decided to capitalize on the popularity of its pecan pies and cheesecakes by opening a bakery. Since that time, the mail order business has flourished. Wrapped tightly in plastic and protected inside a specially designed shipping carton, these pies and cakes are shipped throughout the continental US. It's a gift that is unique and convenient, and one size really does fit all. The folks at the River House Bakery will happily take your order for friends and relatives.

The **Gryphon Tea Room**, ☎ 912-238-2481, Savannah College of Art and Design, 337 Bull Street, has a character unique not only to Savannah, but also to any other town. The charming old-world décor, including a small internal dome, is certainly conducive to a relaxing cup of tea. And the variety of choices is great, whatever the time of day. You may enjoy the beverage alone or as served with any number of goodies, including scones – served with cream and jam of course, tea sandwiches, tea sweets, and/or assorted pastries and sweet delights. But there are other attractions here than tea. Coffees are available, as are bakery delicacies, salads, and deli sandwiches. We would also recommend that you take a look at the very special teapots on display. It is open Monday to Friday from 8:30 am to 9:30 and on Saturday from 10 am to 9:30pm.

Tybee Island

The **Crab Shack**, ☎ 912-786-9857, Estill Hammock Road, is a really neat place to eat. The ambiance is aptly described in their advertisements as "Where The Elite Eat In Their Bare Feet." A visit here may leave you humming *Margaritaville*. It goes without saying that crabs, prepared in a medley of ways, feature on the menu, as do all other kinds of seafood. It is open Monday to Thursday from 11:30 to 10 and Friday, Saturday and Sunday from 11:30 to 11.

■ Visitor Information

The **Savannah Visitors Center**, ☎ 912-944-0460, 877 SAVANNAH, e-mail cvb@savga.com, www.savcvb.com, is at 301 Martin Luther King Jr. Boulevard. It is housed in the restored Central of Georgia Railroad Station, and is open Monday to Friday 8:30 to 5pm, and Saturday and Sunday from 9 to 5 (closed on Christmas Day). In addition to the usual array of brochures, city maps and helpful attendants, you can also enjoy a short audio/visual presentation. And the car park, conveniently, is the point of origin for numerous tours of the city.

Brunswick & the Golden Isles

■ The Ecology of the Georgia Coast

 Georgia's coast is divided into the following six natural ecosystems each with their own very distinctive features: barrier islands, coastal marine, estuaries and sounds, mainland upland, rivers, and swamps. Of these classifications, barrier islands are found along nearly the entire Eastern seaboard. Perhaps you will find it surprising that these are actually geologically younger than, not merely pieces of, the mainland. Some came into existence around 30,000 years ago and others emerged within the last 3,000 years. Dynamic in nature, they are continually reshaped by the powerful forces of nature in the form of winds, ocean currents, waves, storms and tides. But it is the tides that have the greatest impact on their evolution. Geographically, the eastern coastline of Georgia is the end of a massive ocean funnel and, as a consequence, tides here rise higher (six to eight feet) and faster than anyplace else on the Eastern Seaboard.

Behind the barrier islands lie Georgia's salt marshes. Here nutrients from both fresh- and saltwater mix together to provide an organic material that moves into the ocean to become a major link in the marine food chain. The marshes are also the nurseries for countless marine organisms, including shrimp, oysters, and crabs. This area claims to be the shrimp capital of the world. Without the protection of the barrier islands, these great salt marshes and the tidal creeks that meander through them would not exist, and there would be no place for the birth and development of so many delicate species. Such an abundance of life in the salt marshes invites other animals to feed, rest or nest. These Golden Isles are important to migrating waterfowl, especially those displaced from the rapidly disappearing marshes to the north. For the first time ever, the roseate spoonbill, perhaps the most beautiful of the wading birds, can be seen on Little St. Simons Island. And there are many more species difficult to find anywhere else. The islands also provide the ideal habitat for a variety of plants and animals, including endangered species like the greenfly orchid, American alligator, peregrine falcon, loggerhead sea turtle, and the southern bald eagle.

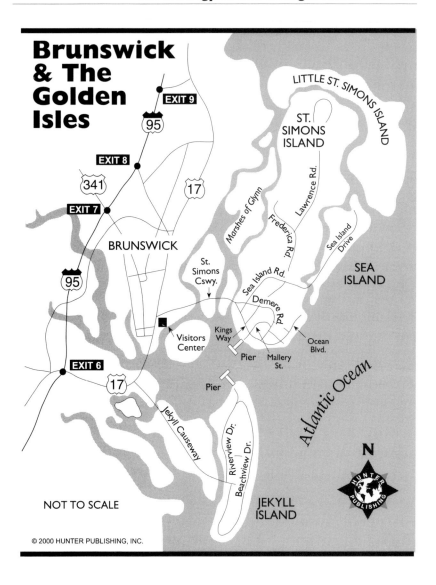

Brunswick & The Golden Isles

LITTLE ST. SIMONS ISLAND

ST. SIMONS ISLAND

EXIT 9

95

EXIT 8

341

17

EXIT 7

BRUNSWICK

Marshes of Glynn

Frederica Rd.

Lawrence Rd.

Sea Island Drive

SEA ISLAND

95

St. Simons Cswy.

Sea Island Rd.

Demere Rd.

Georgia

Visitors Center

Kings Way

Pier

Mallery St.

Ocean Blvd.

EXIT 6

17

Pier

Jekyll Causeway

Riverview Dr.

Beachview Dr.

Atlantic Ocean

N

JEKYLL ISLAND

NOT TO SCALE

© 2000 HUNTER PUBLISHING, INC.

Anyone who has spent time at the beach is aware of the two major forces that influence the ecology of the barrier islands: wind and tides. The energy generated by these two natural elements is awesome, and has battered the Atlantic coastline unceasingly. To counter this irresistible force, nature has developed a remarkable defense system: sand. It offers enough resistance to absorb and dissipate the tremendous energy of the great ocean and its storms. We take it so much for granted. The next time you are at the beach here take a few moments, run some sand through your fingers, and wonder at the significance of those tiny grains so important to the life of the islands and the shoreline just to the west.

The coastal waters off southern Georgia and northern Florida were designated a critical habitat in 1995. During the winter months, they serve as birthing grounds to the northern right whale, the official mammal of Georgia. While adults reach an average of 50 feet long and weigh in at around 60 tons, they are very rare and thought to be close to extinction.

There are 12 barrier islands along the Georgia coastline. A cluster of four of them, listed north to south as Little St. Simons Island, St. Simons Island, Sea Island and Jekyll Island, along with an interesting mainland town, Brunswick, are known, collectively, as Brunswick and the Golden Isles of Georgia.

The flags of five nations have flown over Brunswick and the Golden Isles. The first, the Spanish flag, was hoisted around 1540 when Herman de Soto explored the area. This was supplanted briefly from 1562 to 1564 with the arrival and then departure of French Huguenots, then it flew again until the Union Jack was raised by British General James Edward Oglethorpe in 1736. From 1776 to 1861 the American flag, with its 13 stars symbolizing the original colonies, flew here. In 1861, Georgia seceded from the Union, and from that date until 1865 the Stars and Bars of the Confederate States of America was raised. At the end of that war the American flag flew again, this time with 36 stars. Beyond this shared experience, each of the above-named places is endowed with its own history and characteristics.

■ Visitor Information

Brunswick & The Golden Isles of Georgia Visitors Bureau, ☎ 912-265-0620, 800-933-COAST (2627), fax 265-0629, www.bgislesvisitorsb.com, is at 4 Glynn Avenue, Brunswick, GA 31520. Welcome Centers are located on St. Simons Island and Jekyll Island, both detailed below. There is also a Visitor Center on US 17 at the St. Simons Causeway and a Welcome Center on Interstate 95 Southbound between Exits 8/38 & 9/42.

■ St. Simons Island

History

 This is both the largest and most historical of the islands. It is about the same size as Manhattan, around 24 square miles, but has a population of only 15,000. Its earliest inhabitants were the native Americans of the Muskogean tribes. In the 16th century Spanish explorers settled here and called it "San Simeon." In 1736, General James Oglethorpe, founder of Savannah, established Georgia's first military outpost at Fort Frederica to protect English colonists from Spanish forces. In fact, six years later, in 1742, the Battle of Bloody Marsh, at the southern tip of the island, actually determined the course of Colonial history. The conflict ensued when Spanish forces landed on the south of the island and forced General Oglethorpe's troops back to Fort Frederica. Not to be outdone, English troops regrouped and, though outnumbered five to one, surprised the enemy, chased them back to Fort St. Simons on the coast (which was destroyed by the retreating forces), and won a decisive victory that forever ended the Spanish threat to the colonies.

Rock hard island oaks, indigenous to the island, were put to good use during Revolutionary times. They were milled for use in war ships such as the *USS Constitution*, more fondly known as "Old Ironsides." The ensuing century and a quarter, ending with the Civil War, was one of affluence when crops of indigo and Sea Island cotton were raised on antebellum plantations throughout the island. One of these, **Hampton Plantation** on the island's northern tip, was the hiding place of Vice President Aaron Burr in 1804 after he killed Alexander Hamilton in a duel. Another, **Retreat Plantation**, overlooking St. Simons Sound at the south of the island, is the present site of the Sea Island Golf Club, approached via the famous Avenue of the Oaks, planted by Anna Page King after she inherited the land in 1826. Finally, **Hamilton Plantation**, now the site of the Epworth by the Sea United Methodist Conference/Retreat Center, was originally owned by Captain James Gascoigne who brought Oglethorpe's first settlers to Frederica.

St. Simons Island is connected to Brunswick, on the mainland, by a causeway that runs over vast stretches of the Marshes of Glynn. The latter were immortalized by 19th-century American poet Sidney Lanier in his masterful work of the same name.

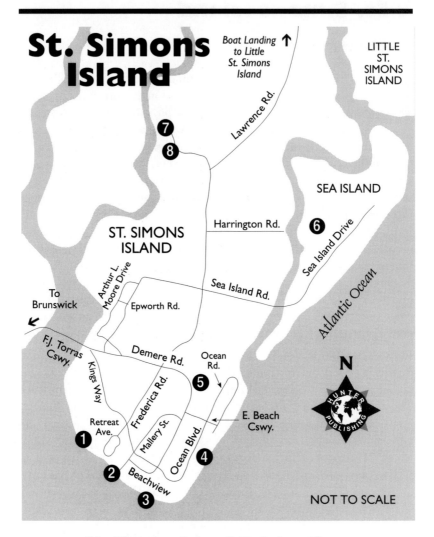

St. Simons Island Driving Tour

The number in parentheses after each stop
indicates the mileage to the next point of interest.

1. Retreat Plantation (.7)
2. Fishing Pier (.2)
3. Museum of Coastal History & St. Simons Lighthouse (1.1)
4. St. Simons Beach (Massengale Park) (1.4)
5. Bloody Marsh Battle Site (National Park Service) (5.2)
6. Sea Island (7)
7. Fort Frederica National Monument (.2)
8. Christ Church, Frederica

Sightseeng

Christ Church

 Christ Church, Frederica, at Frederica Road just past the Lawrence Road fork, is believed to be the second oldest Episcopal Church in Georgia and the third oldest in the United States. Working under the auspices of the Christ Church in Savannah, whose rector was John Wesley, his brother, Charles Wesley, became Frederica's first Protestant minister in the 1740s. In 1808, the legislature granted 100 acres around the town of Frederica for use as a church, and income from rental of the land was used, in 1820, to fund its building. Unfortunately, this was taken over and partially destroyed by Union troops during the Civil War. During the mid-1880s it was rebuilt by Anson Phelps Dodge, Jr. as a memorial to his wife, Ellen, who died during their 'round-the-world' honeymoon. Constructed of wood in the cruciform design with a trussed Gothic roof and steeple, it features beautiful stained-glass windows. Its cemetery is the last resting-place for many of the island's earliest settlers and most of her eminent citizens. It is advisable to visit after 2, when a docent is usually present to lead tours and answer questions. A donation is required.

Lighthouse & Museum

The **St. Simons Lighthouse and Museum of Coastal History**, ☎ 912-638-4666, www.novagate.com/~schoonerman/stsim.htm, is found on the historic site of Fort St. Simons, built to protect the southern tip of the island. The original lighthouse was constructed in the very early 19th century, but was blown up by Confederate forces in 1861 to prevent its use by Federal troops. The present structure, one of only five surviving light towers in Georgia and one of the oldest continuously working lighthouses in the nation, was built in 1872. Visitors are welcome to climb the 129 steps to the 104-foot-high summit, which offers an unparalleled panorama of the Golden Isles. Still in use as a navigational aid, and now fully automated, its Fresnel lens shines up to 20 miles out to sea and guides traffic entering the St. Simons Sound. The Museum of Coastal History has restored the Lightkeeper's Cottage, which contains exhibits chronicling history of the lighthouse and the way of life of a turn-of-the-century lighthouse keeper and his family. Both attractions are open, Monday to Saturday, 10 to 5 and Sunday 1:30 to 5pm.

Georgia

Fort Frederica National Monument

The Fort Frederica National Monument, ☎ 912-638-3639, www.nps. gov/parklists/index/fofr.html, Route 9, is situated on a strategically important bluff on the south branch of the Altamaha River. By now you should be familiar with the fact that General James Oglethorpe founded the Georgia colony and Savannah in 1733. He must have been happy with the results of his efforts, for the new town soon began to prosper. But all was not well in Paradise. True, the building of Savannah was proceeding, but Oglethorpe knew that it was vulnerable to attack from the Spanish, who were now firmly established in St. Augustine only 130 miles to the south. For more than 100 years they had ruled Florida with an iron hand, and Oglethorpe knew it was only a matter of time before they would visit Savannah in force. With the defense of his new colony uppermost in his mind, in 1734 he set out down the coast looking for places to fortify against the perceived threat from the south. He found a likely site on St. Simons Island just below the mouth of the Altamaha River. St. Simons in those days bore little resemblance to the idyllic vacation spot it has become today. It was a wilderness island, thick with live oaks draped in moss, but there was good water and fertile upland was available. Two years later Oglethorpe returned to St. Simons Island with the first settlers, 44 men, mostly craftsmen, and 72 women and children. You have to admire the spirit of the settlers, and indeed all of those who ventured into what can only be described as wilderness, to open up the New World. There were no facilities on St. Simons, just a few Indian trails. Imagine what it must have been like for those women and children. Oglethorpe and his settlers laid out a military town on a bluff overlooking a sharp bend on the inland passage between the island and the mainland. He named it for his king's only son, Frederick, and Fort Frederica was to become Oglethorpe's favorite town in the new colony.

First the settlers built the fort, a fairly complicated affair surrounded by a rampart with four bastions that commanded the river in both directions. Next, behind the fort on a large field, Oglethorpe laid out 84 lots, each measuring some 60-90 ft. Each family received one lot and 50 acres outside the town. The first houses were primitive, wooden structures, but these were soon replaced by houses of brick and tabby – a sort of concrete made of powder obtained from burnt oyster shells. The streets were wide and shaded by orange trees. By the mid-1740s the little town had developed to the point that it was indistinguishable from any little town you might have found in the English countryside.

By 1740 the fort and town were established and, with Oglethorpe's troops well entrenched in the fort, probably invulnerable to all but the largest force an enemy might put against them. Still, the threat from Spain was an ever-present one and Oglethorpe, the opportunist, wasn't one to wait for the enemy to come to him. So, with thoughts of conquest in mind, he set out from Fort Frederica in 1740 with a large force of some 900 English veterans and 1,100 Indians to capture St. Augustine. It was not to be; by the mid-summer Oglethorpe was back in Fort Frederica. Now it was the Spanish who felt threatened, and they, too, decided to do something about it. They set out for Fort Frederica with a fleet of 50 ships and some 2,000 soldiers in July 1742. Landing on St. Simons Island they managed to advance within sight of the fort, but Oglethorpe was waiting for them; the Battle of Bloody Marsh was a decisive victory for the English and, within a week, the Spanish were under full sail once more, heading back to St. Augustine.

When Oglethorpe was recalled to England to stand trail for alleged mismanagement of the St. Augustine campaign, things continued in Frederica just as they had been, for a little while at least. But with peace between England and Spain, the little community's usefulness became a thing of the past. Oglethorpe's regiment was disbanded in 1749 and, like any small town deprived of its main source of income, Frederica soon became something of ghost town. By 1758 it had been abandoned altogether and soon fell into ruin. Its bricks and masonry were carried off to form the foundations of other structures. Today, all that's left of the fort and the once-bustling little town is the remains of the magazine, and the excavated foundations of some of the houses and shops. Still, it's a neat experience to wander the tiny streets, devoid of buildings though they may be, and try to imagine Frederica as it was. See through the windows of imagination the brightly colored uniforms of the garrison, the gaily dressed ladies and courtly gentlemen going about the business of the day, and the children playing among the trees on warm summer days.

Fort Frederica, as preserved and maintained by the National Park Service, is a quiet place now, rarely very busy, and just the spot to spend a few moments on the banks of the river with a picnic lunch. A stop by the fort's Visitor Center, which houses a museum and an auditorium where you can see the informative film *This is Frederica*, is recommended. The park's grounds are open from 8 to 5 daily, with the Visitor Center opening one hour later.

Georgia

The Battle of Bloody Marsh

The site of the Battle of Bloody Marsh, located off Demere Road and operated by the National Park Service in conjunction with the fort, is well marked and open to the public from 9 to 5. It was here on July 7th, 1742, that a largely outnumbered force of British soldiers under the command of General James Oglethorpe defeated Manuel de Montiano's Spanish invasion. De Montiano, the governor of Florida, wanted to destroy Fort Frederica and the town around it, and lay waste the coast as far north as Port Royal in South Carolina. His fleet of 50 ships successfully ran the gauntlet of British guns at Fort St. Simons and landed troops east of Frederica on the shores of the inlet. Oglethorpe pulled back to Frederica, leaving the way open for the Spanish advance. He surprised a force of about 200 Spaniards advancing toward Frederica. These he swiftly routed, then waited. De Montiano responded by sending reinforcements to support the remains of his retreating advance force; the battle that followed was fierce, bloody, and a decisive victory for Oglethorpe and his outnumbered force of veterans. Within a week, De Montiano and his army were back aboard ship, making for St. Augustine and safety.

Private Homes & Gardens

St. Simons Island and Sea Island have more than their fair quota of beautiful homes and gardens but, unfortunately, the majority of these are owned privately and not open to the public. However, if you have your heart set on an insider's view, plan a visit to coincide with the third Saturday in March. On that day, the Episcopal Churchwomen of Christ Church sponsor the annual **Tour of Homes and Gardens**. The tour was held for the 47th consecutive time in 2000. Most recently, the price of a ticket was $25 if purchased on the day of tour, with the ticket proceeds benefiting local charities and tax deductible. ☎ 912-638-8683.

The **Village**, found on Mallery Street, at the southern end of the island and close to the fishing pier and the lighthouse, is the social center of the island. It is here, in addition to an interesting collection of small stores and restaurants, that you will find the **St. Simons Visitors Center**, in the Old Casino Building at Neptune Park. It is open daily from 9 to 5.

National Historic District

As with most historic towns and, Brunswick has its own downtown Historic District, complete with sidewalks, tree-lined streets and monuments. The streets here are not lined with live oaks, they make way for them. You're just as likely to find one growing out of the middle of the pavement as on the sidewalk. The great limbs stretch from one side of the street to the other, festooned with Spanish moss, shading the walkways, and creating the effect of an urban botanical garden that encompasses the entire downtown district. **Lover's Oak**, at Albany and Prince Streets, is a giant oak tree said to be more than 900 years old, at a point just three feet above the ground the great tree is more than 13 feet around. Old Town Brunswick was laid out according to General James Oglethorpe's standard grid pattern, and so it remains today, a city of streets and squares lined with homes noted for their turn-of-the-century architecture and eclectic mix of styles, all nicely restored and kept in pristine condition. The **Courthouse**, built in 1907, is an impressive old building, with moss-hung live oaks surrounding it.

Museums

The **Brunswick History Museum**, ☎ 912-264-0442, 1327 Union Street, is housed in the Lissner House and its exhibits detail the history of this interesting port city.

Plantations

The **Hofwyl-Broadfield Plantation**, ☎ 912-264-7333, between Brunswick and Darien on Highway 17, one mile east of I-95 at exit 9, has its roots set deep into what once was the Old South. In 1807, William Brailsford of Charleston established a rice plantation here among the swamps along the Altamaha River. When the rice industry reached its zenith, the plantation had grown to more than 7,300-acres and employed more than 350 slaves. The Civil War brought about the beginning of the end for the great plantation. At war's end the slaves were freed and labor to plant rice became short, as a consequence rice was last planted at Hofwyl-Broadfield in 1915. After that Brailsford's descendants converted the plantation into a dairy, and that closed in 1943. Eventually, in 1973, the family willed the plantation to the state of Georgia and it was turned into the State Historic Site it is today, a window onto Georgia's turbulent past. Today, you can wander among the magnolias and the camellias, stroll beneath the oak trees, and visit the fine old antebellum home. The old house is filled with fine antiques and memorabilia of times gone by. In the museum, you'll find a model of a working rice plantation, many exhibits, and you can view a slide show depicting the lives and times of the

Georgia

plantation's slaves and their owners. It is open Tuesday to Saturday, 9 to 5 and Sunday, 2 to 5:30; closed Thanksgiving and Christmas.

Adventures

On Foot

Shopping

 There is, certainly, no shortage of shops on St. Simons Island, and some of the more interesting ones are found at the **Shoppes at Redfern Village**.

What's in a Name?

The Redfern name carries with it an interesting anecdote. Paul Redfern, one of the nation's early aviators, took off from Sea Island's beach in 1927 attempting an historical first flight to Brazil. Unfortunately, he didn't make it, and many years later his plane was discovered in an impenetrable mountainous area of that country. Later in the year of his fateful journey, the first airport on St. Simons Island was named in Redfern's honor. Though McKinnon Airfield replaced the original airfield in 1938, the village retains the name of the unfortunate aviator.

In keeping with the aviary theme, you will find among the village shops **Wild Birds Unlimited**, ☎ 912-638-1442, 888-638-1422, fax 634-9231 or e-mail wbussi@technonet.com, at 312 Redfern Village. And if you have enjoyed birdwatching in the island's natural environment, there is no reason why you might not develop a bird paradise in your own backyard. There are birdfeeders in every shape and size imaginable, food for your feathered friends, a corner for hummingbirds, and deterrents to those pesky seed-stealing squirrels. John E. Johnson, the store's owner, has numerous other items that of interest. The prints adorning the walls are by a local artist who just happens to work in the store. There are decorated mailboxes, small decoys, chimes, clocks, thermometers, outside water fountains for birds, indoor and outdoor decorative fountains, flags, candles, cards and books. Also look for an all-natural, non-poisonous, insect repellent, Swamp Buddy, which might leave you with fewer unpleasant reminders of your time on the island.

On Wheels

Cycling

Benjy's Bike Shop, ☎ 912-638-6766, 1300 Retreat Plaza (Winn Dixie Shopping Center), will rent you a bike for four hours ($7), eight hours ($11), 24 hours ($15) or one, two or three weeks ($34, $48 and $58 respectively). It is open Monday to Saturday from 10 to 6.

Trolley Ride

To see and learn more about the above places, and for a good overview of the island, sign on with **St. Simons Trolley Island Tours**, ☎ 912-638-8954. Tours last 1½ hours and depart from the Pier Village daily from March 16th to September 30th at 11 and 1. The rest of the year they are conducted Tuesday to Saturday at 1. They cost $12 per person. Among the stranger things that will be pointed out to you on the tour are the Tree Spirits of St. Simons Island. Majestic oak trees proliferate over the island and, if you look closely at some of them, you will see the image of a weathered face staring back at you. These images, usually wearing sad, forlorn expressions, have been carved by skilled craftsmen to immortalize the countless sailors who lost their lives at sea aboard the mighty sailing ships once made from St. Simons oak.

Resurrection Ferns

Many of the oaks and other trees here are adorned with clusters of resurrection ferns. As with the moss, these ferns are not parasites and, being epiphytic, produce their own food by photosynthesis. In times of drought they can lose up to 70% of their water. They curl up and turn brown, often thought to be dead at such times. With the onset of rain, however, they spring back to their natural shape and color; thus their name, resurrection ferns.

On Water

Airboats, Jet Skiing & Parasailing

If your idea of fun leans more towards participation sports, make contact with **Golden Isles Watersports**, ☎ 912-638-SAIL (7245). Located at the Golden Isles Marina, they offer airboat rides for $15 per person, parasailing – up to a height of 600 feet – for $50, and Jet Ski rentals and tours at $40 a half-hour and $65 for one hour.

Diving

Two sites are popular with dive operators in this region, but there are more. Shipwrecks litter the ocean floor from one end of coastal Georgia to the other, but finding them is another task entirely and well beyond the scope of this book. Both popular sites are well out to sea and require a boat and some fairly specialized local knowledge.

Gray's Reef National Marine Sanctuary: Also known as the Sapelo Live Bottom, Gray's Reef was awarded National Marine Sanctuary status by President Jimmy Carter in 1989. The site is located some 20 miles east of Sapelo Island, and constitutes the largest nearshore live bottom off the Georgia coast; it's also the most accessible. Covering a 17-square-mile area, the underwater terrain ranges from low relief hardpan to rocky ledges rising up to eight ft from the ocean floor; live bottom occurs here and there across the entire area. Certain activities are prohibited on the reef, including trapping and collecting. The live bottom is delicate; don't touch.

"G" Reef: This is the largest of Georgia's artificial reefs. It is 26 miles east of Little Cumberland Island and consists of 3,000 old tires located 100-250 yards to the north, northeast, south and west of the marker buoy. There are also several shipwrecks on the site: a 441-ft Liberty Ship, the *Nettleton*; a 33-ft utility boat; the 100-ft tugboat, *Tampa*; and another tugboat, the 108-ft *Recife*. The wrecks *Nettleton* and *Recife* are some distance from the buoy in deeper water but are often identifiable by the schools of baitfish that surround them.

Dive Operators

Island Dive Center, ☎ 912-638-6590, 800-940-3483, e-mail dive@ thebest.net, www.thebest.net/island_dive, 101 Marina Drive, St. Simons Island GA 31522, is a PADI 5 Star Dive Center. It offers two and three tank dives to Gray's Reef and Reef G at $95/$140 and $85/ $95, respectively. These prices do not include tanks or scuba equipment rental (available at the store), are based on five paying customers and include water and snacks on the boat ride. The depth ranges from 40 to 80 feet on "G" Reef and 55 to 75 feet on Gray's Reef, with visibility varying from 25-100 feet, depending on environmental conditions. Specialty and certification upgrades are available with advance notice.

Fishing

Fly & Light Tackle Fishing

Fishing is an ever-popular pastime, and today it seems that more and more people are getting hooked on fly-fishing. In this neck of the woods, the main man to see is Captain Larry Kennedy, who operates out of his store, the **Bedford Sportsman South**, ☎ 912-638-5454 or fax 638-5493, at 3405 Frederica Road. Either he or his son Mike will be pleased to take you fly fishing or light tackle fishing where the inshore action offers redfish to flounder, and the offshore holds treasures of tarpon, shark, redfish, sea trout and mackerel. Rates range from $250 to $300 for a half-day, and catch and release fishing is encouraged. As they like to say, "wild fish are too valuable to be caught only once." You don't have to worry if you've come unprepared. This Orvis-endorsed outfitter has on display a full range of fly fishing equipment and accessories, offers casting and tying instruction, and stocks a wide range of hiking boots, backpacks, sports clothing, gifts, and Battenkill luggage.

Kayaking

Kayaking, is becoming increasingly popular. **SouthEast Adventure Outfitters**, ☎ 912-ME-TO-SEA (638-6732), e-mail southeastadventure@coastalgeorgia.com, www.gacoast.com/navigator/sea.html, at 313 Mallory in The Pier Village, has many tours available, complete with knowledgeable guides. The two-hour Introduction to Sea Kayaking, exploring the Marshes of Glynn, costs $30; a three-hour St. Simons Sea Kayak Tour is $40; and the fee for a half-day excursion to St. Simons from their other headquarters in Brunswick is $55. They also offer trips to the Altamaha and Satilla rivers, Pelican Split, Cumberland and Sapelo Islands and the Okefenokee Swamp, some with overnight stays.

Motor Yacht Charters

If you are in search of a way to celebrate a really special occasion and are prepared to pay for such memories, look to **Lady Patricia Charters**, ☎/fax 912-638-8450, 511 Marsh Circle, St. Simons Island, GA 31522. The 48-foot classic motor yacht *Lady Patricia*, built by the renowned Elco Boat Works in 1936, is the recipient of numerous awards, including recognition as the "Best Classic Powerboat" from the Museum of Yachting in Newport, Rhode Island. She went to war with the US Navy in 1942, and served for several decades as a pleasure craft in upstate New York before undergoing a decade-long restoration process beginning in 1987. The combination of her classic

Georgia

lines and period detailing with state-of-the-art electronics and lavish guest comforts have created a grand expression of vintage motor yachting. Onboard, you will find three staterooms, a delightful salon, an open-air fantail at the stern, an ample galley with a stocked beverage bar and full air conditioning. If your dream is to set sail in an ambiance of gracious elegance, floating along as the setting sun slips below the horizon, giving way to a glistening lunar sheen upon the waters, this is for you. However, you will disembark, two hours later, with a wallet $350 lighter and a lifetime of memories.

In the Air

 Now that we are acquainted with the aquatic side of St. Simons, it is time to consider getting a birds-eye perspective of the barrier islands. **Air Tours**, ☎ 912-222-2448, operating out of McKinnon Airport, will take you up and over nine barrier islands, while the pilot gives an intriguing narrative of the rich history and the ecological and recreational opportunities of coastal Georgia. Rates begin at $25 per person, and vary according to the itinerary selected.

Eco/Cultural Adventures

If you would like a guided tour of the narrow tidal creeks between St. Simons and Sea Island, with a running commentary and anecdotes about the wildlife, and a chance to discover the unique features of the marsh ecosystem, contact **Salt Marsh Nature Tours**, ☎ 912-638-9354, www.marshtours. com. In their 24-foot pontoon boat, with a shallow draft ideal for getting close to the cordgrass spartina alterniflora, Captains Jeanne or Jim supply binoculars and books in all seasons and lined parkas in the colder weather, on a 1¾-hour ride that costs just $40 per person. You will get a close look at the beautiful birds of the marsh, probably see bottlenose dolphins and possibly catch sight of a river otter, mink or alligator. At low tide you may even get to handle oysters. If you have different sorts of adventures in mind, Salt Marsh offers a variety of other cruises: a Dolphin Quest, a Sunset Cruise, Moonlight Boat Rides, two- or three-hour Excursions to Pelican Split, and a three-hour History Tour to Hampton Point. These range in price between $30 and $55 per person, depending upon their length.

Where to Stay

The King and Prince Beach & Golf Resort, ☎ 912-638-3631, 800-342-0212, fax 638-7699, www.kingandprince.com, Arnold Road at Downing Street, PO Box 20798, St. Simons Island, GA 31522. First opened in the fall of 1935 as a private club, it was designed to reflect a regal atmosphere. Only three months later, a fire attributed to arson burned it to the ground. It was subsequently rebuilt in the lovely Spanish Colonial style for which it is famous today. On July 2, 1941, a festive five-day celebration marked the opening to the public of the King and Prince Hotel. Designed with lovely views of the ocean and oriented to take full advantage of the breezes, its 110 guestrooms are equipped with ceiling fans and circulating ice water. These days guests may choose from among 140 guestrooms and 44 two- and three-bedroom beach villas. The indoor pool and hot tub are joined by four outdoor pools; four Rubico tennis courts; an exercise room; bike, sailboat and kayak rentals; and the 18-hole Hampton Club golf course. Rates for an oceanfront or poolside room are $120, $140 or $185, according to season, with other rooms priced seasonally at $95, $115 or $155.

The **Holiday Inn Express**, ☎ 912-634-2175 or 800-ST SIMONS (787-4666), 299 Main Street, Plantation Village, St. Simons Island, GA 31522, offers modern, clean accommodations and is wheelchair-accessible. There is a complimentary breakfast buffet and outdoor pool. Rates start at $72 a night.

Where to Eat

St. Simon's Island, unlike the other three Golden Isles, has some dining options apart from those of the hotel variety, although the King and Prince has a very fine, pleasant restaurant of its own. But for those of a mind to "dine out," we offer the following options.

J Mac's Island Restaurant and Bistro, "In The Village" at 407 Mallory Street, ☎ 912-634-0403, fax 912-638-0814 or jmac@technonet.com, is open for dinner Monday through Saturday from 5:30 until late, and boasts of offering St. Simon's "Finest Dining Experience." Seafood dominates the menu, but with a Southern flare.

A bit more laid-back is **Frederica House**, ☎ 912-638-6790, 3611 Frederica Road, built of aged cedar and cypress wood and frequented by locals. The atmosphere is cozy with seating both on the main floor and the balcony. Seafood and steaks predominate and the grilled seafood special is offered nightly. Dinner is served from 5:30-9:30.

Visitor Information

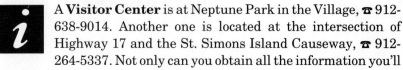

A **Visitor Center** is at Neptune Park in the Village, ☎ 912-638-9014. Another one is located at the intersection of Highway 17 and the St. Simons Island Causeway, ☎ 912-264-5337. Not only can you obtain all the information you'll need to make your visit a special one, you can also see a replica of one of the Liberty Ships built here during World War II, and the pot in which Brunswick Stew was first made. You can also view a short video that will give you a rundown on the sights and sounds of Brunswick and the Golden Isles. Open daily from 9 to 5.

■ Sea Island

History

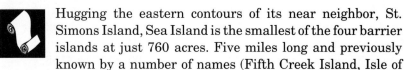

Hugging the eastern contours of its near neighbor, St. Simons Island, Sea Island is the smallest of the four barrier islands at just 760 acres. Five miles long and previously known by a number of names (Fifth Creek Island, Isle of Palms, Long Island, Glynn Isle and Sea Island Beach), it owes its fame to wealthy visionary Howard E. Coffin, who pioneered the idea of opening a resort hotel here, which became **The Cloister**. He formed the Sea Island Company, which was managed by his friend and cousin Alfred William (Bill) Jones Sr.

The Cloister

An initial obstacle to the resort's development was a lack of public utilities. They resolved this problem by building their own electricity plant and installing a local telephone system. In addition, as there was no railroad service to Brunswick at that time, a transport company was formed to shuttle guests to and from the nearby hubs of Savannah and Jacksonville. It was some time later that Mr. Jones persuaded the Seaboard Air Line Railroad to add a stop at Thalman, just 12 miles north of Brunswick, for the convenience of Cloister guests. The resort itself, a hotel of 46 rooms, was designed by acclaimed architect Addison Mizner, who originated the name **Cloister**. He created a low, sprawling, Mediterranean-style structure, set back from the ocean, with cloistered terraces and a grand lounge with high beamed ceiling and clerestory windows. A young landscape architect, T. Miesse Baumgardner, was commissioned to complement the design, which he did – transforming the island into a subtropical balance of natural and cultivated beauty. Simultaneously, work continued on a residential colony whose street names honor Indians, Frenchmen, Spaniards, Colonists, and even pirates.

The Cloister opened on October 12, 1928. Not long after, in 1937 and upon Mr. Coffin's death, ownership passed to Alfred W. Jones. To this day, the Jones family controls the Sea Island Company, which continues to manage the resort. Although the first decade of its operation was not an overwhelming success, persistence paid many dividends. Over the ensuing decades, the hotel was expanded to 286 rooms, refurbishments and renovations were undertaken faithful to the original style, and activities – golf, tennis, horseback riding, sailing, boating and shooting – were added. In recent times and in keeping with popular trends, a modern, state-of-the-art spa joined the Cloister's menu of amenities. The spa has been given the "Jeffrey Joseph Spa of the Year Award" by readers of *Spa Management Magazine* annually since 1993.

Throughout the years, with an ambiance that combines the carefree balance of luxurious living with casual comfort, the Cloister has gained an international reputation as a first-class resort. This, in turn, has attracted a wide array of American presidents, royalty and other dignitaries. It is also a favorite honeymoon destination. Since a register was first kept, in the early 1940s, over 36,000 honeymoon couples have begun their wedded life at the Cloister. Many of them, President and Mrs. Bush for example, have returned to celebrate their anniversaries.

There is an anomaly here. All activities are under the auspices of the Cloister, although many, such as golf, shooting, tennis and riding, are actually located on St. Simons Island.

Adventures

On Foot

Golf

Sea Island has three legendary golf courses – two are found at the Sea Island Golf Club and the other at the adjacent St. Simons Island Club. Playing fees for 18 holes are $115 per

Georgia

person daily and $70 for n5ne holes, including cart, practice range, club cleaning and storage.

Shooting

The Sea Island Shooting School is one of only a handful of shooting facilities that offer all three types of clay target shooting – a five-stand sporting clay field, two skeet ranges and one trap field. You can take aim for $45 a round, including all equipment.

Tennis

The Cloister tennis facilities have been recognized by *Tennis Magazine* (in their list of America's 50 Best Tennis Resorts) and *Racquet Magazine* (in the Best 100 Resorts in the World). The court fee is $15 per day, doubles or singles, and if courts are available play is unlimited.

On Wheels

Bicycling

Biking is a popular way of getting around the island, and the side streets also offer a tour of beautiful homes. Cycles can be rented at $5 for the first hour, $9 for a half-day, $14 for the first full day and $6 per day after that.

On Water

Boat Rentals & Boat Rides

Rent a catamaran for $45 per hour, a single sea kayak for $18 per hour, or a tandem kayak for $25 per hour.

Boat and nature cruises are also available at $30, $40 or $55 per person for one, two and three hours respectively, and with a minimum of the equivalent dollar price for four people.

Fishing

Waterway fishing, either from the Cloister Dock opposite the hotel motor entrance or from the saltwater creeks, rivers and adjoining inlet and sounds, is a popular pastime. According to the season, the catch may include speckled sea trout, tarpon, bass, drum, flounder, whiting, croaker or sheepshead.

On Horseback

 The Cloister also has private stables, from which you can embark on a one-hour Marsh Ride for $30, a two-hour Beach Ride at $58, or a Guided Nature Ride for $75. Instruction is also available. If you bring your own horse along, the boarding fee is $30 per night.

Spas & Fitness Centers

 The Cloister has a state-of-the-art day spa. The Spa Retreat package offers couples two massages each, a soothing Sea Stones massage, multi active vitamin facial, one-hour reflexology session, nutritional consultation with body composition analysis, fitness consultation and a half-hour of personal training. The Ultimate Relaxation allows you three massages, seaweed gel facial, Thermal Mineral Kur, one-hour reflexology session and peach paraffin hand treatment. The cost for either of these, above and beyond the room rate and spa service gratuities, is $510 per person, plus tax. A spa package coordinator will tailor a visit to your specific needs and you will have the use of all spa facilities, entry to exercise classes, wellness lectures and demonstrations, and the option of spa cuisine. As space is limited, package reservations must be made four weeks in advance. Alternatively, consider one of the spa's day programs.

If a package doesn't fit your itinerary or budget, at least pamper yourselves with a singular treatment. Whether you choose an exotic body treatment, a soothing massage, or a skin, hand or foot treatment, a visit to the spa is guaranteed to relax you.

Where to Stay

 The Cloister, ☎ 912-638-3611, 800-SEA-ISLA (732-4752), www.seaisland.com, synonymous with Sea Island, is an international institution in its own right. The history of The Cloister is given above in detail above, and it remains today a resort of rare charm and distinction. You will find here an artful combination of gracefulness, manners and charm of bygone eras, coupled with modern amenities and facilities. The 286 guestrooms, including 32 suites, are all elegantly furnished. Prices are dictated by location (either riverside or oceanfront), type of room, the building in which it is located and the season. Prices range from a low of $141 for the smallest room in the lowest season, up to $433 for an Oceanfront Parlor Suite in the high season. Rates are quoted per person per day,

Georgia

and are subject to state and local taxes, a 15% service charge and, for stays of less than five days, a surcharge of $4 per person per day. The Cloister operates on the Full American Plan, which allows three meals daily, featuring an unusual range of menus served in a variety of settings. A host of other bonuses are included as well.

Guests may avail themselves of Beach Club privileges such as the salon, lockers, steam room and dry sauna, all at no charge. Adjacent to the Beach Club, on a section of the miles and miles of unspoiled beach, you can rent a cabana for $20 a day.

Where to Eat

All restaurants on Sea Island are a part of the Cloister complex.

■ Little St. Simons Island

At 10,000 acres, this is the northernmost of the islands and, being accessible only by boat from St. Simons Island, it is certainly the most secluded. During the 1800s, it was a part of the Hampton Rice Plantation, whose owners were prominent citizens in this part of coastal Georgia. In 1908 it was bought by the Eagle Pencil Company, with the aim of harvesting the red cedar trees for pencil making. When these proved to be unsuitable, Mr. Philip Berolzheimer, the company's owner, purchased the island as a family-owned private retreat, which it still is today. Finally, in 1979, the Lodge on Little St. Simons Island was opened to the public, although the current owners, intent on preserving the natural state of the island, limit the number of guests to just 30 at a time.

Adventures

On Foot

Beaches

You will find seven miles of private beaches for swimming, sunbathing, shelling and strolling. This is one of the few places left in coastal Georgia where you can find seashells easily in quantity and in all shapes and sizes.

Georgia's state shell, the knobbed whelk, can be found here. Approximately eight inches long when fully mature, it's a whorled shell with heavy spines and knobs, brownish in color on the outside, pastel orange in the mouth, with a semi-gloss surface. They are found mostly at low tide and within 30 foot of the shoreline.

Even the elusive sand dollar lies liberally scattered across the ocean shallows and sandy beach. Be careful as you wade. Although the shallows stretch outward from the beach for hundreds of feet, rarely more than ankle-deep, they are a favorite haunt of the stingray.

Although most stingrays are fairly small – not much bigger than the average serving plate – there are lots of them and they can inflict a nasty wound if stepped upon; so keep your eyes open.

Trails

Across the acre upon acre of ancient forests there are 15 miles of trails suitable for hiking, biking (bikes are supplied free), and horseback riding with free guided tours and explorations. Along one of the more scenic of these trails, the two-mile **Old House Road** follows the western side of the maritime forest and passes through the island's largest prehistoric archaeological site. The island was once a seasonal camp for the Guale Indians, who in the winter months foraged for oysters in the local creeks and rivers. Their legacy is a vast area of oyster shell "middens" that date from 700 to 1650 AD.

Aside from their historical interest, the oyster middens have served to enhance the ecology. Calcium that has leaked from the oyster shells over the centuries has buffered the acid soil, giving rise to dense growths of Southern red cedar, and providing perfect growing conditions for two rare plants – the Florida privet and tiny-leafed buckthorn.

A little to the south of the middens, a tabby and brick chimney stands on a slight bluff overlooking the marshes and Old House Creek, all that remains of one of the earliest structures built here by European settlers in the early 1800s. You'll find all sorts of rare plants and birds, and this is one of only two barrier islands on the entire East Coast where you can see the rare and endangered greenfly orchid.

On Water

By Boat

If you want to explore the waterways on your own, your choice of canoes or 14-foot Carolina skiffs will take you deep into the marshes and along the shoreline. This is an ideal way to see the dolphins that reside in these waters.

Fishing

Gear and bait are provided and there are plenty of fish awaiting your attention. Fly fishing is gaining popularity, and some of the best salt-water fly fishing on the Georgia coast can be found on and around Little St. Simons Island. You can, of course, go it alone, but the **Lodge at Little St. Simons** offers instructional programs and excursions that can be tailored to any level of expertise. These, though, are not included in the basic rates.

Eco/Cultural Adventures

With a goal of deepening understanding of and appreciation for the wonderful workings of nature, The **Lodge at Little St. Simons** offers the opportunity to participate in guided interpretive programs, hiking and other activities. Scheduled daily and touring the island by truck, foot, watercraft, horseback, or any combination thereof, these are designed to expose guests to each of the four distinct ecosystems on the Island: maritime forest, wetlands, salt marsh and beach.

Birds

This 10,000-acre island, virtually unchanged for centuries, provides a home to the most eclectic array of birds and animals imaginable. Bird lovers can fashion numerous avian adventures involving the over 240 different species, some of which are endangered, that have been recorded on the island. Each spring, colorful **songbirds** alight on the island during their northward migration, while in the fall the **shorebird** migration begins and the brightly colored neo-tropical species begin their southward journey. The ongoing accretion of the island results in large areas of inter-tidal flats and sandbars that are attractive feeding areas for shorebirds. The best time for shorebirding is at high tide, when they retreat to the upper reaches of the sandbars and beaches, or just afterward as the water is receding. The north end of the Main Beach, near the mouth of Bass Creek, provides an ideal location from which to study these birds. Especially fascinating are the tall and elegant **wading birds**, such as herons and egrets, best spotted in the island's marshes, tidal creeks and rivers – especially at Myrtle Pond, at the old airstrip, and in the high marsh area east of Marsh Road. If you are keen enough to wake early in the morning, join up with one of the island naturalists who lead tours and can assist in locating the birds and providing identification.

Other Wildlife

You are quite likely to see **European fallow deer**. These were introduced to the island in the 1920s by the original owner and now roam freely. Romantic weekenders visiting in the fall, the deer's mating season, if they listen closely, will hear the lovelorn creatures "barking." Spring visitors will delight to see the tiny fawns, born in late spring and early summer, springing after their mothers on unsure, spindly legs. **Tree frogs**, **armadillos** and the shy **river otters**, too, can sometimes put in an appearance, as can the intriguingly appealing, but rather dangerous, American alligator.

The Alligator

The alligator is a living relic of the dinosaur age and has essentially remained unchanged for 65 million years. These creatures abide in the coastal plain region of the southeastern US, from the Carolinas through Texas, with the only other member of its genus residing in the Yangtze River basin of China. By the middle of the 20th century, the alligator population in the US had declined to an alarming low – in sacrifice to the lucrative market for alligator hide and meat. Its numbers have, however, increased remarkably since protective laws were enacted by both state and federal legislatures in the mid-1960s. Many will not realize that the alligator's purpose in these areas goes far beyond biological ornamentation. They are a critical component of the ecosystems where they reside, particularly the seasonal freshwater wetlands found on the barrier islands. During the summer months, when the water level subsides, the "wallows" they dig as a refuge for themselves, serve to protect neighboring fish and amphibians. On Little St. Simons Island they play a complicated and important role in the ecology of colonial-nesting wading birds. The rookery of great and snowy egrets at Willow Pond is one example. Here, wily alligators lie in wait beneath the rookery for the occasional egg or chick to fall from the safety of its nest. Far from damaging the rookery, this is actually a benefit to it. The alligators' presence acts as a deterrent to foraging raccoons that would cause much more damage.

In mid-April, the males' deep growls emanating from ponds and sloughs, signaling the onset of the courtship season. Within domed nests built in June, 35 to 50 eggs incubate for approximately 65 days. The hatchlings, six to eight inches long, are extremely vulnerable and the mortality rate approaches a staggering 80%. The young live in close proximity to their birthplace for two to three years, and survivors of early days may live as long as 35 to 50 years. As water is essential to regulation of their body temperatures, they are seldom found far from an aquatic habitat. Smaller ones eat frogs, insects and small fish, while older ones enjoy a diet of turtles, snakes, small mammals and even a smaller alligator. Though grisly tales abound, alligators have a natural fear of humans. Most negative encounters with humans have arisen from our offering food. Visitors here should keep their distance and not feed the animals. They can travel faster than most humans on the ground over a short distance and can be dangerous when cornered or provoked.

Where to Stay

The **Lodge on Little St. Simons Island,** ☎ 912-638-7472, 888-733-5774, fax 634-1811, e-mail lssi@mindspring.com, www.littleStSimonsIsland.com, PO Box 21078, St. Simons Island, GA 31522, is privately owned and accommodation is limited to just 30 overnight guests. Accessible only by boat from the Hampton River Club Marina on neighboring St. Simon Island 15 minutes away, it is the ideal place to go for nature lovers who are seeking complete privacy in an unspoiled wilderness. All guestrooms feature air conditioning, ceiling fans and use of washer/dryer, with most having a fireplace, screened porch and deck. You won't find televisions, telephones or other such modern communications, and an alarm clock is superfluous as well. The folks on this private island wake each day to the tolling of a cast iron bell that announces breakfast – a sumptuous meal served family-style in the Hunting Lodge Dining Room around long oak tables supported by local cedar tree trunks. Lunch can be taken in the same room or, if you prefer, the kitchen staff will prepare an island picnic replete with regional specialties for you to savor beachside or overlooking the rivers and marshes. You won't need a blanket, at least not for the meal. The staff has set up picnic tables at some of the island's more scenic spots for just such occasions.

Later comes the time-honored tradition of the cocktail hour. When held indoors in the hunting lodge, it features delicious regional fare such as fried green tomatoes or roasted quail with a sweet and sour dipping sauce. Weather permitting, guests are invited outdoors onto the front lawn where bushels of oysters, along with cocktail sauce, crackers and lemons, will be waiting beside a bonfire. Barge cruises aboard the *Captain Doug*, weather and tides permitting, are another cocktail hour favorite. You can take a sunset cruise along the island's waterways with unobstructed views of the famous Marshes of Glynn, while partaking of delicacies such as local blue crabs and fresh steamed Georgia shrimp. A feast, to be sure, for all your senses.

Dinner, again taken communally in the Hunting Lodge Dining Room, is an abundance of home-style cuisine, often featuring wild game and local seafood. Once each month, The Lodge offers a full-moon beach picnic, with baskets of blue crabs, in a pavilion overlooking a seven-mile stretch of beach so pristine and so deserted that it is easy to imagine that yours are the first feet ever to grace the sand.

But there is much more here than accommodations and meals. In fact, there is an extensive array of activities (detailed above), all of which are included in the price. Dress on Little St. Simons is decidedly casual, with even cocktail hour and dinner being "dress as you like" affairs.

The High Season on Little St. Simons is October through June, and the Summer Season is July through September. There is a minimum two-night stay on weekends and during the holidays of Easter, Thanksgiving and Christmas. Daily rates for two people during the High Season are $450 for the Hunting Lodge, $500 for Cedar House/River Lodge or Helen House, and $550 for Michael Cottage. Summer Season rates are $325, $375 and $425, respectively. These include all activities, boat transportation to and from the Hampton River Club Marina, three home-cooked meals each day – with picnic lunches available, and complimentary mixed drinks, beer, wine, soft drinks and juices. The only services that carry additional charges are the charter fishing guide, fly fishing school, overnight dockage for private boats, golf and tennis, historical tours and shopping trips on neighboring St. Simons and Sea Island.

Georgia

■ Jekyll Island

This, the southernmost of the islands, is 10 miles long by 1½ miles wide. As dictated by a 1995 law, development is limited to no more than 35% of its 5,565 acres – over 4,200 of which are above the mean high water line – thus preserving a mostly undeveloped, pristine environment that is rich with wildlife.

History

 Jekyll Island's first known inhabitants were the Guale Indians, who called it "Ospo," which means "toward the marsh." Subsequent to Spanish missionaries' habitation of the island in the 16th and 17th centuries, General James Oglethorpe, passing by the island in 1734, renamed it after a friend, Sir Joseph Jekyll, who had contributed generously toward his campaign to colonize Georgia. One of Oglethorpe's most trusted officers, Major William Horton, established a home and a prosperous plantation on the island. These were destroyed in 1742 by the retreating Spanish, following their defeat at the Battle of Bloody Marsh on St. Simons Island. By 1746 Major Horton had rebuilt both with "tabby" – a building material native to coastal Georgia, using crushed oyster shells as its main ingredient. The shell of that home and the ruins of Georgia's first brewery, which he also built, can be seen to this day. After the Major's death in 1749, his son had no inclination to operate the plantation himself. As subsequent owners fell short in their efforts to develop the property, it was sold several times for the payment of outstanding debts and taxes prior to its acquisition by Christophe Poulain du Bignon around 1800. He raised Sea Island cotton there until his death in 1825. It was in 1858 under his son's ownership that the slave ship *Wanderer* arrived at Jekyll Island with the last major cargo of slaves ever to land in the United States. The Civil War destroyed the plantation way of life here, as it did elsewhere. Finding it impractical during Reconstruction to continue operation of a cotton plantation, the du Bignon family subdivided the land, selling it off section by section.

Postwar entrepreneur John Eugene du Bignon, a descendant of Christophe Poulain, purchased one of these sections. He and his brother-in-law, the well-connected Newton S. Finney, formulated a plan to purchase the island and to sell it to northerners seeking warmer climes during the winter months for their use as a private hunting club. To their advantage, Finney, as a member of New York's Union Club, a meeting place for some of America's wealthiest and

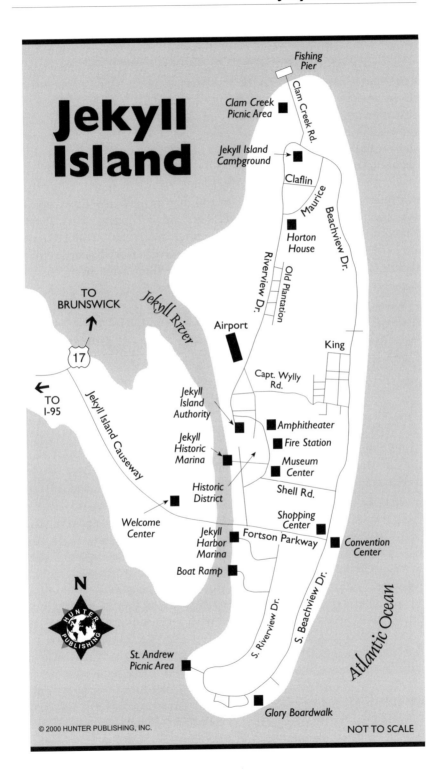

Jekyll Island

Georgia

NOT TO SCALE

most influential men, was in an ideal situation to arrange hunting trips for his affluent friends. By June 16, 1885, the men had succeeded in purchasing the entire island at a cost of $13,100 and were in a position to negotiate with the prospective Jekyll Island Club. A purchase price of $125,000 was agreed upon and on January 8, 1886 the Jekyll Island Club was officially incorporated with a limit of 100 shares of stock. They expected 50 subscribers, with each taking two shares, but by April 1st demand was so great that the charter list had expanded to 53. Subsequently, the Club management limited the purchase to only one share of stock and, requiring election by other members, held the membership to 100. The formation of the new club was announced in the April 4, 1886 edition of *The New York Times*, who noted, presciently, that it was going to be "the 'swell' club, the crème-de-la-crême of all, in as much as many of the members are intending to erect cottages and make it their Winter Newport."

Over the next half-century this became the winter home for the visionaries, mainly from New York City, who led the technological and economic revolution that transformed the United States of America from an agrarian society to an industrial world power. Men such as William Rockefeller, J.P. Morgan, Joseph Pulitzer, Vincent Astor and William K. Vanderbilt, household names to this day, spent the season, between January and early April, here. Indeed, so exclusive was the club that, during its active existence from 1886 until 1942, only 361 men and women were privileged to hold full membership.

Acclaimed landscape artist Horace W.S. Cleveland was retained to lay out the grounds and the building plots for members, with the mission of creating a "paradise" that would enhance the natural beauty of the island. And with the completion, by November 1, 1887, of architect Charles A. Alexander's elegant yet unpretentious clubhouse, the Jekyll Island Club was ready for the 1888 season, its first. It was during that first year that members began construction of their private residences, which, rather euphemistically, were referred to as "cottages." To most people, they would have been considered mansions! Slowly, club facilities were expanded and improved, with telephone communications established with the mainland in 1892, a golf course added in 1898, and electricity replacing the antiquated gas lighting system in 1903. By the end of World War I, in 1918, the operation of the club had become so complex that it catered for the physical needs, through medical services, and spiritual needs, by way of a small church, of its members. It boasted oyster beds, a full-scale dairy, a large vegetable garden, a collection of vintage wine, a steam launch for guest excursions, and a taxidermist. And the library made available whatever newspapers the members required, regardless of where they were published.

Life at the Jekyll Island Club was tranquil and gracious indeed. The Vanderbilts' and Astors' splendid yachts became familiar sights. The hub of social life was the Club House, where most members enjoyed sumptuous cuisine and one another's company for activities such as whist, bridge, billiards and the occasional dance. Outdoor recreations included hunting, cycling, horseback riding and tennis. All in all, for the wealthy, Jekyll was a total escape from the hectic daily routine in the north.

History at the Jekyll Island Club

Jekyll Island would host several events of national importance during the "Club Era." In 1910, Senator Nelson Aldrich arranged a meeting on the island to draft a plan for sweeping bank reforms. So secret was the transaction that the use of full names was forbidden, and participants thus became known as the "First-Name Club." The resulting agreement was the Aldrich Plan that, with some modifications, in 1913 became the Federal Reserve System. Also of import was the first transcontinental telephone call, which, on January 25, 1915, connected Bell Telephone General Manager Theodore N. Vailon on Jekyll Island with Alexander Graham Bell in New York, President Wilson in Washington DC, and Bell's assistant, Thomas Watson, in San Francisco.

Georgia

The Club's future was not, however, impervious to the ravages of the Great Depression, when all but the very wealthy suffered. Following the entry of the United States into World War II in December 1941, the 1942 season was forced to close a few weeks early for lack of supplies. The intention was to open again after the war; but fate would have it that the Club never reopened its doors.

In 1946, Governor Ellis G. Arnall set up a committee to consider one of Georgia's Sea Islands for use as a state park. When it decided upon Jekyll Island the committee was told that it was not for sale. The state, though, was empowered to condemn the Island and to confiscate it for public use. On October 8, 1947, with the consent of the Club, which received a settlement of $675,000, Georgia took possession of Jekyll Island. It promptly established the Jekyll Island Authority and assigned as one its first tasks responsibility for building a causeway to the mainland. For some time the state attempted to operate the Club House and apartments but, as there was less concern in those days with historic preservation, little effort was put into maintenance of the buildings and some fell into a sorry state of disrepair. In 1969, after recognizing the historic value of these turn-of-the-century treasures, the Authority instituted the restoration of the McKay-Rockefeller Cottage, continuing work on other structures into the early 1970s. In recognition of these ongoing efforts, the Secretary of the Treasury designated the 240-acre Jekyll Island Club Historic District as a National Historic Landmark in June 1978.

During the era that spanned the late 1950s through the early 1970s, much development, including hotels, golf courses, a shopping center and convention complex, took place on the island. But this construction was done with scant regard for its environmental impact, because the developers knew little about the importance of sensitive dune networks and undisturbed natural areas.

In 1978, a new era began when the state amended the structure of the Jekyll Island Authority, replacing political favoritism with a business approach to the island's management. The new board, consisting of private citizens from throughout the state, ended tax revenue support and imposed a mandate that the Authority should become self-supporting through revenues generated on the island. Thus, since 1983, no state taxes have been used to support Jekyll Island's operations. The Authority also established a Museums and Historic Preservation Division to implement a professional approach to preservation and collections management efforts. At the same time, work continued apace in restoring, stabilizing and interpreting the structures and sites within the Historic District, culminating, in 1985, with the newly renovated and restored Jekyll Island Club Hotel. In the mid-1980s the golf facilities were vastly improved, and in 1988 the Jekyll Island Tennis Complex opened, along with Summer Waves, an 11-acre water-park.

Concurrently, the Jekyll Island Authority worked to reverse the damage caused by earlier development. In the early 1980s, it rebuilt the dune systems and installed crossovers to the beach at the South Dunes Picnic Area. It also oversaw the replacement of six acres of an asphalt parking lot with dune networks and attractive parking and picnic areas. To further protect the island and guarantee its preservation for future generations, the Georgia General Assembly passed legislation in 1995 that limits development on Jekyll Island to no more than 35% of the land above mean high water.

Visitors to Jekyll Island may be surprised that, after crossing the causeway from the mainland, they are assessed $3 parking fee per day upon entering the island. The revenue received is one source of funding for the island's operations and maintenance.

Sightseeng

National Historic Landmark District

 Visitors to Jekyll Island will be curious about the 240-acre National Historic Landmark District, which consists of 33 structures, including the Jekyll Island Clubhouse and numerous mansion-sized cottages. A behind-the-scenes tour provides an inside look at the craftsmanship involved in the restoration of **Moss Cottage**, circa 1896. For tour information, call ☎ 912-635-2119.

Instead of hoofing it, an informative and relaxing option is a narrated horse-drawn carriage ride operated by **Victoria's Carriages & Trail Rides**, ☎ 912-635-9500. Daytime tours, between 10 and 3pm, last approximately 40 minutes and depart from the Visitors Center on Stable Road. Evening carriage rides, between 5:30 to 9:30pm, last approximately 30 minutes and depart from the Jekyll Island Club Hotel. The regular fare for either is $10 per person.

Once you have been suitably introduced to the exterior of these historic landmarks, track back to the very beautiful **Faith Chapel**. Constructed in 1904 as a non-denominational church for Club members, its main claim to fame is a pair of exquisite stained-glass windows. The one in the west façade, an original by the incomparable Louis C. Tiffany, is one of few of such works signed by him. The other window, above the altar and also signed, is the work of David Maitland Armstrong, Tiffany's protégé, who served as Second Counsel General to Italy, and his daughter, Helen Armstrong.

Adventures

On Foot

Beaches

 Jekyll Island is blessed with more than 10 miles of public beaches, sand dunes, and sea oats, all of which are accessible by motor vehicle. Here, you can enjoy endless opportunities for shell and driftwood collecting, beachcombing, swimming, fishing, windsurfing, or just relaxing. Except at the height of the vacation season, the sands are quiet with plenty of room to stretch out in comfort. The Authority keeps everything clean and in good order. Public restrooms and showers are located at several beachfront sites and picnic areas.

Golf

Jekyll Island claims to be Georgia's largest public golf resort, with 63 holes on four courses; three with 18 holes and one with nine holes. The Oleander was designed by Dick Wilson and measures 6,679 yards; Indian Mound designed by Joe Lee and measures 6,596 yards and Pine Lakes, also designed by Dick Wilson, is 6,802 yards. Ocean-side has nine holes, and was originally laid out for the members of the Jekyll Island Club in 1898. It was remodeled in the 1920s by Walter Travis and measures some 3,298 yards. The clubhouse has a full-service pro shop where you can rent equipment and carts, have a lesson, or tune up your swing on the driving range. Call ☎ 912-635-2368 or 635-3464 for tee times.

Hiking

With more than 10 miles of beach and several thousand acres of parkland, unspoiled Jekyll Island provides a unique opportunity for hiking, strolling and walking, and learning about the area's delicate ecosystems.

Shopping

If shopping is your favorite sport, you will find within the National Historic Landmark District a collection of shops that blend easily with this environment and are of some interest. A good second-hand bookstore is not easily found these days, so it is a pleasant surprise to come across the **Jekyll Books and Antiques Inc.,** ☎ 912-635-3077, at 101 Old Plantation Road. The shop makes its home within the old, twice moved, Infirmary and seems to have an ethereal resident – a young girl with long dark hair, wearing a silver brooch, who has been seen by many wandering around. Alongside the assortment of new, used and rare books, you will find an array of antiques, photographs, prints, maps, bookends, huge puppets, and even a children's room. Interestingly, this is the only place open on Jekyll Island on Christmas Day, when it becomes the social center for the island, and guests, fortified by cheese and wine, often give impromptu poetry readings. On all other days of the year it is open from 9:30 am to 5:30 pm.

Nature's Cottage, ☎ 912-635-3933, at 21 Pier Road, offers a fine array of art, books and gifts devoted to the beauty of nature. It is a Harmony Kingdom Royal dealer, and has, among a proliferation of items, animals made by Big Sky Carvers from Montana, beach scenes hand-painted by Rex Dugger, Baltic Amber, fine Maruri Porcelain collectibles, US-made puppets, attractively carved fish, nature jewelry, numerous soft toys and an educational children's corner. It is open from 10 to 5 daily. On the same street, but with an entirely different theme, is **The Cottage on Jekyll**, ☎ 912-635-2643, at 32 Pier Road. The emphasis is on specialty gifts and crafts, and you will find collections of Russian and Limoges Boxes, classic Pooh Bears and, as it is a Boyds Bronze Paw dealer, all kinds of nattily dressed bears. Look, also, for teapots, both miniature and full-sized, spirit chasers from Bali, Lithopane porcelain lamps and interchangeable light shades. Angels, too, are predominant, and coexist with dolls and fairies, which might be found hiding among the very unusual collection of miniature Victorian shoes. And, to occupy daughters while mothers are shopping, there is an innovative corner where little girls can play dress-up.

Tennis

If you like to play tennis, you'll love it here. The **Jekyll Island Tennis Center**, ☎ 912-635-3154, just off Captain Wylly Road in the center of the island, was selected by *Tennis Magazine* as one of the 25 best municipal tennis centers in the country. There are 13 clay courts tucked away among the live oaks and pines; seven of them are lighted for play at night. They rent for $14 an hour during the day and $16 at night. There's also a full-service pro shop where a USPTA professional offers private or group lessons, and arranges games for players without a partner. The facility organizes junior summer tennis camps and numerous other programs.

On Wheels

 There are more than 20 miles of scenic paved bicycle paths on Jekyll Island. They wind through the marshes, beside the beaches, under the massive moss-draped live oaks, and through the Historic District. Rental bikes are available at a number of locations on the island, ☎ 912-635-2648.

On Water

Boating

 Two marinas serve Jekyll Island. **Jekyll Harbor Marina**, ☎ 912-635-3137, has dockage and boat ramps, and also offers a number of other services. You can go parasailing, charter a fishing boat and captain, join a sightseeing cruise, rent a jetski, or enjoy a snack and a drink at **Seajay's Waterfront Cafe and Pub.** The **Jekyll Island Historic Wharf,** ☎ 912-635-3152, opposite the Jekyll Island Club in the Historic District, can set you up with a fishing charter, sightseeing cruise, jet boat ride, or a sea kayaking trip.

Water Park

Summer Waves, ☎ 912-635-2074, an 11-acre water park with many attractions, opened in 1988 and received its 1,000,000th visitor in 1996. This facility, a deluxe water park, is one of the best of its type and a real bargain. The 11-acre park is a vast, watery fairyland of pools and rides, a playground for kids and grown-ups of all ages. The Pirate's Passage is a five-story, totally enclosed tube ride that, the first time at least, takes you on a high-speed ride into the unknown. Force 3 is a thrilling combination of two enclosed body slides and one double tube slide. The Frantic Atlantic is where you can ride ocean-like waves in the water-park's 500,000-gallon wave pool. Then there's the Hurricane and Ternade, 300-foot side-by-side body slides, and the Slow Motion Ocean, where you can relax in an inner tube and drift with the current for hours. For the younger set, the Kiddie Pool provides endless hours of carefully supervised fun in the water, where many of the rides available to the adults are reproduced in miniature for the kids. There's even a McDonald's (the only one on the island) inside the park, along with a gift shop where you can buy a souvenir T-shirt complete with funny logo. Open daily, in season, Sunday to Friday from 10 to 6 and Saturday from 10 to 8. Slightly shorter hours out-of-season. Admission, $12.50; under 48 inches, $10.50.

On Horseback

 If you are partial to horseback riding, head for **Victoria's Carriage's & Trail Rides,** ☎ 912-635-9500, at the Visitor's Center on Stable Road. In addition to the carriage rides mentioned above, they offer either a one-hour beach ride at $30 per person or a 1½-hour beach ride at $40 per person.

Eco/Cultural Adventures

 The **Coastal Encounters Nature Center,** ☎ 912-635-9102, 100 South Riverview Drive, deserves your attention. Open Monday through Saturday from 9 to 5, the site includes an indoor educational center with aquariums, touch tanks and a variety of displays. Outdoors, a 17-acre salt pond is bordered by salt marsh and the Intracoastal Waterway to the west, with maritime forest and the Atlantic Ocean to the east. In other words, it provides an ideal environment for bird watchers and, as Jekyll Island plays host to migrating birds on the Atlantic Flyway in the spring and fall, it offers spotters a chance to see species not usually found in these climes. If you have the time and interest, their Barrier Island Ecology walks should not be missed. A three-hour walk taking in three ecosystems – the marsh, the maritime forest and the sea – costs $18 per person, or you can explore the ecosystem of your choice at a rate of $10 per hour.

Turtles

Jekyll Island is also home to the endangered loggerhead sea turtle during the nesting season from mid-May to mid-August. Mature female turtles, weighing 175-350 pounds and measuring 21-45 inches, have been laying just over 100 nests per year in recent years. The count usually amounts to 90-130 each season. Females are capable of laying four to six clutches of eggs consisting of 80 to 160 eggs each during a nesting season. They dig a hole 18-20 inches deep, lay their eggs, and cover them with sand before returning to the ocean. Interestingly, the sand temperature in the nest will determine the sex of the hatchling – warmer for females and cooler for males. After an incubation period of 58-60 days, 60-90% of the eggs actually hatch, emerging with a swimming motion through the sand in their haste to reach the ocean. Males never return to shore after hatching, but it is thought that the females carry with them a chemical imprint of the beach where they hatched, coming ashore to play their part in procreation 15-20 years later.

If this brief explanation has piqued your interest, you can participate in guided **Turtle Walks**, held Monday to Saturday nights, from June through August, beginning at 9:30 pm. They depart from the Visitors Center, and may last until 11 pm or midnight, depending upon the number of sightings. The cost is $5 per adult, no flashlights or cameras are permitted and reservations are required. Call ☎ 912-635-2284 in advance of your trip to avoid disappointment. If you prefer to wander out on your own, here are a few turtle tips.

- Never disturb a turtle crawling to and from the ocean.
- Once one has begun nesting watch only from a distance.
- Never attempt to ride a turtle.
- Don't shine a light in a turtle's eyes or take flash photos.
- If you see a dead or injured turtle, or come upon someone harassing one, call ☎ 800-2-SAVE-ME or the DNR at 912-264-7218.

Georgia

Adopt a Turtle

Though these fascinating creatures have been in existence for over 250 million years, exploitation, commercial fishing and beach development have put them on the endangered species list. But you can play a part in ensuring their future success. For $35 you can adopt an adult mother through the **Adopt A Loggerhead** program,. This includes an official certificate, photograph, all sighting dates, hatching announcements, turtle sticker and a poster. For $25 you can adopt a nest, receiving an official certificate, information on the mother, hatching announcement, success rate and a turtle sticker. For $15, adopt a hatchling, and receive an official certificate, nest information, hatching announcement, and success rate. To adopt, or for further information, contact the **Jekyll Island Authority Turtle Patrol**, ☎ 912-635-2284, 196 Stable Road, Jekyll Island, GA 31527.

Where to Stay

The **Jekyll Island Club Hotel**, ☎ 912-635-2600, 800-535-9547, fax 635-2828, e-mail jiclub@technonet.com, www.jekyllclub.com, 371 Riverview Drive, Jekyll Island, is both Mobil Four-star and AAA Four-diamond-rated. It offers guests an unusual opportunity to experience a way of life that is all but forgotten. The first sight of this distinctive hotel will enchant you, with its charming American Queen Anne-style architecture, bay windows and verandas. Restored to its Victorian splendor in 1985, it has been designated a National Historic Landmark and a Historic Hotel of America. Guests may choose from 134 rooms, including 21 one-bedroom suites.

The Jekyll Island Club Hotel has three seasons: high, March through the third week in August; shoulder, fourth week in August through November; and low, December, January and February. Room rates vary according to season and the type of room, of which there are eight. We suggest that you consider a suite at $199, a king jacuzzi at $209, a deluxe king suite at $229, or the presidential suite at $279, with those prices being per night in the high season. Each of these rooms is discounted $20 in the shoulder season and another $20 in the low season.

Although there are other restaurants on the island, none have the charm and ambiance of those within the hotel. It is suggested, therefore, that you choose either the Modified American Plan, at $54 per person per night, or the Full American Plan, at $72 per person per night. The latter allows you to take breakfast, lunch and dinner in the acclaimed, and very beautiful formal restaurant. The Grand Dining Room, elegantly restored in Victorian style and dominated by Ionic columns and gleaming white woodwork, has three handsome fireplaces with intricately carved mantle pieces and marble surrounds.

The Jekyll Island Club Hotel offers a host of complimentary recreational activities. Take a dip in the near-Olympic-sized pool surrounded by beautiful landscaping, try your luck at the putting green or tournament-level croquet, where serious players wear white and you must sign up in advance, or lob a few over the volleyball net. Bicycle rentals are available from dawn to dusk, at $9 a half-day, $18 a day or $4 per hour; and, if all of this exercise stresses your body, arrangements can be made for a massage at $62.50 per hour.

The **Beachview Club**, ☎ 912-635-2256 or 800-299-2228, 721 North Beachview Drive, is the newest hotel on the beach at Jekyll Island. Surrounded by a canopy of century-old oak trees and palms, it has 38 rooms and suites appointed to create a casual but luxurious beach ambiance reminiscent of Bermuda traditions. A nice bonus is that the hotel provides a complimentary shuttle to any restaurant on the island. Rate schedules, based on four different seasons and several categories of accommodation, are challenging. The most economical choice, a King Efficiency, rents for $89-$189 depending on season; the rate for the much more romantic Deluxe Luxury Suite ranges from $169 to $359.

Camping

Jekyll Island Campground, ☎ 912-635-3021 or 800-841-6586, North Beachview Drive, is one of the best campgrounds in Georgia. It has 220 places for campsites and RV camping, with full hookup at $17 per night or $102 a week and partial hookup at $15 a night and $90 a week. Cable TV ($2 per day) and firewood are available. There's a camp store where you can stock up on food, ice, bait, propane, and other supplies. There are two bathhouses with hot showers and restrooms. You can rent a bike at the camp store.

Where to Eat

Dining options are extremely limited here. When staying at the Jekyll Island Club Hotel, for the best in food and the best in value, it is strongly recommended that visitors opt for either the Full or Modified American Plan. While the Beachview Club does not have a restaurant, free shuttle service is provided to and from the Grand Dining Room of the Jekyll Island Club Hotel, one of the nicest restaurants you are likely to find.

Visitor Information

For more information on other attractions and events, contact the **Jekyll Island Welcome Center**, on the Jekyll Island Causeway, ☎ 912-635-3636, 877-4JEKYLL (453-5955) or visit them on the web at www.jekyllisland.com.

■ Brunswick

History

Brunswick, the gateway to the Golden Isles, was founded as a Colonial outpost and named for Braunsweig, the German ancestral home of King George II, grantor of Georgia's original land charter. Laid out in 1771 and based on General James Oglethorpe's famous grid system, its streets and squares were named in honor of the King and House of Hanover and, unusually, were not changed after the American Revolution. The town flourished during the resort era a century ago, and the fine array of Victorian architecture in the Old Town National Register Historic District reflects this period. Today's urban renewal has spawned many new businesses, including numerous antique stores in the downtown area. The city claims to be the official home of Brunswick Stew. Brunswick is also a busy port.

Liberty Ships

Following the disastrously high number of ships and cargo lost to enemy U-boats during the early years of World War II, the US Maritime Commission selected Brunswick and 15 other sites around the country to build what would later be known as "Liberty Ships." Incredibly, the J.A. Jones Construction Company, which employed over 16,000 people in the shipyards, produced 99 of these 447-foot ships in less than two years between 1943 and 1945.

Nowadays, in addition to welcoming ocean-going freighters from around the world, the city's waterfront district is famous for its fleet of commercial shrimp boats that supply the area's large seafood industry. The backwash from the marshes, rivers, inlets and estuaries provide all the necessary nutrients for the prized crustaceans to breed, multiply and thrive. During the shrimp season, which runs from early June to the end of February, it is fascinating to wander, from Bay Street between Gloucester and Prince Streets, to the docks, to watch the shrimpers unload their catches in the late afternoon.

Getting Here & Getting Around

 From north and south, I-95 passes the city five miles to the west and Highway 17, the scenic route, lies east of and runs parallel to I-95 and through the city itself.

Getting around on the Golden Isles is easy; there are no rush hours as we know them, and even in Brunswick the roads are never very busy. There's plenty of parking available. You'll do quite a lot of walking here, but you'll need a car to get around. On St. Simons Island you can take a guided trolley tour; the pickup point is near the lighthouse in the Village.

Adventures

On Foot

Shopping

 There is one place most of you will pass on your way to this region that will appeal to many. This is a manufacturers outlet mall, in fact the largest one in all of Georgia. And if you find you have a rainy morning or afternoon on your hands, it is a perfect place to escape the weather. **Prime Outlets**, ☎ 912-437-2700, 888-545-7224, www.primeretail.com, formerly Magnolia Bluff Factory Shops, is just 10 minutes from Brunswick off I-95 at Exit 10 in Darien. Opened in 1995 and since expanded, it now has 80 name-brand outlet stores that feature a unique upscale mix of leading women's and men's designers, the hottest names in children's wear and toys and the main brand names in house wares and electronics, including the only Bose store in Georgia. All are at attractive prices that can be reduced even more, provided you stop by the Customer Service Center in the Food Court for a free coupon book worth over $400 in discounts. Prime Outlets, Darien, is open Monday

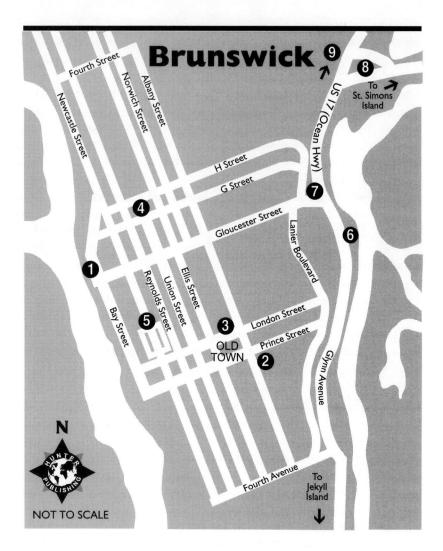

Brunswick Driving Tour

The number in parentheses after each stop
indicates the mileage to the next point of interest.

1. Shrimp Docks (1.1)
2. Lovers' Oak (.4)
3. Old Town National Register
   District (.7)
4. Courthouse (.1)
5. Main Street Brunswick (1.1)
6. Overlook Park (.2)
7. Lanier Oak (.2)
8. Visitors Center (14.7)
9. Hofwyl-Broadfield Plantation

through Saturday from 10-9 and Sunday from 11-6; it is closed Easter, Thanksgiving Day and Christmas Day.

The Fort King George Historic Site

The nearby town of Darien has an interesting history. In 1721, a small band of scouts from the English colony in South Carolina pushed the boundaries of the King's holdings in the Americas to new limits when they established a small fort on the banks of the Altamaha River. Darien, a small coastal town established near Fort King George in the late 1730s, is another of General James Oglethorpe's creations. It was to be a stronghold to protect the English colonies' southern borders at the mouth of the Altamaha River from attack by the Spanish, French and Indians. Populated by Scottish settlers, the little town soon became the center of a thriving plantation economy. By the 1800s timber was being shipped in large quantities from the little river port, and over the next 200 years Darien was to become one of the largest timber exporters in the world. The export continued until the early years of the 20th century, and the ruins of three of the old sawmills can still be seen.

Today, with one exception, the great plantations are all gone, and the port, once bustling with great ships, is a haven for the local shrimping fleets. But it's still a great little place, a little out of the way, quiet, and not on most lists of popular places to visit. You'll be delighted with this picturesque little town. Unfortunately, most of the original city is gone; victim of a fire that swept through the community in 1863. The **Fort King George Historic Site**, ☎ 912-437-4770, is a mile east of Highway 17 and three miles east of I-95. Established in 1721 by a band of scouts from the colony in South Carolina to prevent expansion into the area by the French and Spanish, it was the first English settlement in Georgia. It was a frontier fort in every sense. An earthwork topped with a stout wooden blockhouse was built on a peninsula on the Altamaha River. For more than 10 years, from 1721 to 1732, Fort King George marked the southernmost limits of the British Empire on the North American continent. Of course, the original fort is long gone, but the reconstruction that stands on the site is considered to be a faithful representation of the one garrisoned by His Majesty's 41st Independent Company and is open for you to visit. There's also a museum where you can view exhibits that interpret the history of the fort and surrounding area from the earliest times through Indian, Spanish and English occupation. Open Tuesday to Saturday, 9-5pm, and Sunday, 2-5:30; closed Thanksgiving, Christmas and New Year's.

Georgia

On Water

Casino Cruise

 Golden Isles Cruise Lines, Inc., ☎ 800-842-0115 (for tickets and reservations), based at Brunswick Landing Marina, Newcastle and K Streets, in Downtown Brunswick, operates the nearly 200-foot *Emerald Princess* as a casino and dinner cruise ship. She sails Tuesday to Saturday between 7 pm and 1 am ($35), on Saturday from 11 am-4 pm ($19.98) and on Sunday from 1-6 ($35). Prices are per couple with daytime cruises including a brunch buffet and evening cruises offering a dinner buffet. All cruises include at no additional charge shipboard entertainment ; music and dancing; access to casino gambling games such as roulette, blackjack, Caribbean poker, craps, live poker and slot machines; and a return-to-port appetizer. Advance reservations are required, boarding begins one-hour prior to departure time and any tickets not claimed 45 minutes before sailing will be subject to forfeiture.

Fishing

Captain Vernon Reynolds, ☎ 912-265-0392, 3202 East 3rd Street, Brunswick, GA 31520, has 30 years' experience in local waters. He offers fishing offshore for tarpon, shark, king mackerel, Spanish mackerel, cobia, amberjack and barracuda, with half-day trips costing $250 for two people, and $50 for each additional person up to six. Inshore fishing for trout, flounder and bass costs $225 for two people, with $35 for each additional person. Captain Reynolds also leads dolphin watch tours; coastal birding excursions to see the great blue heron, white egret, wood storks, ospreys and mvany others; sand dollar wading tours along the Pelican Split sand bar in St. Andrews Sound; marsh nature tours; sunset cruise and moonlight cruises. He operates out of Brunswick, Jekyll Island and St. Simons Island.

Eco/Cultural Adventures

The Marshes of Glynn

 The Marshes of Glynn, spectacular and unspoiled, separate Brunswick from the Golden Isles of St. Simons, Sea Island, Jekyll Island and Little St. Simons. The best vantage point to see this vast saltwater biosphere is from Overlook Park. Indeed it was from under the Lanier Oak here that Georgia poet Sidney Lanier during the 1870s stood and viewed the marshes that inspired him to write *The Marshes of Glynn*, now considered his finest work. Another good spot is at the Visitors Center at the intersection of Highway 17 and the St. Simons Island Causeway, or even from the Causeway itself.

Where to Stay

Brunswick Manor, ☎ 912-265-6889, 825 Egmont Street, has four rooms that rent for $75-$100 per night.

Cumberland Island & St. Marys

■ History

Located just south of Jekyll Island, Cumberland Island, 17½ miles long and totaling 36,415 acres, is the largest and most southerly of Georgia's barrier islands. Indians lived here 4,000 years ago, called the island Missoe, meaning "sassafras" and controlled it until the Spanish arrived in the latter half of the 16th century. From then, and for another two centuries, the English, Spanish and French competed for the island, until England gained control in the 1700s and renamed it Cumberland. In 1881 an estate at the south end was created by Thomas Carnegie, brother of Andrew, and the ruins of his magnificent home, Dungeness, can still be seen today. In 1972 the island's residents decided, in return for various rights of use and occupancy, to sell their land to the National Park Service, who established the Cumberland Island National Seashore.

St. Marys history goes back to the mid-1500s and it was established as a town by the English in 1787 – making it, so they claim, the second oldest city in the United States. A picturesque little town, less than an hour south of Brunswick, with many old homes and historic structures, it is also the departure point for the ferry to Cumberland Island. The First Presbyterian Church was built in 1808, and is the second oldest church in Georgia.

Georgia

■ Cumberland Island & St. Marys Today

The island is now a part of the South Carolina-Carolinian Biosphere Reserve, and this wonderfully unspoiled environment will now be permanently protected in its primitive state. It is a complex ecological system of interdependent animal and plant communities, where wild horses and other wildlife roam freely. Visitors, limited to about 300 a day, enjoy scenes of breathtaking natural beauty, walk deserted beaches beyond the massive sand dunes and, if you're lucky, spot some of those wild horses. As there are no concessions here, no facilities other than restrooms and drinking water, you'll want to take along a picnic lunch; there are plenty of places to enjoy it. You should also wear appropriate clothing, considering the weather and the season; bug spray and sunscreen are also a good idea.

St. Marys is the home of the vast King's Bay Naval Submarine Base and the US Navy's fleet of nuclear-powered submarines.

■ Getting Here

Access to Cumberland Island is by a limited ferry service from St. Marys, seven miles and 45 minutes away. The ferry and the basic camping facilities are operated by the National Park Service, and it is wise, in fact necessary, to book some months ahead of your visit. For reservations call ☎ 912-882-4335, Monday through Friday from 10-4. Faxed reservations are accepted 24 hours a day at 912-673-7747, but a copy of the NPS fax form is required; this can be requested by fax or downloaded from www.nps.gov/cuis/index.htm. The ferry schedule is such that you can expect to be on the island for at least six hours. Remember that there is no transportation for visitors, other than your own two feet. If you want to stay in some luxury, the Greyfield Inn is the place to be.

From I-95, St. Marys is approximately eight miles east of I-95 and is 32 miles north of Jacksonville and 45 miles south of Brunswick. Georgia State Road 40 is a direct link from I-95 to the National Park Service Visitor Center in downtown St. Marys on the waterfront.

■ Sightseeng

The **Cumberland Island National Seashore Museum** will open in 2000 and be dedicated to providing a glimpse of life over the centuries on Cumberland Island.

The **Submarine Museum**, ☎ 912-882-ASUB, 102 West St. Marys Street, St. Marys, GA 31558, is housed in a converted historic movie theatre on the waterfront. Among the many exhibits is a working periscope, models, working solar panels, a display dedicated to the eight submariners who received the Medal of Honor and much other submarine memorabilia.

■ Visitor Information

The **St. Marys Tourism Council**, ☎ 912-882-4000, 800-868-8687, www.gacoast.com/navigator/stmarys.html, PO Box 1291, St. Marys, GA 31558. It is housed in Orange Hall, a wonderful example of Greek Revival architecture, and is open Monday through Saturday from 9-5 and Sunday, 1-5.

■ Adventures

Eco/Cultural Adventures

Crooked River State Park, ☎ 912-882-5256, 10 miles north of St. Marys on Georgia Spur 40, or east of Kingsland, 12 miles off Highway 17, or eight miles off I-95, is on the banks of the river from which it takes its name. The freshwater fishing is good year-round, though private boats are limited to 10 hp. There are more than seven miles of canoe trails to explore, as well as the 400-acre lake. Of special interest are the ruins of the old **McIntosh Sugar Works**. The mill was built around 1825 and was used during the Civil War years to produce starch. For active outdoors people there's swimming, hiking, camping, fishing, hiking, and miniature golf, all of which make Crooked River an exciting and unique outdoor experience. Major facilities at the park include 21 tent and trailer sites, a winterized group shelter, four picnic shelters, and canoe and fishing boat rentals. The park is open from 7 am until dark, and the park office is open from 8 until 5.

■ Where to Stay

Cumberland Island

The **Greyfield Inn**, ☎ 904-261-6408, is the only place to stay on the island – but what a place! That's why it was chosen by the late John F. Kennedy Jr. as the perfect romantic setting for his wedding.

St. Marys

Goodbread B&B, ☎ 912-882-7490, 209 Osborne Street, St. Marys, is in a house that dates from around 1870 and has much charm. Rates: $75 weekdays and $85 on weekends.

Spencer House Inn B&B, ☎ 912-882-1872, fax 882-9247, www. spencerhouseinn.com, was constructed in 1872 and at one time was the finest hotel in town. These days it has 14 individually decorated guestrooms.

■ Camping

Cumberland Island

 Facilities are fairly basic, a day use fee of $4 per person per visit is required, and it is $4 per person per day to use the **Sea Camp Campground**. It has restrooms, cold water showers and drinking water, with campfires permitted. The charge is $2 for backcountry camping, where only drinking water is available and campfires are not allowed.

See also *Crooked River State Park*, above.

Okefenokee National Wildlife Refuge

Although it's not on Georgia's coast, the Okefenokee is on the coastal plain, well within daytrip distance of Savannah and the Golden Isles. It is a vast, primitive world of water and cypress swamp that covers an area of more than 600 square miles in southeast Georgia. The swamp is a watershed fed almost entirely by rainfall and the origin of two of Georgia's great rivers, the Suwannee and the St. Marys. But it's not really a swamp at all. The word swamp means a low-lying area of stagnant wateru, but the Okefenokee is more than 100 feet above sea level and its waters are constantly on the move, flowing through the thousands of channels that meander through the great wetland.

Nearby, the surrounding towns of Folkston and Waycross are of most interest, with a range of restaurants, motels and other attractions.

■ The Water

The Okefenokee's waters are dark and mysterious, the color of old tea, giving the impression of dirt and contamination; in fact the opposite is true. The waters are pure and quite drinkable. The discoloration comes from tannic acid, the by-product of decaying vegetation in the water, and there's plenty of that. The bed is a layer of peat at least five feet thick, more in places. The dark color of the water provides photographers with many unique opportunities. It gives the surface a mirror-like quality, and when the waters are still and silent, as they are almost everywhere in the interior, the images of the water produced on film are so clear and sharp that it's often difficult to determine which way is up.

■ Habitats

The Okefenokee is a strange land of diverse habitats: hammocks, islands, lakes, and great open expanses of shallow water covered with aquatic plants and surrounded by dense stands of cypress. The Grand Prairie is some five miles long and more than three miles wide; the Chase Prairie is a little larger. But they are not the only ones. There are thought to be at least 60,000 acres of them in the swamp, all quiet, all populated by an abundance of wildlife, and all beautiful in their own right. The lakes, 60 of them large enough to have names, are famous for good fishing, and for the wildlife that makes a home around them. The sandhill crane, osprey, anhinga, great egret, great blue heron, white ibis, and yellow crowned night heron are just a few of the delights awaiting birdwatchers.

There are approximately 70 islands in the Okefenokee; most of them are large enough to have names and many have been inhabited by settlers for more than 150 years. Before that there were only Indians and wildlife. The Indians are long gone now, chased away by soldiers during the early part of the 19th century, but the wildlife remains very much intact.

The American Alligator

The Okefenokee is home to the American alligator. Once hunted almost to extinction for its skin, it is now protected and there are many of them in the swamp. The female lays 30-60 eggs at a time, and when they hatch the baby alligators are a little less than six inches long. They grow about a foot a year for the first six years or so. Those that make it through those early years into adulthood can reach 12-15 feet in length and weigh as much as 700 lbs. The alligator looks deceptively slow, even clumsy; but it's not. They feed on small animals, birds, fish, turtles, snakes, and just about anything they can catch or sink their teeth into, even baby alligators.

Other Wildlife

The Okefenokee is also home to a wide variety of other animals: the white-tail deer, otter and the black bear, along with 27 species of snakes, including the venomous water moccasin, which can strike, empty its venom sacs, and return to its coiled position in about a half-second. Keep a sharp lookout for them.

■ Getting Here

There are several entrances to the Okefenokee Swamp, a couple of state parks, and several points of special historical interest.

From the north: The easiest route into the swamp is via the city of Waycross, just to the north of the swamp on **Highway 82**, going east and west, and **Highway 84** from the northeast and southwest. From there you'll take **Highway 23** and the **121 Spur** to the eastern entrance at the Suwannee Canal Recreation Area.

From the south: For a quick visit, you can head for the Okefenokee Swamp Park just eight miles south of Waycross on **Highways 1** and **23**.

From the southwest: You can enter the swamp at Stephen C. Foster State Park via **Highways 441** and **177**.

■ Adventures

Eco/Cultural Adventures

State Parks

The **Stephen C. Foster State Historic Park**, ☎ 912-637-5274 or 800-864-7275, Fargo, GA 31631, situated on Jones Island, is the western entrance to the wild and wonderful world of the great Okefenokee Swamp. Named after the famous songwriter, this is the mysterious, quiet side of the Okefenokee where the numbers of visitors are but a fraction of those from the more easily accessible entrances to the north and east. This is your introduction to an alien land set deep in the heart of southern Georgia.

The lush vegetation of the cypress swamp and its waterways is inhabited by a population of more than 200 species of birds, 40 species of mammals, at least 50 different reptiles and some 60 species of amphibians. Stephen C. Foster is a lonely place, approached by a long, often deserted, road that seems to go on forever. At night, when the hot, southern sun has disappeared below the treetops to the west, this subtropical world comes to life with all the sounds of the swamp, reminiscent of the African rainforests of the old Tarzan movies. Here, you can enjoy the Okefenokee from the comfort of an elevated boardwalk, or get really close to nature by taking a guided boat tour through the maze of waterways. Stephen C. Foster is a world of its own. This is not really hiking country. However, the quarter-mile **Trembling Earth Nature Trail** offers an easy walk through the swamp and a close-up look at the birds and other wildlife that inhabit it. You can also take a guided boat tour, or rent your own (canoes, motorboats, and jonboats are available at the Visitors Center) to go off on your own. Nature study, birdwatching, wildlife photography, and exploring more than 25 miles of public use waterways are all popular pastimes. It is open daily, between March 1st and September 14th from 6:30 am-8:30 pm, and from 7-7 the rest of the year.

The **Laura S. Walker State Park**, ☎ 912-287-4900, 5653 Laura Walker Road, Waycross, GA 31503, is a 300-acre park, nine miles southeast of Waycross on Route 177, and is named for one of Georgia's most famous citizens. A naturalist, teacher, writer, and civic leader, Laura Walker was a lover of nature and the outdoors, especially trees. She was also a dedicated worker for the preservation of Georgia's natural beauty. The park is located close to the Okefenokee Swamp and is famous for its birds, animals, and wildflowers. Hiking is a popular pastime at Laura Walker. The nature trail offers a nice easy stroll and opportunities for nature study, birdwatching and wildlife photography. Picnicking is also popular, and the picnic area is big enough for family reunions and group outings. There is also a 120-acre lake, a pool, nine picnic shelters, four group shelters and a nature trail. The fishing here is good: lots of bass, bluegill, crappie and catfish, you can bring your own boat, or you can rent one at the park office. If you like to water ski, that is also available. It is open daily from 7 to 10 pm.

Swamp Park

The Okefenokee Swamp Park, ☎ 912-283-0583, on Cowhouse Island, has been the headquarters for this 1,600-acre wilderness park since 1945. It is operated by a private non-profit organization created for the purpose of making the great swamp accessible to the public. Aside from providing easy access to the Okefenokee, the park has its own museum with all sorts of interpretive exhibits. The **Swamp Creation Center** interprets the evolution of the swamp through dioramas, animated exhibits, aquariums and charts. The **Living Swamp Ecological Center** provides insight on the wildlife; there's an exhibition of carnivorous plants native to the swamp, insects, a serpentarium, bear observatory, and films that interpret the ecosystem of the swamp. Out in the park, a 90-foot observation tower provides a panoramic view of the swamp. It is open from 9-5 and the admission price is $10 for adults and $7 for children. A half-hour boat ride costs $14 and a one-hour ride $18, both of which include admission to the park.

■ Where to Stay

Folkston

The **Georgia Motel**, ☎ 912-496-7767, US 1 & 301 North, Folkston, GA 31537, has 15 rooms and efficiencies and has overnight and weekly rates.

The **Inn at Folkston**, ☎ and fax 912-496-6256, 888-509-6246, e-mail info@innatfolkston.com, www.innatfolkston.com, 509 West Main Street, Folkston, GA 31537, is found in a charming house that was built in 1922. It offers four distinctly different rooms that rent for $75-$125 a night.

Camping & Cabins

Stephen C. Foster State Historic Park, ☎ 912-637-5274 or 800-864-7275, Fargo, GA 31631, has 68 tent and trailer sites, $13 for tent and $15 for RV and nine cottages that rent for $61, Sunday through Thursday, and $71 on Friday and Saturday, and a bathhouse with hot showers and restrooms.

Laura Walker State Park, ☎ 912-287-4900, 5653 Laura Walker Road, Waycross, GA 31503, has 44 tent and trailer sites that rent for $15, a bathhouse, a group camp, picnic tables and grills.

■ Where to Eat

Nearby Folkston has the better options in what is a limited selection of places to dine in the area. Outside of the usual fast food choices of Burger King, McDonalds, Dairy Queen

Brazier, you might check out one of the following. The **Okefenokee Restaurant**, ☎ 912-496-3263, located at 103 S. Second Street, is open from 6 am to 9 pm, Monday through Saturday, with a noon buffet each day. Foods include various types of chicken, pork, fish, shrimp, and beef. Prices range from $5 to $10. The **Family Restaurant**, ☎ 912-496-2208, at 1201 S. Second Street, is open from 6 am to 8:30 pm, Monday thru Thursday, 6 am to 9 pm, Friday and Saturday, and 8 am to 2 pm on Sunday. There is a varied buffet at lunch and dinner, or you may order from a menu that features chicken, beef, fish and shrimp priced from $4 to $10. The **Fleming House**, located at 113 S. First Street, ☎ 912-496-7958, is open from 11 am to 2 pm for lunch only and serves home-cooked meals, including chicken, pot roast, chicken pot pies, crêpes and home-made desserts in the $5 range. The **Rose Garden Chinese Restaurant** at 105 Main Street, serves a luncheon buffet and menu items range from $5 to $13. Hours are Monday through Friday and Sunday from 11 am to 2 pm; Friday and Saturday nights from 5 to 9 pm. **Quick Chic** of Folkston, located at 107 N. Second Street, ☎ 912-496-7044, is open Monday through Saturday from 10 am to 9 pm. On offer for lunch, 11 am to 2 pm, is a varied hot buffet of meats and vegetables. Chicken, as you would surmise, is the main feature and the chicken strips are highly recommended by the locals. **Mikey's Pizza**, located at 1003 S.Second Street, ☎ 912-496-2721, serves all types of Italian food. It is open Monday through Thursday from 11 am to 9 pm and Friday and Saturday from 11 am to 10 pm and is closed on Sunday.

For more information, surf on over to www.folkston.com.

Georgia

NOT TO SCALE

North Carolina

N

VIRGINIA

THE OUTER BANKS

Elizabeth City

95

85

Raleigh

Burlington

Winston-Salem

77

Boone

40

85

Fayetteville

HIGH COUNTRY

Charlotte

Asheville

26

95

SOUTH CAROLINA

GEORGIA

TENNESSEE

Greenville

Morehead City

THE CRYSTAL COAST

40

Wilmington

Atlantic Ocean

North Carolina

History

As far back as 1524 the North Carolina coast was explored by some of Europe's greatest adventurers. Men like Giovanni da Verrazano, Hernando de Soto, Sir Walter Raleigh, and many others first set foot on the islands of the Outer Banks in search of riches and fame. Many of them found it, many more lost their lives in the search; their bones lie there still, lost and forgotten. It was Raleigh who established the ill-fated English colony on Roanoke Island in 1585, and it was he who died at the hands of his king in 1618, headless and alone. Two years after Raleigh's abortive attempt to settle North Carolina, Sir John White, having established a second colony, sailed to England for supplies. He returned to Fort Raleigh in 1590 to find no trace of the settlement or the men and women he'd left behind, among them White's granddaughter, Virginia Dare. Born on August 18th 1587, she was the first English child born in America. Only the word "Croatoan" carved into the trunk of a tree offered any clue to what had happened. The Lost Colony is as much a mystery today as it was when John White returned to the site more than 400 years ago.

■ The First Settlement

King Charles I granted the territory south of Virginia a charter in 1629, and it was named Carolina – the "Land of Charles" – in his honor. The first permanent settlement was established by settlers from Virginia on the shores of Albemarle Sound in 1653. In 1663, a much beleaguered **Charles II**, newly restored to the English throne, granted the Carolina region to eight Lords Proprietors. The colony prospered, but the settlers became discontented over feudal laws and neglect by the owners. Finally, in 1712, North and South Carolina became separate provinces; North Carolina became a crown colony in 1729. For almost 50 years the state continued to prosper, but by the 1760s discontent with British rule in general, and British taxation in particular, had already planted the seeds of revolution deep in the hearts of most North Carolinians. By 1765 they were openly defying the tax laws, and the fight for independence, though still very much a shadowy one, was already under way. Physical defiance and other acts of resistance all but nullified the Stamp Act in North Carolina. By 1768 the western counties, led by a group of backcountry farmers known as the **Regulators** (so called because they pledged to "regulate" the local government), were in open rebellion against royal rule. They were defeated by Governor William Tryon's militia on May 16, 1771, in a battle along Alamance Creek, but the die had been cast.

■ Declaring Independence

North Carolinians organized a provincial congress on August 25th 1774, to plan resistance against royal rule. When war broke out at Lexington and Concord, North Carolina's last royal governor fled, and a provincial council took over. On May 20th, 1775, the citizens of Mecklenburg County drew up the first declaration of independence in the colonies, the **Mecklenburg Declaration of Independence**. The date of their meeting is on the state seal and flag. Equally significant was a meeting of the Mecklenburg Committee on May 31st, also in Charlotte, that adopted more moderate resolutions known as the Mecklenburg Resolves. North Carolina's militia gained a victory over Loyalist troops at Moore's Creek Bridge near Wilmington on February 27th, 1776. On April 12th the provincial congress, meeting at Halifax, directed its delegates to the Continental Congress to vote for independence. With these Halifax Resolves, North Carolina became the first colony to authorize a vote for freedom from England; the first battle of the Revolution fought on North Carolina soil took place at Moore's Creek Ridge on April 12th, 1776, and was a decided victory for patriot forces. The Battle of King's Mountain in October, 1780, was another victory for North Carolina frontiersmen. But the British won the biggest battle in North Carolina, at Guilford Courthouse on March 15th 1781. But heavy losses in both battles, especially of officers at Guilford Courthouse, helped force Cornwallis's surrender at Yorktown. North Carolina refused to ratify the new Constitution until November 21st 1789, after the Bill of Rights had been introduced in Congress. In 1790 the state ceded to the federal government its western section, which became the state of Tennessee.

■ The Civil War

For more than 70 years after the end of the American Revolution North Carolina struggled through periods of political unrest, ineffectual local government, and economic depression. Slow to prosper, it struggled on until, finally, the winds of war blew it reluctantly into the heart of the Civil War.

In the period before the Civil War, two future presidents were born in the state: James K. Polk, in Mecklenburg County, and Andrew Johnson, in Raleigh.

North Carolina did not secede from the Union until after the fall of Fort Sumter in 1861. When finally it did become a part of the fledgling Confederacy, it did so wholeheartedly. The state furnished some of the Confederacy's greatest and most heroic regiments – certainly it supplied more troops that any other state and its losses accounted for more than one-fourth of the South's total casualties – and such Confederate military leaders as Braxton Bragg and James Johnston Pettigrew. The last major action of the Civil War occurred near Durham, when General Joseph E. Johnston surrendered to Sherman on April 26th 1865.

■ Reconstruction

The years of Reconstruction were hard for the people of North Carolina. Many of the farms had been destroyed in the fighting, the countryside laid waste, the towns devastated, and the economy was a disaster. North Carolina was readmitted to the union on July 20th, 1868, but Reconstruction continued. The postwar government was run by the Republican party and corrupt carpetbaggers until 1876, when Reconstruction in North Carolina officially ended. The Democrats gained complete control with the return to office of Zebulon B. Vance, who had been governor in 1862-65 during the Confederacy.

By the turn of the 20th century North Carolina was involved in yet another war, at least of sorts. Race relations in the state had become a major issue; many North Carolinians were pushing for white supremacy, and the state was on the verge of apartheid. A constitutional amendment barring all illiterates from voting was passed and prevented most blacks from exercising their constitutional rights; the amendment was eventually repealed, but the bad feelings among blacks remained. In 1903, near Kitty Hawk, the Wright brothers launched the new age of transportation when they made the first flights in a self-propelled aircraft.

■ Today

Today, the troubles of the past have brought a new prosperity to North Carolina. The state abounds in attractions for its expanding tourist industry. Fort Raleigh National Historic Site marks the scene of the first attempt at English settlement in the New World. Historic areas in North Carolina include important battlefields of the Revolution and the Civil War.

What's in a Name?

The people of North Carolina may have received their nickname of **Tarheels** during one of those wars. When the British forces of Lord Cornwallis waded across the Tar River in 1781, the soldiers supposedly found their feet blackened with tar that had been dumped into the water. According to another popular tradition, North Carolina soldiers said that Jefferson Davis, the president of the Confederacy, was going to put tar on the heels of troops who had retreated during battle in order to make them stick better. Robert E. Lee, commander of the Southern forces, reportedly commented, "God bless the Tarheel boys." Most historians, however, believe that the term dates from Colonial days, when the area was the leading producer of naval stores — tar, pitch, resin, and turpentine — and from the tar riverfront where they were loaded on rafts.

North Carolina is also a leader in many other fields. It is first in the nation in tobacco growing and in the manufacture of cigarettes, textiles, and wooden furniture. And, although it ranks second in population among the South Atlantic states, it leads in industry and agriculture. Fontana Dam, in the far-western part of North Carolina near the Tennessee border, is the highest dam built by the Tennessee Valley Authority, at 480 feet. Fort Bragg is one of the largest military reservations in the United States. Mount Mitchell, in the northwestern part of the state, is the highest mountain east of the Mississippi.

Geography

 North Carolina is made up of three natural regions: the **Mountain Region** to the west; the **Piedmont Region** in the center of the state; and the **Coastal Plain** in the east. The Coastal Plain, cut by many rivers, including such navigable streams as the Cape Fear, Neuse, Tar, and Roanoke, is the largest of the three regions, including some 25,000 square miles and all or part of 46 counties. Most of its soil is rich, level, and sandy. About two-thirds of the region is in timber. On its eastern side, the plain has an inner coastline separated by the Intracoastal Waterway, a vast tidal area that includes **Pamlico Sound** near the center and **Albemarle Sound** to the north. This tidewater region is characterized by low and swampy terrain. In the northeast the aptly named **Dismal Swamp** is a marshy area that extends into Virginia. The **Whiteoak, Angola, Holly Shelter**, and **Green swamps** stretch into the southern part of the state. Here, too, are the largest natural **lakes** in North Carolina: **Mattamuskeet, Phelps** and Waccamaw.

The outer coastline is a long chain of narrow sandy reefs and fragile barrier islands called the **Outer Banks**. Major projections into the Atlantic are, from north to south, **Cape Hatteras, Cape Lookout**, and **Cape Fear**. The easternmost of these capes, Hatteras is an area vulnerable to dangerous storms. Here the warm winds from the Gulf Stream meet cooler land breezes. The waters off the cape have been so dangerous to ships that they are called the "Graveyard of the Atlantic." The state has two major seaports for worldwide commerce – **Wilmington** on the Cape Fear River and **Morehead City** on Bogue Sound. It also has fisheries, fine beaches and other scenic vacation spots, plus plenty of waterpower for hydroelectric development.

North Carolina

Climate

One of North Carolina's greatest natural resources is its favorable climate, which ranges from subtropical in the southeast to temperate in the northwest. In the east the climate is tempered by the Atlantic Ocean, landlocked sounds, and the warm Gulf Stream that approaches to within 12 miles of Cape Hatteras. The average annual temperature on the east coast is 63°, although extremes have ranged from a high of 110° to a low of -34°. The growing season may be as long as 295 days a year along the Atlantic coast and at least 240 days a year throughout the coastal plain. The average annual rainfall on the Atlantic coast is about 50 inches; the heaviest rains fall in July and August. Average yearly snowfall in the area is about two inches.

Recreation

North Carolina has been called the "variety vacation land" because of its great diversity of recreation spots. For outdoor sports fans there are streams, lakes, and woodlands in every part of the state, but especially so in the coastal areas. The Atlantic Ocean and the barrier islands provide more adventure than you can handle, including hiking, backpacking, windsurfing, jetskiing, sailing, surfing, scuba diving and snorkeling, kayaking, canoeing, nature and birdwatching, inshore and deep-sea fishing, camping, sightseeing and, of course, shopping. Vast areas of the coast are set aside for preservation and recreation, including a number of state parks, Cape Lookout National Seashore, and the Cape Hatteras National Seashore, which covers about 25,000 acres on the Outer Banks.

The Outer Banks

The Outer Banks are a string of barrier islands and peninsulas that lie between the Atlantic and the great sounds along more than 125 miles of North Carolina's coast; they are not unique. Barrier islands are a part of America's coastline from Maine to Galveston and provide a number of essential services, not the least of which is protection

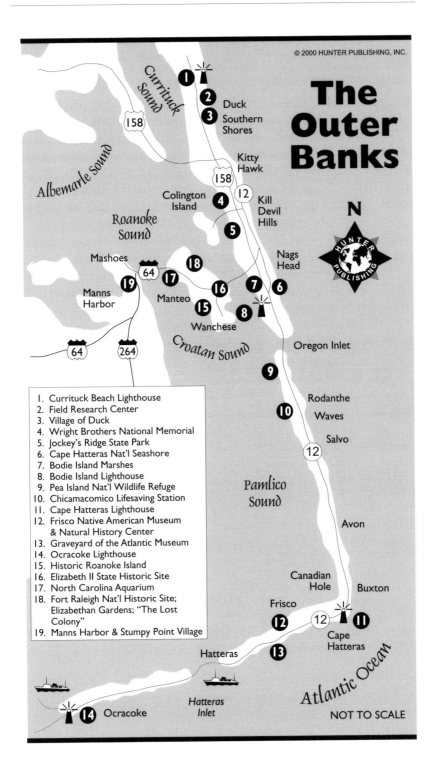

© 2000 HUNTER PUBLISHING, INC.

The Outer Banks

N

HUNTER PUBLISHING

Currituck Sound

158

Duck
Southern Shores

Kitty Hawk

158

Albemarle Sound

Colington Island

12

Kill Devil Hills

Roanoke Sound

Nags Head

Mashoes

64

Manteo

Manns Harbor

Wanchese

64   264

Croatan Sound

Oregon Inlet

Pamlico Sound

Rodanthe
Waves

Salvo

12

Avon

Canadian Hole

Buxton

Frisco

Cape Hatteras

Hatteras

Hatteras Inlet

Ocracoke

Atlantic Ocean

NOT TO SCALE

1. Currituck Beach Lighthouse
2. Field Research Center
3. Village of Duck
4. Wright Brothers National Memorial
5. Jockey's Ridge State Park
6. Cape Hatteras Nat'l Seashore
7. Bodie Island Marshes
8. Bodie Island Lighthouse
9. Pea Island Nat'l Wildlife Refuge
10. Chicamacomico Lifesaving Station
11. Cape Hatteras Lighthouse
12. Frisco Native American Museum & Natural History Center
13. Graveyard of the Atlantic Museum
14. Ocracoke Lighthouse
15. Historic Roanoke Island
16. Elizabeth II State Historic Site
17. North Carolina Aquarium
18. Fort Raleigh Nat'l Historic Site; Elizabethan Gardens; "The Lost Colony"
19. Manns Harbor & Stumpy Point Village

North Carolina

from the ravages of the ocean and the great storms it produces. Aside from the protection they provide, the Outer Banks are a land of wind, sand and fun, a thin line of great natural beauty drawn along the edge of a deep blue sea, remote, often swept by great winds and angry seas, but always lovely and inviting.

Although the entire area is sometimes referred to as **Nags Head**, that is really a misnomer. Nags Head is only one of a number of small cities and towns that line the Outer Banks from Corolla on the northern end to Hatteras on the south, including: **Duck, Kitty Hawk, Kill Devil Hills, Nags Head, Oregon Inlet** and **Hatteras**. Each of these is a delightful destination in its own right with its own unique local history. But much of the information that will be helpful to visitors and many types of adventures (such as four-wheeling explorations, fishing and wreck diving) are common to all. So before we outline a tour for you, we will set forth below an overview of the history, visitor information, and adventures that are applicable to the Outer Banks as a whole.

■ The Natural History of the Outer Banks

The barrier islands are a relatively new creation, perhaps not more than 20,000 years old. That was when the last ice age ended, and the seas in those prehistoric times were at least 400 ft lower than they are today. At that time, the area we know now as North Carolina extended some 30 miles farther to the east. As the great ice flows melted, the seas began to rise, covering the low-lying areas. The Outer Banks probably began as dunes on the edge of what had been the mainland. As the seas rose and covered them, they became sandbars. Under the action of the tides they moved westward and broke the surface once again. It was a long process, taking many thousands of years to complete; even today, the system is fragile and ever-changing.

Best known for its pristine, windswept, white sand beaches, the Outer Banks really offers much more. And, while thoughts of the beach naturally equate to summer fun, and there is plenty here, each season offers it own particular brand of charm. Visitors will discover in the Outer Banks a year-round destination where national parks, wildlife refuges and maritime forests, tucked between the tumultuous ocean on the one side and the peaceful sound on the other, offer a host of adventures: bird watching, fishing, kayaking, hiking, windsurfing, and parasailing, to name but a few. History lovers will thrill to tales of Indian lore, colonies lost and brave brothers who broke our bond to earth on a windy strip of dune at Kill Devil Hills on December 17th, 1903. But, most importantly, life here runs on island time. The pace of life is slower. Sleep late, enjoy barefoot walks on the beach, work on your tan, feast on seafood until you pop, and shop until you drop. The options are many and the choices are yours.

■ History

 It was in 1548 that **Sir Walter Raleigh** sent out the first expedition to explore this section of the Carolina coast. On July 4th, his captains, Philip Amadas and Arthur Barlowe, landed just to the north of what is now Kitty Hawk and began exploring the Banks. There they encountered friendly Indians from a settlement on the northern Roanoke Island, who gave the English a warm welcome. When Amadas and Barlowe returned to England after a brief stay, they took with them two local Indians, Manteo and Wanchese.

The Captains' report to Raleigh and his contemporaries aroused such interest that Raleigh immediately organized and equipped a fleet of seven ships to sail under the command of **Sir Richard Grenville**. After some consideration,Grenville determined that Roanoke Island would be the site of the first English settlement on the Outer Banks. He and his crews, which totaled 600 men, arrived in the summer of 1585 and spent several months clearing ground, building the earthworks of Fort Raleigh, and erecting houses to protect the 107 men who would stay behind. At the end of the summer, Grenville set sail for England, leaving Governor Ralph Lane in command and promising to return early the following year with reinforcements and supplies.

Grenville, however, was delayed. Governor Lane and his men had a difficult winter. There were skirmishes with the Indians, during which their chief and a number of warriors were killed. When **Sir Francis Drake** visited the fort in the spring of 1586, Lane and his men, believing Grenville's return was uncertain and fearing the hostility of the Indians, decided it best to leave while they had friendly transport home. When Grenville finally arrived, he was dismayed to find Fort Raleigh deserted. After a short stay and leaving 15 soldiers behind to guard the fort, he returned once again to England.

The following winter, 1586-87, Raleigh made the necessary preparations to colonize the Outer Banks. When the sailing conditions were favorable, **John White**, in command of three ships bearing 120 men, women and children, departed Plymouth for the New World. When they arrived at Fort Raleigh, it was once again deserted. The only clue as to the fate of Grenville's 15 men was a lone skeleton beside what was left of the fort.

Nevertheless, White's settlers began the task of putting things to right. After reconstructing the fort and building new homes, they settled in for their first winter on the island. On August 18th, a baby girl was born to John White's daughter and son-in-law. She was the first English child born in the New World and her parents named her, quite appropriately, **Virginia Dare**. White set sail for England in the early fall of 1587, vowing to return with supplies the following year. England was at war with Spain, however, and those hostilities delayed White's return for three years. When White dropped anchor again on Roanoke Island in 1590, he found the village and fort deserted, the colonists gone and a single word and three letters, CROATOAN and CRO, carved on a nearby tree. The search that followed revealed nothing, leaving a mystery that has never been solved. With a heavy heart, White returned to England, leaving Roanoke, once again, to the Indians. And so it remained until in 1665 colonists from Virginia arrived on the Outer Banks.

Present-day Roanoke Island is a busy fishing community and a popular tourist destination. In addition to its beauty and the many activities that flow from its natural attributes, visitors will find inviting options for accommodations and dining and a host of other attractions.

■ Weather & Storms

Storms are always a possibility on these islands. You need to keep an eye on the weather and an ear to the reports. Rough seas along the beachfronts on Highway 12 can flood the road and, on windy days, living in an RV, or towing a large trailer, can be more than a trial. Many's the trailer that lies in bits and pieces by the side of the road. Even the bridges in stormy weather aren't always safe, and ferry service is suspended during a storm.

■ Getting Here & Getting Around

From Ocracoke: Take the North Carolina Ferry from Ocracoke to Hatteras (this is more fully explained in the Ocracoke chapter, page 179).

From I-95: Exit at Rocky Mount and follow **Route 64** through Manteo island to Nags Head.

From the Norfolk, VA, area: **Route 158** to **168** brings you to the Outer Banks by way of the Wright Memorial Bridge.

It is helpful to understand that towns, hotels, restaurants and attractions often designate their location relative to the closest "milepost" marker along the main road that runs the length of the islands.

■ Special Events

A variety of special events are scheduled at different spots along the Outer Banks throughout the year. Some of the highlights are listed here.

In May, Hatteras hosts the **Hatteras Village Offshore Open Billfish and Gamefish Tournament**. Also in May, the **Hang-Gliding Spectacular and Air Games** are held at Jockey's Ridge State Park. The year 2000 will mark the 28th anniversary of this event, the oldest continuous hang gliding competition in the country.

In June, Jockey's Ridge hosts the **Rogallo Kite Festival**, honoring Francis M. Rogallo, inventor of the Flexible Wing Flyer. For 17 years, the **Wanchese Seafood Festival** has been a favorite for locals and visitors alike.

A variety of fun-filled activities are scheduled around the July 4th holiday, including the **Independence Day Fireworks Display** at the Ferry Docks in Hatteras and, later in the week, the **Best Body on the Beach Contest**.

The **Pirate's Cove Billfish Tournament** is held in August, as is the **Virginia Dare Birthday Celebration**, a day-long series of special events sponsored by the National Park Service, which culminates with the Virginia Dare Night Performance of the *The Lost Colony*. **National Aviation Day** is celebrated in August at the Wright Brothers' Monument.

In September, the Weeping Radish Brewery & Bavarian Restaurant in Manteo hosts the **Weeping Radish Oktoberfest**, complete with German oompah band. Celebrating its 50th anniversary in the year 2000 will be the **Nags Head Surf Fishing Club Invitational Tournament**.

The Christmas holidays are celebrated by the **Lighting of the Town Tree**, with caroling, Yule log, cake and hot chocolate, on the Waterfront at Manteo; **Kites With Lights**, when you can watch the antics

North Carolina

of lit stunt kites, sing carols and snack on hot cider and cookies at Jockey's Ridge State Park; and the **Anniversary of the First Flight**, at the Wright Brothers' Memorial.

■ Visitor Information

More information about the Outer Banks can be obtained ahead of your visit by contacting the **Dare County Tourist Bureau**, ☎ 252-473-2138, 877 BY-THE-SEA (298-4373), e-mail dctb-info@outer-banks.com, www.outer-banks.com/visitor-info. Once in the Outer Banks, the **Aycock Brown/Outer Banks Visitor Center**, Milepost 1½, and the **Kitty Hawk and Dare County Tourist Bureau**, Highway 64/264, Mateo, are open year-round. The **Nags Head Visitor Center** at Whalebone, located at the northern entrance of the Cape Hatteras National Seashore, and the **Roanoke Island Visitor Center** at Fort Raleigh, located on Highway 64/264 on the north end of Roanoke Island, are open from April through October.

■ Lighthouses

In 1789, in an effort to make the Eastern Shore of this then-fledgling nation safer, President George Washington and Congress passed legislation to establish buoys, lighthouses and other warning devices along the coastlines of the 13 original states. Of these, Cape Hatteras, Bodie Island, Ocracoke and Currituck were constructed along the Outer Banks. Overseeing the preservation of these towering sentinels today, in conjunction with the National Park Service, is the **Outer Banks Lighthouse Society**, PO Box 305, Kill Devil Hills, NC 27948, ☎ 252-441-9928. The sites of all four lighthouses are open to the public; keeper's quarters at Hatteras, Bodie, and Currituck have small museums and shops; and Hatteras and Currituck, weather permitting, are open for climbing. Interestingly, the Hatteras lighthouse was moved, very slowly indeed, from its endangered position to a new, safer one in the summer of 1999. For opening hours, contact the National Park Service at ☎ 252-473-2111.

■ Shopping

This area is not short on outlet malls and other such places, and these are readily identifiable when driving around. It is also famous for its specialty stores. As these are somewhat more difficult to find, some of the better ones are detailed below.

A Southern shopping tradition that shouldn't be missed is just 11 miles north of the Wright Memorial Bridge on Highway 168 in Jarvisburg. In a building that opened in 1929 as a working cotton gin is a unique shopping adventure in an atmosphere of bygone days. Aptly named, **The Cotton Gin** might best be described as a country marketplace – colorful, a bit on the rustic side, quaint and with country friendly service. Room after room, from attic to cellar, is chock full of items that will set your shopping senses reeling. There are North Carolina loomed textiles; handmade quilts; waterfowl carvings; soaps and candles; stuffed animals; collectible dolls; wicker baskets; gourmet kitchen wear and accessories; men's and women's classic clothing; adorable country crafts and accessories; jams, jellies and candies; jewelry; knicknacks and a variety of items that feature a seaside theme. Look for a number of specialty displays such as: "Teddy's Place," "Gnome Hollow," "The Mug Room" and the "Wildfowler Store. " If you want a foretaste of what to expect, you can order a full color catalogue. Write The Cotton Gin, Deep Creek Farm, Post Office Box 414, Jarvisburg, NC 27947, ☎ 800-637-2446, e-mail info@corrongin. com, www.cottongin.com. The Cotton Gin is open 364 days a year (closed on Christmas) and remains open until 8 pm during the season.

■ Adventures

On Wheels

Off-Road

The Outer Banks, with their spectacular natural beauty and unique environment, offer a vast number of opportunities to enjoy pleasures that are far from commonplace. Not all the best places to visit are on well-paved roads. On these shores, you can drive your off-road vehicle along many miles of accessible beach in search of the perfect fishing spot, picnic ground, secluded place to swim, or explore the pristine beaches as the waves lap your tires. Yes, off-roading here is a great experience, but there are a few rules and regulations you'll need to observe.

General Rules

■ The speed limit is 25 miles per hour. Enter and leave the beach only at designated open ramps, never between or over the dunes.

- Drive only on that portion of the beach that lies between the foot of the dunes and the ocean. Proceed with caution and consideration for other beach users.

- Open containers of alcohol are prohibited in vehicles. Your vehicle must have a state road registration and valid license plate. The operator must have a current driver's license.

- The use of off-road vehicles (ORVs) on the beaches along the Cape Hatteras National Seashore is permitted year-round, with some limitations.

- No permit is currently required to drive on National Park Service beaches, but it might be best if you checked with a ranger to make sure you understand NPS guidelines, and to ensure you are not entering a closed zone. Driving in the Pea Island Wildlife Refuge is strictly prohibited. For current information on open zones and guidelines, contact the National Park Service Headquarters at Cape Hatteras Group, ☎ 252-473-2111, or visit any NPS Visitors Center located throughout the park.

- Each township north of the Cape Hatteras National Seashore has its own requirements for beach driving. The towns of Southern Shores and Kitty Hawk do not allow ORVs on the beaches at any time. The towns of Kill Devil Hills and Nags Head do allow beach driving, but only between October 1 and April 30. If you want to drive your ORV on the beach in Nags Head, you must apply for and receive a permit from the Nags Head town hall. You do not need a permit at Kill Devil Hills.

- For more information, contact the following administrative offices: Southern Shores, ☎ 252-261-2394; Kitty Hawk, ☎ 252-261-3552; Kill Devil Hills, ☎ 252-480-4000; Nags Head, ☎ 252-441-5508.

4WD Rental

If you don't have a 4WD of your own, then contact **Midgette Auto Sales, Inc.,** ☎ 252-491-8500, 800-685-9938 (out-of-state-only), fax 491-2169, one mile north of the Wright Memorial Bridge, on the side heading to the beach at Harbinger. Here, a 4WD rents for about $90 a day, plus insurance, collision insurance and tax. The rate allows 100 free miles a day, with extra miles charged at 20¢ per mile.

Bicycling

A great way to see and enjoy the scenery and sites on the Outer Banks is to do it by pedal power. Because the roads can be a little dangerous for cyclists, the best way is to take advantage of the new **bike paths** located throughout the islands on Roanoke Island, in South Nags Head, Kill Devil Hills, and Southern Shores. You can bring your own bicycle or rent one when you get there. The path on **Roanoke Island** runs six miles from the Washington Baum Bridge to Manns Harbor Bridge. You'll get plenty of exercise and fresh air, can take your time and do it right. It's the best way to see all of downtown Manteo and visit the North Carolina Aquarium, Elizabeth Gardens and Fort Raleigh.

Kill Devil Hills has a one-mile bike path. It begins, depending upon where you happen to be, at either Colington Rd. near the First Flight School, or at West First St. **Nags Head** has a new multi-use path for cyclists or walkers that runs along Old Oregon Inlet Rd. in South Nags Head. It begins at Whalebone Junction and parallels Rte 1243. The path is paved, eight feet wide, and almost five miles long. The bike path in **Southern Shores** is a short one, about a mile, that runs from the Kitty Hawk Elementary School, along Highway 12/158, to the Southern Shores Town Hall.

On Water

Fishing

 As you might expect, the Outer Banks are considered a sportsman's paradise. Fishing is available in a variety of forms – surf, pier, freshwater and sound, offshore and inshore – with the season continuing throughout the year. The Outer Banks are also known for crabbing, clam digging, oyster catching and shrimping. Dining outside on fresh-caught seafood cooked over an open campfire or picnic grill is an experience you won't soon forget.

Every year thousands descend on the Outer Banks to enjoy some of the finest fishing anywhere in the world. In 1996, the North Carolina Division of Marine Fisheries recognized more than 6,300 anglers for their outstanding achievements in saltwater fishing by issuing citations for large catches, as well as for catch and release, recognizing some 33 species of fish and seven catch and release categories.

So what's available? You name it, the likelihood is you'll find it cruising the waters somewhere off the Outer Banks. You can expect all the great game fish, such as blue and white marlin, tarpon, amberjack, swordfish, sailfish, bigeye tuna, bluefin and yellowfin tuna, dolphin, wahoo, red drum, sea bass, bonito, spanish mackerel, king mackerel, bluefish and more. In the waters of the great sounds the catch includes flounder, sea trout, croaker, spot, sheepshead and striped bass.

 Outer Banks Weather and Fishing Hotline: *☎ 800-446-6262.*

Fishing Licenses

No license is required for saltwater fishing. A North Carolina fishing license is required, however, for freshwater fishing. Guest passes are available for short-term visitors covering one to three days at greatly reduced rates. These and all other fishing licenses may be obtained in advance by writing the **North Carolina Wildlife Resources Commission**, License Section, 512 N. Salisbury Street, Archdale Bldg., Raleigh NC 27604-1188. Licenses may also be obtained by telephone, using a credit card for payment. Call ☎ 888-2HUNTFISH. When ordering by telephone, an identification code and license number are issued to the caller and the license is thus valid immediately. For detailed information on the types of licenses, costs and the various ways to procure a license, visit www.wildlife.state.nc.us/.

Offshore & Inshore Charter Fishing

The Outer Banks are known as the "Billfish Capital of the World," and for good reason. Hundreds of white and blue marlin and sailfish are caught and released in the surrounding waters every year. The billfish season is a long one, peaking for blue marlin in June, and for white marlin and sailfish in August; all three can be caught throughout the period from late spring until early fall.

The Gulf Stream runs approximately 30 miles off the Outer Banks, providing the offshore angler with a wide variety of fish throughout the year. Probably most sought after is the yellowfin tuna, which is abundant throughout the year. Giant bluefin tuna have also made an impact in recent years. Ranging from 200 to 1,000 lbs, they will put up a real fight and will challenge even the professional angler. The bluefin season ranges from January through late March. Let the boat captain know if you are interested in this particular species.

Trolling is the offshore method of choice. Most boats carry a maximum of six people and a full day of fishing will cost $850 or more. All charters are run by professional captains and mates and, while tackle, bait and equipment are provided, you will need to bring your own food and drink, and a cooler for taking home your catch. Inshore charters are available for half-day trips. Fish caught inshore are smaller than those from the Gulf Stream, but the experience can be just as exciting. You can expect to catch king mackerel, big blues, cobia and amberjack during the spring and fall, and tailor blues and Spanish mackerel from late April through September. Most inshore boats carry a maximum of six people, and the cost for a half-day is about $350.

Both inshore and offshore charters can be booked through any of the local marinas. If you are unable to arrange a group, make-up charters, where the marinas put together the group, are available. So, even if you're traveling alone or with your family, you can still enjoy a day or half-day of charter fishing.

Sound & Head Boat Fishing

Another great way to fish the Outer Banks is by small boat in the Pamlico, Croatan, Albemarle and Roanoke sounds. Either from your own boat or from one rented in the area, you can expect to catch a wide variety of fish, including flounder, sea trout, croaker, spot, sheepshead and, at night, even red drum. Tarpon can be caught in the southern areas of the Outer Banks, though they are not as plentiful in the sounds as they are in the ocean. Cobia, too, can be caught in the great sounds; they are a hard-fighting fish sure to give you an exciting run, especially when they hit their peak in late May or early June. In recent years, there have been good catches of striped bass during the fall, winter and early spring.

You can hire a guide and boat, or set out in your own rig from one of the many public boat ramps, including those at the Manteo waterfront, Oregon Inlet, Pirate's Cove, Kill Devil Hills on Durham St, and throughout Hatteras Island.

Another excellent choice, and a lot of fun too for both novice and experienced anglers, is head boat fishing. The head boats carry 40-50 people, run half-day trips, and stay in the sound and inlet waters. Depending on the season, the catch is usually spot, sea trout, croaker, and/or sea bass. These boats are popular, manned by an experienced and helpful crew, supplying all bait, tackle and equipment; they even have restroom facilities and a drink and snack bar. Best of all, the cost for a half-day of fishing is extremely reasonable – usually on the order of $40 for adults, with discounts for children.

North Carolina

Brackish/Freshwater Fishing

The Outer Banks offer great freshwater fishing at the northern end of the beach in Currituck Sound, in Kitty Hawk Bay, and Colington Bay. These stretches of freshwater support a large population of Largemouth Bass. The bass season begins in April and lasts through November, with the peak season occurring from mid-April to early June and again in September and October.

During the summer months, you can catch white and yellow perch, perhaps even the odd catfish. Along the marshy shorelines and weed beds of the sounds, a fly rod can be a good companion. Whether you prefer to fish from a small boat or wade out into the water, you can expect some great sport; you'll be sure to take home your limit and release many more fish than you keep.

Recommended baits in the spring months are crank and spinners, with worms a good choice in the summertime. Freshwater licenses are required and can be obtained from many of the area bait and tackle shops or seafood shops.

Pier & Surf Fishing

There are fishing piers from Kitty Hawk to Hatteras. The season begins in March, increases to its peak in May, tapers off somewhat in the summer, reaches another peak in November, then slows again into January. The spring season, beginning around mid-March, is often best for red drum, which can weigh as much as 60 lbs. Good catches of mullet, spot, flounder, sea trout, croaker and others can also be expected during the spring season. You can also see small bluefish, perhaps even a "big blue," although these are not around in big numbers until the late fall. In summer, flounder, croaker, and small bluefish are the norm, although spot and gray trout can be caught.

For the surfcaster, there are more than 100 miles of accessible beach, but surf fishing on the Outer Banks is not considered good until August when the pompano and Spanish mackerel begin to make an appearance, along with a few elusive tarpon. Generally, however, September is considered the best month for all three. Fishing really gets serious, as the locals say, after Labor Day when the red drum and the big blues return to the waters of the Outer Banks. Blues weighing in at 15 lbs or more can be caught consistently throughout the fall months. The drum is prevalent under a series of names depending upon the size: the "puppy drum" is the youngest and smallest; next in age and size is the red drum, ranging from 35-70 lbs, and then comes the really big fella known as the channel bass, which can weigh in at

75 lbs or more. Other species available during the fall are the spot, flounder, croaker, sea trout and, occasionally, the striped bass.

The most popular baits are cutbait, bloodworms, squid and shrimp. Metal casting lures can be used for big blues and mackerel. Red drum can be caught with mullet heads and whole spot or whiting. A longer rod is the equipment of choice for surfcasting, with heavy line for big blues, channel bass and stripers. Shorter rods with lighter line are best for flounder and the smaller inshore species. For all-around use, a nine-foot rod with an open-faced reel spool and 250 yards or more of 17 lb test line is best. Tackle and bait shops on the piers can advise you about bait and equipment for any given location. And if you don't have equipment of your own, you can rent what you need at most shops and piers.

Swimming

Always use caution before entering the ocean. Be alert for red warning flags and red and white warning posters. If red flags are flying, it means swimming is prohibited. Although you may find flags flying when the weather seems calm and fine, it's always difficult to know when the water is safe.

Trust the experts. Ocean swimming is not like swimming in a lake or pool; strong currents and shifting sands can make the waters dangerous. Read all safety tips and rules posted at lifeguard locations. Lifeguards are on the beaches from Memorial Day Weekend through Labor Day, from 9:30 to 5:30pm. All beach areas have roving lifeguards and supervisors, although hours and locations are subject to change. The sound access areas do not have lifeguards. Specific lifeguard locations are pinpointed throughout this section.

Wreck Diving

The waters along the Outer Banks were regarded by early mariners as among the most treacherous in the world. From the time of the first European explorers to the present, over 2,000 ships, falling prey to storm-driven waters and shifting sands, have found their final resting-place in the "Graveyard of the Atlantic." Among these, the most famous is the **USS Monitor**, the iron-clad Civil War vessel sunk in 1862, rediscovered in 1973, and credited with ushering in our present age of naval warfare. A number of shipwrecks are visible at low tide and still others are on display at various locations. If this subject in-

North Carolina

trigues you, we suggest you pay a visit to Hatteras' museum, **The Graveyard of the Atlantic**, dedicated to the preservation, interpretation and understanding of shipwrecks and maritime history through multimedia presentations and exhibits.

They say there are more than 600 wrecks lying at the bottom of the sea off the Outer Banks. There are many you can visit, but you'll need a lot of stamina; this is not fun diving. The deep waters offshore are almost always cold, plagued by strong currents, populated by sharks of every shape and size, and visibility is often little more than a few feet. Add to all that the changeable weather, the shifting sands that cover and uncover the wrecks, and you have a very difficult diving situation. The list of wrecks is long, too long to cover in detail here, but there are a few worth mentioning that you can visit without the aid of a guide. The local dive shops along the Banks are familiar with the best sites. They stand ready and willing to take you out to them, which is by far the best way to go. Following are some of the interesting wrecks to be explored:

- The **Triangle Wrecks**: the *Josephine*, lost in 1915, the *Kyzickes*, in 1927, and the *Carl Gerhard*, in 1929. All lie in about 20 feet of water off Milepost 7 at Kill Devil Hills, south of the Sea Ranch.

- The **USS Heron** was a Federal screw-driven steamer lost off Nags Head in 1877. She lies at a depth of 25 feet.

- The **U-85**, a German submarine sunk in 1942, lies almost intact off Bodie Island northeast of the Oregon Inlet in 100 feet of water.

- The **Oijental**, thought to be the remains of a Federal steamer that sank in 1862, lies about four miles south of the Oregon Inlet. Her boiler can be seen in the surf.

- The **LST 471**, sunk in 1949, lies just north of the Rodanthe Fishing Pier in 15 feet of water 100 yards offshore; she is partially visible at low tide.

Beach Diving

There are more than 12 wrecks in the shallow waters between Duck and Hatteras Village. These can be visited without scuba gear; a snorkel and mask is all you need. Ask at any of the local dive shops for locations.

■ Touring the Outer Banks

 To help you discover the individual attractions and adventures of each fascinating town along the way, we have given under each town a little local history, the sightseeing highlights and the adventures you will find there. We also provide a listing of the hotels and places to dine in each community.

Start at the Wright Memorial Bridge, and the first destination is Corolla. To get there, however, you'll have to turn north at the junction of Highways 158 and 12 just on the northern edge of Kitty Hawk, where you'll also find the Dare County Aycock Brown Welcome Center just beyond the stoplight.

A WORD TO
THE WISE

You'll want to drop in at the Welcome Center. It's open year-round and there are picnic facilities and a rest area; you can also stock up on brochures and maps.

From here you'll drive north to Corolla and then turn and make the drive south again, this time at a more leisurely pace, with stops along the way to visit the beaches and sights, taking time out to eat or picnic.

From Aycock Brown, take Highway 12 through Southern Shores and Duck to Corolla. Don't bother to stop along the way, unless you see something too unusual to miss, you'll return and be able to visit all the sights on your drive south. From Aycock Brown the drive to Corolla is about 18 miles. The drive north offers some spectacular scenery with views of the dunes, Currituck Sound, and the ocean.

Corolla

Corolla, the northernmost point on the Outer Banks, once famous for its hunting clubs and well-dressed millionaire sportsmen, is undergoing change. Tourism has arrived here in a big way. The once deserted beaches, marshes and waters of the sound are visited each year by thousands of modern-day adventurers. Even so, it's more a stop on the way south than somewhere to stay for any length of time. The beaches are fabulous, deserted in the early mornings and late evenings, but getting busier during the day as the word continues to spread.

North Carolina

Sightseeing

Currituck Beach Lighthouse

The focus of Corolla must be the wonderful old Currituck Beach Lighthouse, ☎ 252-453-4939. It stands some 158 feet high above the beach and flashed its first warning beacon on December 1st, 1875. It is a first-order lighthouse, and filled the last remaining "dark spot" on the North Carolina coast between Bodie Island to the south and Cape Henry to the north. Prior to its institution, hundreds of ships foundered in the 80-mile stretch of darkness between the two lighthouses; the Currituck, its light visible for more than 18 miles, solved the problem. Lighthouses in earlier times were used by sea captains to identify their exact location, and so were distinctive both in style and decoration. Currituck was left unpainted in its natural red brick state. The Lighthouse Keeper's House, a Victorian "stick-style" dwelling, was built from pre-cut and labeled materials, then shipped to the site by barge. It was a duplex shared by two keepers and their families. When the light was automated, the keepers were no longer required and the house was abandoned; by 1980, it was in ruins. That year it was taken over by the Outer Banks Conservationists who were charged by the state to restore it. The work goes on, although restoration of some of the smaller buildings is complete, and they are open to the public. The lighthouse itself is also open to the public, and you can climb all the way to the top, if you so desire; certainly the view is well worth the effort. There are 214 steps to the top. Open daily for climbing, weather permitting, Easter through Thanksgiving, from 10 to 5 pm.

Adventures in Corolla

On Wheels

4WD/ATV

Few will realize that the dunes in the off-road area north of Corolla are home to wild Spanish mustangs. These have survived over 400 years of inclement weather and poor food to roam free on these beaches. The best way to see and learn about these magnificent creatures is through **Corolla Outback Adventures**, ☎ 252-453-0877, www.corollaoutback.com, next to the Corolla Post Office at Wink. A 4WD two-hour Wild Horse Safari, priced at $39 per person, winds through the petrified forest, Penny's Hill, and Carova. As you learn of area legends, you may be lucky enough to observe local wildlife such as whitetail deer, goats and, possibly, wild boar. Other adventures include a three-hour combination 4WD/ kayak expedition for $49 per person; a two-hour paddling excursion into the Salt Marsh Eco-Zone in Whalehead Bay at $34 per person; and a 20-mile guided adventure to Carova Beach and back behind the wheel of an ATV for $45 per person.

Where to Stay in Corolla

The **Inn at Corolla Light**, ☎ 252-453-3340, 800-215-0772, fax 453-6947, e-mail the-inn@outer-banks.com, www. corollainn.com, 1066 Ocean Trail, Corolla, has a delightful location nestled beside Currituck Sound. Each of the 41 guestrooms or suites are luxuriously appointed with either a king-sized or two queen-sized beds, refrigerator, TV, video player, AM/FM tape radio, and coffee maker. Many feature a fully equipped kitchenette and dining facilities. The Inn has a private pool and hot tub overlooking peaceful Currituck Sound, plus a 400-foot sailing pier. In summer, from the gazebo at the pier's end, guests can rent wave runners, kayaks, paddleboats, pontoon boats, and other watercraft. Other outdoor facilities include seven outdoor tennis courts, two oceanfront pools, a grass putting course, walking and biking trails. Indoors, there is a sports center with competition pool, hot tub and saunas, racket and volleyball courts, exercise room, tennis pro instruction and aerobics. Rates range from $85 to $295 per night.

Where to Eat in Corolla

Northbanks, ☎ 252-453-3344, at the TimBuck II Shopping Center, Corolla, is a petite and very personal restaurant where the highest priority is placed upon freshness of ingredients. Local and regional docks are scoured daily for prime fish and shellfish. Nearby Wanchese, one of the largest fishing communities on the East Coast, offers a plentiful variety. Meat dishes feature hand-selected beef from Allen Brothers in Chicago, and lamb and veal raised without hormones by Summerfield Farms in Culpeper, Virginia. Northbanks Restaurant, on the Northbanks, or so it was called originally, is open daily for lunch, 11:30 to 3:30 and for dinner from 5 to closing.

Steamers Shellfish To Go, ☎ 252-453-3305 or fax 453-0879, 798-B Sunset Boulevard, TimBuck II Soundside, Corolla, offers unique options for a gourmet take-out meal or snack, or purchase a customized Steamer Pot to enjoy back home.

Sorrel Pacific Cuisine, ☎ 252-453-6979, www.sorrels.com, TimBuck II Soundside, is an intimate, non-smoking restaurant, with a limited number of outdoor patio tables and a sound view. Most enjoyable also is the bar, the Tiki Tavern, where sushi is prepared and frozen island drinks and a supply of Pacific beers are on offer. Dishes reflect a variety of influences – Japanese, Thai, Polynesian, Australian, New Zealand, and South and North American, prepared in concert with East-West fusion cooking techniques. Sorrel is open seven days a week in season, from 11 to 10pm.

Duck

From Corolla, we travel back southward through Sanderling along Highway 12 to a point just a short distance north of Duck. This is where you'll find the **US Army Corps of Engineers Duck Pier Research Station**, a 1,800-foot long concrete pier from which the Corps investigates the ocean and the forces that create and destroy the beaches. It's an interesting place to visit, with lots of displays, but you'll have to be there by 10 in the morning, June 1 through August 12, Monday through Friday, when the walking tour begins. Otherwise, the facility is strictly off-limits.

Duck is still the tiny island community it has always been. Although they have long been dependent on the sea and its bounty for their livelihoods, the people here are turning more and more toward tourism. Where once was a lonely little fishing village, new upmarket shops, stores and cafés are springing up everywhere; there is even a large (by Outer Banks standards) shopping center and new outlets are opening all the time. Even so, Duck still manages to hang on to its old-world atmosphere, and it's difficult to believe that will ever change. The sea is quite close on the eastern side, and can be reached from almost anywhere in the village. Park your vehicle and walk into a world of dunes and sea oats where the seabirds wheel and squawk above the sands, crabs scurry hither and thither among the dunes, and the waters of the Atlantic seem to stretch away into the distance without end.

Adventures in Duck

On Foot

Shopping

 The **Scarborough Faire Shopping Center** in Duck is home to the studio of **Sara De Spain**, ☎ 252-255-0633 or 261-5591. Sara, a graduate gemologist from the

Gemological Institute of America and trained in the identifying and grading of diamonds and colored gemstones, has been creating jewelry for residents of, and visitors to, the Outer Banks since 1974. She transforms the nature she sees around her into precociously beautiful, free flowing and colorful jewelry. Sara aspires, in her own words, to echo the beauty, precision and grace she observes in God's living work all around her, and describes her works as small sculptures. She believes that jewelry should fit the look, personality and body of the wearer, and be versatile enough to make a fashion statement, whether worn with an evening dress or with jeans. The pieces are multi-dimensional in color, shape and substance, more often than not reflecting movement and motion. Sara De Spain's work has been shown in the North Carolina Museum of Art, and her name appears in *Who's Who of American Women*. Prices range from around $100 up to $15,000 for a heart-shaped diamond ring.

One of the delights of a visit to the Outer Banks is the opportunity to observe the amazing number of birds, in their many species, that either live on or migrate along these shores. You will also soon realize that these often exotic creatures, reproduced in the form of decoys or other carvings, are on display in numerous local shops. These are highly collectable and, in selecting one for your home, you will want to look for quality and authenticity. Head to **The Wooden Feather**, ☎ 252-261-2808, 1171 Duck Road, Suite B3, Duck, in the Scarborough Lane Shoppes. The proprietors, two sisters and a brother, Amy, Wendy and Lance Lichtensteiger, come with a carving pedigree; their father, Lance, has some 20 years experience in the craft. When all three came to the conclusion that they wanted to start a business of their own in 1998, they relocated to the Outer Banks, from Vermont, Arizona and New Jersey, respectively, and assumed ownership of The Wooden Feather, which had been in business for over a decade. At any given time, you will find here work by over 75 artists from throughout the nation, though many are local to the Outer Banks, North Carolina, Chesapeake and the Eastern Shore of Virginia. The amazingly diverse array of pieces includes antique and new decoys, sculptures, paintings, prints, photography, model boats, stained glass and other unique home furnishings. These original pieces of art may be created of wood, metalwork, clay, glass or driftwood. The Wooden Feather is open daily from 10 to 6, with hours extended until 10 in the summer.

Toy-Rific, 1171 Duck Road, Suite 1-5 in the Scarborough Lane Shoppes, Toy@interpath.com, is a hands-on store where everyone is invited to come in and play. In fact, this store is not really just for children – their slogan is "Specialty Toys for Big and Little Girls and

Boys." A wonderful train layout, visible to shoppers inside and browsers outside, actually runs around the store, passing through exterior walls and out onto the walkway. Filling every nook and cranny are toys from around the world, including an interesting selection handmade in the old world tradition by toy craftsmen.

Where to Stay in Duck

The **Sanderling Inn Resort and Conference Center**, ☎ 252-261-4111, 800-701-4111, fax 261-1638, e-mail sanderlinginn@outer-banks.com, www.outer-banks.com/ sanderling, 1461 Duck Road, Duck, is actually five miles north of the town of Duck at the narrowest point between the Atlantic Ocean and Currituck Sound. This 12-acre private resort is comprised of three inns which, combined, house 88 luxury rooms, a restaurant and bar housed in a restored 1899 coast guard lifesaving station. There is a fully equipped health club and one of the most extensive collections of fine wildlife art and sculpture in the country. The Main Inn, opened in 1985, blends the understated elegance of traditional Outer Banks architecture with spectacular antiques and artwork. The North Inn, opened in 1988 and was completely renovated in 1994. The South Inn, opened in 1994, offers deluxe suites and an array of all oceanfront and ocean view accommodations. The Sanderling Inn Resort bases rates upon two seasons and type of accommodation, with prices ranging from $123 to $504 a night for double occupancy.

Advice 5¢ - A Bed & Breakfast, ☎ 252-255-1050, 800-ADVICE 5, e-mail advice@theouterbanks.com, www.theouterbanks.com/advice5, is at 111 Scarborough Lane, Duck. Located in the secluded and quiet neighborhood of Sea Pines, it is a short walk from Duck's shops and restaurants. Built in 1995, it offers a pleasant getaway in an atmosphere of casual simplicity. Each of the four guestrooms has private bath and deck, and a singular suite also offers a sitting area with cable TV and stereo, and a master bath featuring a Jacuzzi-style bathtub. Rooms range from $95 to $140, and suites from $120 to $175.

Where to Eat in Duck

Elizabeth's Café & Winery, ☎ 252-261-6145, e-mail elizcafe@pinn.net, www.elizabethscafe.com, 1177 Duck Road, Suite 11, Scarborough Faire Shops in Duck, has been described as having one of the finest restaurant wine lists in the world by *Wine Spectator*. The dinner menu, designed totally around fresh ingredients that can be found at market, changes nightly and usually is not published until around 5 pm. Reservations for dinner are scheduled at 6, 6:30, 8:15 and 8:45, and reservations are a necessity. The restaurant is open every night during the high season, and as long afterwards as there is sufficient business, although it does close for one month in the winter. Diners may order à la carte or opt for either the prix fixe wine dinner at $80 per person or – the house's real specialty – the premier wine dinner at $125 per person. Such gourmet cuisine deserves to be paired with a fine wine list, and it is. In fact, in the 10 years since its inception, Elizabeth's Café & Winery has established a worldwide reputation for its wine selections. The selection at Elizabeth's includes between 1,200 and 1,500 different vintages at any given time. To assist-up-and-coming connoisseurs in what can prove to be a difficult selection, owner Leonard Logan has fashioned the prix fixe wine dinner and the premier wine dinner. Why not taste the very best cuisine and wine when you have the opportunity? It isn't something most of us get a chance to do every day. The menu is too large to reproduce here, but the culinary experience will be first class.

The **Duck News Café**, ☎ 252-261-6117, 1564 Duck Road, Duck, is located on the waterfront of Currituck Sound, across from the Sanderling Inn. This innovative eatery, with a newspaper theme, has the scoop on tasty cuisine. The house specialties, though, are the real breaking story, with crab imperial, fresh pasta and slow-roasted prime rib most deserving of a byline. For the comfort of non-smoking patrons, smoking is limited to the bar, lounge and outdoor area. The Duck News Café is open for dinner daily in season from 5 to 9:30 pm.

The **Duck Deli**, ☎ 252-261-3354 or 255-0861, 1378 Duck Road, Duck, opened in 1988 and took little time in establishing itself as the area's favorite small country barbecue restaurant. Success didn't stop there, however. The owner, Ron Forlano, a retired dentist from Pennsylvania, realized quickly that fish were suitable for smoking too, and he pioneered Carolina Blue Smoked Wildfish, www.smokedfishnc.com, www.theouterbanks.com/wildfish. Historically, fishermen in these parts had been paid rather scantily for their catches. Ron, however, offered premium prices for the best quality fish, smoked them and then wrapped them in deliciously appetizing packages suitable for shipping anywhere in the country. Tuna, salmon fillet, shrimp, scallops, king mackerel and wild bluefish can be seen in their catalogue or on the web. Once you have made a selection, call ☎ 800-589-1690 24-hours-a-day, seven-days-a-week to place an order. It should go without saying that the Duck Deli is famed for smoked food.

North Carolina

Kitty Hawk

From Duck as you continue south toward Kitty Hawk, the next stop along the way is **Southern Shore**s, the oldest planned development on the Outer Banks. It's basically a residential community, but the scenery is lovely with occasional views out to the sound between the dunes, and some very expensive oceanfront dwellings. The first point of entry to the Outer Banks from the north, Kitty Hawk is booming. Once a remote island fishing village, it is isolated and swept by strong offshore breezes. Both factors must have been high on the Wright brothers' list of priorities when deciding where to test their flying machine in 1900. Even though it's always busy and crowded, it's still a good place to visit. It still has the sun, sand and sea, and you can still find a place to sit and enjoy them.

Adventures in Kitty Hawk

On Foot

Golf

 SeaScape Golf Club, ☎ 252-261-2158, on Highway 158 Bypass at Milepost 2, is on the sound side of the bypass amid rolling dunes and sand hills. This is a typical links-style course, not quite as rugged as those in Scotland, but challenging enough. There are no water hazards or trees, which makes it somewhat bleak, but the greens are fresh and well-kept; you will, however, need a good bug repellent during the summer, especially just after wet weather. The par is 72 over 6,200 yards. There's a 19th hole where drinks are available by the glass.

On Water

Fishing

 Kitty Hawk Fishing Pier, ☎ 252-261-2772, if you're an angler, you'll want to stop by and try your luck here. The pier stretches out into the ocean more than 700 feet, and the fishing is good, very good, in fact. All inshore species are available, including bluefish, sea trout, flounder, spot, king mackerel, cobia and stripers. You can go at night; the pier is lighted. Once on the pier, you don't have to leave. There is a little restaurant, restrooms, and a bait and tackle shop where you can rent all the equipment you need for a great day out fishing, Open daily, April 1 until Thanksgiving, from 5 until 5 (they just close the doors and then open them again).

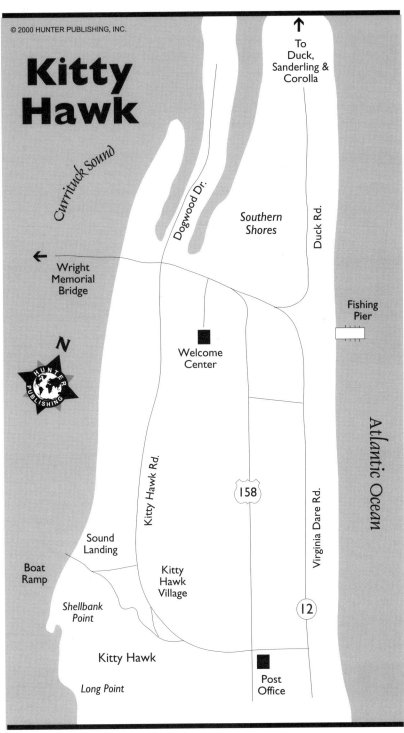

© 2000 HUNTER PUBLISHING, INC.

Kitty
Hawk

Currituck Sound

To
Duck,
Sanderling &
Corolla

Dogwood Dr.

Southern
Shores

Duck Rd.

←
Wright
Memorial
Bridge

N

HUNTER
PUBLISHING

Fishing
Pier

Welcome
Center

Kitty Hawk Rd.

158

Atlantic Ocean

Virginia Dare Rd.

Sound
Landing

Boat
Ramp

Kitty
Hawk
Village

Shellbank
Point

12

Kitty Hawk

Long Point

Post
Office

North Carolina

Where to Eat in Kitty Hawk

The **Black Pelican Oceanfront Café**, ☎ 252-261-3171 or fax 261-1437, Milepost 4, Beach Road, Kitty Hawk, comes by its name from the Legend of The Black Pelican, which is described on the back of the menu. Over the years this informal restaurant has become an Outer Banks' institution. Seating is in one of several dining areas or in a sizeable sports bar.

Kill Devil Hills

Kill Devil Hills is a busy little community some six miles south of the Wright Memorial Bridge. And, like all the other small communities along the way south, it's worth a visit, especially if you like the beach.

Sightseeng

Wright Brothers National Memorial

You will surely want to investigate just how the Wright Brothers managed their amazing feat on December 17, 1903. The Visitor Center at Wright Brothers National Memorial, ☎ 252-441-7430, relates, through exhibits and full-scale reproductions of their 1902 glider and 1903 flying machine, the full story of the Wright Brothers. Nearby are two reconstructed 1903 camp buildings, one of which duplicates their hangar and the other reminiscent of, and furnished much like, Orville's and Wilbur's workshop and living quarters. A large granite boulder marks the spot where the first craft left the ground, while numbered markers indicate the distance of each of the four flights taken on that momentous day. The Wright Brothers National Memorial, easily spotted and dominated by a massive granite monument on the crest of a 90-foot-high sand dune, is open daily from 9 to 6 in the summer, but closes an hour earlier during other seasons.

Adventures in Kill Devil Hills

On Foot

Shopping

Hammocks are a popular and useful souvenir from the Outer Banks. Just imagine lazily rocking to and fro in the shade of an ancient tree, a cold drink nearby, on a hot and sultry summer afternoon or caressed by a crisp autumn breeze. Indulge your fantasies with **Nags Head Hammocks**, ☎ 252-441-6115, 800-344-6433, fax 480-0415, e-mail sales@nagshead.com, www.nagshead.com. The main store is at 1801 Croatan Highway, 158 Bypass, Kill Devil Hills, but there are other locations at TimBuck II in Corolla; 1212 Duck Road in Duck; at Highway 158 in Point Harbor; and at Avon on Hatteras Island. Owners Chuck and Susan Sineath are proud that the original, high-quality rope hammocks are made here by their own craftsmen. While you are probably most familiar with the standard rope hammock, available in single, double or extra-wide sizes, these are not the only products they make. Look for hammock chairs, slingshot swings, rope furniture (including folding single or double rockers), captain's chairs, double recliners, folding rope foot stools, and even a toy chest hammock. The price within each range depends largely on color, as some hues are more costly to produce. Accessories, too, are intriguing. Who could, for instance, buy a hammock without taking a drink caddy as well? And if the promise of such relaxation can't wait for a visit, Nags Head Hammocks is open for telephone and fax orders from 9 to 6 daily, or you can order from their website at any time.

On Water

Fishing

Avalon Fishing Pier, ☎ 252-441-7494, is just as big and well served as the one farther to the north in Kitty Hawk; in fact, it's owned and operated by the same outfit. More than 700 feet long, lighted for night fishing, it has a restaurant, tackle and bait shop, ice, gear for rent and rest rooms. It never closes during the season, April 1 to Thanksgiving.

In the Air

Air Tours

In an area famous for the site of man's first powered flight, what could be more appropriate than taking to the air yourself on an air tour that departs from that very same spot. For just $58 a couple, **Kitty Hawk Aero Tours**, ☎ 252-441-4460, will whisk you aloft from the airstrip at the Wright Brothers Monument for an informative 25-minute, 50-mile tour. You will soar over land and water, enjoying spectacular views of sea creatures, shipwrecks, lighthouses and Jockey's Ridge, at the same time becoming better acquainted with the unusual geographical features of the Outer Banks. Upon landing, your pilot will present you with a signed First Flight Certificate.

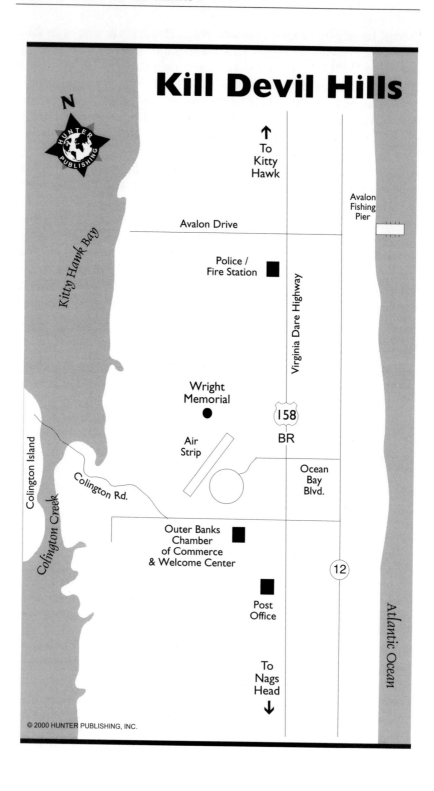

Kill Devil Hills

N

HUNTER PUBLISHING

To Kitty Hawk

Kitty Hawk Bay

Avalon Fishing Pier

Avalon Drive

Police / Fire Station

Virginia Dare Highway

Wright Memorial

158 BR

Air Strip

Colington Island

Colington Creek

Colington Rd.

Ocean Bay Blvd.

Outer Banks Chamber of Commerce & Welcome Center

12

Post Office

Atlantic Ocean

To Nags Head

© 2000 HUNTER PUBLISHING, INC.

Eco/Cultural Adventures

Colington Island

Just a half-mile south of the Wright National Monument, near Milepost 8, a narrow road runs west to the heavily wooded and very pretty Colington Island, one of the lesser-known attractions on the Outer Banks. In 1665, this site was colonized by English settlers under the leadership of Peter Carteret, thus becoming the first permanent settlement on the Outer Banks. The five-mile drive into Colington is scenic indeed, a photographer's dream, passing over old arched bridges and through forests of holly, oak and pine as it winds its way to the shores of the sound. Once you arrive, you will enjoy beautiful countryside and peace and quiet. This is an ideal spot for a picnic lunch. Before leaving, pack yourselves a hamper, tucking in a bottle of your favorite wine, and plan for an afternoon of rest and relaxation.

Where to Eat in Kill Devil Hills

The **Flying Fish Café**, ☎ 252-441-6894, Milepost 10, Highway 158 Bypass, Downtown Kill Devil Hills, is a sophisticated but casual restaurant serving American and Mediterranean cuisine. Although seafood is on the agenda, there is a wider range of offerings than most other restaurants in the area. It opens for lunch from 11:30 am to 5 pm, and for dinner from 5 to 10 pm, daily.

Goombay's Grille and Raw Bar, ☎ 252-441-6001, 1608 North Virginia Dare Trail, Milepost 7.5, Kill Devil Hills, has a crazy décor and an enjoyably lighthearted atmosphere that are a perfect match for the beach environment. They have combined a tropical taste with a casual place for the maximum of fun. Not surprisingly, the menu is eclectic. Before leaving, check out Goombay's colorful T-shirts, which are of very high quality.

Mako Mike's, at Milepost 17, 158 Bypass, Kill Devil Hills, ☎ 252-480-1919, serves up killer food and a healthy dose of fun. A cheerfully casual ambiance is created by brightly colored, crisply modern furnishings; murals from which whimsical underwater creatures seem to swim right off the walls; an array of imaginative local artwork; and a 200-gallon aquarium, which is home to a variety of multi-hued ocean fish. The Octopus Lounge, cooled by the rhythmic whir of antique paddle fans, is a relaxing place to enjoy your favorite beverage. And fun souvenirs, including Mako Mike's specialty items, are sold in the gift shop. Mako Mike's is open year-round, with the feeding frenzy beginning at 4:30 pm.

Nags Head

Traveling southward from Kill Devil Hills, you'll enter the Nags Head city limits near Milepost 11. If not the premier vacation spot on the Outer Banks, this seaside village must come close to it. Always busy, always crowded, it can be a bit hectic at times, but it has all you need for a pleasant afternoon on the beach. But Nags Head is much more than that. It's also a major recreation center where you can fish, boat, surf, and enjoy the arts; you can even hang glide, if you like. There are more galleries, art studios, shops, and stores here than anywhere else on the Banks.

The Legend of Nags Head

Nags Head first became a resort in the early 1800s, when wealthy plantation owners began taking their summers on the Outer Banks away from the heat and humidity farther inland. Before that, however, it was a dangerous place to visit, at least for mariners. Legend has it that "wrecking" was a popular pastime and source of income for the early inhabitants. It seems that certain ne'r-do-wells would tie lanterns to their horses' necks (could this be the origin of the name?) and walk them back and forth along the beach at night. The bobbing lights, easily mistaken for ships riding safely at anchor in harbor, would be seen by captains at sea and they would steer for them, only to run aground – easy pickings for the wreckers.

Today, the wreckers are long gone, and Nags Head is one of the safest resorts on the East Coast. If you intend to stop and rest for a couple of days to enjoy the beaches, this is as good a place as you will find... unless you're looking for solitude, that is.

Sightseeing in Nags Head

Jockey's Ridge State Park

Just off South Croatan Highway, Highway 158 Bypass, at Milepost 12, you will come to the 414-acre Jockey's Ridge State Park, ☎ 252-441-7132 or fax 441-8416.

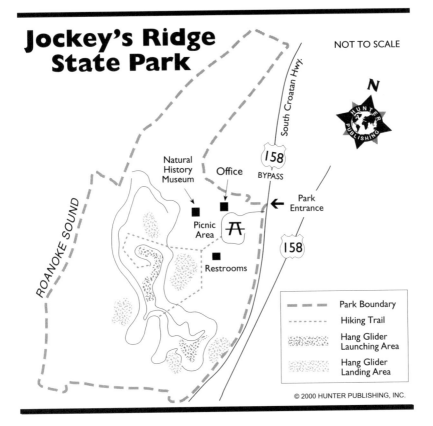

Jockey's Ridge
State Park

NOT TO SCALE

South Croatan Hwy.

N

HUNTER PUBLISHING

158
BYPASS

ROANOKE SOUND

Natural
History
Museum

Office

← Park
Entrance

Picnic
Area

158

Restrooms

- – – – Park Boundary
- - - - - Hiking Trail

Hang Glider
Launching Area

Hang Glider
Landing Area

© 2000 HUNTER PUBLISHING, INC.

North Carolina

*This is home to the tallest natural sand dune
system in the Eastern US, 80-100 feet above sea
level, depending on weather conditions, and
with dune peaks of up to 140 feet high.*

Jockey's Ridge is an example of a **medano**, defined as a huge hill of
shifting sand that lacks vegetation. Maritime winds from differing directions are constantly changing both the shape and the size of the
dune. The reason it doesn't blow away completely is that prevailing
winds in summer and winter come from exactly opposite directions,
constantly blowing the sand back and forth. Still, the ridge is moving
very slowly in the direction of the stronger winds, most recently over-
taking a miniature golf course, purchased by the state so that the natural movement of the dunes could continue unobstructed. In fact,
during winter months, the gusty winds often uncover turrets of the
cement castle that, not so long ago, reigned over the putt-putt.

Hiking on this huge pile of sand, perhaps along the self-guided 1.5-
mile Tracks in the Sand Trail, can be a lot of fun.

Remember to wear properly protective shoes as the sand temperature can be as much as 30° higher than the air temperature.

If you make it to the top you will have a glorious view over the sand and Roanoke Sound; and, on a clear day, though you can't see forever, you can see for miles, both to the north and south, along the Outer Banks. When on the dunes keep an eye out for the little glass tubes formed when lightning hits the sand. These are called **fulgurites**, and are named after the Roman goddess Fulgera. Don't remove them from the park. On the same topic, but on a rather more serious note, be warned that this park is exposed to lightning during thunderstorms. Very recently, the park opened a visitor center and museum with informative exhibits on sand and sand movement. A variety of programs, including star-gazing, kite building and bird watching, are offered throughout the year. The park opens at 8 all year round, closing at 6 between November and February, 7 in March and October, 8 in April, May and September and 9 from June through August.

Adventures in Nags Head

On Water

Dive Shops

Nags Head Pro Dive Center, ☎ 252-441-7594, Kitty Hawk Connection, Milepost 13.5, Nags Head. This is the oldest dive facility on the Outer Banks, offering a full line of services. Located just across from Jockey's Ridge, they sell and rent equipment, air fills to 5,000 lbs, and offer PADI instruction. The also run their 50-foot dive boat, the *Sea Fox*, from the Manteo waterfront to the historic wrecks. They're open seven days a week from 10 to 5 during the season.

Dolphin Watch

Visitors to the Outer Banks are not alone in their fascination with the dolphin population. Research teams track the creatures up and down the coast, taking photo IDs and keeping a record of their numbers and travels. In order to finance their studies, the scientists take paying passengers along on their excursions. Can you think of a better way to see and learn about the dolphins? **Nags Head Dolphin Watch**, ☎ 252-449-8999, www.dolphin-watch.com, is based at Willett's Wetsports on the Causeway beside Caribbean Corners. They offer three trips daily between Memorial Day, when the dolphins are just arriving, and the end of September, when the dolphins migrate south to Beaufort, NC. You will learn from those that know them best about the dolphins' feeding and social habits and you may be able to participate in one or more of the ongoing studies. Other wildlife, such as osprey and pelicans, will put in an appearance too, no doubt, and expert naturalists will provide an in-depth commentary on local ecology and history. We think you will agree that this is an opportunity too good to pass up – see the dolphins and help them at the same time. Just after Memorial Day, when sightings are likely but less frequent, the cost is $15 per person. For the balance of the season, the cost increases to $20.

Fishing Piers

Nags Head Fishing Pier, ☎ 252-441-5141, is near Milepost 12 on the Atlantic side. It's 750 feet long, with all the usual facilities, including a tackle and bait shop and clean, well-kept restrooms. There's also a nice restaurant, where the staff will clean and cook your catch for you. There's a games room to keep the kids occupied when they've had enough fishing. You can rent gear on the spot and the fishing is good. Bluefish, sea trout, spot, croaker and flounder are all available. Open 24 hours daily year-round.

Jennette's Pier, ☎ 252-441-6116, is four miles south of Nags Head Pier, near the intersection of Highways 64/264 and 12 at Whalebone Junction. Jennette's is 540 feet long. It's quite old, first built in 1939 and rebuilt several times since then, but it has all the facilities necessary for a great day out. There's a snack bar where you can get cold drinks, including beer on tap, and light food, a games room with coin-operated machines, and a bait and tackle shop where you can rent equipment. Open 24 hours daily from mid-April through November.

Tackle

If you are need of tackle, there is a shop that can we can recommend. Recognizing that not all ladies are fisherwomen but that they do often accompany their men folk to the shop, the management of **Capt. Marty's**, ☎ 252-441-3132, 1800 MARTYS-9, fax 441-3841, www.captmartys.com does their level best to make them feel welcome. They are in the Outer Banks Mall at 5151 South Croatan Highway, Milepost 141/2, Nags Head. There is a "ladies' corner" in the light and spacious 5,700-square-foot store, with fireplace, easy chairs, magazines and coffee. The range of fishing and hunting supplies is comprehensive and the staff is friendly and helpful. They will assist you in building a custom rod, give you hands-on instruction in bait rigging and, if you call ahead, custom-rig your offshore baits. What's more, if you catch a few keepers, Capt. Marty's has a rental freezer locker where you can keep your prizes fresh until your trip back home.

In the Air

Hang Gliding & More

 Among the more colorful and intriguing sights along the Outer Banks is the host of hang gliders that float gracefully upon the currents above Jockey's Ridge. Gusty winds and a naturally soft landing field of sand made conditions ideal for the sport, even for first timers. Each May the **Hang Gliding Spectacular**, the oldest continuous hang gliding competition in the US, is held in this park. Those of you adventurous enough to try it yourselves will not have far to travel for assistance and the proper equipment. **Kitty Hawk Kites**, ☎ 252-441-4124, 800-334-4777, fax 441-7597, e-mail catalog@kittyhawk.com, www.kittyhawk.com, has its main store and flight center at Milepost 13, Jockey's Ridge. In addition to a complete range of dune hang gliding packages and experiences, they offer comprehensive opportunities for paragliding, aerotowing and boat-tows. Kayaking is another of their specialties; and they offer are a full range of guided kayak eco-tours and sunset tours, kayaking and sailing instruction, and bare boat rentals. The folks at Kitty Hawk Kites accommodate landlubbers, too, with biking tours or bike rentals, in-line skate lessons and rentals and climbing on two indoor walls (one outdoor wall and a portable wall). Kiting, as you will have noticed, is also a popular pastime on these windy shores; and, as the name implies, this company offers kite-making workshops and demonstrations. If you take a more permanent shine to any one of these sports, equipment is for sale as well as for rent, alongside a full range of goods from shirts to sailboats and including such novelties as windsocks, spinners and banners, boomerangs, the ever popular yo-yo and stunt kites.

Kitty Hawk Kites operates other stores (in their own name, in conjunction with Carolina Outdoors, or designated solely as Carolina Outdoors) at the following locations: Kitty Hawk Kites at Corolla, ☎ 252-453-8845; Currituck Airport, ☎ 252-453-3540; and Duck, ☎ 252-261-4450; Kitty Hawk Kites & Carolina Outdoors at Avon, ☎ 252-995-6060; and Carolina Outdoors at Corolla, ☎ 252-453-3685, Hatteras and Manteo, ☎ 252-473-2357. The range of adventures offered at these other stores, however, is less comprehensive than at the parent store.

Where to Stay in Nags Head

The **Surf Side Motel**, ☎ 252-441-2105, 800-552-SURF, fax 441-2456 or e-mail surfside@pinn.net, Milepost 16, Nags Head, with its wonderful oceanfront location and array of unusual room layouts, has long been a family favorite. There are 76 well-appointed guestrooms designated standard, king room, loft room, efficiency and honeymoon suite with Jacuzzi. The loft room offers a unique layout, designed for a family, but conducive to privacy. The main level consists of a bedroom/sitting room with full bath and balcony. Upstairs, by way of wooden stairs, is a balcony bedroom with double bed, chest of drawers of and skylight. Rates range from $39 to $209 per night.

The **First Colony Inn**, ☎ 252-441-2343, 800-368-9390 (reservations only from 8 to 10), fax 441-9234, e-mail innkeeper@firstcolonyinn.com, www.firstcolonyinn.com, 6720 South Virginia Dare Trail, Mile Post 16, Nags Head, is a AAA Four-Diamond inn with a fascinating history. When first opened in 1932, during an era when Nags Head was considered "the summer capital of Albemarle Society," the First Colony Inn was considered the place to stay on the beach at Nags Head. By 1988, however, this distinctive structure with its wide two-story encircling verandas had fallen into a state of disrepair and was in danger of being swallowed up by the sea. It was saved that year through the efforts of the Lawrence family of Lexington, North Carolina who, overcoming a myriad of obstacles, had the structure cut into three pieces and reassembled three miles to the south. Each of the 26 guestrooms has TV/VCR, telephone, refrigerator, air conditioning, and heated towel racks in the bathrooms. Rates here are governed by three seasons and four types of rooms: A rooms (first floor), B rooms (third floor), C rooms (second floor), and D rooms (deluxe). Most recent rates for A rooms were $75, $110 and $150; for B rooms, $100, $135 and $180; for C rooms, $125, $160 and $210; and for D rooms, $150, $185 and $240, depending on season. Weekend and holiday night rates include a surcharge of $15, $20 or $25, depending upon the season.

Where to Eat in Nags Head

The **Windmill Point Restaurant**, ☎ 252-441-1535, Milepost 16½, Highway 158 Bypass, is set well back from the road and overlooks Roanoke Sound. This is a delightful and interesting place to dine, and for more reasons than the imaginative American cuisine. Dr. Sarah E. Forbes, the proprietress, has amassed the largest collection of memorabilia from the SS *United*

States, the most luxurious, fastest and the largest ship of its time. This forms the decor of the restaurant, creating one of the most unusual ambiances on the Outer Banks. Nowhere is this truer than in the upper level lounge, the perfect place to enjoy a before-dinner cocktail. In fact, this room replicates the lounge aboard the *SS United States*, and the furnishings, including the bar, cocktail tables and chairs, are the originals from that ship.

Owens' Restaurant, ☎ 252-441-7309, Milepost 161/2, Beach Road, Nags Head, a AAA Three-Diamond Award recipient for the past 20 years, has been owned and operated by the Owens and Shannon families, Nags Head natives, for over a half-century. The menu, which offers Miss O's crab cakes and hush puppies, features classic local Southern coastal cuisine, with fresh-off-the-boat seafood and shellfish, whole Maine lobster, tender aged Angus beef, ribs, pasta and outrageously delicious homemade desserts, complemented by an extensive wine list.

Tortuga's Lie Shellfish Bar & Grill, ☎ 252-441-RAWW, Milepost 11.5, Beach Road, Nags Head, is a Caribbean-style restaurant whose ambiance fits easily in to the beach environment. Here, seafood, chicken, beef and vegetarian dishes get a tropical twist. Rounding out the fare is a nice selection of pasta and steamed seafood dishes and a sushi menu. The full-service bar serves specialty drinks, wine, and buckets of beer and microbrews.

Roanoke Island

From Nags Head, continue southward to the intersection of Highway 12 and 64/264 at Whalebone Junction; turn west on 64/264 and head out across the bridge to Roanoke Island.

Manteo

Reached by way of the Nags Head and Manteo Causeway (Highway 64/264), Manteo is as good a place as any to begin your visit to Roanoke. The downtown area directly fronts Shallowbag Bay. The waterfront there is a great place to stroll, watch the boats, eat, shop and stay. It's a very attractive area, with lots of quaint little shops and stores, and any number of photo opportunities; the view over the bay is wonderful. Just off the Waterfront in the downtown area there are more shops and outlets, all worth a visit.

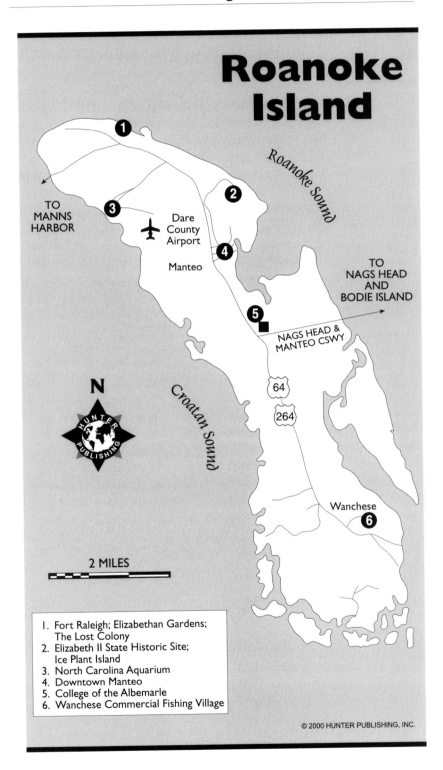

Roanoke Island

TO MANNS HARBOR

Dare County Airport

Manteo

Roanoke Sound

Croatan Sound

TO NAGS HEAD AND BODIE ISLAND

NAGS HEAD & MANTEO CSWY

64

264

Wanchese

N

2 MILES

1. Fort Raleigh; Elizabethan Gardens; The Lost Colony
2. Elizabeth II State Historic Site; Ice Plant Island
3. North Carolina Aquarium
4. Downtown Manteo
5. College of the Albemarle
6. Wanchese Commercial Fishing Village

© 2000 HUNTER PUBLISHING, INC.

North Carolina

Sightseeing

The North Carolina Aquarium

 The North Carolina Aquarium, ☎ 252-473-3494, is located on Airport Road, Manteo, just three miles north of Manteo. An expansive renovations should be completed by the time of your visit. The new 68,000-square-foot aquarium features a massive 180,000-gallon centerpiece tank, which includes a replica of the *USS Monitor*. The theme is "Waters of the Outer Banks," and the exhibits and activities examine habitats of the Alligator River, the fresh- and saltwater marshes of the region and the Gulf Stream waters offshore.

Festival Park

History lovers will also want to check out Roanoke Island Festival Park. This exciting art and history complex is located directly opposite the Manteo waterfront on an island within an island. Tickets and information on park exhibits are available at the Arrival Center. The highlight, unquestionably, is the *Elizabeth II*, a reproduction of a three-masted bark, similar to those used by the colonists of 1586 to cross from England to the New World. You will likely be surprised by its small size – just 69 ft long and 17ft wide. She was rated in 1586 as a 50-tunne ship, when the average merchant ship was 125 tunnes, an English warship might go as high as 800 tunnes, and a Spanish galleon considerably more. *Elizabeth II* was small by any standards, and a voyage of several months across seas that seemed to stretch on forever must have been a harrowing experience. Guides and interpreters dressed in Elizabethan costume will tell you just how harrowing it was as they escort you about the ship and discuss the lifestyles of her passengers. Other noteworthy attractions at the park are a 230-seat theatre showing *The Legend of Two Paths*, a film that depicts their first encounter with the English from a Native American perspective. There is an 8,500-square-foot hall with an array of historical, cultural, economic and natural interactive exhibits. An outdoor Pavilion seats 3,500 and offers one-act plays, Shakespearean dramas, dance recitals, concerts (from jazz to symphonic), country music or R&B shows, and vaudeville-style reviews. Open Tuesday through Sunday, hours are 10 to 6 between April and October and 10 to 4 the remainder of the year. Admission for adults is $3; for children six-12, $1.50. For more information, call ☎ 252-473-1144.

Outdoor Drama

No summertime visit to the Outer Banks would be complete without taking in *The Lost Colony*. Reservations are required and may be made by calling ☎ 919-473-3414 or 800-488-5012. This is a symphonic outdoor drama that vibrantly recounts the story of the 120 English settlers who made their homes at Fort Raleigh in the summer of 1887 and disappeared sometime before John White's return in 1590.

The drama grew out of the frustrations of several Roanoke Island citizens seeking to refute the historical fallacy that Jamestown and Plymouth were America's first English settlements. Their first efforts resulted in a 1921 vintage silent film that told the story of the Roanoke voyages of 1585-87. By 1934, the newly-formed Roanoke Island Historical Association had ambitious plans to commemorate the 350th birthday of Virginia Dare, the first English child born in the New World, with a pageant. They commissioned native North Carolinian and Pulitzer-Prize-winning playwright, Paul Green, to pen the script and began construction of an outdoor theater near the site of the ill-fated colony. Green created a masterpiece of innovative theater, bringing the tragic tale to life through a cleverly woven tapestry of music, dance and high drama. On July 4, 1937 the show debuted beneath the stars in the Waterside Amphitheater for two performances before over 8,000 patrons. And the production has gone on to write its own chapter in the history of Roanoke Island. Surviving the economic depression, fire, hurricanes, war and financial challenges, *The Lost Colony* has played each summer season to the present (except for a three-year suspension during World War II) to appreciative audiences. And so, a production that was envisioned to run just one season is, as of 2000, in its 63rd. Of this phenomenon, current director Drew Scott Harris says "This is a story of human values. Courage, compassion, survival, these are things that never go out of style."

Today's patrons are enthralled as over 125 actors, singers, dancers and technicians tell the story of history's most enduring and endearing mystery.

Performances of this, the nation's premier and longest-running outdoor drama, are given Sunday through Friday at 8:30, mid-June through late August. Tickets are $18 for Producers Circle seats, $16 for adults, and $8 for children under 12, with additional discounts offered on Sunday nights. For a really special treat, inquire about "Tea with the Queen," a special package that includes a formal backstage tour, sumptuous dessert and tea, an audience with the actress portraying Queen Elizabeth I and Producer's Circle tickets to the show.

Gardens

The **Elizabethan Gardens**, within The Lost Colony complex, were created by the Garden Club of North Carolina as a memorial to the lost English colonists. Opened in 1960, the beautiful and peaceful garden paradise designed by Innocenti and Webel and created through the largest garden club project in the country, fittingly graces the grounds hallowed by locals as the birthplace of America. Passing through the Great Gate and continuing past the Gate House at the entrance, you can stroll, sit or wile away the hours amid the beauty of the azaleas, dogwoods, rhododendrons, gardenias, roses, magnolias, crape myrtles, lilies, hydrangeas, hibiscus, chrysanthemums, impatiens and a variety of herbs, bulbs and annuals. The gardens are open from 9 to 5 daily, with closing extended until 8 when *The Lost Colony* is playing. Admission is nominal and there is no charge for children under 12. For more information, call ☎ 252-473-3234.

Adventures on Roanoke Island

On Foot

Shopping

At the other end of the beach at 207 Queen Elizabeth Avenue on the Manteo Waterfront, is a jeweler, **Diamonds 'n Dunes**, ☎ 252-473-1002, fax 473-1195, e-mail diamonds@beachlink.com. This establishment is owned and operated by Ken Alexanian Kelley, a jeweler-designer, and his wife, Eileen Kelley Alexanian, a graduate gemologist. Both belong to the American Gem Society and to the Independent Jewelry Organization, with membership in the latter allowing them to hand-select diamonds from the international market at Antwerp, Belgium. Among a glittering array of jewelry, we found the following exclusive collections, many with an appropriate seaside flair, to be of particular interest. Lighthouse bracelets have each been custom-designed by Ken and depict the numerous lighthouses of the Outer Banks and North Carolina. Original lighthouse lens cut rings, incorporating beautiful gemstones, are fashioned after lighthouse beacons. The "sea life" jewelry collection, most crafted in 14 kt. gold, includes pelicans, crabs, jumping dolphins, mermaids with pearls, seashell pendants with blushing pink enamel interiors, detailed seahorses, and sterling silver fish finished out in bright enamel. A particular favorite are the Akteo watches, which have Swiss movement, leather or metal bands, are water-resistant to 99 feet, carry a two-year warranty and cost $89 to $99. The real novelty, however, is that you can choose from over 300 different models, each styled to reflect on the face of the watch an individual's interests, hobbies or occupation.

At the Waterfront Shops on Roanoke Island, Jennifer McGaha and Christine Webster, owners of **The Poop Deck**, ☎ 252-473-6171, fax 473-3535, e-mail t07boat@one800.net, have created a kid-friendly environment. Name brands such as Learning Curve International, Educational Insights, and World-Class Learning Materials, give a quick clue that educational toys are highlighted here. And in addition to keeping up with the latest toy innovations and trends, traditional (and not so easy to find) favorites like wooden doll furniture and wooden puzzles are in stock. The Toy Boat targets kids of all ages; their slogan is "Toys for the Young and the Young at Heart." They also will wrap your purchases free of charge and will ship anywhere that the US Mail or UPS delivers.

Within the past decade, all manner of shops dedicated to the celebration of the Christmas season have sprung up throughout the country, with most major tourist areas having (maybe more than) their share. The Outer Banks, though, has a shop of this genre that is unique among the many and was attracting visitors in droves long before the current trend began. **The Christmas Shop and Island Gallery**, ☎ 262-473-2838, 800-470-2838, e-mail santa@outerbankschristmas. com, www.outerbankschristmas.com, Highway 64 in Manteo, NC 27954, has been a must since 1967 for most area vacationers. Entry into this wonderland of seasonal sights, sounds and aromas is through a spacious re-creation of Mann's General Store, which closed its doors in the 1930s. There is a veritable treasure trove of old-fashioned merchandise here. The 25,000-square-foot store incorporates 36 rooms, filled to overflowing with gifts, collectibles, music boxes, toys, jewelry, stationery, candles, decoys, pottery, Outer Banks souvenirs, home decor items, and, in the galleries, the work of over 100 regional artists and craftsmen. The real magic is found, however, in the six Christmas rooms, with 30 light-bedecked, fully decorated trees, Christmas ornaments by the thousands, and other decorations that are sure to dazzle. The variety and the presentation are enchanting. You are sure to leave with a Christmas carol in your heart and an armful of packages. The Christmas Shop is open during June, July and August from 9:30 to 9, Monday through Saturday, and from 9:30 to 8:30 on Sunday. At other times of the year, as the hours vary, it is best to call ahead for the schedule.

North Carolina

On Water

Fly & Light Tackle Fishing

 If fly fishing and light tackle charters are more to your liking, the specialist in Nags Head is USCG-licensed Captain Bryan Dehart, who runs the **Coastal Adventure Guide Service**, ☎ 252-473-1575, 141 Brakewood Drive, Manteo, NC 27954. Bryan, born and raised in Manteo, comes from a line of local fishermen. His grandfather was one of the first to run a hook and line charter trip out of Oregon Inlet shortly after the turn of the century. As you can imagine, Bryan knows the intricacies of area lakes, rivers and sounds, including just where to take you for a safe and rewarding fishing trip. A committed naturalist, he will take particular delight in sharing the natural history of the region with you. In testimony of Bryan's way with all types of tackle, he has caught and documented over 50 species of game fish. His preference, though, is to share with clients the joys and intricacies of his favorite – fly-fishing. Striped bass (rockfish) are at their peak in the Roanoke River during April and May, can be found throughout the rest of the year in the sounds and inlets, and reach up to 30 lbs. Speckled trout (spotted sea trout), weighing up to six lbs, are around all summer with peak seasons being early spring and fall. The state salt water fish, red drum (aka puppy drum), spot-tail bass and red fish are caught all summer, with a peak in early fall. They routinely weigh in at around 40 lbs. The largest summertime population of adult tarpon (silver king) on the East Coast populates the Pamlico Sound in July and August. Finally, those visiting later in the year will be likely to hook fat albacore (fat alberts), which peak from October through November. Trip prices, for one or two people, are $200 for a half-day and $350 for a full day, including everything you need except food and drink.

If you are here in October and November you might want to consider a really mixed bag. Captain DeHart, who runs the **Coastal Adventure Guide Service**, ☎ 252-473-1575, 141 Brakewood Drive, Manteo, NC 27954, also conducts Fall Duck Hunting Trips. For a total of $350, he will take you on a morning (4:30 to 10:30) duck hunt and an afternoon (1 to sunset) fishing trip. Indeed, he is the only one in the area to offer such a blast and cast combination. And, if only the duck hunting takes your fancy, that will cost $125 per person with a minimum of $250.

Sailing

A less energetic and more relaxing experience is a cruise on *The Downeast Rover*, ☎ 252-473-4866. This 55-foot modern reproduction in steel of a traditional topsail schooner sets sail, in season, from the Manteo waterfront for two-hour cruises at 11 and 2 and for an extended sunset cruise at 6:30 pm. Once out on the Roanoke Sound you will delight in the cavorting of dolphins, the ethereally graceful movements of the heron, and see numerous other species of birds. Would-be sailors can assist in trimming the mighty sails or take a turn at the wheel. Others can simply sit back, relax and enjoy these historical waters. The price is $20 per person and, although sodas and snacks are available for sale on board, passengers are encouraged to bring along with them whatever they wish to eat and drink, including alcoholic beverages.

Eco/Cultural Adventures

Canoeing

 Guided canoe trips can be a fascinating experience, especially in an area so rich in nature. The owner/operator of **Wilderness Canoeing**, ☎ 252-473-1960, PO Box789, Manteo, NC 27954, Melvin T. Twiddy, Jr., has many years of experience leading trips and knows all the best spots. For $39 per person, he will take you on a 3½- to four-hour excursion through, among other places, the Alligator River Wildlife Refuge and Sawyer Lake. As the sounds of civilization give way to the sounds of the wilderness, you will get an up-close look at alligators, beavers, reptiles and other amphibians, black bear, red wolves, deer, and a plethora of exotic birds, including bald eagles, ospreys, wood ducks and pileated and red cockaded woodpeckers. The variety of trees and plant life, too, is stunning, especially when dressed in their glorious fall colors.

Where to Stay on Roanoke Island

 The **Tranquil House Inn**, ☎ 252-473-1404, 800-458-7069, fax 473-1526, e-mail djust1587@aol.com, www.1587.com, Queen Elizabeth Street, is located in quaint downtown Manteo, right on the waterfront and overlooking the sailboats bobbing on Shallowbag Bay. The original inn, constructed on this same site in 1885, catered to a variety of sophisticated clientele from around the world. Fate intervened in the 1950s, however, in the form of a fire. The current structure was built in 1988 to carry on the tradition. There are rooms with canopy beds, four-poster beds, queen-sized beds, and king-sized beds, as well as mini-suites with cozy sitting areas. Rates run from $79 to $169 per night, double occupancy, depending on the season, and include full continental breakfast each

Downtown Manteo

© 2000 HUNTER PUBLISHING, INC.

N

Ananlas Dare St.

Cora Mae Basnight Bridge

→
To
Elizabeth II
State
Historic Site

Wingina Ave.

Lord Essex Ave.

Tranquil
House

Budleigh St.

64

264

County
Courthouse

Sir Walter Raleigh St.

The Waterfront

Old Town St.

Agona St.

Queen Elizabeth St.

Bicentennial
Park

Fernando St.

To Wanchese
& Beaches
↓

Shallowbag Bay

NOT TO SCALE

morning and a wine reception each evening. Add an extra $20 a night during holidays.

The **White Doe Inn Bed & Breakfast**, ☎ 252-473-9851, 800-473-6091, fax 473-4708, e-mail whitedoe@interpath.com, www.whitedoeinn.com, 319 Sir Walter Raleigh Street, Manteo, is listed on the National Register of Historic Places and has recently been awarded the AAA Three-Diamond rating. The home, set in the middle of this quaint village and just a short walk from the bustling waterfront, was built as a family residence for the Meekins at the turn of the century. As the family prospered, additions were made until, by 1910, it had evolved into the Queen Anne-style Victorian house with wrap-around balconies that you see today. There are seven rooms and one suite, each with its own personality and furnished with turn-of-the-century antiques, reproductions and special architectural features that complement the décor. Rates, per room/suite, range from $120 to $150 during the winter season, from $130 to $180 during the spring and fall seasons, and from $145 to $195 during the summer. Suites rent for $170, $200 and $225.

Where to Eat on Roanoke Island

While staying on Roanoke Island, a good choice for fine dining is **1587**, found in the Tranquil House Inn, described in the *Where to Stay* section above. Here, in a sophisticated setting, the chefs have created a menu offering the freshest fare from the sounds and the sea, delicious soups, meats, fowl and truly decadent desserts. You will find a copy of the current menu posted in the lobby of the hotel. For a more casual dining experience and a taste of what the locals enjoy, pop just around the corner to the **Duchess of Dare**. Here, in the morning, you will find residents gathering for coffee, a hearty homecooked breakfast and conversation. At lunch and in the evenings, families come here to enjoy a variety of down-home recipies offered up at reasonable prices with a side-order of friendly service.

Back To The Banks

From Roanoke Island, take the Nags Head and Manteo Bridge east across the water, and rejoin Highway 12/158 at Whalebone Junction. Continue your journey southward onto Bodie Island.

North Carolina

Cape Hatteras National Seashore

Cape Hatteras is the edge of the world where the ocean meets the sea. The National Seashore, instituted to preserve and protect the three islands to the south of Nags Head, stretches north and south for 75 miles across Bodie, Hatteras and Ocracoke, linked together by Highway 12 and the Hatteras Inlet ferry. The National Seashore offers many activities: hiking, camping, fishing, and swimming. The Park Service Information Center is off Highway 12 at Whalebone Junction, and there are others at Coquina Beach and on Hatteras Island. ☎ 252-473-2111.

Adventures on Cape Hatteras

On Foot

Hiking

Cape Hatteras has something special for dedicated hikers. From Whalebone Junction on Bodie Island, south through the Pea Island National Wildlife Refuge, across Hatteras and Ocracoke Islands to Ocracoke itself, the **Cape Hatteras Beach Trail** provides 75 miles of fine hiking. The trail is divided into eight sections, with plenty of parking, rest areas and comfort stations. Going south from the Whalebone Junction Information Center, the sections are as follows:

Section 1: Nags Head to Oregon Inlet. Eight miles.

At the Whalebone Junction Information Center, head south on the left shoulder of Highway 12 for 5.3 miles, then turn left onto the access road to Coquina Beach. Continue past the Interpretive Center at Coquina, returning to Highway 12 at 5.9 miles. Cross the highway and follow the paved access road to the Bodie Island Lighthouse and Visitors Center at 6.9 miles. From the Visitors Center, follow the paved loop road south for 0.1 mile to a gate; turn left and follow the red-topped markers for 0.2 mile over a small bridge and freshwater overflow. Make a sharp left and continue on through the old dune area for 1.3 miles; back to Highway 12 at 8.5 miles.

Section 2: Oregon Inlet to Rodanthe. 19 miles.

Take Highway 12 across the bridge onto Hatteras Island. Continue on through the Pea Island Wildlife Refuge to Rodanthe.

Section 3: Rodanthe to Salvo. Three miles.

Follow the beach from Rodanthe south to Salvo. Salvo Public Campground is at 31 miles. The beach exit and parking area are at 35.4 miles.

Section 4: Salvo to Avon. 13 miles.

Follow the beach south from Salvo to Avon. Beach exits and parking areas are at 37.6 and 41.9 miles.

Section 5: Avon to Cape Hatteras Lighthouse. Eight miles.

Follow the beach south from Avon. At 46.8 miles, cross the dunes for 100 yds to the parking area at the Old Beach Road; Highway 12 is another 100 yds beyond. Take Highway 12 and follow it south for 0.2 mile to an old off-road vehicle trail on the right. Turn right and follow the old road for 2.6 miles. Cross Highway 12 to the beach at 49.6 miles. Continue for 1.4 miles and turn right to the Cape Hatteras Lighthouse at 51 miles.

Section 6: Cape Hatteras Lighthouse to Hatteras Village. 10 miles.

From the lighthouse, go west to the Visitors Center at 51.2 miles, then continue along the road to the Buxton Woods parking area and Nature Trail. At 51.7 miles, the Hatteras Island maintenance road is on the left; you'll take the Open Pond Rd. to the right at 51.9 miles. Cross the stream at 53.2 miles and you'll reach a fork in the road at 53.3 miles. Take the right fork, where a sign restricts ORV, use and follow the south side of the lakes at 53.4 miles. Then follow the sandy road to the Frisco Campground at 55.8 miles. Beyond the campground is a gate at 56.1 miles; turn left there and follow a ramp to the beach at 56.3 miles. Turn right onto the beach and follow it to an ORV ramp on the right. Take the ramp and follow it 0.1 miles to Highway 12; turn left and follow 0.1 miles to the Hatteras Ferry.

Section 7: Hatteras Village to Ocracoke Campground. Eight miles.

Take the Hatteras Ferry to Ocracoke Island – it takes about 40 minutes to cross – and then take Highway 12 for 0.7 mile to a parking area on the left. Turn left and go to the beach, reaching the ocean at 63.6 miles. Follow the beach south; at 68.1 miles cross the dunes from the ocean for about 100 yds to a parking area and observation deck to see the Ocracoke Ponies at the Pony Pen. Turn left there and follow the shoulder of Highway 12 for .7 mile to another observation deck at 68.8 miles. Turn left, crossing Highway 12, and return to the beach via another ORV ramp, and follow it to Ocracoke Campground at 72.4 miles.

Section 8: Ocracoke Campground to Ocracoke Town. 6.5 miles.

From Ocracoke Campground, return to the beach and follow it to the ORV ramp at Ocracoke Airport at 75.3 miles. Then follow Highway 12 to the Ocracoke town limits at 75.8 miles; the hike to the ferry is another 1.3 miles.

North Carolina

Camping on Cape Hatteras

 Cape Hatteras, ☎ 252-987-2777, PO Box 10, Waves, NC 27968, is open all year and has 50 tent sites with water access, restrooms, showers, laundry, heated indoor and outdoor pool, game room and boat ramp.

Cape Hatteras National Seashore

Camping is only permitted in four campsites, which are usually open between early April and late September. Three of them, **Oregon Inlet** (120 sites), **Cape Point**, near the Cape Hatteras Lighthouse (202 sites), and **Frisco**, between the villages of Buxton and Hatteras (127 sites), are available on a first-come first-served basis. The other, **Ocracoke**, on Ocracoke Island, has 136 sites that must be reserved by calling ☎ 800-365-2267. All are within walking distance of the beaches and ocean and have centrally located washhouses with flush toilets and cold water showers, but no hookups are available. Fees are $14 at Ocracoke, and $13 at the others.

Colington Park Campground, ☎ 252-441-6128, 1608 Colington Road, Kill Devil Hills, NC 27948, is open all year and has hot showers, cable TV, a small store and is just five minutes from the beach.

Cypress Cove Campground, ☎ 252-473-5231, 818 Highway 64, Manteo, NC 27954, is open all year, has camper cabins and trailer rentals, hot showers, restrooms, some hookups, electric and water, cable TV, camp store and laundry, playground and sports facilities and a nature walk and wildlife observation deck.

Hatteras Sands Camping Resort, ☎ 252-986-2422 or 800-323-8899, is open between March 1st and December 1st and offers camping condos, chalet rentals, cable TV, two bathing units, clubhouse, TV lounge, Olympic and kids pools and mobile cottage rentals.

Bodie Island

From Whalebone Junction, Bodie (pronounced body) stretches southward to Oregon Inlet, occupying a great chunk of the Cape Hatteras National Seashore. Bodie was once, though not now, an island in its own right; heavy seas, hurricanes and shifting sands closed the inlets south of Nags Head. At Whalebone Junction the islands merged but the name remains.

Sightseeing on Bodie Island

The Bodie Island Lighthouse

 The Bodie Island Lighthouse, ☎ 252-441-5711, is the second of the great lights on the Outer Banks. It stands at the end of a side-road to the west of Highway 12, opposite Coquina Beach some six miles south of Whalebone Junction. To ensure correct identification from the sea, it's painted with two black and three white bands. The 156-foot-high lighthouse is not open for climbing but is worth a visit just the same, for the old keeper's quarters have been restored and opened as a Visitors Center with interpretive exhibits. There's also a self-guided nature trail that leads through the marshes behind the light. Open daily, May through September.

Adventures on Bodie Island

On Foot

Beaches

 Coquina Beach, some five miles south of Whalebone Junction, is a special place. If you like to swim, you won't find a better place. Often busy, but not unbearably so, the sands are clean and well kept, and the dunes must look as good today as they did 400-years ago when Raleigh's men first set about exploring these islands. And, because it's now a part of the National Seashore, it will remain that way. Lifeguards are on duty during the summer season. There are picnic shelters, restrooms, showers and plenty of room to park. This is the ideal place to stop for an hour or two on your journey south; don't miss it. On Coquina Beach lies a victim of the Graveyard of the Atlantic. The *Laura A. Barnes*, a 120-foot schooner built in 1918, went down in heavy seas that drove her onto the beach some distance north of where she now lies. As with all shipwrecks, time has given her a romantic image. In order to save her, the National Park Service moved what was left of her in 1973 to the present location. Now she lies high and dry, protected from the buffeting of the waves at the southern end of the parking lot. Be sure to visit the old girl.

On Water

Deep-Sea Fishing

 The last stop on Bodie Island is Oregon Inlet. It wasn't always an inlet, however. It opened during a hurricane in 1846 and was named, according to the custom in those days, after the first ship that made it through into the sound. Due to the action of the ocean and shifting sands, it always seems in danger of closing, but the US Corps of Engineers wages a constant, some say futile, battle to keep the way clear.

This is fishing country. Everything here is dedicated to the sport and those who engage in it. A National Park Concession, the **Oregon Inlet Fishing Center**, nine miles south of Whalebone and west of Highway 12, is home to one of the largest fleets of sportfishing boats on the mid-Atlantic coast. You can charter an inshore or deep-sea fisherman for a day's sport in the coastal waters of the Gulf Stream. They can be reached at ☎ 252-441-6301, 800-272-5199, e-mail oregon-inlet@outer-banks.com.

Eco/Cultural Adventures

Marshes

 Bodie Island Marshes are near the north entrance to the Hatteras National Seashore, on Highway 12. There's a parking area that allows access to the marshes, where you can view a great number of wild birds, especially during the winter: egrets, heron, glossy ibis, and any number of wading birds from spring through fall.

Hatteras Island

Most of Hatteras Island is part of the Cape Hatteras National Seashore and is administered by the National Park Service. Just as with all National Parks, the emphasis here is on the great outdoors and all the activities associated with it. Camping is a big part of Hatteras, as is fishing, swimming and hiking. In the early days on Hatteras, the islanders lived out most of their lives cut off from the rest of the world. Since 1964, however, the Oregon Inlet Bridge has changed all that, but Hatteras is still very different from the other islands in the Outer Banks. The locals are for the most part a friendly lot, but wary – as only long winters spent on a lonely island, with little more than the wind, seas and ever-wheeling seabirds for company can produce. The villages of **Rodanthe**, **Waves** and **Salvo** are small communities, and lonely too, with perhaps just 200-300 people living in each during the winter. In the milder months, however, they come alive: the bait and tackle shops fill, the gift shops open again, the small cafés and restaurants are full of hungry tourists. Even so, these tiny villages are often bypassed on the long drive south. You should stay for a while, especially if you like to fish; if you're a camper, you'll find more opportunities here than anywhere else on the Banks. Farther south are the villages of **Avon**, **Buxton** and **Frisco**. Avon is the last town on the northern section of Hatteras Island. It was once one of the most remote little villages on the island. With the opening of the Herbert Bonner Bridge, however, it has become much more accessible. Here you'll find the island's movie theater, a few convenience stores, several gift shops, a fishing pier and a couple of campgrounds. A little farther to the south on the southern arm of the island, Buxton is a neat little village where fishing, closely followed by tourism, is the mainstay of the local economy. From Buxton it is but a short drive west through the forest to Frisco and yet another fishing pier. Hatteras village lies at the western tip of the island, a tiny community where fishing is king. Here, everything from trout to tuna to king mackerel is brought ashore each day, iced down, and sent to the great fish market in New York, and all is done within 24 hours of the fish coming ashore. Sport fishing is also a big part of Hatteras's economy. You can charter a boat and take to the seas for a day, even a half-day, and head out in search of the big one. The highlight of the year is the **Annual Hatteras Marlin Tournament**, hosted each year in the second week in June by the Hatteras Marlin Club.

Sightseeing

Cape Hatteras Lighthouse

The lighthouse, ☎ 252-995-4474, stands 208 feet high and is the tallest lighthouse in the United States. From the sea it is easily recognizable by its black and white painted spirals. Its light can be seen for more than 20 miles, warning ships of the dangerous shoals and sand bars offshore. Cape Hatteras was the second of three to be built on the cape, the first having fallen victim to Confederate soldiers in 1861. This one was built in 1869 and its first order Fresnel lens magnified the light of a small oil lamp first lit in 1870. It fell victim to vandals when it was abandoned by the Federal Government in 1935. Its great lens was damaged and a temporary light was built in 1936, just northeast of Buxton. It wasn't until 1950 that the great light here was put back in action. When it was reactivated, the small oil lamp had been replaced by a rotating beacon with two 1,000-watt lamps on each wing. The new light could easily be seen 20 miles out to sea, but there have been reports of 50 miles, and 115 miles from the air.

The lighthouse was moved from its original location, which was in danger of being overrun by the elements, in 1999, and it was reopened in 2000. The more energetic visitors can again climb the 268 steps to its summit.

Chicamacomico Lifesaving Station

On Highway 12 in Rodanthe, this was once one of the most famous of the life stations on the Outer Banks. There were seven of them and their purpose was to provide aid to shipwrecked sailors. Each station was manned by a crew of six strong surfmen. During bad weather and high seas, they would take up positions along the coast and watch for ships foundering on the shoals. Once a ship was spotted, they would run back to the station for their equipment. From that moment the fight was on, sometimes on foot, sometimes in a heavy, oar-driven boat, but always in high seas that threatened to kill at the first break in concentration. With Lyle gun, ropes and breeches buoy, they would bring the sailors ashore, one by one, if they were successful, hanging high above the pounding surf. It was perhaps the most dangerous occupation a man could choose, and many of those that did paid with their lives.

The Lyle gun shoots a projectile with a rope attached to it. The line is used to pull a rope to the stricken ship. The breeches buoy runs on the rope and is pulled one way then the other by more ropes.

Today, the old life saving station, which was constructed in 1874 but converted in 1911, is no longer in service but has been restored and opened as a monument to those brave men who manned it and as an interpretive center to tell their story. Admission is free in summer.

Frisco Native American Museum & Natural History Center

This museum, ☎ 252-995-4440, located off Highway 12 in Frisco, is the place to learn all about the Indians that once inhabited these islands, as well as the natural history of the area. Exhibits include displays of artifacts, tools and several unusual items. There are self-guided woodland trails and a picnic area – just the place to take time out and enjoy an outdoor lunch. Admission is free, but donations are accepted.

Graveyard of the Atlantic Museum

This is the Outer Banks' newest attraction, ☎ 252-986-2995, adjacent to the Hatteras-Ocracoke Ferry Terminal and the US Coast Guard base at the south end of the village. Opened in the spring of 1997, the museum's purpose is to "preserve, interpret and enhance the understanding and knowledge of the maritime history associated with the Outer Banks." In short, it's the place to learn all about the sea and the shipwrecks. The exhibits include a multimedia presentation, displays that interpret the geographic and natural forces at work in the ocean off the Outer Banks, and the courage of the men and women who spend their lives working there. Artifacts from many of the shipwrecks are also on display, including some from the *Monitor*, mentioned earlier. Other exhibits trace the toll in wrecked vessels, from those of the first European explorers and colonists, through the Civil War, then the two World Wars, to modern commercial and passenger ships – all lost in the uncertain waters off the Outer Banks. The museum is open daily.

Adventures

On Water

Diving

Diamond Shoals Dive Center, ☎ 252-995-4021, e-mail gunsmoke@interpath.com, www.outer-banks.nc.us/gunsmoke, 52436 Highway 12 in Frisco, is Hatteras Island's only full-service dive facility. Operating from the *M/V Gunsmoke,* they can take you wreck diving, artifact hunting, spear fishing or even on underwater photography dives. In season, the water temperatures are 70-82° and the visibility range is 50-150 feet.

Fishing

Hatteras Landing, ☎ 252-986-2205, 800-551-8478, fax 252-986-1140, e-mail marina@hatteraslanding, www.hatteraslanding.com, PO Box 728, Highway 12, Hatteras, NC 27943, has a hotel, full-service ships store, deli-market and coffee shop onsite. It is also the place to go if you want to get out and do some serious fishing, whether in the Gulf Stream, inshore, fly fishing, bottom fishing, sight casting or even on an overnight trip.

The **Hatteras Island Fishing Pier**, ☎ 252-987-2323, is the first of the three piers as you drive south from Oregon Inlet. It is on Spur Road 1247 east of Highway 12. It's on the left, south of Rodanthe and well sign posted. The pier is more than 1,100 ft long and the water averages some 15 feet deep. This pier is famous for its large channel bass. In 1973 Elvin Cooper caught the then world's record channel bass here; it weighed in at 90 lbs and is on view for you to see. All the usual facilities, and more, are available: there's a bait and tackle shop where you can rent all sorts of fishing equipment. There is also a restaurant – the food is good – and even a motel, should you decide to stay the night and try your hand again tomorrow. The pier is handicapped-accessible.

The **Avon Fishing Pier**, ☎ 252-995-5049, is not quite so long as the Hatteras Island Pier, being only 852 feet, and is just off Highway 12 on the south side of the village. It's a modern pier, well lighted for fishing at night, with all the usual services: bait, rental tackle, ice and a snack bar where you can get cold drinks and a sandwich. Here you can expect to catch channel bass, sea trout, and blue fish, to name just a few. Open through the spring, summer and fall.

The **Cape Hatteras Fishing Pier**, ☎ 252-986-2533, also known as the Frisco Pier, is about two miles west of Frisco, and is the closest pier to the Gulf Stream. It's small by Outer Banks standards, just 600 feet long and made of wood, but it stands, at its head, in some 24 feet of water, so you can expect to catch the larger species found at the other piers, perhaps even a king mackerel or two. It's well lit for night fishing and has all the usual facilities: restrooms, snack bar, bait, ice and tackle for rent. Open during the spring, summer and fall.

Windsurfing

This is one of the fastest growing sports in the United States, and there's no better place to do it, or to learn how, than here on North Carolina's Outer Banks. It's not the easiest sport to learn, especially if you try to do it on your own. The best way is to take a lesson or two, and there are several surf shops on the islands that sell all the necessary equipment and will teach you how to use it.

Eco/Cultural Adventures

Nature Trail

 The **Buxton Woods Nature Trail**, is claimed to be one of the best little trails on the Outer Banks and is certainly worth a mention here. Located at Cape Point, it leads from the road through the dunes, vinelands, and freshwater marshes of Buxton Woods for a little more than three quarters of a mile. It's easy going, with some of the most scenic views on the islands. The trail begins on the right side of the road and runs south from the lighthouse to the point. It won't take more than an hour to hike it both ways; don't miss it.

Underwater Marine Sanctuary

There are literally hundreds of wrecks lying at the bottom of the sea off Hatteras Island – some in deep water, some high and dry on the sandbanks. Of all of them, the most famous must surely be that of the *Monitor*, the first of the modern warships, a true ironclad. *Monitor* was the Union's answer to the Confederate ironclad, *Virginia*, a converted Union frigate once named the *Merrimack*; she was stripped of her wooden superstructure and clad with a sheath of four-inch-thick armor plating, making her almost invulnerable to the heavy guns of the day. *Monitor*, however, was a true ironclad, built when news of *Virginia* filtered through to the north. She was a strange looking craft; her superstructure was barely above water, and her revolving turret looked for all the world like a great "cheesebox on a raft." She was slow and sluggish in the water, barely maneuverable even in calm seas. On March 28th, 1862, *Virginia* steamed out from Norfolk into Hampton Roads; her mission was to sink the Union fleet of conventional wooden warships blockading the port. And so she did, at first. But *Monitor* arrived just in time to save the bulk of the fleet. The battle between the two giants lasted for more than four hours and culminated in a stalemate. *Virginia* retreated back upriver, never to leave it again, and *Monitor* was called out and ordered south. She fell victim to the Graveyard of the Atlantic on New Year's Eve, 1862, foundering in heavy seas and sinking. For 120 years she lay on the bottom, upside down with her turret stuck deep in the mud. In 1973, she was rediscovered. Today, she is the main feature of a National Underwater Marine Sanctuary, lying some 17 miles southeast of Cape Hatteras. For more information, visit www.sanctuaries.nos. noaa.gov/natprogram/natprogram.html. For those wishing to explore this fascinating sanctuary, we suggest you contact **Diamond Shoals Dive Center**, ☎ 252-995-4021, e-mail gunsmoke@interpath.com, www.outer-banks.nc.us/gunsmoke, 52436 Highway 12 in Frisco.

Wildlife Refuge

The **Pea Island National Wildlife Refuge**, ☎ 252-473-1131, is between the Oregon Inlet and Rodanthe; the Visitor Center, ☎ 252-987-2394, is seven miles south of the inlet off Highway 12. On the Refuge's more than 6,000 acres, some 265 species of wild birds find a haven, including Canada geese, snow geese and 25 species of duck. From

North Carolina

spring through fall, there's always a large variety of wading, shore and upland birds, but the best time to do your birding is spring. Observation platforms near the parking areas provide the best vantage points. Walking tours are offered on Tuesdays through Fridays at 9 between June and the Labor Day Weekend; between mid-September and early November there are walks on Saturdays, also beginning at 9. Admission is free.

Ocracoke Island

Fourteen-mile-long Ocracoke Island, one of a host of barrier islands of the Outer Banks of North Carolina, is accessible only by water or air. When the first Europeans arrived in the 1500s, they found it inhabited by Indians. By the early 18th century, it had been incorporated into Bath County, of which the main town, Bath, is the oldest town in North Carolina. In 1705, Bath County was divided into three. The section containing Ocracoke initially was dubbed Wickham, although that subsequently was changed to Hyde, in honor of Edward Hyde, a cousin of Queen Anne, who was made Colonial Governor of North Carolina. In 1715, the North Carolina Colonial Assembly recognized a settlement here, which had been established by seafaring pilots who guided vessels through Ocracoke Inlet. During this era the inlet became a favorite haunt of the notorious pirate Blackbeard, who met his end in hand-to-hand combat and then was beheaded off the shore of Ocracoke in 1718.

Ocracoke Village, with a population of 700, is nestled around a natural harbor formed by Silver Lake on the southwest tip of the island. The village's designated Historic District was listed on the National Register of Historic Places in 1990. It includes the Ocracoke Lighthouse, the 1942 Coast Guard Station, several historic commercial buildings and over 100 homes. Actually, for a place so small, it has more than its share of things to do. Not the least of these is a simple stroll around town to enjoy the very unusual old-world ambiance and charm which, thankfully, has managed to avoid commercial corruption. Peeking out from any number of unassuming nooks and crannies are an array of specialty and craft stores. When you are ready for a bit of refreshment, have a seat at one of many harborside cafés, where you can observe the comings and goings of boats and the antics of seabirds frolicking overhead. The balance of the island is an integral part of the Cape Hatteras National Seashore, which is owned by the National Park Service and virtually undeveloped.

Getting Here & Getting Around

 All of the other destinations along the Outer Banks are easy to get to. Just take the appropriate turn off the main road that runs their length. Getting to Ocracoke Island, however, involves taking a ferry and that is half the fun of going there. A system of ferries, which for many years were privately operated, has connected the coastal communities of eastern North Carolina since the mid-1920s. By 1934 the state had begun subsidizing these services and, after World War II in 1947, the North Carolina Transportation Department established the North Carolina Ferry Division. Working in five different bodies of water – the Pamlico Sound, Currituck Sound, Neuse River, Pamlico River and Cape Fear River – the 24 current ferry vessels operate at an average speed of 10 knots and can maneuver in as little as five feet of water. The shortest crossing, between Cherry Branch and Minnesott Beach, is just 2.3 miles and takes 20 minutes, while the longest, from Swan Quarter to Ocracoke Island, is 27 miles and takes 2½ hours. Together, these comprise one of the largest ferry systems in the US; each year, over two million residents and visitors ride the seven routes in the system.

To reach Ocracoke Island, you can take any one of three ferries. From the north, leave Hatteras (☎ 800-368-8949 for information) for a 45-minute ride. It is free of charge and employs a first-come, first-served, no-reservations policy. From the west, depart from Swan Quarter (☎ 252-926-111 or 800-773-1094 for reservations) for a 2½-hour sailing. From the south, set sail from Cedar Island (☎ 828-225-3551 or 800-856-0343 for reservations) on a 2¼-hour crossing. Reservations are suggested for the latter two options, especially in season. Departures from Ocracoke can be arranged by calling ☎ 252-928-3841 or 800-345-1665 and, with the exception of the Hatteras route, we recommend that reservations be made ahead of time. Contact the **North Carolina Ferry System**, ☎ 800-BY-FERRY (800-293-3779), www. dot.state.nc.us/transit/ferry.

Such trips, especially for first-timers, can be a real adventure. Among our abiding memories is a late afternoon fall sailing from Ocracoke Island to Cedars Island. We were crossing just before nightfall when the sky went black as countless thousands of seabirds, including a host of brown pelicans, arose from the water in flight to their nightly homes. These birds follow along the stern of the ferry, wheeling around and around as they try to catch tidbits of food you toss up for them. It's a lovely and very relaxing way to travel.

No problems getting around here, at least as far as the village itself is concerned; it is so small that you can walk just about everywhere.

North Carolina

However, it is hard to imagine anyone coming to Ocracoke without their own car.

Sightseeng on Ocracoke Island

Ocracoke Lighthouse

This lighthouse stands on one of Ocracoke Island's highest spots. Built in 1823 by Noah Porter, it is both the oldest lighthouse still in operation on the East Coast and the shortest lighthouse on the North Carolina coast. It is so small, in fact, that it can be seen only from a 14-mile distance.

While lighthouses are, and have been, instrumental in safely steering myriad craft safely through these treacherous waters, no lighthouse could have saved the *HMC Bedfordshire* when a German submarine torpedoed it on May 14, 1942. The ship sank and all hands were lost, with only four bodies subsequently washing onto the Ocracoke shore. These sailors were buried in what, to this day, is a well-tended grave-yard surrounded by a white picket fence that stands as a memorial to the British Royal Navy. The graves are marked by bronze plaques on concrete crosses. Thus the British Cemetery stands as a memorial to the British Royal Navy – a curious bit of Blighty in North Carolina!

Pirates

Although the dastardly pirate Blackbeard has long ago gone to his eternal unrest, his legend lives on in Ocracoke Village. If you want to learn more about the man and his exploits, head to **Teach's Hole - Blackbeard Exhibit and Pyrate Specialty Shoppe**, ☎ 252-928-1718. George and Mickey Roberson founded this establishment in 1992, with the intention to educate the public about Blackbeard through numerous exhibits. The shop features anything and every-thing to do with piracy. The opening hours are Monday through Sat-urday from 10 to 6 in the summer and from 11 to 5 in the winter.

Adventures on Ocracoke Island

On Water

Boat Rentals

Should you prefer to skipper your own craft, contact **Island Rentals**, ☎ 252-928-5480 or e-mail cbmville@aol.com for a fiberglass, flat-bottom motor boat or catamaran-style motor boat just perfect for exploring the shallow waters of Pamlico

Sound. You can then find your own spot to fish, clam and shell. Each boat is equipped with anchor, life vests and safety equipment and, depending upon the vessel you select, the cost will be $70 to $95 for a half-day (anything up to four hours) or $99 to $125 for a full day. Reservations must be made a week ahead of time, and craft must be returned one hour before sunset (use after dark is not allowed).

Fishing

On Ocracoke Island, surrounded by the Atlantic Ocean on one side and the Pamlico Sound on the other, water activities dominate the recreational options. Fishing is, obviously, a popular pastime here. If you are in the market for a bit of professional assistance, we recommend you contact **Captain David Nagel**, ☎ 252-928-5351 or 800-825-5351. Captain David is a licensed skipper and expert fishing guide, who can get you just where you need to go and help you to catch the fish of your dreams. A full day's inshore fishing costs $650 and if a full day's wreck or gulf stream fishing, either trolling or bottom fishing, will set you back $750. Between December and March he specializes in giant bluefin tuna fishing, which will cost you $850. If you want to keep the cost down and don't mind a bit of company, you can join a party of fellow fisherpeople at $70 for a half-day or half-night. All trips depart from The Anchorage Marina and fees include all bait and tackle.

On a less serious note, you may enjoy a trip on the ***Miss Ocracoke***, ☎ 252-928-6060 or 921-0107. Half-day fishing trips, either from 8 am to midday or from 1 to 5 pm, both with bait and tackle provided, depart on Monday to Saturday and cost just $25. Dolphin Cruises leave on Wednesday through Saturday from 6:30 to 8:30 pm, and are an affordable $20 per person.

Sailing

If sailing interests you, check out the ***Windfall***, ☎ 252-928-SAIL (928-7245), a modern replica of the sort of vessel that plied these waters in days gone by. Inspected and certified by the US Coast Guard for transport of 30 passengers, she sets sail three times during the day for a one-hour trip that costs just $10 per person. The Sunset Cruise, priced at $15 each, lasts approximately 1¼ hours. Easily identified by its pirate flag and red sails, this ship departs from the Community Store docks in Ocracoke Village.

North Carolina

Eco/Cultural Adventures

Kayaking

The more adventuresome and environmentally minded, will want to sign up for a Kayak Eco-Tour through **Ride the Wind Surf Shop**, ☎ 252-928-6311 or fax 928-3267, located on Highway 12 at Silver Lake Harbor. $30 per person buys three hours of exploration, guided by an experienced naturalist who will instruct you in the handling of your kayak, choose the best area for the tour, and provide a wealth of information on the local wildlife and nature. Among the specialty tours, the birdwatching trip will be of interest to those of avian tendencies, as Ocracoke is on the eastern flyway of many migrating water and land birds and the winter home of the Canada goose. If you so desire, the accommodating folks at Ride the Wind will customize a tour.

Wild Ponies

Ocracoke's herd of wild ponies will fascinate equestrian lovers. The origins of these, dubbed the Banker Ponies, are disputed, although some historians believe that they descended from the ponies that came ashore with the Raleigh expeditions and were left on Roanoke Island when the Lost Colony mysteriously disappeared. Visitors can get a closer look on the north of the island, where many are corralled and cared for by the National Park Service.

Where to Stay on Ocracoke Island

The **Berkley Manor Bed & Breakfast**, ☎ 252-928-5911, 800-832-1223, e-mail berkley@beachlink.com, www.berkleymanor.com, Silver Lake Road, enjoys a prime location just across, but concealed from, the harbor. The four-story tower is the focal point of the house, and from its comfortable lounges there are marvelous vistas of the island. Each of the 12 guestrooms has been individually designed with a decidedly Caribbean flair. Eight of these, designated standard accommodations, have private bath, TV, telephone and individual climate control. The other four, designated luxury accommodations, feature space, private bath, and luxury bedding, with two having a private two-person Jacuzzi tub. Standard rooms range between $75 and $135, while luxury rooms cost $125-$175.

The **Anchorage Inn & Marina**, ☎ 252-928-1101, e-mail info@theanchorageinn.com, www.theanchorageinn.com, is an impressively designed four-floor, soon to be five-floor, structure just across the road from the marina. There are 34 guestrooms, a mix of smoking and non-smoking, with modern décor and the expected amenities of cable TV and telephone. Its best feature, however, is the fabulous view out over the harbor – especially of the fiery sun as it sizzles into the horizon above Pamlico Sound. Rates vary according to season and room choice, but expect to pay somewhere between $79 and $125 a night.

The **Ocracoke Harbor Inn**, ☎ 252-928-5731 or 888-456-1998, Silver Lake Road, opened in 1998 and just across the harbor from the center of the village, has 16 guestrooms and seven suites. Each is nicely appointed with either two queen-sized beds or one king-sized bed, and features cable TV, telephone with modem port, coffeemaker and refrigerator. Summer and spring/fall rates are governed by floor, with first-floor accommodations ranging from $60 to $95 and second-floor accommodations from $70 to $105. Suites, on the higher floors, run from $109 to $170. In the winter, rooms cost between $49 and $79, with suites priced at $90-$125, no matter which floor they are on.

Where to Eat on Ocracoke Island

 The **Cockle Creek Restaurant**, ☎ 252-928-6891, www.cocklecreek.com, on Highway 12 just outside of the village proper, is operated by native islanders David and Kari Styron. It is considered one of the finest eateries on Ocracoke. The wine list is primarily American, but has some international selections, and a few are available by the glass. It is open for dinner, seven days a week, from 5 to 9:30 pm.

The **Café Atlantic**, ☎ 252-928-4861, just across from the Cockle Street on the northern edge of Ocracoke Village, is housed in a structure that reflects the character of the region. It offers an interesting mix of Italian cuisine and seafood. The Café Atlantic has an extensive wine list and is open for lunch daily from 11 to 3 and for dinner from 5:30 to 9:30 pm. Sunday brunch, a favorite with the locals, is served from 11 to 3 pm.

Creswell

Creswell or, to be exact, Phelps Lake, located in the remote eastern part of North Carolina on the peninsula between the Albemarle and Pamlico sounds, is not a place that most people reading this guide will have heard of, let alone visited. That is, of course, unless they are into hunting and wildlife.

■ Getting Here & Getting Around

From the east or the west: Route 64 connects Rocky Mount and I-95 to the Outer Banks, with Creswell being two-thirds of the way towards Manteo.

From the north: From Norfolk, VA, take Route 17 South to Elizabeth City and onto its junction with Route 37, which will take you over the Albemarle Sound to Route 64. Take 64 east to Creswell.

A vehicle is a necessity in the area.

■ Adventures

On Foot

Hunting

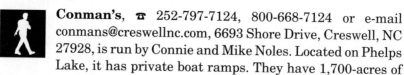

Conman's, ☎ 252-797-7124, 800-668-7124 or e-mail conmans@creswellnc.com, 6693 Shore Drive, Creswell, NC 27928, is run by Connie and Mike Noles. Located on Phelps Lake, it has private boat ramps. They have 1,700-acres of personally owned and managed woodlands and swamp (called the Wildlife Connection), and another 8,000-plus acres of leased property. They offer guided hunts for whitetail deer, black bear and water-fowl, including tundra swans, and also provide and manage for both quail and rabbit hunting and organize dove shoots. There is an on-site sport shop that has most of the necessities for hunters and fishermen, and they are licensed agents for the North Carolina Wildlife Resources Commission.

Eco/Cultural Adventures

Wildlife Refuge

Alligator River National Wildlife Refuge, ☎ 252-473-1131, Box 1969, Manteo, NC 27954, covers 152,000-acres of Dare, Hyde and Washington counties and includes pocosins (brackish marshes), white cedar and cypress swamps and hardwood forests. Here you will find over 145 species of birds, mammals and reptiles, including alligators, bears and red wolves, which were reintroduced into the refuge in the 1970s. It also has nature and hiking trails, plus 13 miles of canoe/kayak trails. The central part of the refuge, 46,000-acres of it, is owned by the federal government, however, and is used for military bombing practice.

■ Where to Stay

Conman's, on Phelps Lake, has lodges and a campground. Contact them at ☎ 252-797-7124, 800-668-7124 or e-mail conmans@creswellnc.com, 6693 Shore Drive, Creswell, NC 27928.

The Crystal Coast

The Crystal Coast, also known as the Southern Outer Banks, runs along the central coastline of North Carolina. Although not the best-known of the resort areas on the Atlantic Ocean, the combination of history, quaint towns and white, sandy beaches is, indeed, alluring. Geographically, too, it is unusual. The 30-mile length of Bogue Banks shares, with Long Island, NY, the distinction of being one of only two coastlines on the Atlantic Ocean that run east to west and face south.

■ Beaufort

The town of Beaufort (pronounced Bow-fort), just across the sound on the mainland, is both historic and charming. It has its fair share of visitors, yet remains very much unspoiled. Particularly tempting are the numerous maritime excursions that set sail from the boardwalk to the small neighboring islands. You can visit **Carrot Island**, now part of the Rachel Carson Estuarine Reserve, a tidal complex in the state estuary system established to protect the fragile ecology. Home to more than 160 species, it is a bird-lover's paradise. On **Shackleford Banks**, comprehensive preservation efforts ensure that wild ponies run free and that dolphins, sea turtles and rare waterfowl thrive. Alternatively, take the ferry to **Cape Lookout**, where tranquil seclusion and an historic lighthouse await.

Established as a fishing village in the 17th century, Beaufort was surveyed in 1713, many years before George Washington's birth and when Ann still reigned as Queen of England. It was incorporated just 10 years later and, since that time, has continued as the seat of Carteret County. Named after Henry Somerset, Duke of Beaufort, its rich history is recalled still today in the street names: Ann Street, in honor of Queen Anne; Craven Street, after the Earl of Craven; Moore

Street, for Colonel Maurice Moore, a South Carolinian who granted aid during the Indian Wars; Pollock Street, after a governor of the time; Turner Street, for Robert Turner, owner of the land that was then surveyed; and Orange Street, for William, Prince of Orange, who later would become William III of England.

Beaufort is the state's third-oldest town.

The **Historic District of Beaufort**, listed on the National Register of Historic Places, boasts over 100 private homes, each displaying a plaque with the date of its construction. The Beaufort Historical Association operates the Historic Beaufort Site, which is comprised of seven period homes and public buildings that are open to the public. More on these later, though (see page 189).

■ Morehead City

A bit to the east, and across a pair of bridges, is a town with a quite different, and decidedly more modern, character. Morehead City is one of only two deepwater port cities in North Carolina. Vessels hailing from the world over negotiate the three miles from the sea through Beaufort Inlet to arrive at the Morehead City docks. This port is also the arrival and departure point for the Second Division of the US Marine Corps, based at nearby Camp Lejeune, North Carolina. The waterfront at Morehead City is famed for boat-to-table seafood restaurants, fish markets where buyers inspect the catch as it is landed, charter fishing boats for those angling to catch a trophy, and cruise boats that allow you to investigate the neighboring islands.

Morehead City is the easternmost of the two entry points to the 30-mile Bogue Banks, a beach-lover's paradise. **Atlantic Beach**, immediately across the bridge, is the most commercial of the areas here. To its east, at the tip of this narrow island and providing a stark contrast, is the historic **Fort Macon State Park**. Following Highway 58 west from Atlantic City, you will find a handful of small communities, easy access to a host of public beaches, and two places of particular interest. As on the Outer Banks, addresses are designated by a mile marker number indicating the number of miles you travel along the main road (here, Highway 58), from a point of origin at number 0, to reach your destination.

At Mile Marker 4 is **Pine Knoll Shores**, bequeathed to the children of Theodore Roosevelt by Alice Hoffman, owner of the island between 1918 and 1953. In consideration of its spectacular location within a maritime forest, wedged between oceanside dunes and the Bogue

Sound, the Roosevelt children developed Pine Knoll Shores in a manner so as to create the minimal disturbance to the island's natural dynamics. Consequently, this is one of the state's most ecologically sensitive towns. Interestingly, just off the coast at Pine Knoll Shores and visible at low tide, is the wreck of the 500-ton Confederate blockade-runner *Pevensey*, run aground by a Federal navy vessel in 1864.

At Mile Marker 7 is the intersection that leads to the **North Carolina Aquarium**. Pause a moment to read the plaque, which will tell you that this was among the first landing sites for a European explorer in the New World.

■ Swansboro

At the western end of Bogue Banks another bridge takes you across Bogue Sound and back to the mainland. Before taking Highway 24 back to Morehead City, a short detour leads to the very quaint town of Swansboro, formerly Swannsborough. First settled around 1730 upon the site of an Algonquin Indian village, the town was incorporated 53 years later and named in honor of former speaker of the North Carolina House of Commons, Samuel Swann. It soon became a major shipbuilding center. In fact, the *Prometheus*, the first steamboat constructed in North Carolina, was fashioned here.

The town prospered until the end of the Civil War but then experienced a decline concurrent with that of the shipbuilding industry as a whole. The effects of the Great Depression were felt severely here. But its seaside location proved advantageous and Swansboro survived through development of a commercial fishing industry. Business from local Marine Corps bases, Camp Lejeune and Cherry Hill, brought renewed economic growth during the Second World War. But progress has not detracted from Swansboro's unique ambiance and it retains the charm of a picturesque Colonial port.

Blackbeard

No history of the Crystal Coast would be complete without a mention of its infamous visitor, Blackbeard, the fiercest pirate of them all. He left many disasters, and many more legends, in his wake when he rampaged through this region in the early 18th century. His first name, we know, was Edward. There is, however, considerable doubt as to his last name. It has been recorded as Teach, Thatch, Tatch or even Tache, although an anchorage inside Ocracoke Inlet confidently bears the name "Teach's Hole." It is believed that he was born in Bristol, England around 1680, and that he served in Queen Anne's War, fought between England and Spain from 1702 to 1713.

Following that war Blackbeard joined up with the pirate crew of Captain Benjamin Hornigold, who operated out of New Providence in the Bahamas. In 1717, he captured the French slave ship *Concorde* off St. Vincent Island in the Caribbean and took command of the vessel, deeming it his flagship and renaming it Queen *Anne's Revenge*. In May of the following year, he made what was probably his most audacious attack, raiding Charleston, South Carolina, then the busiest and most important port in the Southern colonies. He met his end, violently as might be expected, when a military force commissioned by two American colonies lured him into battle off Ocracoke Island on Friday, November 22, 1718.

Throughout the succeeding centuries many efforts were undertaken to locate the remains of the *Queen Anne's Revenge*, but all without success. The tide of fortune changed though in 1996 when a private research firm, Intersal, Inc., discovered a shipwreck near Beaufort Inlet. Since that date, many artifacts have been recovered from the wreck and, although scientific studies continue, it is thought probable that this is indeed what remains of Blackbeard's flagship.

■ Getting Here & Getting Around

 From the north: Take the Ocracoke to Cedar Island ferry, then follow Routes 12 and 70 to Beaufort.

From the west: Take the Route 70 East exit off Interstate 95 and follow it through Goldsboro, Kinston and New Bern to Morehead City and Beaufort.

From the south: Take Route 17 North from Wilmington, then branch off onto Route 172 (that takes you through the Camp LeJeune Marine Base) and, at the intersection with Route 24, head east towards Morehead City and Beaufort. A car is the only viable option here.

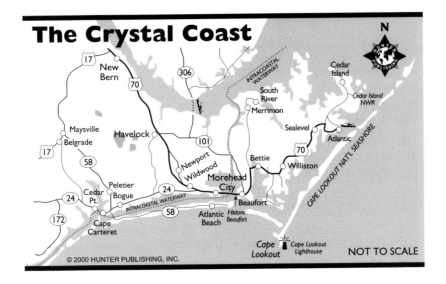

The Crystal Coast

■ **Sightseeing**

Beaufort

A stop at the **Beaufort Historical Association**, ☎ 252-728-5225, 800-575-SITE (7483), fax 728-4966, e-mail bha@bmd.clis.com, 138 Turner Street, is an absolute must. Find them on the Internet at www.nccoastonline.com/bha, www. blackbeardthepirate.com. It is open year-round Monday-Saturday from 9:30 to 5:30. The Association oversees the operation of the two-acre Historic Site, which includes eight historic buildings (six of them restored), dating from 1732 to 1859. To learn more details about this fascinating small town, take one of the guided tours that depart from the Association building at 10 am, 11:30 am, 1 and 3 year-round. Also taking place between April and October are tours of the Old Burying Ground, english double-decker bus tours of the Historic District, architectural walking tours and special Civil War bus tours. Times vary, so call the Association for schedules.

Among the special events they sponsor throughout the year are the Publick Day-Colonial Market Day on the third Saturday in April; the Old Homes Tour & Antiques Show and Sale held on the last weekend in June; the Community Thanksgiving Feast on the Sunday before Thanksgiving; and the Coastal Carolina Christmas Celebration on the second weekend in December.

North Carolina

A WORD TO
THE WISE

Before leaving, stop by The Old Beaufort Gift Shop, which has books, maps and variety of other items that make excellent souvenirs and gifts.

Even if you have passed up the formal tour, you will want to visit the **Old Burying Ground** on Ann Street. Listed on the National Register of Historic Places, it dates from 1731 and is the final resting place for many local legends. Stick close to one another, though. With its ancient headstones and overhanging oak trees you may get spooked.

On the Beaufort waterfront is another attraction that celebrates local traditions. The **North Carolina Maritime Museum**, ☎ 252-728-7317, www.ah.dcr.state.nc.us/maritime/default.htm, 315 Front Street, has a cedar shake design reflecting both 19th-century Beaufort styles and early US Lifesaving Service buildings. Its exhibits chronicle the maritime and natural histories of the North Carolina coast and that of the US Lifesaving Service. Among the displays are full-sized working watercraft, ship models, decoys, tools, fossils, shells, coastal plant and animal life and saltwater aquariums. Across the street but still on the waterfront, is the museum-run **Harvey W. Smith Watercraft Center**. This is a working boat shop, where visitors can view the construction and restoration of wooden boats. It also sponsors a small craft research program dedicated to the preservation of the history of boats and boat building in North Carolina. The museum proper is open Monday through Friday from 9 am to 5 pm, Saturday from 10 am to 5 and Sunday from 1 to 5. The Watercraft Center observes basically the same hours, except that it is closed on Monday.

Bogue Banks

At the far-eastern end of Bogue Banks is the 385-acre **Fort Macon State Park**, ☎ 252-726-3775, www.clis.com/friends, which is comprised of the fort, the swimming area and the park grounds. While all three areas are open daily, the actual hours vary. The fort and the swimming areas are open from 10 to 5:30 pm. The park itself opens at 8:30 each morning and closes at 9 from June through August, at 8 in September, April and May, at 7 in October and March, and at 6 November through February.

The fort itself dates from 1826 and was the culmination of a string of efforts, which began in the mid-1700s, to protect the harbor of Beaufort. During Colonial times, Beaufort was among the first harbors designated as a port of entry, an honor that brought with it many dangers, including a vulnerability to naval attacks. Following its capture in 1747 by Spanish raiders who held the town for several days, defense was deemed a priority. Although attempts to build Fort Dobbs in 1756 never came to fruition, in 1808, over a half-century later, Fort Hampton was completed. Alas, its guardianship was short-lived, being destroyed by hurricane winds and floods in 1825. The following year, construction commenced on the present structure. It was initially engineered by Robert E. Lee, who needs no introduction here, and was named after Senator Nathaniel Macon of North Carolina, whose efforts funded it. The fort was garrisoned in 1834. Although Confederate forces wrestled it from Union forces at the beginning of the Civil War, the Union reclaimed it in 1862 and, subsequently, utilized it as a coaling station for their ships. Following the war, from 1867 to 1876, it served as a Federal prison. It was again garrisoned during the Spanish-American War, but closed in 1903. By 1923, it was considered surplus to Federal requirements and was sold to the State of North Carolina. The price – a mere $1. By 1934, Fort Macon had been fully restored and readied for what would be its final tour of duty, World War II. Today, the five-sided brick and stone structure, with outer walls 4½ feet thick, appears much as it did during the Civil War and is open for self-guided or tour-guided exploration.

Atlantic Beach

Five miles west of Atlantic Beach, at Mile Marker 7, you will find the entrance to the **North Carolina Aquarium** at Pine Knoll Shores, ☎ 252-247-4003, www.aquariums.state.nc.us/Aquariums. This is one of only three such facilities in the state, the others being at Roanoke Island on the Outer Banks to the north, and at Fort Fisher near Wilmington to the south. The variety of exhibits ensures that there will be something of interest to most anyone. The riverbank display, with live alligators, is enough to frighten those who are a bit skittish. If turtles are your thing, then head for the Loggerhead Odyssey, where injured and orphaned turtles are cared for before their release back into the ocean. A turtle release trip is scheduled each May. The Touch Tank allows you to get close up close and personal with common marine animals and the Living Shipwreck, set within a 12,000-gallon display, accurately simulates the real thing. The aquarium is open in the summer daily from 9 to 7 pm, closing at 5 the rest of the year.

■ Adventures

On Foot

Hunting & Shooting

Adams Creek Gun Sports, ☎ 252-447-6808 or 447-7688, mobile 252-241-2961 or fax 447-6902, 6240 Adams Creek Road, Havelock, NC 28532, is about 20 miles north of Beaufort. A wide range of hunts are available, all accompanied by guides. You are welcome to use your own dogs, or they will be provided.

On Water

Catamaran

Cruises on a 45-foot catamaran are offered by **Lookout Cruises**, ☎ 252-504-SAIL, www.lookoutcruises.com. Each day between the Memorial Day weekend and October 1st, they offer the following. From 9:30 to 11:30 am, at a cost of $18, the AM Dolphin Watch will carry you to the place where the Newport River approaches Beaufort to watch these fascinating creatures cavort in the shallows. Next in line is the Cape Lookout Cruise. Departing at midday and returning six hours later, it takes you on a six-mile cruise in each direction, and allows you time to swim, snorkel, sunbathe or simply walk along the unspoiled beach. The $49 fare includes lunch and refreshments. An hour after the catamaran returns, at 7 pm, the ship leaves on a 1½-hour Sunset Cruise, priced at $20 per person. Five nights a month, during the full moon, Lookout operates a Moonlight Cruise. This departs at 9 pm, returns at 10:30pm, and costs $20 per person, including complimentary beer, wine and soft drinks. Lookout Cruises are US Coast Guard-approved for up to 42 passengers. All rates are per person.

Diving

The **Olympus Dive Center**, ☎ 252-726-9432, 800-992-1258, fax 726-0883, e-mail olympus@olympusdiving.com, PO Box 486, is at 713 Shepard Street, Morehead City, NC 28557. Visit their website at www.olympusdiving.com. This is a full-service PADI diving center that offers a range of experiences. It also has a store with all the equipment, and more, that you will need. Wreck diving, of course, is one of the highlights, after all *Rodale's Scuba Diving* rates North Carolina as having the "Best Wreck Diving in North America" and calls it one of the "Top Five" wreck diving locations in the world. Whether you are interested in German U-boats, their victims, historical sites, modern vessels they are all found in local waters. There are also local shore dives, shark dives, night dives, lobster dives and even photographic dives so you can catch images of the abundant tropical and pelagic fish.

Fishing

Deep Sea Fishing

As you cross the causeway between Morehead City and Atlantic Beach you will see, on your left, the **Capt. Stacy Fishing Center**, ☎ 252-247-7501 or 800-533-9417 – the place to go to for deep sea fishing. The center has available for charter a multitude of boats, from 34 to 54 feet in length and with state-of-the-art electronics. Each is piloted by an experienced captain and his highly capable mates. You may take your choice of a Full Day Troll, looking for tuna, dolphin, wahoo, king mackerel, sailfish and marlin, or Full Day Bottom Fishing, aiming to snare red and silver snapper, grouper, triggerfish and others. Both of these depart around 5 and return at about 5 pm. The prices, including bait, ice and all tackle, range between $650 and $1,100 for up to six people. If this is too much, then consider a Half-Day Troll for approximately five hours. January through March is the season for Special Giant Blue Tuna Fishing, at around $1,000 for a full day. Fish cleaning is available, with tuna, wahoo, dolphin and kings being filleted or cut into steaks and all bottom fish filleted and skinned for 40¢ per pound.

Fly-Fishing & Light Tackle

In direct contrast to the deep-sea fishing charters sailing from Morehead City, Captain Dave Dietzler's **Fly Fishing & Light Tackle Charters**, ☎ and fax 252-240-2850, 242 Brant Landing Road, Newport, departs from Beaufort, working the local waters on excursions classified by season. In March and April, at $425 for a full day and $250 for a half-day, the Captain will take you in search of albacore and bonita. From the last week of April through May, at $400 for a full day or $250 for a half-day, the Roanoke River stripers are biting – maybe as many as 100 of them in a day. May through December is the season for wreck fishing. At $500 for a full day or $300 for a half-day, you will be angling for king mackerel, bonita, barracuda or sharks. Whichever one you hook, you are guaranteed a good fight. In the period from May to October redfish occupy waters so shallow that you can actually watch them swim beneath the boat and make a game of picking out the fish you want to catch. A full day will cost you $400 or a half-day $250. July through November, the sport fishing on the Crystal Coast is superb, but forget the frying pan and take the camera, as these trips are catch-and-release only. July, August and September in the southwest corner of Pamlico Sound, the hunt is on for giant red drum, which can weigh 30 to 50 lbs. In July and August, Pamlico Sound is also the place to fish find 70-100 lb tarpon. During October and November, shoals of thousands of False Albacore, also known as "Fat Alberts," arrive at Cape Lookout. Average weights are 8 to 18 lbs, but some world record fish of over 20 lbs have been caught each year. The preceding three trips are offered as daylong outings only, the first two at $500, the latter at $100. December and January trips are not inexpensive, $600 for a half-day, but that may buy you a lot of tuna fish. Giant bluefin tuna will weigh in at an average of 400 to 600 lbs. The fishing is done within a mile off the beach, sometimes in just 15 feet of water. And, incidentally, this is one time when two can live as cheaply as one. Prices are for one or two people. Whatever season you visit, you can rely on Captain Dave for an adventure you will not soon forget.

Kayaking

Whether you are a beginner or a seasoned paddler, kayaking is always fun, and **Coastal Carolina Kayak Tours**, ☎ 252-728-7070, e-mailhollie@coastalkayak.com, www.coastalkayak.com, is your ticket to kayaking adventure on the Crystal Coast. They are on Front Street across from the NC Maritime Museum in Beaufort. If you prefer to explore on your own, kayaks are available for rent at $10 an hour, $30 a half-day or $55 a day, per person. If, on the other hand, you prefer an organized adventure, there are several options. For $5 per person, you can head out to Carrot Island/Sand Dollar; or for $20 more you can take your choice of either Bear Island or the Shackleford Banks. Cape Lookout is another popular destination, but it is a long way to paddle. Never fear. For this trip, kayaks are loaded onto a 45-foot catamaran for transport and, once there, you can paddle the waters searching for dolphin, sea turtles and other wildlife. All rates include the use of kayak, paddling gear and instruction, with some tours having a catered lunch.

Yachting

Sailing can be a serene, and at **The Sailing Place**, ☎ 252-726-5664, 136 Atlantic Beach Causeway, Captain Brenton Creelman offers a choice of sailing lessons, yacht charters (with or without a captain) and an array of boat rentals. Sailboat charters range from $80 for a half-day to $275 a day, with the cost of a captain extra. Other non-power boats, from canoes to catamarans, are also available for hire. Alternatively, if speed is your thing, powerboats can be hired for $60 for four hours or $180 for eight hours.

From Beaufort, between late spring and fall, you have the charming option of cruising the Intracoastal Waterway on the *Good Fortune*, a Dutch custom-built 42-foot yacht. **Coastal Ecology Sails**, ☎ 252-242-3860, based at 1307 Shepard Street, Morehead City, NC 28557, is piloted by Captain Ron White, a marine biologist/diving instructor. Conceptualized in Key West in 1979, this is the oldest sailing charter operation in the Eastern United States, and has been sailing out of Beaufort since 1981. In the winter months you will find Captain White either in the Florida Keys or in the Bahamas. The *Good Fortune* can accommodate up to six passengers. Book early to avoid disappointment.

For nature lovers, we recommend the 2½-hour Dolphin Watch. Even if the creatures don't surface, you will enjoy both the ride and the informative running commentary. The cost is $25 per person. At a slightly higher cost of $30, but ever so much more romantic is the Sunset Sail. Also 2½ hours in duration, the main attractions on this trip are the scenery and the ambiance. Champagne, wine, beer and soft drinks are complimentary. Finally, consider booking a full day of sailing adventure aboard the *Good Fortune* for a very reasonable $280. Captain White will set sail for Cape Lookout, where you can spend your time snorkeling (equipment is provided), swimming, shelling or merely lazing around. Whatever you choose to do, you will have the personal attention of the Captain and the advantage of his vast reservoir of knowledge.

North Carolina

Captain's Best Friend?

On the *Good Fortune*, you will also become acquainted with the First Mate, Lt. Willis, whose duty it is to spot the dolphins and whales. He has even been known to jump overboard and swim with the creatures himself, or to dive for shells. Best not to trust his navigating abilities though. Lt. Willis is a golden labrador!

In The Air

For a different perspective on the Crystal Coast, contact **East Air**, ☎ 252-728-2323 or fax 728-6706, at the Michael J. Smith Field Airport in Beaufort. Any one of their three sightseeing flights will give a spectacular bird's-eye perspective. The Cape Lookout Tour, lasting 30-minutes and costing $65, will wing you over Morehead City, Atlantic Beach, Fort Macon, Shackelford Island and the Cape Lookout Lighthouse. The Beach and Bank Tour, 15 minutes longer and $20 more, flies you over Atlantic Beach and as far as Emerald Isle. The Inland Tour, 40 minutes long and costing $80, is, to our minds, less interesting – as the name implies, you don't get to see much sea.

Eco/Cultural Adventures

Between Morehead City & Swansboro

Between Morehead City and Swansboro, at 3609 Highway 24 in Ocean, you will find the **North Carolina Coastal Federation**, ☎ 252-393-8185, a non-profit organization that works to achieve a healthy coastal environment and offers unique on-the-water kayak experiences. These are variable, however, so we suggest you call for an up-to-date schedule. The Federation also sponsors a gift shop and art gallery, featuring original coastal art, books, educational games and fine gifts – including some really nifty carved birds. It opens, Memorial Day to Labor Day, Monday to Friday from 9 to 5 and Saturday from 10 to 4.

■ Where to Stay

Atlantic Beach

A Place At The Beach, 1090 Fort Macon Road, is part of the Sands Oceanfront Rentals group. Each of the one-, two- or three-bedroom apartments, designated either ocean view or oceanfront, is pleasantly furnished and features a fully equipped kitchen and a private balcony. On-site facilities include an indoor pool and whirlpool, an outdoor pool with a 150-foot waterslide, a game and billiard room, and outdoor grills. Rates are between $50 to $153, with an additional surcharge on holidays. ☎ 252-247-2636, 800-334-2667 or fax 247-1067.

The **Royal Pavilion Resort**, overlooks the ocean three miles west of Morehead City at 125 Salter Path Road. Its 110 guestrooms, whether king, double, studio efficiency or specialty suite, feature island décor, microwave, refrigerator, cable TV, individual climate control, private balcony or deck, and free local calls. Rates: $60 to $150 per night. ☎ 252-726-5188, 800-533-3700, fax 726-9963, www.nccoast.com/royal.htm.

The **Sheraton Atlantic Beach Oceanfront Hotel**, 2717 West Fort Macon Road, boasts a delightful location right by the beach. Each of the 200 rooms and 16 suites is well-appointed and features private balcony, microwave, refrigerator and coffeemaker. There is an indoor pool, outdoor pool, fitness center and, just outside the back door, a private 600-foot fishing pier. Ocean-view rooms are between $49 and $165, depending upon the season. ☎ 252-240-1155, 800-624-8875 or fax 240-1452.

Beaufort

The **Pecan Tree Inn**, 116 Queen Street, is within an absolutely delightful two-story Victorian house, easily identifiable by its verandas, turrets and gingerbread trim. Making the grounds really special is a lovely 5,500-square-foot English-style flower and herb garden, designed, created and maintained by the innkeepers. The Pecan Tree Inn derives its name from the 200-year-old pecan trees on the property. Rates are between $70 and $135, according to room and season. ☎ 252-728-6733, www.pecantree.com.

The **Beaufort Inn**, 101 Ann Street, has three floors with 44 well-appointed rooms, two of which are handicapped-accessible. Each has either a balcony or patio. They offer every bed size and both smoking and non-smoking options. Also on hand are a fully equipped exercise room and an outdoor hot tub spa. Rates are between $59 and $139, according to the season, and include a complimentary breakfast. ☎ 252-728-2600, 800-726-0321, http://www.nccoast.com/bfrinn.htm.

Cape Carteret

The **Harborlight Guest House Bed & Breakfast**, 332 Live Oak Drive, Cape Carteret, is undoubtedly the finest place for many a mile. It offers a great location with 530-foot frontage on the Bogue Peninsula, and an amazing combination of absolutely delightful oversized rooms, with fantastic views and modern amenities such as oversized Jacuzzi tubs. Rates are $75 to $200 per night. ☎ 252- 393-6868, 800-62-4-VIEW, fax 393-6868, www.bbonline.com/nc/harborlight/.

■ Camping

Salter Path Family Campground, ☎ 252-482-2867, PO Box 2323, Atlantic Beach, NC 28512, www.kiz.com/ salterpath, is located at Milepost 11.5 on Bogue Banks, midway between Atlantic Beach and Emerald Island. It opens between late March and early November and has full hookups – including cable TV, grassy and shaded sites, hot-water showers, a convenience store, LP gas, laundry and sports facilities.

■ Where to Eat

Atlantic Beach

The **Paradise Restaurant**, 2717 West Fort Macon Road, is a casual, full-service restaurant in the Sheraton Atlantic Beach Oceanfront Hotel. Of special interest is the seafood buffet served from 5 to 9 on Friday and Saturday night. Don't forget to check out the Champagne Sunday Brunch between 11:30 and 2 ($13.95 per person). ☎ 252-240-1155 or fax 240-1452.

Beaufort

The **Beaufort Grocery Co.**, 117 Queen Street, tucked away on a side street just away from the waterfront, is an ideal place for an informal lunch or a sophisticated dinner. ☎ 252-728-3899.

The **Front Street Grill**, 419-A Front Street, just across from the waterfront, is a bright and airy restaurant offering an interesting selection of soups and salads, sandwiches, small plates and big plates. Dinner is served, Tuesday through Sunday, beginning at 5 pm. ☎ 252-728-3118.

Morehead City

The **Harbor House Restaurant**, 714 Shepard Street, offers fine dining in a relaxed waterfront atmosphere. Lunch is served, Monday through Thursday, from 11 to 2 and, Friday and Saturday, from 11 to 3. Dinner hours are Wednesday and Thursday from 5 to 9 (5 to 10 on Friday and Saturday). Sunday brunch is served from 11 to 3. ☎ 252-247-7009.

The **Channel Marker Restaurant** is on The Causeway between Morehead City and Atlantic Beach. It has marvelous views overlooking Bogue Sound. In addition to spacious dining rooms with picture windows and an attractive bar, this establishment boasts the largest outdoor dining space in the area. The Channel Marker is open seven nights a week, beginning at 5 pm. ☎ 252-247-234.

■ Visitor Information

 More information about this area can be obtained from the **Carteret County Tourism Development Bureau**, ☎ 919-726-8148, fax 726-0990, e-mail cctb@bmd.clis.com, www.nccoast.com/tourism.htm, 3409 Arendell Street, PO Box 1406, Morehead City, NC 28557.

Wilmington & Wrightsville Beach

■ History

 A quarter of a century ago, like many cities of its genre, Wilmington was struggling to establish a new identity. Leaders had already come to the realization that neither its plentiful and interesting history nor the attraction of the battleship *North Carolina* had proved sufficient to entice visitors to the town. Tourism, with its accompanying financial and cultural benefits, needed a proverbial shot in the arm.

These days, however, it is an absolutely delightful city with a revitalized downtown area. That did not come about by chance. Following the formation of the Downtown Area Revitalization Effort Inc. (DARE) in 1977, a large-scale redevelopment of the Central Business District ensued, with investments eventually exceeding $150,000,000.

Wilmington's history stretches back through several centuries – quite a rarity for an American city – to 1524, when explorer Giovanni da Verrazano landed in the area while sailing in the name of the King of France. Strangely, the French showed very little interest, and it was not until two centuries later, in 1725, that the first permanent settlement was established at Brunswick, just across the Cape Fear River. Earlier, in the mid-17th century, settlers from the Massachusetts Bay Colony had attempted to settle the area, but a combination of circumstances forced them south, where they founded the city of Charleston. Finally, in 1732, a new settlement was founded on this,

North Carolina

the higher east bank of the river. The settlement was known by several names – New Carthage, New Liverpool and Newton – before it was dubbed Wilmington in 1739 as an endowment of Governor Gabriel Johnston in honor of his friend Spencer Compton, Earl of Wilmington, . During the following year, it was incorporated by the North Carolina General Assembly.

Wilmington's strategic position at the junction of the two branches of the Cape Fear River and high upon a bluff protected from the Atlantic Ocean naturally created a safe port. This led to very favorable trading conditions, which were capitalized on by both settlers and ocean-going vessels. In short order, Wilmington became a thriving seaport, and soon had captured the distinction of being North Carolina's largest city.

Strangely though, it was the area's abundance of pine trees, the world's largest collection at the time, which led to the city's affluence. By-products of the pine trees were the tar, pitch and turpentine so necessary to keep wooden ships afloat. The demands of the British Navy (the world's largest) for these goods was enormous and, as a result, the Wilmington region flourished. By 1768, more naval stores passed consistently through Cape Fear than any other port in the British Empire.

This, of course, was also the era of the Revolutionary War, and among the prominent patriots who called the area home was William Hooper, a signer of the Declaration of Independence. In January of 1781 Wilmington was taken by the British, an occupation that lasted until October of the same year. During that period, Cornwallis used the residence of John Burgwin, located on the most prominent corner of downtown Wilmington, as his headquarters.

Growth rallied slowly after the war, and it was not until the 1840 opening of the Wilmington and Wheldon Railroad, at that time the longest in the world, that the economy once again flourished. It was also soon recognized as the site of the largest cotton exchange in the world. In the succeeding decades many of the city's most enduring and impressive structures were completed. Among these were the Town Hall, Thalian Hall, the Bellamy Mansion, and the Zebulon Latimer House – all of which will be detailed later.

During the Civil War, massive defenses were erected to protect the city and, as a result, Wilmington remained open longer than any other Atlantic port city of the Confederacy. Then, blockade-runners, with their multinational crews and abundance of monetary resources, brought with them a strange epoch of international influence and one unwelcome immigrant – a dose of yellow fever, which in 1862 took the lives of 300 citizens. It was near the end of the conflict, on January 15th, 1865 and after the most extensive naval bombardment of the century, that Fort Fisher fell and Wilmington was overrun.

Recovery was not long delayed after the war. Cotton again became a major economic factor and a building boom ensued. Rice, though, suffered a decline, as did the business in naval stores. The latter was brought about by the decreasing pine forests and the advent of metal-clad vessels. The expansion continued through the early part of the new century as, during World War II, the need for ships and the maritime skills of the Wilmington citizenry brought shipbuilding to prominence again. In fact, the Cape Fear area's population increased rapidly and dramatically to nearly 100,000 as the region played host to a major military base and construction area.

Post-war years, however, saw the city's sharp decline and in the 1950s two unfortunate events seemed to spell doom for the floundering metropolis. First, Hurricane Hazel physically devastated the downtown area in 1954. In the following year, the area's 10th largest employer, the Atlantic Coast Line Railroad, removed its corporate headquarters from the city.

The future, though, would be brighter. The expanding technologies of the 1960s brought new industries to the city with economic recovery in their wake. Concurrently, there came a resurgence of appreciation for Wilmington's heritage. In 1974, over 200 city blocks, stretching from the Cape Fear River to Ninth Street, were listed in the National Register of Historic Places, making it the largest neighborhood then so recognized. More recently, since 1983, Wilmington has attracted the attention of filmmakers, whose industry now contributes over $100 million annually to city revenues. Presently, the population of Wilmington is slightly over 60,000, a considerable proportion of whom are students at the University of North Carolina, Wilmington.

It is believed that Wrightsville Beach and the Masonboro Islands were the first of this area's locations to be explored by the European adventurers. Whether true, or not, this particular area was not readily accessible until the middle of the 19th century, when the first road to the beach was completed. The Tidewater Power Company subsequently took an interest and began investing in the beach, which is named for the prominent landowners of their day, the Wright family. It was incorporated as a resort community in 1899, and three years later the power company began operation of a trolley service, which replaced an earlier railroad. This ran a 12-mile, 35-minute route from downtown – until 1935, the sole land link with Wrightsville Beach. In early 1903, Tidewater Power Company

North Carolina

bought an oceanfront lot next to the end of the trolley line. Following up on a bright idea, they commissioned the building of The Lumina pavilion. Bedecked with thousands of lights, it was visible far out to sea. Made entirely of heart pine, this three-story structure became an entertainment mecca. It served as a beach house by day; by night, its huge dance floor attracted renowned big bands of the day. The Lumina remained a major landmark until its demolition in 1975.

This narrow island, just over 4½ miles long and with an area of not quite one square mile, has been battered untold times by hurricanes. The most serious storm blew through in 1954, followed by two in 1996. Fires also have caused much damage. Each calamity, however, has been followed by timely repair. Coastal erosion, though, especially at the north end of the island (near the Shell Island Resort Hotel and many condominiums), is a source of major concern.

Wrightsville Beach has over 3,000 permanent residents, and attracts huge numbers of overnight visitors and day-trippers in the high season. It has managed to avoid the overt commercialization seen in such places as Myrtle Beach, Virginia Beach and Ocean City. This really is best categorized as a family place. Most of the buildings are single-family cottages, interspersed with only a handful of hotels and high-rises. What's more, a nature reserve has been created in the middle of Harbor Island.

 The exotic Venus fly trap, a perennial plant called by Charles Darwin "the most wonderful plant in the world," is found only within a 100-mile radius of Wilmington. Not only does this amazing plant have a primitive nervous system similar to that of animals, it is both insectivorous and carnivorous. Don't try taking one home with you, though; that will get you arrested.

Notwithstanding the occasional hurricane, the weather in this area is pleasing indeed. The Gulf Stream, some 45 miles offshore, keeps the weather on this part of the Eastern Coast unusually mild. Even in the height of summer, the temperature generally reaches only the upper 80s, with the mean average temperature a very mild low 60s. On a culinary note, seafood lovers will be in their element. Local restaurants pride themselves on serving some of the freshest seafood on the Atlantic Coast.

■ Getting Here & Getting Around

From the north: Take the I-40 exit from I-95, then follow it south to Wilmington.

From the northeast: Take Route 24 West from Morehead City, then Route 172 south through the Camp LeJeune Marine Base and follow Route 17 South to Wilmington.

From the west: Exit I-95 at Lumberton, then follow Routes 211 and 74 East to Wilmington.

From the south: Follow Route 17 North from the South Carolina state line to Wilmington.

In Wilmington itself everything, apart from the *Battleship North Carolina*, can be reached on foot. Otherwise, you will need private transportation.

■ Sightseeing

Wilmington

Begin with a little history lesson on Wilmington; you don't have go very far and it is entertaining as well. Stroll to the junction of Market and Water Streets, by the Cape River Fear, and look for the flagpole announcing "**Wilmington Adventure Tours** BEGINS HERE" – ☎ 910-763-1785. Of course, you will have to, for the moment, discipline yourselves to ignore the hulking hull of the *Battleship North Carolina*, whose presence on the opposite riverbank unquestionably dominates the scene. She is, though, inaccessible from this point. In the meantime, you won't have any trouble identifying the Adventure Tour guides. Their canes and hats easily set them apart. Between April and October, at 10 and 2 and without prior appointment, they will introduce you to Wilmington by way of a guided walking tour, for a fee of just $10 each.

Historic Buildings

One of Wilmington's most enduring monuments is **Thalian Hall**, ☎ 910-343-3664 or 800-523-2820. Built in 1858, this building housed the town government, a library and a theater or, as it was called then, an "opera house." The latter seated 1,000 people, which was more than 10% of Wilmington's population at that time. Beginning at end of the 18th century, the city welcomed productions by professional touring companies as a major staging post on the theatrical circuit that included New Orleans, Charleston and Richmond. At other times, the theatre hosted shows by a local gentlemen's acting society, the Thalian Society, hence its name. After a small fire in 1973, it was restored to its Victorian grandeur. The building is open for tours Monday to Friday at 11 and 3 and on Saturday at 2. As it still stages shows of international, national and local repute, it is considered to be the oldest continuously operating community theater in the United States.

Wilmington has an uncommonly large district listed on the National Historic Register. This boasts an array of meticulously restored antebellum, Italianate, Victorian and Georgian homes and, while not all are large and grand, few are without interest. Even for those not overly inclined towards history, the plaques mounted on these homes make for interesting reading. Unfortunately, most are not open to visitors, but the following three are well worth a look.

The **Bellamy Mansion**, ☎ 910-251-3700, at 5th Avenue and Market Street, is a truly magnificent example of antebellum architecture that was built in 1859, just before the Civil War, by prominent planter Dr. John D. Bellamy. During those hostilities the home was taken over by the Union army, but the family managed to reclaim it after the war and actually lived there until 1946. Presently, its 22 rooms on four floors house a museum, with exhibits that document the home's history. Visit Wednesday to Saturday from 10 to 5 and Sunday, 1 to 5.

Of an altogether different style is the **Burgwin-Wright House**, ☎ 910-762-0570, built in 1770 by merchant, planter and Colonial official John Burgwin. The Wright family purchased it for 3,500 Spanish milled dollars in 1799 and it remained in their possession until 1869. Interestingly, the foundation of ballast stone upon which this Colonial home stands today at one time belonged to a jail, and its antique furnishings, outside kitchen and lovely gardens make for a fascinating tour. Situated at 3rd and Market Streets, this has the distinction of being the oldest museum house in the lower Cape Fear region. It is open from February to December, with guided tours on Tuesday through Saturday between 10 and 4.

The Victorian/Italianate-style **Latimer House**, ☎ 910-762-0492, fax 763-5869, www.wilmington.net.org/latimer, dates from around 1852 and was built by the prosperous businessman Zebulon Latimer upon his marriage to a local lady. In 1963, it passed out of that family's hands, and became the headquarters of the Lower Cape Fear Historical Society. At 126 South 3rd Street, and open Monday to Friday 10 to 10:30 and Saturday and Sunday from midday to 5, the museum exhibits chronicle the history of the house. There are walking tours on Wednesday and Saturday at 10 am. If you are lucky enough to be visiting during the first weekend of December, be sure to avail yourself of the Historical Society's romantic Historical Candlelight Tour of this area's finest homes.

In the 19th century, the largest cotton exporting company in the world operated from Wilmington. The buildings in that complex were converted into a three-story shopping and restaurant center in the late 1970s, the popularity of which paved the way for the downtown redevelopment. As a complement to its commercial enterprises, **The Cotton Exchange**, ☎ 910-343-9896, 321 North Front Street, displays photographs and exhibits of its history. With its glorious views overlooking the Cape Fear River, this is a "must see" for visitors to Wilmington. An informative brochure available at various stations throughout The Cotton Exchange details the history of each building and gives a listing of their present occupants.

While en route to Chandler's Wharf, the second of the historic shopping sites, you will stroll along North Front Street, where numerous bright and colorful window displays vie to distract you from your mission. One in particular deserves a dalliance. **Nautical Hangups Gift & Gallery**, ☎ 800-545-1847, fax 763-8874, e-mail mooreart@ nauticalhangups.com, www.nauticalhangups.com, at 24 North Front Street, offers all manner of maritime wares. There are models of lighthouses and items with a lighthouse motif, model wooden sailing ships, hand-carved fish, Afghans, tapestries, t-shirts and much, much more.

Notwithstanding such enticements, Nautical Hangups is most recognized as the homeport of the famous Waterways Collection by artist Terry Moore. Terry, a native of Wilmington, and holder of B.A. degrees in History, Philosophy and Religion from the University of North Carolina at Wilmington, is a self-taught artist who had a vision of capturing for posterity the spirit and beauty of America's spectacular coastline. Terry introduces into his works elements of cartography and history, resulting in what he has dubbed geographic/or geo-art. To date he has covered 95% of America's coastline, and the collection is growing. Accompanying each of Terry's paintings are two things, a rabbit and a poem. Why? Well, as to the rabbit, Terry had learned that, in ancient cultures, this creature was associated with good luck. To him, each rabbit is a personal reminder of his own luck in making his living from doing something he loves so dearly. Also, he hopes the

North Carolina

lucky rabbit will bring some of the same to those who support his artwork and personal dream. Insofar as the poem is concerned, multi-talented Terry is a guitarist, a lutenist, and a lover of language. He, therefore, enhances each visual interpretation with a short but intense composition reflecting his thoughts on the area.

Those as captivated as we were by the Waterways Collection will be able to purchase prints, note cards and other accessories, but never one of the original oil paintings. You see, Terry Moore is also philanthropic in his outlook. Fully expecting that, upon completion, the collection's worth will escalate dramatically, he plans for the originals to be auctioned off, with the receipts donated to children's charities in each of the regions.

Time now to disengage yourself from distractions and make your way to the corner of Water and Ann Streets and the rather charming area known as **Chandler's Wharf**. Here, a restored warehouse, dating from the late 19th century, and the surrounding cobblestone streets have been cleverly transformed into a preserve of specialty stores and restaurants, some of which we will describe later. Here, you shop to your heart's content, dine or snack in pleasant surroundings, and enjoy lovely views overlooking the Cape Fear River.

Museums

The *Battleship North Carolina*, ☎ 910-350-1817, www.city-info.com/ncbb55.html, won 15 World War II battle stars in Pacific Ocean combat zones between 1941 and 1945. It is truly the star attraction of this city. Most impressive at night as the sun slowly slips below the horizon, the silhouette of this massive vessel is awesome indeed. She is maintained in much the same condition as during the war, being 728 feet in length and displacing over 44,000 tons. Putting this in amazing perspective, if two of these ships stood end to end they would be as tall as the Empire State Building in New York City! She was manned by a crew of 2,339, spread throughout her nine decks, and on a self-guided tour you can see how they lived, worked and played. To get a glimpse of her power, you can climb inside a 16-inch gun turret and imagine that it could fire a 2,700 lb shell (the weight of a medium-sized car) as far as 20 miles. Astounding indeed! At her stern sits one of the few Kingfisher floatplanes still in existence; when these planes were pressed into service they were actually catapulted from the ship's deck. The *Battleship North Carolina* now serves as a fitting World War II memorial to the 10,000 North Carolinians who did not return from battle. It is open daily in the summer months from 8 to 8 and at other times from 8 to 5 pm. The last tickets are sold an hour before those closing times, but bear in mind that a tour takes approximately two hours.

The **Cape Fear Museum**, ☎ 910-341-4350 or fax 341-4037, at 814 Market Street, and handicapped-accessible, bears investigation. It was established in 1898 as a Confederate Museum and these days it documents the social and natural history of the area. Everyone, and sports lovers in particular, will be fascinated by the hands-on adventures in the Michael Jordan Discovery Gallery. It highlights, with photographs and memorabilia, the majestic career of hometown hero and international legend Michael Jordan. Although Michael is, arguably, the most famous, he is not alone in calling the Cape Fear area home. Other notable sportsmen and women who grew up here are: Meadowlark Lemon, of the Harlem Globetrotters; NFL quarterbacks Sonny Jurgensen and Roman Gabriel; boxing champion Sugar Ray Leonard; and female tennis star Althea Gibson. Non-sporting notables include journalists Charles Kuralt and David Brinkley; Charlie Daniels and Sammy Davis, Jr.; and painter Minnie Evans. The museum is open every day in the summer on Monday through Saturday from 9 to 5 and Sunday 2 to 5, but closed on Monday the rest of the year.

The **St. John's Museum of Art**, ☎ 910-763-0281, at 114 Orange Street, is the primary visual arts center in southeastern North Carolina. Located in three restored and distinctive buildings that date from the beginning of the 19th century, its permanent art collection includes works by three centuries of North Carolina masters. These are complemented by works in paper, sculpture and Jugtown Pottery and by one of the world's largest collections of romantic color prints by the 19th-century American artist Mary Cassatt. Explore its treasures Tuesday through Saturday from 10 to 5 and Sunday, noon to 4.

■ Adventures

On Water

Boat Trips

Wilmington

If you spent any time at the waterfront, perhaps while awaiting the guided tour, you most probably noticed the *Henrietta II*, North Carolina's only true sternwheel riverboat. Although not an original (built in the late 1980s), she will surely evoke visions of a romantic 19th-century riverboat fantasy. The operators, **Cape Fear Riverboats, Inc.**, ☎ 910-343-1611 or 800-676-0162, offer a choice of cruises. A 1½-hour Narrated Sightseeing Cruise departs at least once daily between April and October at a cost of $10 per person. Perhaps an Entertainment Dinner Cruise is more to your taste. These run on Friday and Saturday evenings between April and December, for 2½ hours, starting at 7 pm, on Fridays; a Southern Buffet is served and the cost is $32 per person. On Saturdays, expect a full spare rib meal and a price of $35 per person. Also of interest is the Moonlight Cruise, departing in June, July, August and September at 10:30 for a 90-minute cruise beneath the stars, and costing $10 per person. In addition, a number of special events cruises are scheduled throughout the year. With all cruises, guests are asked to board a full half-hour before sailing time.

Wrightsville Beach

Another maritime option is a trip with **Wrightsville Beach Scenic Cruises**, ☎ 910-350-2628. This company operates out of the Blockade-Runner Resort at Wrightsville Beach and offers a selection of very interesting sailings. Most popular is the one-hour narrated harbor cruise for $10 per person, but romantics among you would do well to consider, at $15 per person, a 1½-hour narrated sunset cruise. Immediately to the south of Wrightsville Beach is a very beautiful, fascinating and uninhabited (at least by humans) barrier island. Best described as pristine, **Masonboro Island** is a wonderland of nature. It is among the most successful nesting grounds for loggerhead turtles, protected by the Endangered Species Act, who visit the area between mid-May and late August. The female of this species can weigh from 200-500 lbs, and lays an average of 120 eggs in the dunes closest to the sea. Look for otters, raccoons, a variety of birds and several species of aquatic life as well. You may enjoy shelling, crabbing and clamming, or simply sunbathing and relaxing. Whatever your plans, take everything you will need with you, including food and drink and, very importantly, sunscreen and bug spray. You are responsible for packing out everything you pack in. Wrightsville Beach Scenic Cruises has three ways to acquaint you with Masonboro Island, a mere 20-minutes sail away. A shuttle service departs at 10 and returns at 1 for $10 each; the Masonboro Island Nature Excursion includes three hours of fun and information with a marine biologist for $20 per person and, if you are real adventure lovers, arrangements can be made to camp out overnight.

In the Air

For a bird's eye view of Wilmington and Wrightsville Beach, give Ken Vojta of **ISO AERO of Wilmington, Inc.,** ☎ 910-763-88998 or fax 763-8820, a call. You may choose your flight of fancy from two options, each departing from New Hanover International Airport, just a short distance from downtown. A "figure 8" formation around the city and coastal beaches will cost $42 per couple; double that fee allows for a one-hour flight overlooking the coastal beaches, Masonboro Island, Fort Fisher, Bald Head Island and the *USS Battleship North Carolina.*

■ Where to Stay

Wilmington

The **Graystone Inn,** ☎ 910-763-2000, 888-763-4773, fax 763-5555, e-mail paulb@graystoneinn.com, www.graystoneinn.com, at 100 South Third Street, is an incredibly imposing mansion. An historic landmark and one of the most beautiful structures in Wilmington, the "Bridger's Mansion," as it was once known, was built in 1905-06, and is easily the most impressive place to stay in Wilmington. The new owners, Paul and Yolanda Bolda, undertook a very stylish and elegant remodeling that has enhanced what was already a gracious home. Traditional décor and extremely spacious rooms with every modern amenity go hand-in-hand here. Rates are between $179 and $289.

The **Front Street Inn,** ☎ 910-762-6442, fax 762-8991, www.frontstreetinn.wilmington.net/front.html, is housed in a converted Salvation Army building of classical Italianate style with large arched windows, balconies, and glorious Cape Fear River views. The interior, though, colorfully decorated throughout with American art gathered at galleries, fairs, auctions and attic sales, is far from old-fashioned. Among the public areas is the enticing Sol y Sombra, which doubles as a bar and breakfast room. Rates range from $95 to $155.

The **Rosehill Inn,** ☎ 910-815-0250, 800-815-0250, fax 815-0350, www.rosehill.com, 114 South Third Street, occupies a beautiful house built in 1848 by distinguished businessman and banker Henry Russell Savage. These days, this 7,000-square-foot home has been lovingly restored to serve as an elegant, yet comfortable, bed & breakfast. The six guestrooms, three with king-sized and three with queen-sized beds, are uniquely designed and decorated to incorporate a mix of antiques accented with fine fabrics. Rates are between $109 and $169.

The **Worth House, A Victorian Bed and Breakfast Inn**, ☎ 910-762-8562, 800-340-8559, fax 763-2173, e-mail worthhse@ wilmington.net, www.bbonline.com/nc/wworth, 412 South Third Street, makes its home in a gracious Queen Anne-style building that dates from 1893. Each of the seven guestrooms, most named after a type of flower, has a distinct personality. Rates vary between $80 and $120.

The **Wilmington Hilton**, ☎ 910-763-5900 or fax 763-0038, 301 Water Street, was at the time of writing undergoing a huge expansion. The location on the banks of the Cape Fear River across from The Cotton Exchange shopping center is superb. You can take your choice of 178 beautifully renovated guestrooms, including six Executive Suites and three Presidential Suites. Rates vary greatly; call to inquire.

Wrightsville Beach

The **Blockade-Runner Beach Resort & Conference Center**, ☎ 910-256-2251, 800-541-1161, fax 256-5502, www.blockade-runner. com, 275 Waynick Boulevard, is the only oceanfront hotel on Wrightsville Beach. This distinguished position allows 90 guestrooms Atlantic Ocean views (30 with private balconies), while the other 60 guestrooms face Wrightsville Sound and the Intracoastal Waterway. The oceanfront terrace heated pool is open year-round, and an adjacent indoor health club features a large Jacuzzi that accommodates 12, a sauna and the latest in Hydrafitness Exercise equipment. Sports lovers will feel very much at home at the Blockade-Runner. Perhaps you would like to try your luck at windsurfing. Alternatively, kayak and Hobie Cat rentals and instruction, and bicycle rentals are coordinated through the health club. Parasailing is also available, and several deep-sea fishing charter boats pick up guests at the hotel dock. Golfers aren't forgotten; they receive full privileges at 14 of the area's finest courses, as well as discounts on carts and green fees. Rates vary greatly; call for information.

■ Camping

Wilmington

 Camelot Campground RV Park, ☎ 910-686-7705, 800-454-7705, www.wilmington.net/camelot, 7415 Market Street (Highway 17 North), Wilmington, NC 28405, is just nine miles north of downtown Wilmington. It is AAA approved, open all year and has a pool, playground, nature trails and sports facilities.

■ Where to Eat

 The **Pilot House Restaurant**, ☎ 910-343-0200, at Chandler's Wharf, is in the historic Craig House, which dates from 1870. It overlooks the Cape Fear River and offers spectacular sunset views while dining either inside or alfresco on a covered porch. It strives for innovative, high-quality Southern regional cuisine in an ambiance best described as casually elegant to formal. The restaurant is open for lunch daily from 11:30 to 3, for dinner, Sunday through Thursday, from 5 to 10, and Friday and Saturday from 5 until 11.

Elijah's, ☎ 910-343-1448, 2 Ann Street, is another colorful restaurants at Chandler's Wharf. Its nautical décor and location directly on the Cape Fear River are reminiscent of the building's former life as a maritime museum. And, as it has been designed, it seems as if there are two restaurants in one – an enclosed indoor dining room and an Oyster Bar with outdoor seating on the deck. No matter where you are seated, if your timing is right, you are guaranteed a remarkable view of the sun slipping beneath the horizon, with the *USS Battleship North Carolina*, at peace now, moored on the opposite bank. Elijah's, a good choice either for lunch or dinner, is open daily from 11:30 to 3 and from 5 to 10 – closing an hour later on weekends. Sunday brunch is served from 11:30 to 3. The Oyster Bar is open from 11:30 until midnight.

Deluxe, ☎ 910-251-0333, in the center of downtown at 114 Market Street, is a relative newcomer to the Wilmington scene, but it has very quickly earned a reputation befitting its name and become a favorite. Unlike many trendy restaurants, there is ample space between tables, and the cuisine is certainly novel. Deluxe is open for lunch, Monday through Saturday, from 11:30 to 2:30, for dinner Sunday through Thursday from 5:30 to 10 and Friday and Saturday from 5:30 to 11. Or try the Sunday brunch between 10:30 and 2:30.

Roy's Riverboat Landing, ☎ 910-763-7227, in a very central location on the corner of Market Street and the Cape Fear River, has become a Wilmington tradition. They offer an interesting mixture of seafood and steak dishes. Roy's is open for lunch, Tuesday through Saturday from 11:30 to 4, for dinner seven nights a week between 4 and 10. Sunday brunch is served from 11 to 4 and the Lounge Bar is open to accommodate night owls, generally, until 1 am.

Grouper Nancy's, ☎ 910-251-8009, 501 Nutt Street, is in the old Coast Line Railroad freight terminal on the Cape Fear River. The ambiance indoors is light and airy, and a deck outside overlooking the river provides alfresco dining. It is open for dinner, Tuesday through Saturday, from 5:30 until late.

The **Nuss Strasse Café**, ☎ 910-763-5523, 316 Nutt Street, is on the first floor of the Cotton Exchange, and there are no prizes for guessing its ethnic origin. Owner Caroland McFarlane has been serving authentic German specialties here since 1985. Adding to the ambiance are old brick walls, exposed rafters and comely waitresses in traditional German costume. This is about as close to a Bavarian small town inn as you are likely to find this side of the Atlantic.

■ Visitor Information

The main office of the **Cape Fear Coast Convention Bureau** is at 24 North Third Street ☎ 910-341-4030, 800-222-4757, fax 341-4029, e-mail info@cape-fear.nc.us, www.cape-fear.nc.us. Its hours are Monday to Friday, 8:30 to 5; Saturday, 9 to 4; Sunday, 1 to 4. It also operates a Visitors Booth on the downtown waterfront, which is only open seasonally (from April to October) between 9 and 4.

Bald Head Island

Have you been saving your pennies for a tropical vacation? Well, paradise is closer than you might imagine. Just two nautical miles off the southeastern tip of North Carolina, and 25 miles south of Wilmington at the mouth of the Cape Fear River is a semi-tropical island, with miles of pristine beaches and a wealth of exceptional animal and plant life, just begging to be explored.

■ History

Not just a pretty island, its strategic location has endowed Bald Head Island with an interesting history as well. In fact, the abundance of shellfish and fish found in the waters and marshes surrounding the island attracted Native Americans to build a campsite here as early as 300 AD. Many, many centuries later English settlers discovered these natural resources, establishing colonies upstream on the Cape Fear River and on the coast to the southwest. The growth of trading and shipping logically followed, as did the scourge of the day, pirates, who weren't long in discovering that Bald Head Island made for a perfect base. The most famous of these bandits, Blackbeard (see page 187), certainly stopped here on several occasions. A more frequent visitor, however, was a retired British officer from Barbados, Major Stede Bonner. The trademark trick of Bonner, the area's chief pirate, was to position lights along the beaches, thereby luring ships to shore. It was reported that in July and August of 1718 alone he captured 13 ships in that fashion. Ironically, later that year, he ran aground off the island and was captured himself.

In the years leading up to the Revolution, the Cape Fear area, as has been more fully detailed in the *Wilmington and Wrightsville Beach* chapter, was a major supplier of naval stores for the British fleet. So vital were these supplies that during the Revolutionary War the British stationed 5,000 troops on Bald Head Island, first under the command of General Sir Henry Creighton and then under General Charles Cornwallis, to protect their interests. Later, during the Civil War, Confederate forces built Fort Homes along the western edge of the island, with the aim of preventing Union forces from gaining access to, or taking possession of, the Cape Fear River.

What's in a Name?

The treacherous waters of Cape Fear, and the **Frying Pan Shoals**, an area of sandbars extending miles into the Atlantic Ocean from the cape, have profoundly influenced the island's character. In early days, river pilots who lived on the island would stand watch atop the dunes on the south beach. Upon sighting a vessel, they would row out to guide them safely across the sandbars and up the river. Eventually, this traffic wore the dune free of grass, and to approaching vessels it resembled a bald head. Thus the name, Bald Head Island – at least, so the story goes. Later, lighthouses replaced the pilots as the main navigational aids. Three were built on the island: Bald Head Light in 1796, Old Baldy in 1817, and the Cape Fear Light in 1903. In 1882 a lifesaving station was constructed, and by the end of that decade, the population, including lifesaving servicemen, fishermen, river pilots, and lighthouse keepers and their families, had swollen to 150. This intriguing past is recalled to visitors today by way of several carefully restored structures, including light keepers' cottages, a lifesaving station and, most famous of all, Old Baldy.

In 1983 the very prescient George P. Mitchell family, through their Bald Head Island Limited company, purchased the island. They have overseen its development into a tasteful and ecologically aware resort, keeping careful control of all aspects of life on the island and of transportation to, from and around Bald Head Island.

Bald Head Island is very small. It has just two thousand acres, although another 10,000 acres of protected salt marsh creeks and maritime forest have been deeded to the State of North Carolina. There are, however, a surprising number of activities available to guests here, most of them centered around the water.

■ Getting Here & Getting Around

 No cars are allowed on the island, leaving the roads traffic-free and the air as pristine as the beaches. In fact, you couldn't drive if you wanted to. There is no bridge. The only way in is by ferry, operated by **Bald Head Island Transportation, Inc.** from the Bald Head Island Ferry Landing at Indigo Plantation and Marina, off West 9th Street in Southport, North Carolina. When making your plans, set aside ample time to arrive early, driving directly to the baggage area to allow the outfitters plenty of time to get your luggage onto the ferry dollies. Drive your car back to the gated and secure parking lot, where you will pay a daily parking charge. The price of the voyage is $15 per person (round-trip), and the 20-minute voyage to the island is most enjoyable.

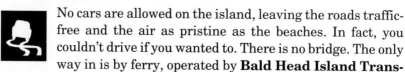 *Remember to pack as though you will be traveling by plane when you go on the Bald Head Island Ferry. In other words, everything should be secured in suitcases, not left loose.*

If you are in luck, statuesque pelicans sitting on wooden poles jutting from the water will form a guard of honor for your arrival.

You need to make an advance reservation for the ferry, and confirm it three days in advance, by calling ☎ 910-457-5003. This not only ensures your place in heavy traffic (especially critical in the high season), it also guarantees you seats on the tram from the harbor to your accommodations.

To get around, use the golf cart provided by the B&B, a bicycle or walk.

■ Sightseeing

Old Baldy Lighthouse

The highlight of a stay on Bald Head Island will almost certainly be a visit to itself. It is open for self-guided tours daily from dawn to dusk, and the observation tower at the top has the most splendid views over the island.

■ Adventures

On Foot

Guests on Bald Head Island are deemed temporary members of the resort for purposes of tennis, croquet, golf and swimming. While entry to the pool is free, you are responsible for the payment of greens or court fees.

Sometimes the simplest plans are best, and a visit to Bald Head Island certainly lends itself to enjoyment of the simple pleasures. Here the hustle and pressures of day-to-day living will seem a distant memory as you leisurely explore the 14 miles of pristine beaches.

On Water

Boating/Sailing

Fishing isn't the only thing that's happening out on the water. Maybe you want to be in charge of your own craft. If so, contact the **marina dockmaster**, ☎ 910-457-7380, or **Island Passage**, ☎ 910-457-4944, and arrange to rent a vessel. If you want a canoe, **Island Wheels** rents 17-footers suitable for a creek safari, with basic instruction provided.

On the other hand, leave the navigation to the professionals at **Winds of Carolina Sailing Charters**, ☎ 910-278-7249 or 612-0222, while you unwind with the winds. Between March 15th and December 1st a number of daily outings are offered aboard their 37-foot sailing boat, the *Stephanie*. The Morning Tour Sail departs at 9:30 am, takes you to local points of interest and includes a narration on Oak Island history. The Afternoon Sail leaves at 1 and, weather permitting, allows time for a swim when it lays anchor off Caswell Beach. Each of these lasts approximately three hours and costs $38 per person, including complimentary beverages. The Sunset/Dolphin Watch Sail sets out at

5:30 pm. If your timing is right, you can enjoy a Full Moon Cruise, available for the five nights before and five nights after this lunar phase. These last two escapades includes a cheese and fruit tray, hors d'oeuvres and complimentary beer, wine and soft drinks for $41 per person. While all of these cruises leave from *Stephanie*'s home slip at Dock B, Southport Marina, those based on Bald Head Island may request, when making reservations, a pick-up at the Island Marina. This will cost an extra $10 per person, but saves both travel and hassle.

Fishing

Of course, a bit of fishing is always a tempting thought. And you can succumb to temptation even if you neglected to bring your equipment with you. Either the **Island Chandler**, ☎ 910-457-7450, or **Island Passage**, ☎ 910-457-4944 (their store), can supply you with whatever you need to go fishing or with crab nets or clam rakes.

Deep Sea Fishing/Backwater

Or maybe you dream of catching a really big fish. If so, call Captain Paul Thompson of **Impulsive Charters**, ☎ 910-457-5331, pager 457-TUNA, fax 699-1234, www.charternet.com/fishers/impulsive, Marina Row, Slip A-11, PO Box 3264, Bald Head Island, NC 28461. Paul operates the 38-foot twin 375 hp turbocharged Bertram, which is equipped with the best in electronic equipment and outfitted with Penn International or Tiagra rods and reels. Choose either a half-day at $475 or a full day at $900. You'll experience some ultra-exciting fishing, in search of giant king mackerel, wahoo, cobia, dolphin, tuna or bluefish. And you may cross paths with some ferocious looking sharks. The really adventurous will want to make the 45- to 60-mile trip out into the Gulf Stream itself, a privilege that will cost you $1,100 for a full day. OK, so it's a tad expensive. But just think of the adventure and excitement, and if you get lucky out there you can live off of the stories and the photographs for a lifetime. Captain Paul also offers trips on a 17-foot Scout flat boat for backwater fishing that may appeal to those who are prone to seasickness on rougher seas. Just give him a call for more details.

Eco/Cultural Adventures

 You can expect to come face-to-face with the wide variety of animals that call Bald Head Island home. Who could fail to be charmed by the cavortings of the omnipresent brown pelicans, a species so recently near extinction? Loggerhead sea turtles also are common, no doubt because of their prolific reproductive habits. Typically, a female will lay over 100 eggs in the dunes each season. Amazingly, the temperature of the sand determines the sex of the hatchlings – warmer sand produces more males and cooler sand produces more females. Try a midnight Turtle Walk. These, and the Alligator and Bird Walks each morning, are led by **Bald Head Island Conservancy**, ☎ 910-457-0089. Blue crabs, so-called because of their brightly colored claws, inhabit the creeks. Take a little more care around the freshwater lagoons, where you might spot an American alligator. Back on land you might come across a gray fox, but are unlikely to meet the plentiful, mainly nocturnal, white-tailed deer. In the warmer months, you may spot the fascinating white ibis, a very impressive wading bird that flies to the island to feed on fiddler crabs in the marshlands.

A good way to acquaint yourself with the flora is a gentle walk along the **Kent Mitchell Nature Trail**. Begin at the marker on the Federal Road, just past its intersection with Muscadine Road, and allow approximately 20 minutes to maneuver through maritime forest, salt marsh and tidal creek. You will find that many of the plant species are identified along the way.

■ Where to Stay

Bald Head Island Management, Inc., manages real estate development and sales, as well as resort and island operations, and offers a wealth of attractive properties for rent, either by the day or the week. If you are in the market for space (multi-bedroom) and privacy, and if money isn't a major consideration, call ☎ 800-234-1666 for information or 800-432-RENT for reservations. The company also owns the Marsh Harbor Inn, which offers a couple of interesting packages for visitors.

The privately owned **Theodosia's – A Bed & Breakfast**, at Harbor Village, on the opposite side of the harbor to the dock, is a better option. Its delightful architectural design, with numerous porches and balconies, fits perfectly in this maritime environment. Inside there are 10 lovely rooms, each with a private bath/shower, cable TV and telephone, and it boasts views out over the harbor, the river or the island marshes from either a private porch or balcony. Following in the family tradition, the son of the owners is an accomplished chef. For an additional $130 he will prepare a gourmet meal for two, which may be taken by the soft glow of candlelight on your private balcony. For this, an advance reservation is necessary. There are other extras as well. Guests enjoy free use of a golf cart and bicycles. Keep in mind, though, that the speed limit on the island is just 18 mph. Bald Head Island is becoming increasingly popular as a shooting location for both movies and television programs, so you never know whom you might run into. ☎ 910-457-6563, 800-656-1812, fax 457-6055, www.theodosias. com. Rates are between $150 and $225 a night.

■ Where to Eat

Bald Head Island Management Inc. has incorporated in its plan a variety of eateries. The most prestigious is the **Bald Head Island Inn**, where patrons can enjoy cocktails and light snacks in the lounge, or a full meal in the dining room. In keeping with the resort atmosphere, dress shorts or dress jeans are acceptable here – but t-shirts, cutoffs and short-shorts are not. The **River Pilot Café and Lounge** is more casual in style as to both cuisine and dress, although shoes and shirts are required. Lunch and dinner are served year-round, and a full breakfast can be enjoyed during the summer. The **Pelicatessen**, found near the pool and also known as the "Peli Deli", and **Eb & Flo's**, a harborside place, are open only seasonally. The latter, an open-air pavilion, features such delicacies as a Carolina steampot of shrimp, clams and spiced sausages. Finally, the **Island Chandler Deli** is integrated into a well-stocked grocery store, and has all of the typical deli delights.

South Carolina

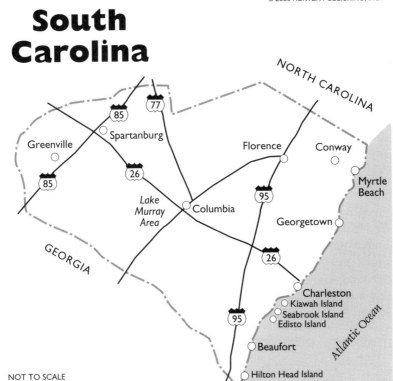

NOT TO SCALE

South Carolina

The leading state of the Old South, and once predominantly agricultural, South Carolina today has become an industrial leader of the New South. A state with a turbulent history, it was a major battleground of the American Revolution and suffered severely during the Civil War, a conflict into which it led the other Southern states in its futile attempt to preserve the aristocracy of the plantation culture. South Carolina was the first state to secede from the Union, and the Civil War's first guns sounded over the harbor at Charleston in the Confederacy's bombardment of Fort Sumter. South Carolina was named first for King Charles IX of France and then for Charles I and Charles II of England.

South Carolina extends over three natural regions: the **Blue Ridge**, the **Piedmont Plateau**, and the **coastal plain**, which is the section we are concerned with. South Carolinians refer to the coastal plain as "**Low Country**." The rest of the state is "**Up Country**."

The coastal plain occupies most of the eastern two-thirds of the state. The coast itself is a land of a thousand tiny bays and inlets, of barrier islands just beyond a hinterland of rich swamplands. Here, since the state's beginnings, the large plantations produced rice, then indigo, then cotton. Now tobacco and truck crops are also grown.

The Low Country is separated from the Up Country by the **fall line**, a line of low hills where the soft rocks of the plain meet the hard rocks of the plateau. It runs diagonally across the state from Chesterfield County to Aiken County. Wherever a river crosses this line, there are rapids and falls. Below the fall line runs a narrow belt of sandy ridges and troughs, covered with scrubby oaks and pines. These are the dunes of an ancient beach. The soil is poor and provides an uncertain living.

History

■ Early Settlements

 South Carolina has a long and checkered history. For a thousand years or more, prior to the arrival of the first European adventurers, the coastal territory and the sea islands had been inhabited by Indians of one tribe or another. The first Europeans to visit were **Spaniards** from Santo Domingo. They put ashore from a single ship in 1521, took on slaves and supplies, but didn't stay for long. A second Spanish expedition arrived the following summer: it, too, sailed away with captured Indian slaves. Then, in 1526, **Don Lucas Vasquez de Ayllon** arrived in Winyah Bay with 500 settlers and established the ill-fated settlement of **San Miguel**. After a dreadful, disease-ridden winter, with frequent attacks by Indians who remembered well the previous Spanish visits, the Spanish were forced to abandon San Miguel, taking with them just 150 survivors of the original 500.

Hernando de Soto, the ultimate adventurer, stopped by in 1540, took more slaves, then headed off again on his search for the legendary lost city of El Dorado. Was there anywhere this man didn't visit?

The **French** arrived in South Carolina in 1562. **Jean Ribault** came here with a group of Protestants fleeing from their Catholic king in France and from the Spanish in St. Augustine. Following an abortive landing on Amelia Island, they sailed into Port Royal Sound and established Fort Charles near what was to become the US Marine Corps' Parris Island Recruit Training Depot. The French settlement lasted all of four years, until the most able Spanish military commander of the 16th century, conquistador **Don Pedro Menendez de Aviles**, routed the garrison, causing great loss of life, and destroyed the fort. Aviles established a new Spanish settlement in the Carolinas and built Fort San Felipe to defend it; they, too, were forced to abandon their attempts at colonization when **Sir Frances Drake**, pursuing his lifelong persecution of all things Spanish, sacked the settlement of St. Augustine in 1586.

■ British Settlements

The **English** arrived in 1670 and established the first permanent settlement. Iit flourished – so much so that by the outbreak of the American Revolution South Carolina had already become a prosperous colony. But before that, in 1729, after long years of dispute between the colonists and the eight Lords Proprietors, Carolina was granted a Royal Charter by King George, became a Crown Colony, and divided itself into northern and southern provinces. Georgia was established in 1731 by General James Oglethorpe, with the intention of acting as a buffer between the English colonies in the Carolinas and the Spanish territories in Florida.

From 1730, South Carolina, now a safe and attractive place to live, experienced an explosion in the population. Settlements sprang up everywhere, from the sea islands to the fall line, and the great plantations continued to prosper, due almost entirely to the employment of slave labor, most of which was imported from the West African nations of Sierra Leone and Senegal. By the 1740s, the slave population in South Carolina had risen to more than 22,000, outnumbering the white population by more than three to one. The slaves cleared swampland, built dikes and canals to protect it, and then planted and harvested the crops. These were good times for the Low Country planters, but the first rumblings of revolution could already be heard echoing across the coastal plain.

■ The American Revolution

South Carolina played a pivotal role in the War of the Revolution. Among the men who represented her in the Continental Congress and signed the Declaration of Independence were Edward Rutledge, Thomas Lynch, Jr., Arthur Middleton, and Thomas Heyward, Jr. Following the signing of the Declaration, a temporary state constitution was drafted in 1776. A second constitution, adopted in 1778, declared the state independent of England.

Many crucial engagements of the American Revolution were fought on South Carolina soil. In fact, more battles and skirmishes were fought here than in any other state. Charles Town was saved from the British in 1776 when Colonel William Moultrie sailed into the harbor; but it was finally surrendered in 1780. South Carolinian patriots such as Francis "the Swamp Fox" Marion, Thomas Sumter, and Andrew Pickens, led small bands of fighters throughout the state. They and others won decisive battles such as those of Cowpens and Kings Mountain.

These were hard times for the people of South Carolina, but prosperity soon returned after the Revolution. The cotton gin had been invented and the Up-Country people grew wealthy raising cotton. Wealthy as they were, however, the Up-Country planters were not happy. They claimed that those in the Low Country were controlling the government. And so, in 1786, legislation was passed to move the capital from Charleston, as Charles Town was called after 1783, to Columbia.

The years that followed brought even more prosperity to South Carolina, but were punctuated by a series of events that brought on the Civil War.

■ The Civil War

By 1800, several Northern states had passed laws abolishing **slavery**, and by January 1808 the importation of slaves into the United States had ended. This, however, did not end the breeding, buying and selling of slaves already within the country. In 1822, a slave revolt planned by Denmark Vesey was discovered before it could be carried out, but it helped create a climate of anxiety among plantation owners. Then, in May 1824 and again in April 1828, Congress passed harsh, discriminatory Protective Tariff Laws that favored the interests of the Northern states over those of the Southern slave-holding states. This caused the president of South Carolina College in Columbia to ask, "Is it worthwhile to continue this Union of States, where the North demands to be our masters and we are required to be their tributaries?" These new laws, even then, were considered by many southerners to be reason enough to declare the Union dissolved. Vice President John C. Calhoun and Senator Robert Y. Hayne, both of South Carolina, led the faction that demanded states' rights and fought the high tariffs framed to protect Northern industries.

In January of 1831, William Lloyd Garrison began publishing *The Liberator*, a newspaper dedicated to the abolition of slavery, and in November 1832 South Carolina nullified the Tariff Acts of 1824 and 1828, declaring itself prepared to secede from the Union if the government decided to use force.

By 1856 events were rapidly approaching a boiling point and the situation was made even worse when Senator Charles Sumner of Massachusetts rose in the Senate and delivered a blistering attack on the South in general, and on Senator Andrew P. Butler in particular. The situation deteriorated even further when representatives from South Carolina walked into the Senate and beat Sumner into unconsciousness.

Things came to a head on October 16, 1859, when abolitionist John Brown, together with a group of five blacks and 16 whites, including his own sons, launched an attack on the Federal arsenal at Harper's Ferry in Virginia. The US Marines sent to put down the insurrection were led by a man who, within just a couple of years, was to become legend: **Colonel Robert E. Lee**. Finally, on December 20, 1860, the following was published in the *Charleston Mercury*:

> "Passed unanimously at 1:15 o'clock, PM December 20, 1860. An Ordinance to dissolve the Union between the State of South Carolina and other states united with her under the compact entitled 'The Constitution of the United States of America.' We, the people of the State of South Carolina, in Convention assembled, do declare and ordain, and it is hereby declared and ordained, that the ordinance adopted by us in Convention, on the twenty third day of May, in the year of our Lord one thousand seven hundred and eighty eight, whereby the Constitution of the United States of America was ratified and also, all acts and parts of Acts of the General Assembly of this State, ratifying amendments of the said Constitution, are hereby repealed; and that the union now subsisting between South Carolina and other States, under the name of United States of America, is hereby dissolved. THE UNION IS DISSOLVED."

South Carolina

And so South Carolina became the first of 11 Southern states to leave the Union. In so doing, it claimed that secession entitled it to all government property within its boundaries, including the Federal military installations at Forts Moultrie and Sumter. The opening shots of the war were fired almost in a holiday atmosphere. Fort Sumter fell to the Confederacy on April 13, 1861. Two days later President Lincoln issued a proclamation that called into service 75,000 militia for three years and in effect declared war on the Confederacy.

■ Reconstruction

South Carolina suffered greatly during the war, and the years of Reconstruction that followed were long and bitter. The plantation system that had brought prosperity to the state collapsed, thrusting it into a long economic depression. The leading landowners lost their property, and the era was marked by military occupation, disenfranchisement of former Confederates, and corrupt government. After its re-admission to the Union in June 1868, however, the state developed steadily.

In 1876, with the support of white militants (called Red Shirts) who intimidated black voters, Wade Hampton, a popular Confederate general, was elected governor. After Hampton's election, the leadership of the old guard planters and merchants was reestablished, until a farmers' movement led by Benjamin Tiliman fought for and won certain rights for small farmers, including provisions for agricultural and vocational education.

The development of industry, which began on a large scale late in the 19th century, was accelerated by an **industrial revolution** that began in the 1920s when many New England **textile mills** relocated to the South. Most of them were attracted by low wages, the lack of unions and the nearness of raw materials. Manufacturing soon became the major industry and has been the key to the state's gradual return to prosperity. Since then, **farming** has improved, and **cattle raising** has become important. The growth of **hydroelectric power** has been rapid, and with it have come new industries. Manufacturing is still the backbone of South Carolina's economy, but the Palmetto State is as famous today for the federal government's nuclear materials plant on the Savannah River as it once was for its cotton plantations and beautiful tropical gardens.

The palmetto has been the emblem on the state's flag as well as the state seal since the late 1700s. It is a symbol of the defeat of the British fleet at Fort Moultrie near Charleston in 1776. The ramparts of the fort were made of palmetto logs.

Getting Here

Coastal South Carolina is served by a major airport at Charleston, and by smaller regional airports at Myrtle Beach, Georgetown and Hilton Head. **I-95** is the main artery north and south. **I-26** provides fast access from the northwest, while **Hwy 17** hugs the coast, providing a scenic route north and south.

How Transportation Developed in South Carolina

In colonial days plantations and towns were built on tidal streams near the South Carolina coast. The planters always had river frontage and a wharf at which boats could moor. Road building came late because nearly all the produce was raised within a few miles of a navigable stream. The Up Country, or interior, had to depend on old **Indian trails**. The first **toll road** was completed between Columbia and Charleston in 1829. Highways were in poor condition until the State Highway Department was organized in 1997.

In 1827 work was begun on a **railroad** from Charleston to Hamburg, a village just across the Savannah River from Augusta, Georgia. For a time the Charleston-Hamburg line, with a 136-mile run, was the longest passenger-carrying steam railway in the world. Its purpose was to divert Up-Country produce from the port of Savannah to Charleston. Service opened on Christmas Day 1830, though the line was not completed to Hamburg until 1833. The first engine used on the line was one of the earliest American-built locomotives, the Rest Friend of Charleston, which came to a violent end when a fireman, irritated by the hiss of escaping steam, sat on the lever controlling the safety valve. The engine blew up, killing him.

Interest in water transportation was revived in the early 20th century. Some of the main rivers were dredged to the fall line. The Intracoastal Waterway was created to provide a protected passageway for small boats along the entire coastal border, and so it still does today.

Major highways running north and south and east and west are complemented by a network of minor roads that provide easy access to all the coastal resorts, towns and sea islands. Public transportation, except in and around Charleston, can be a bit of a problem. So, unless you intend to stay in town, it's best to rely either on your own vehicle or a rental from one of the major companies; all are represented at Charleston Airport, and most at the regionals.

Climate

 The coastal areas of South Carolina are favorites with winter vacationers because of the mild to subtropical climate. Westward and up into the mountains the temperatures dip below zero occasionally and snow may linger for a few days.

Activities

South Carolina's mild climate, inviting seacoast, wooded hills and mountains, and wealth of historic sites offer lots of opportunities for outdoor recreation. The strategic location of each of South Carolina's state parks, especially those in the coastal areas, means that there is at least one within an hour's drive of every home in the state. The National Park Service maintains several areas of historic interest, including Fort Sumter National Monument, Cowpens National Battlefield, Kings Mountain National Military Park, and Ninety Six National Historic Site.

South Carolina is also famous for its magnificent gardens. Many tourists visit Charleston during azalea season, mid-March to mid-April. Not far from the city, Middleton Place Gardens, laid out by slaves in 1741, are the oldest landscaped gardens in the United

States. Even closer are Magnolia Plantation and Gardens and Cypress Gardens. Between Georgetown and Myrtle Beach on the north coast are the Brookgreen Gardens on the site of an old rice and indigo plantation. They were created as an outdoor museum to display the sculpture of Anna Hyatt Huntington and other American sculptors. Among the sculptures displayed in garden settings are works by Frederick Remington and Augustus Saint-Gaudens.

Popular ocean resort areas are Myrtle Beach and Hilton Head Island. Both have large golf and tennis facilities. The sea islands, left to the freed slaves after the Civil War, offer unlimited opportunities for hiking, fishing, nature and bird-watching, and a host of other outdoor adventures.

Fishing, swimming, sunbathing and boating are available at Hilton Head, Myrtle Beach, and the islands of Seabrook, Kiawah and Edisto. Want to try fishing offshore? Deep-sea charter fishing for the major sportfish, tarpon, sailfish, king mackerel, amberjack, barracuda and bonito is excellent, and there are plenty of charter captains to see to your wants and needs.

The Grand Strand

The so-called Grand Strand starts at the Little River on the Atlantic coast near the North Carolina border and runs some 60 miles south to the Santee River. Along with the coastal communities, it also includes several inland towns: Loris, Conway, Andrews and Georgetown. On the coast itself lie Cherry Grove, Windy Hill, Atlantic, Pawley's Island, Murrells Inlet and, of course, Myrtle Beach. The coastal scenery is beautiful almost everywhere, spectacular in some areas. Here, anglers find the action outstanding, golfers do as well, you can go snorkeling and scuba diving, hiking, sailing, swimming, birdwatching and observing turtles. The shopping, too, is exceptional and, for those to whom a grand meal means adventure, there are restaurants galore.

■ Getting Here

By Air

The Grand Strand is served by airports at Charleston and Myrtle Beach.

By Road

From north and south: Highway 17 is the artery that runs the length of the Grand Strand and connects Charleston with Myrtle Beach. It is fed from the west by Highway 501 to the north, and by I-26 to the south, with a number of minor roads in between.

■ Myrtle Beach

History

The Grand Strand, a 60-mile stretch of beach reaching from the North Carolina state line to Georgetown, has its fair share of history. Most of that, though, centers on Georgetown County, to the south, and is described in detail in the Georgetown chapter. We will focus here on the history of the beaches themselves.

Until the turn of the 20th century, the beaches of Horry County were largely uninhabitable due to their geographical inaccessibility and the poor economy. This began to change, albeit slowly, in 1901 when the Burroughs & Collins Company, a timber firm with extensive beachfront land, built the beach's first hotel, the Seaside Inn. Visitors were encouraged to travel to the inn on a new railroad that had been built originally for use in timber transport. The fledgling community was called **New Town** and, as incredible as it now seems, oceanfront lots sold for just $25! What's more, citizens who constructed a house valued at $500 or more were given an extra lot free.

What's in a Name?

New Town, though, wasn't deemed an inspirational name for an up-and-coming resort, so the local newspaper, the *Horry Herald*, held a contest to rename the town. Coincidentally or not, and who will ever know, the winner was Mrs. F. E. Burroughs – yes, you've guessed it, the wife of the founder of Burroughs & Collins. Having noticed the many wax myrtle trees growing wild on the beach, her winning entry was **Myrtle Beach**. And while on the topic of names, it is said that Claude Dunnagan, a gossip and publicity columnist for the weekly *The Myrtle Beach Sun*, originated the name Grand Strand in 1949.

In 1925 a major advance in tourism was made when John T. Woodside, a textile magnate from Greenville, SC, planned an upscale resort called Arcady, at the north end of the beach. This featured the Grand Strand's first golf course, the legendary Ocean Forest Hotel, and was the birthplace of the famous magazine *Sports Illustrated*. In 1936, pleasure boats and commercial shipping began using the newly opened Intracoastal Waterway and, just two years later, Myrtle Beach was incorporated. The Air Force Base, used for training and coastal patrols during World War II, was built here in the early 1940s and remained open until 1993. Myrtle Beach, elevated to city status in 1957, reaped the benefits of the 1960s golf boom – a trend that continues to this day – and the Grand Strand, in turn, became a nationally known resort, with a burgeoning infrastructure to match.

When we first visited Myrtle Beach on our honeymoon in 1975, we found a place with two sides. The downtown area with funfairs and other similar flashy attractions, and North Myrtle Beach with upmarket hotels, plush golf courses and miles of beautiful beaches.

When setting out to research this guide, we realized immediately that Myrtle Beach had grown significantly in size and scope. Even so, we were totally surprised at exactly how much it had grown. Our first clue came when, out of curiosity, we tried to locate the hotel we had stayed in those many years ago, at the time a magnificent new Hilton in North Myrtle Beach. We caught on very quickly that Myrtle Beach had grown so much it had literally swallowed North Myrtle Beach and now stretched nearly to the state line. We eventually found our hotel. It is no longer a Hilton, however, having been bought by the Wyndham group in 1998.

Myrtle Beach Today

Today Myrtle Beach hosts over 13,000,000 visitors annually, has over 490 hotels, with many more under construction, lists approximately 1,500 places to eat, boasts of 102 golf courses, has 46 more miniature golf courses and 11 live entertainment theaters that seat a total of 17,700 people. Adding to this array are other places of entertainment, including a wonderful aquarium, an alligator adventure, a NASCAR Speedpark, a number of water parks, and a zoo – to name a few.

Getting Here & Getting Around

From Charleston or Wilmington, take Route 17 north or south, respectively.

From I-95, exit at Florence, and then take Routes 76/301, 76, 576 and 501 to Myrtle Beach.

A car is the only viable option for getting around.

Visitor Information

The **Myrtle Beach Area Chamber of Commerce**, ☎ 843-626-7444, www.myrtlebeachlive.com, PO Box 2115, 1200 North Oak Street, Myrtle Beach, SC 29578, provides information on the area. There is also a North Myrtle Beach Office, ☎ 843-249-3519, 213 Highway 17 North, North Myrtle Beach, SC 29582, and a South Strand Office, ☎ 843-651-1010, 3401 South Highway 17 Business, Murrells Inlet, SC 29576.

Adventures

On Foot

Aquarium

Ripley's Aquarium, ☎ 843-916-0888 or 800-734-888, 29th Avenue North at Broadway at the Beach, is where you can see sea life in a different way. This 74,000-square-foot aquarium is filled with thousands of fish. At the Dangerous Reef a moving pathway carries you along inside one of the world's longest underwater tunnels, past large sharks, poisonous predators and other beautifully colored fish. It also offers educational experiences for the entire family. It is open Sunday to Thursday, 9 to 9; Friday and Saturday, 9 to 10 pm.

Beaches

The waters are warmed by the Gulf Stream just a few miles offshore, but the beaches are cooled by an ever-present ocean breeze, making Myrtle Beach one of the most popular seaside resorts on the Atlantic coast. Mile after mile of pristine sands provide plenty of space, even on the busiest days, to enjoy the sun and the sea. The boardwalk and connecting streets offer a range of amusements and entertainment second to none. The surf offers all sorts of opportunities for fishing, parasailing, waterskiing, jetskiing and windsurfing. But it's the beaches that attract most people – more than 13 million each year.

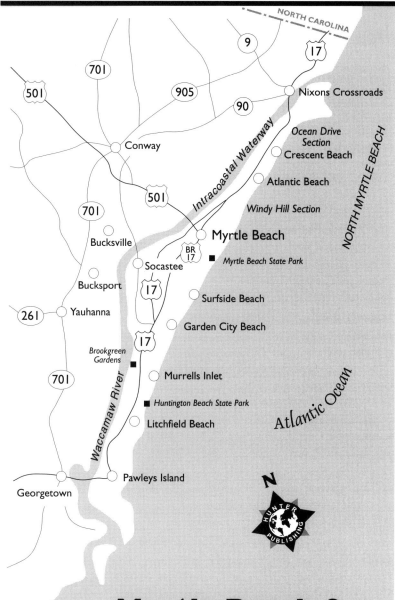

Myrtle Beach &
The Grand Strand

NOT TO SCALE

Golf

With a multitude of courses to choose from, Myrtle Beach is a special place in the world of golf. To list and describe all the courses and opportunities available would require a volume all of its own, and there are plenty of those already available. To get your complete breakdown of Myrtle Beach's extensive golfing opportunities, call the Myrtle Beach Chamber of Commerce, ☎ 800-845-4653, and request the Myrtle Beach Golf Holiday's free 172-page *Golf Vacation Planner*.

Shopping

When you are not frolicking on the miles of glorious beaches, the name of the game in Myrtle Beach is entertainment and shopping. Shopping is a big industry in Myrtle Beach. Although there are only 70,000 permanent residents in the city, it has to cater to millions of visitors each year. So you'll find more shops, stores and malls here than in most cities five times its size.

There are specialty stores in all sorts of diverse places – side streets, oceanfront strip malls, and on almost every corner. The **Myrtle Square Mall**, a 530,000-square-ft complex famous for its gigantic neon clock, has all the usual department stores, a food court, and an arcade, even a carousel. **Briarciffe Mall**, near North Myrtle Beach, opened in the spring of 1986; it's slightly smaller than Myrtle Square, but lacks nothing its bigger sister has to offer. Bigger even than Myrtle Square, however, is the Grand Strand's newest mall, **Inlet Square**, a vast complex of department stores, specialty shops, theaters, restaurants and more. There are also over 200 factory outlet stores in the area. A popular one is **Myrtle Beach Factory Stores**, ☎ 843-236-5100, 888-SHOP-333, www.charter-oak.com/myrtle, at 4635 Factory Stores Boulevard. It has over 50 stores.

Beyond the malls, Pawleys Island has a number of unique beachfront shops and stores housed in buildings that resemble old-fashioned Low-Country cottages. Then there's the **East Coast Outlet Park**, which consists of a movie theater and three large malls offering an incredible array of clothing, shoes and other goods for men, women and children, along with books, sporting goods, pottery, and toys.

Not content with ordinary shopping, enterprising entrepreneurs have created two all-purpose complexes. **Broadway at the Beach**, Highway 17 Bypass, between 21st and 29th avenues, features more than a hundred unique specialty shops, 16 restaurants, including the Hard Rock Café, NASCAR Café, Planet Hollywood, the Palace Theater, Ripley's Aquarium, an IMAX theater, and Celebrity Square – a New Orleans-style night club district. And there is a 23-acre freshwater lake right in the center of it! In 1996 the complex earned the state's top tourism award; a year later it won the state's top honor, the South Carolina Governor's Cup, and it was recently chosen by *Destination Magazine* as "America's Best New Attraction." It moves with the times, too; gift certificates may be purchased on-line at www. broadwayatthebeach.com.

At the other end of Myrtle Beach, in North Myrtle Beach actually, just off Highway 17 to the west, you'll find **Barefoot Landing**, www. bflanding.com. Opened in 1988, and winner of many prestigious awards, this complex is creatively constructed around a 27-acre freshwater lake teeming with wildlife. Over 100 specialty shops, 14 factory-direct stores and 15 or so restaurants line the boardwalks that circle the lake. It is also home to the famous Alabama Theater, the House of Blues, the curious Alligator Adventure and the *Barefoot Princess*, which will take you cruising on the adjoining Intracoastal.

If you have enjoyed feasting on fresh seafood during your stay, why not take some back home? When heading south, or leaving town by way of downtown, stop by the **Strand Seafood**, ☎ 843-448-6511, 803 Highway 17 South. Ed Richardson, the owner, has been in business for 18 years – the longest in town. In addition to a huge selection of fresh fish and other seafood, which he will pack to travel, you will find a variety of spices and beers. Alternatively, if you are based in North Myrtle Beach and will be heading north, make a beeline for **Berry's Food Inc.**, ☎ 843-249-2534, just off Highway 17 on 1122 Sea Mountain Highway, at Little River. Catering to the wholesale and retail markets, this rather large store has, in addition to the expected fish and seafood packed for travel at no extra charge, a really interesting selection of condiments and outdoor cooking gadgets, including many unusual items that would make a great addition to your barbecue.

Theme Parks

If you want to put some snap into your visit, at least metaphorically speaking, stop by the **Alligator Adventure**, ☎ 843-361-0789, 800-631-0789 or fax 361-0742, at Barefoot Landing. This 15-acre park, a reptile zoo, houses one of the largest collections in the world. Besides the over 800 American alligators, including some extremely rare albino American alligators, you will find the Komodo dragon, the world's largest land-dwelling lizard, and an amazing array of reptiles, lizards, turtles, giant snakes (including king cobras that can grow to over 13-feet long), frogs, other amphibian life and exotic birds. Finally, although it may seem incongruous, there are two giraffes that, because they migrate from the park seasonally, are called Spring and Autumn. All of these fascinating creatures may be viewed from a boardwalk that meanders through ponds landscaped with native and exotic plant life. There are interactive exhibits as well. Which one of you will be brave enough to hug a giant python? Rounding out the activities are venomous snake demonstrations and live gator feedings. Alligator Adventure is open daily, but hours vary by season.

Zoo

Waccatee Zoo, ☎ 803-650-8500, Enterprise Rd., is a 500-acre farm that provides a natural habitat for more than 100 species of exotic and domestic animals, including miniature horses that stand no more than 36 inches high, leopards, buffalo, llamas and alligators. There's a nature trail, and a petting zoo where the kids can get to know the smaller domestic animals. Open 10 to 5 daily.

On Wheels

 NASCAR Speedpark, ☎ 843-626-TRAK or 877-626-TRAK, Highway 17 Bypass at 21st Avenue North (across from Broadway at the Beach), is a 26-acre miniature grand prix entertainment complex. Speed is the name of the game here, and you can match times with racing's elite. You can start at the Qualifier and Young Champions tracks, then move up to the France Family 500 or Intimidator outdoor slick track. If you want to try the faster stuff, then head for 5/8-scale Thunder Road or the top-of-the-line D-oval Competitor track. In the SpeedDome you will find the hottest new race simulators, kids rides and 36 holes of challenging miniature golf on race-style courses.

On Water

Cruises

 The ***Barefoot Princess***, ☎ 843-272-7743, Barefoot Landing, Highway 17 North, is a river boat that offers sightseeing, sunset and dinner cruises with entertainment. Call for schedules.

Diving

Scuba Syndrome, ☎ 843-626-DIVE or fax 626-5723, 515-A Highway 501 (at the Sports Corner), Myrtle Beach, SC 29577, is a full-service PADI shop with 17 years of experience and its own 17-foot training pool. The waters off Myrtle Beach, with temperatures ranging from the 80s in the summer to the 70s in the fall and spring, offer beautiful diving on natural shallow and deep live bottom ledges. They are strewn with wrecks, from historical to post-Civil War, World War II and storm wrecks just 30 minutes offshore. Other diving opportunities include spear fishing, photography, fish collecting, exploring history and underwater sightseeing. All gear can either be rented or purchased from the store.

Fishing

As might be expected, there is no shortage of companies offering cruises and fishing adventures in the Myrtle Beach area. If this interests you, contact the **Hurricane Fleet**, ☎ 843-249-5371 in South Carolina and ☎ 910-579-3660 in North Carolina, or fax 249-2416. The fleet (really a fleet and not just one vessel) sails under the control of a professional crew from the Hurricane Fleet Marina in Calabash, North Carolina. Several great fishing opportunities are offered, with a half-day fishing at $26 per adult, sailing at 8 or 1 pm, the most popular. For the more serious among you, Gulf Stream fishing at $60 per person departs at 7 for 11 hours of fishing 40 to 50 miles offshore, and overnight Gulf Stream trips at $125 per person will long be remembered. Prices include fishing license, rod, reel, bait and tackle. There are also a number of charter and specialty trips designed for groups of seven to 10 people and with prices from $475 to $1,200. A more genteel adventure and one that is a little easier on the wallet is the daily Adventure Cruise, which sails at 2 or 4 and costs just $15 per person. All the vessels are designed to accommodate the physically challenged and wheelchair clients.

Water Park

Wild Water Water & Race Theme Park, ☎ 843-238-WILD, www.wild-water.com, on the South Strand, has the area's only Wipeout Wave Pool, as well as the beach's best scary ride, The Dark Hole.

Eco/Cultural Adventures

Myrtle Beach State Park

Located in the heart of the Grand Strand, at 4401 South Kings Highway, Myrtle Beach State Park is one of the most popular public beaches on the East Coast. This 312-acre oceanfront preserve is one of the best-kept secrets and loveliest natural areas in South Carolina. Its beaches are kept in pristine condition. There always seems to be room to stretch out, relax, play in the sand or in the water, or go fishing. The surf is excellent for casting, and there's a fishing pier that provides an even better opportunity to catch dinner. You can take it from pier to picnic grill in a matter of minutes; seafood doesn't come any fresher than that. Park hours are 6 to 10 year-round; the office is open from 9 to 5, Monday through Friday, and from 11 to noon and 4 to 5 on Saturday and Sunday. Myrtle Beach State Park, 4401 South Kings Hwy, Myrtle Beach SC 29575. ☎ 843-238-5325.

Theaters

When the sun goes down you can be certain that the stars will come out, whatever the weather. Myrtle Beach boasts 11 beautiful theaters, with a seating capacity of 22,000.

The man held to be responsible for this galaxy of entertainment is Calvin Gilmore, who, in 1986, opened his show **The Carolina Opry**, ☎ 843-913-1400, in the stunning 2,200-seat theater at the junction of US 17 Business and US 17 Bypass. Now in its 14th season and still going strong, it serves up a combination of country, bluegrass, Western swing, big band and gospel music, with patriotic and show tunes and comedy completing the mix. To this day, Calvin Gilmore himself often appears to sing and play the guitar.

Next door, in a 35,000-square-foot arena, is an entirely different kind of show. **The Dixie Stampede - Dinner & Show**, ☎ 843-497-9700, 800-433-4401 or fax 497-6767, 8901-B Highway 17 Business, owned by Dolly Parton, treats guests to two shows for the price of one. The Dixie Belle (non-alcoholic) Saloon features a pre-show that is a mix of Dixieland music and comedy. The main show, staged by more than 30 cast members and 32 horses with spectacular star-spangled variety and a dazzlingly patriotic finale, presents a new look at the "Old South." Following the show and a four-course meal, patrons participate, by way of friendly contests, in a north/south rivalry. Believe it or not, there are even ostrich races. Admission, including the meal and soft drinks, is $29.99 per person.

In a similarly equine theme, but with 25 rare Andalucian stallions, is the **Medieval Times Dinner & Tournament**, ☎ 843-236-8080, 236-4635, 800-436-4386, www.medievaltimes.com, 2904 Fantasy Way, in the Fantasy Harbor behind Waccamaw Pottery. Once inside The Castle, a 1,300-seat Grand Ceremonial Arena, you will be transported back through a millennium to feast on a four-course banquet and witness a royal tournament where careful attention has been given to the faithful recreation of each chivalrous detail. And fittingly – but not for you we hope – there is a Museum of Torture, with a collection of torture instruments from the Middle Ages. The show, including the feast, costs $32.75 plus tax per person.

On a more serious note, many will want to check out (preferably before you finalize your trip) who is playing at the magnificent **Palace Theater at Myrtle Beach,** ☎ 843-448-9224, 800-905-4228 or fax 626-9659, 1410 Celebrity Circle, Broadway at the Beach. This relative newcomer to the Myrtle Beach scene is easily distinguished by its large cupola dome. The magnificent interior is graced by a luxurious foyer with winding stairs, massive marble columns, gold laced ceilings and a 30-by-75-foot burgundy velvet curtain over the stage (the curtain weighs 5,000 lbs.). The 2,700-seat theater regularly attracts a glittering array of the biggest names and brightest stars in the entertainment world. Recent shows featured Manhattan Transfer, Wayne Newton, Willie Nelson, Julie Andrews, Kenny Rogers and the Bolshoi Ballet. If you are in Myrtle Beach during November or December, look for the Christmas Spectacular, starring the world famous Rockettes from Radio City Music Hall.

Give serious consideration, also, to a night at the 2,000-seat **Alabama Theater,** ☎ 843-845-1646, 800-557-8223, fax 845-5650, www.wildcountry.com. It is at 4750 Highway 17 South, North Myrtle Beach, at Barefoot Landing. Carolina's best-attended theater, it is owned by country music's number-one band, Alabama. This amazing group, named "Artist of the Decade for the 1980s" by American Country Music Awards, has to its credit 42 number-one singles and worldwide record sales totaling over 59 million. Alabama performs here several times throughout the year and their theater also hosts some of the most famous country and western names in the business. During the holiday season the "Christmas in Dixie" show is not to be missed.

The **Gatlin Brothers Theater,** ☎ 843-236-8500, at 2901 Fantasy Way, features the famous country group performing a family-oriented act nightly at 8, Monday through Saturday, and on Wednesday at 3. Times vary according to the season.

Legends in Concert, ☎ 843-238-7827, Highway 17 South in Surfside Beach, is a lot of good, clean fun suitable for all the family. Here, the emphasis is on impersonations. Imitators and look-alikes present impressions of Dolly Parton, Elvis Presley, Michael Jackson and many more. Performances are held Tuesday through Sunday at 8; other days and times according to the season.

The **Eddie Miles Theatre,** ☎ 843-280-6999, 701 Main Street, North Myrtle Beach, is certainly the place for lovers of "The King." Eddie

South Carolina

Miles portrays Elvis at his Las Vegas peak and performs a different selection of Elvis favorites at each performance.

The **IMAX Discovery Theater**, ☎ 843-448-IMAX or 800-380-IMAX, Broadway at the Beach, 21st Avenue North & Highway 17, is the ultimate film experience, and has an ever-changing menu of fantastically realistic movies.

Spas & Fitness Centers

The **Spa at Jordan Marsh Salon**, ☎ 843-448-6750, 411 Broadway (not to be confused with Broadway at the Beach), in downtown Myrtle Beach, offers all kinds of ways to relax.

Susan Taylor, esthetician and owner, has put together an interesting menu of treatments that will appeal to those of you wishing to be indulged for an hour or two, or maybe more. Therapeutic massages cost $35 for a half-hour or $55 for a full hour, and an aromatherapy massage is available for $60. Facials are in the $40 to $60 range, and body masks, either with seaweed or hydrating, cost $80 and $75, respectively. We would suggest, though, that you treat yourself to a Spa Excursion, which begins with a stimulating shower followed by an hour-long massage, manicure, and pedicure, and finishes with a facial – all for just $140.

Where to Stay

The **Yachtsman Resort**, ☎ 843-448-1441, 800-868-8886, fax 626-6261, www.yachtsmanhotel.com, just four blocks from the Pavilion Amusement Park at 1400 North Ocean Boulevard, is an ultra-modern 20-story structure wrapped in mirrored glass. It has 142 luxuriously decorated suites, each with two TVs, kitchenette with refrigerator/ice maker, range, microwave, coffee maker, dishwasher and eating utensils, a garden-sized whirlpool bath and a private balcony. The views from the top suites stretch for miles on the Grand Strand and are simply incredible. Rates most recently ranged from $59 to $190 a night, with surcharges of up to $50 a night during most holidays.

The **Atlantica**, ☎ 843-448-8327, 800-248-0003, www.atlantica-resort.com, 1702 North Ocean Boulevard, Myrtle Beach, was new to Myrtle Beach in 1999 and is within easy walking distance of the Pavilion Amusement areas downtown. It has one- or two-bedroom condos with deluxe furnishings, two TVs and telephones, full kitchenettes with all expected accessories, and oceanfront balconies. Rates range from $53 to $265.

The **Wyndham Myrtle Beach Resort and Arcadian Shores Golf Club**, ☎ 843-449-5000, 800-248-9228, fax 497-0168, www.wyndham. com, 10,000 Beach Club Drive, Myrtle Beach, is well off the main road in a very nice beachfront location with 600 feet of white sand beach. In an impressively styled tower and set around a 15-story atrium lobby, you will find 385 luxurious guestrooms, each with a private balcony and ocean view, cable TV, telephone with voice mail and dataport, re-frigerator, radio alarm clock, in-room safe and shower massager. Rates vary according to four seasons with an oceanfront king-bed room renting for $49 to $179, a one-bedroom suite for $119 to $289, and a two-bedroom suite from $219 to $389.

The **Seawatch Resort**, ☎ 843-918-000, 800-879-5908, fax 918-8599, e-mail info@seawatchresort.com, www.seawatchresort.com, is just north of the Wyndham at 161 Sea Watch Drive. It has glistening twin towerst, with the northern one opened in 1999. This resort hotel of-fers very modern and fully equipped studio, one-bedroom, two-bedroom and three-bedroom condominiums with an array of layouts and views to choose from. Rates vary widely, from $39 to $190, accord-ing to the room chosen and the season. For some of the accommoda-tions there is a weekly minimum stay between June 5th and August 13th, but a 10% discount is given for five- to six-day stays if you arrive on a Sunday. On the other hand, expect to pay a surcharge of $10 to $20 per day on some holiday weekends.

Shore Crest Vacation Villas, ☎ 843-361-3600, 800-361-8141, fax 361-3601, www.shorecrest.com, 4709 South Ocean Boulevard, North Myrtle Beach, literally towers over the beach in this less crowded sec-tion of the Grand Strand. There is a choice between one-bedroom or two-bedroom ocean-view or two-bedroom oceanfront accommodation. Rates are between $59 and $255 a night.

Serendipity an Inn, ☎ 843-449-5268 or 800-762-3229, 407-71st Av-enue North, Myrtle Beach, is an elegant Spanish mission-style com-plex set within private gardens of palmetto trees and bright flowers. And though just 300 yards walk from the beach, family-owned and operated Serendipity is far enough off the beaten path to offer quiet nights and peaceful days. Rates vary, between $45 and $129, by sea-son.

Camping

Barefoot Camping Resort, ☎ 800-272-1790, Highway 17 South, North Myrtle Beach, is open year-round and has a variety of oceanfront and wooded sites with full hookup ca-pabilities. There is also a clubhouse, lazy river, indoor pool and whirlpool, outdoor pool, fitness center, free cable TV, laundry facilities and rental trailers.

Myrtle Beach State Park, ☎ 843-238-5325, has the largest campground in the South Carolina system. There are 350 campsites, rented on a first-come, first-served basis. Each site has water and electric hookups, a picnic table, and is within easy reach of a comfort station with hot showers and restrooms; all facilities are handicapped-accessible. For those campers who like to keep a roof overhead, there are five cabins and two apartments, all fully equipped with linens and utensils for preparing and serving food. The high-season rate is $16 per night; from October 1st through March 31st the rate is $12 per night. The rate for a cabin with two bedrooms is $56 per night, or $306 for the week. A one-bedroom apartment is $40 per night or $210 for the week; two bedrooms will cost you $56 per night or $306 for the week.

Where to Eat

Downtown Myrtle Beach

As Indian restaurants are not yet that popular in most parts of the United States, it was a pleasant surprise to come across the **Taj Mahal**, ☎ 843-916 4-TAJ (916-4825) or fax 445-2900, at 702 North Kings Highway. Both vegetarian and non-vegetarian dishes are freshly cooked on the premises and served to your taste, spicy, mildly spicy or without spice. It is open daily for lunch from 11:30 to 3 and for dinner from 5 to 10:30.

Myrtle Beach

The **Roma Italian Restaurant**, ☎ 843-449-9359, 5815 North Kings Highway, Myrtle Beach, has a colorful history. Since its construction in 1935, the building has been a bordello, speakeasy, and bed & breakfast before, in 1956, being purchased by the Diminich family for use as a restaurant.

The Melting Pot, ☎ 843-692-9003 or fax 692-9004, 5001 North Highway 17 Business, in the Rainbow Harbor Shopping Complex, is an excellent example of this fondue restaurant chain. Choose a Traditional Kirschwasser, Swiss, Cheddar or even a Fiesta Cheese fondue ($9.95 or $10.95), blended tableside and served with French rye and pumpernickel breads, apple wedges, assorted fresh vegetables and your choice of a mushroom salad or chef's salad.

Little River

The Parson's Table, ☎ 843-249-3702 in SC or 910-579-8298, Highway 17 Little River, has earned an enviable reputation. It has received the 1998-99 International Award of Excellence, a Mobil three-star rating and a ranking as the number one historic restaurant in South Carolina, among others. It was named Parson's Table because the main dining room was the original Little River Methodist Church, which was built in 1885. When the congregation moved to a new location, this structure was converted into a community meeting place. Then, upon its purchase in 1978 by Toby Frye, it was moved two blocks south to its present location and converted to a restaurant.

Toby's Lakeside Restaurant & Lounge, ☎ 843-249-2624, Highway 17 Little River, 2½ miles north of the Intracoastal Bridge and Highway 17, offers fine dining in a casually relaxed ambiance with live entertainment and dancing. During happy hour in the bar, between 4 and 8 pm, you can order from a special bar menu and eat your fill of free chicken wings. There is music for dancing here six nights a week.

Breweries are fun places to eat and drink, and at either end of Myrtle Beach you will find two that, while quite different in ambiance, offer great beers and menus that are typical of their genre. The **Liberty Steakhouse Brewery**, ☎ 843-626-HOPS, is at 1321 Celebrity Circle in Broadway at the Beach. At Barefoot Landing, the other shopping and entertainment center at North Myrtle Beach, you will find the **Mad Boar Restaurant & Brewery**, ☎ 843-272-7000, www.madboar.com, at 4706 Highway 17 South.

Theme restaurants, too, although they aren't to everyone's taste, are very popular here at the beach. Most everybody will have heard of the **Hard Rock Café**, ☎ 843-946-0007, and **Planet Hollywood**, ☎ 843-448-STAR (7827), and they are each found in the Broadway at the Beach complex. You will also find the **Official All Star Café** here, ☎ 843-916-8326, open from 11 to 2 am, daily; and the **NASCAR Café**, ☎ 843-946-RACE, which will be lapped up by the ever-increasing number of lovers of that sport.

You would have to ride through Myrtle Beach with blinders on to miss the proliferation of signs advertising a Calabash-style, all-you-can-eat seafood buffet. These places are, for the most part, family-oriented. Calabash itself, rather grandly self-styled as The Seafood Capital of the World, is a very small town at the southernmost point in North Carolina and just a few minutes from North Myrtle Beach. Located on the river, its docks are home to numerous fishing boats

South Carolina

who bring ashore bountiful supplies of fish, shrimp and crabs. The numerous local restaurants then serve the catch Calabash-style – copious amounts of it, lightly breaded and fried, along with French fries, coleslaw and hush puppies. More than one restaurant makes claim to being "The Original," but it is anyone's guess as to which one really is. That said, if you want to experience this local phenomenon, one establishment is pretty much the same as another.

Surprisingly, there aren't too many beachside bars or cafés, but one you won't want to miss is the suitably named **Bummz Beach Café**, ☎ 843-916-9111, at 2002 North Ocean Boulevard. Here, you will find a lively, engaging, and casual atmosphere, with typical bar food and drinks served either inside or on the vast beachfront deck.

■ Georgetown

History

 Native American Indians were the earliest inhabitants of the tidelands in this area, living nomadically, fishing from the ocean and inland waters and hunting on the forested land. But few reminders exist today of that era, with the exception of Indian names such as Pee Dee, Wee Nee, Waccamaw, Winyah and Santee. The first Europeans, under the leadership of Spaniard Lucas Vasquez de Ayllon, are thought to have arrived around 1526 and founded a colony in the Winyah Bay. Within a year, though, the twin threats of Indians and disease had forced them to abandon the site. Over a century later, the first permanent English settlers arrived and set up business trading with the Indians. In 1721, Prince George, later to become King George II, declared the territory a royal province and land was granted to the settlers for the asking. The history of Georgetown proper began in 1729, when Elisha Screven founded George Town, named after King George II, laying out, across 174½ acres, a five-block-by-eight-block grid that he subdivided into 220 lots. Thus, Georgetown is the third oldest town in South Carolina, falling behind only Charleston and Beaufort.

George Town quickly became a thriving seaport, with the main source of business being "naval stores" such as pitch, turpentine, resin and timber, all products taken from the numerous local pine trees. Business, though, was impeded by the fact that all foreign exports and imports, by decree, had to pass through Charleston, where duties and freight were paid. This was a particular source of aggravation to the George Town citizenry, whose town had both a port and a navigable ocean inlet. A petition for relief was made directly to the King of England, who declared George Town an official port of entry in 1732 and forthwith dispatched to the town a King's "Collector of Customs."

Indigo Trading

A faraway European dispute between English, French, Spanish and Portuguese traders left England without a source for the much-prized royal blue dye indigo – a turn of events that led to untold riches for George Town. The indigo plant was indigenous to the surrounding area and, in fact, grew wild along the coastal plains. It didn't, therefore, take long for local planters to realize the huge profits that could be made through its cultivation. Because blue is the most difficult color to produce in a dye, indigo was highly coveted, and the George Town County variety produced not just one but three fine colors known as copper, purple and fine flora. Trade was so profitable that an aristocratic society developed around indigo plantation owners, whose wealth rivaled that of European royalty. These planters formed the Winyah Indigo Society, and the grand hall that they built still stands as a monument to this era. The Revolutionary War, however, brought greater changes to George Town. The subsidy by Britain to indigo farmers, which began in 1742, was, of course, withdrawn subsequent to that conflict and the lifestyle it had fostered collapsed shortly thereafter. Wild indigo plants, though, still bloom, undaunted, every spring, more than two centuries after the industry's demise.

Georgetown Patriots

On the subject of the Revolution, the area wasn't short of patriots. Thomas Lynch, Jr., one of George Town's most powerful planters, was among the first to sign the Declaration of Independence. His home, **Hopsewee**, a combination of the names of the Hop and See Wee tribes, can be visited, but unfortunately for visitors, only during the week. Another planter, Francis Marion, the legendary "Swamp Fox," harassed the British endlessly with his followers until they abandoned George Town in 1781. A decade later, in 1791, on his famous tour of the Southern states, President George Washington acclaimed these heroes from the steps of the Masonic Lodge in George Town. It was shortly thereafter, in 1798, that the town's name was changed to its present form, Georgetown.

South Carolina

Rice Production

Local geographical conditions, a network of tide-controlled freshwater rivers and rich marshy areas, were soon found favorable for cultivating rice. The profitability of that crop came to rival that of its predecessor, indigo, though it would itself fall afoul of another war. Rice production was extremely labor-intensive and, of course, slaves supplied the labor. In fact, throughout the 1880s the slaves comprised as much as 85% of the total population. Over 40,000 acres were cleared and more than 780 miles of canals dug as rice plantations cropped up across the region. Each plantation was serviced by, on the average, 200 to 500 slaves, with the largest utilizing over 1,000.

By the 1840s nearly half the rice eaten in the United States was grown around Georgetown. The local variety, Carolina Gold, gained such popularity that Georgetown exported more rice than any port in the world, sometimes as much as 56,000,000 bushels each year. Affluence came with such success, and the planters and their families led a life of extreme elegance in plantation mansions. After the crops were harvested, they would journey to equally opulent homes in Charleston, for the "social season" in February. In the summer, they would retreat from the coastal heat to homes on Pawleys Island and Litchfield Beaches, which became the first resort area in America. The romance of those days has been recreated in such movies as *Gone With The Wind* and *Old South*.

The scourge of the Civil War physically destroyed much of this lifestyle and the liberation of the slaves sounded the death knell for the rice industry. Vicious hurricanes in 1893 and in the early 20th centurydamaged the fields, and there simply wasn't the manpower available to repair them. The last commercial harvest was brought in just after World War I in 1919.

Industry

The natural resources of the Georgetown area, abundant forests and plentiful water, supplied the economic rescue. **Lumber mills** took over the inheritance and, by 1914, the Atlantic Coast Lumber Company was the largest producing plant on the East Coast. That company did not survive the Depression of the 1930s, but in 1936 the International Paper Company built a factory that, within six years, became the largest kraft paper mill in the world. The management of International Paper took on the responsibility for preservation and renewal of local agricultural forests, which still thrive today. So, while the factory silhouette does little to improve the skyline of an otherwise charming small town, in concert with commercial fishing and other small industries, it has fostered a successful business climate to Georgetown. Also contributing to the economic and social health of the area in recent years has been an influx of retirees and vacationers who have come to appreciate its charms.

Murrells Inlet, on the Waccamaw Neck, is a nearby town that shouldn't be overlooked. This small fishing village, known as the "Seafood Capital of South Carolina," has a fascinating history. It was once an Indian fishing ground. Later, it was a port of entry during the Revolutionary and Civil Wars and often provided a haven for pirates.

Getting Here & Getting Around

From the north or south, **Route 17** is the best option.

From I-95, exit at Manning, then follow **Route 521** east to Georgetown.

This area is so widespread that anything other than a car for getting around is impractical.

Visitor Information

Georgetown County Chamber of Commerce, ☎ 843-546-8436, 800-777-7705, fax 527-9866, www.myrtlebeachlive.com/tidelands, PO Box 1776, Georgetown, SC 29442.

There is also a visitor information center on Highway 17 at Pawley's Island.

Sightseeing

Historic Area

The four-by-eight block grid, originally laid out by Elisha Screven and now listed in its entirety on the National Register of Historic Places, is an excellent place to begin. Within the area bounded by **Wood**, **Church**, **Meeting** and **Front streets**, the latter running parallel to the Sampit River, there are many fine examples of pre-Civil War homes and public buildings. These clearly reflect the wealth that indigo and rice once brought to this still-attractive town.

On Prince Street, between Orange and King, you will find the home of **Joseph Hayne Rainey**. In Georgetown, even in pre-Civil War times, slaves could purchase their freedom, and that is what the parents of Joseph Hayne Rainey were able to do. He went on to become a citizen of some prominence and was the first Black American to sit in the House of Representatives, serving from 1870 until 1879.

Not to be missed, either, on the corner of Canon and Prince Streets, is the **Winyah Indigo Society Hall**. Dating from 1857 this housed the society formed in the 1740s to promote indigo.

Visitors, for the most part, are relegated to appreciating the homes, now privately owned, from the exterior. An exception is made, however, during two occasions each year. The Women of Prince George Winyah Parish sponsor **Annual Plantation Tours** on one Fridayand Saturday at the end of March. These tours have been held for over 50 years and take in many of the nearby plantation houses, which are also normally out of bounds to visitors. Houses are open from 9:30 to 5 daily, histories and maps are provided with the tickets, and trained hostesses are happy to answer any questions. Visitors are also invited to tea at the Winyah Indigo Society Hall each afternoon. In traveling between sites you will be responsible for your own transportation; only cars and vans are allowed in consideration of low-hanging oak limbs and soft roadbeds. Be advised also that ladies must wear low-heeled shoes – for their own comfort and for the protection of the old floors – and no photographs may be taken inside the houses. For more information, precise dates and ticket prices, write to Annual Plantation Tours, PO Box 674, Georgetown, SC 29442, or contact Mrs. Perry R. Collins, PO Box 1476, Georgetown, SC 29442, ☎ 843-527-2603.

Later in the year, usually the second Saturday in December between 9:30 and 4:30, the Mental Health Association in Georgetown County sponsors a **Christmas Tour Of Homes**. Contact them directly for details of this event: MHAGC, PO Box 2097, Georgetown, SC 29442; ☎ 843-546-8101 (call on Monday or Wednesday between 9 and 11 am).

Cemetery

At 400 Broad Street is the **Beth Elohim Cemetery**, which was established by South Carolina's second oldest Jewish community around 1772. Although it is not generally open, you can see from the sidewalk that the older graves, set in the center, face Jerusalem to the east, while the newer ones are laid perpendicular to the cemetery's borders.

Church

The **Prince George Winyah Episcopal Church** congregation was established in 1734. The first service in the present building, constructed of red ballast brick transported from England, was held in 1747. It was occupied by troops during the Revolutionary War, when it is said that British troops quartered their horses in the box pews, and during the Civil War, when it was badly damaged. When the church was subsequently rebuilt, English stained-glass windows rescued from a decimated plantation chapel were installed.

Museums

The **Rice Museum**, ☎ 843-546-7423, www.the-strand.com/rice, at the intersection of Front and Screven Streets, by Lafayette Park, is easy to find. The structure itself, originally built in 1842 on the site of the original wooden market which dated from 1788, has become symbolic of the town by virtue of a distinctive bell tower and clock that was added three years later. Also used as a market during the 18th and 19th centuries, this site was where the town council, at the close of the Civil War, surrendered to Federal troops. Since 1970, the building has been dedicated to giving visitors an understanding of the rice and indigo production that brought such wealth to the district. An extension to the museum, **Kaminski Hardware**, next door at 633 Front Street, was built around 1842. It was upon its upper level and towards the end of the Civil War, that Captain Daggett, a Confederate commander of coastal defenses, built the powder keg torpedo that sank the *Harvest Moon*, the only Federal flagship sunk during that war. Its remnants can still be seen at low tide at Belle Island on Winyah Bay. The building now holds local art exhibitions. The museum complex opens Monday through Saturday from 9:30 to 4:30, and there is a small admission fee.

Not too far away, on a bluff overlooking the river at 1003 Front Street, you will find the **Kaminski House Museum**, ☎ 843-546-7706. Dating from pre-Revolutionary War times this has, in its over 200-year history, been home to an eclectic array of people – including the woman for whom it was built, Magdalene Elizabeth Trapier Keith, the aforementioned Captain Daggett and three of the city's mayors. Among these, Harold Kaminski and his wife Julia, who purchased the house in 1931, took great pride in furnishing their home with a wonderful array of antiques collected by Harold's mother, Rose Baum Kaminski. Upon her death in 1972, Julia bequeathed the home and grounds to Georgetown, with the proviso that it should become a his-

South Carolina

toric house museum. It is open for tours Monday through Saturday from 10 to 4 and Sunday 1 to 4.

Adventures

On Foot

 Few will want to leave Georgetown without exploring the many shops and restaurants dotted along **Front Street**. Quite enjoyable also is a stroll along the 1,100-foot boardwalk, known as the **Harborwalk**, which runs alongside the Sampit River.

Shopping

Seafood lovers know that the fresher the catch, the tastier the dish. So, why not take back home a delicious seafood dinner. On your way out of town, stop by **Murrells Inlet Shrimp & Fish Co.**, ☎ 843-651-1730 or fax 651-2027, Murrells Inlet, where owner Rick Baumann likes to boast that all of his seafood was swimming just the day before.

Hunting

Duck hunting, too, is an option, at least during the season that runs for four days over Thanksgiving and 46 days between early December and late January. **Mansfield Duck Hunting Club** will take you on an excursion where you get to keep what you shoot. They are at ☎ 843-546-6961, 800-355-3223, fax 546-6961, www.mansfieldplantation.com, Route 8, Box 590, Highway 701 North, just five miles from the center of Georgetown. The fee is $225. At the close of your trip you may be able to stock your freezer with both duck and fish.

The **Back Woods Quail Club**, ☎ 843-546-1466 (day), 527-8429 (night), www.backwoodsquailclub.com, 647 Hemingway Lane, Georgetown, SC 29440, is actually on Old Morrisville Plantation with over 15,000 acres of open fields, timber lands and wooded areas. It is about 30 minutes from the town of Georgetown.

Deer hunting is available from September 1st to January 1st. You use tree stands with your preference of weapon, at a cost of $275 per person per full day.

Quail hunting is available from October 1st to March 20th. An experienced guide accompanies each party – a maximum of three guns with only two shooting at any one time – with trained dogs supplied or use your own if you wish. Full-day hunts are either for 30 birds per person per day at $400 per person, or 50 birds per person per day at $500 per person. Half-day hunts are for either a 30-bird hunt at $330, a 50-bird hunt for $430, a 75-bird hunt at $575 or a 100-bird hunt at $700. All rates are per person, with the price including guide and dogs and dressing and packaging of birds.

Turkey hunting takes place in the spring and is dependent upon South Carolina laws, but usually runs during the month of April, and costs $350 per person per full day.

All full-day hunts include guide and dogs; dressing and packing of birds; breakfast, lunch and dinner; a night's lodging and an open bar.

If you are interested in sporting clays, courses of either 50 or 100 shots are available and cost $17 and $30, respectively.

On Water

Diving

Scuba Express, ☎ 843-357-DEEP (3337), Murrells Inlet, runs a PADI basic open water course as an introduction for a new diver to the underwater world. They also hold basic open water dive classes and offshore dives at one of the many local dive sites. Call for prices and dates.

Fishing

It is natural in such a setting for thoughts to turn to fishing. For those so inclined, we are happy to introduce **Salt Marsh Guides, ☎** 843-650-4469, owned and operated by Captain Jim Gnozzio, an Orvis-certified guide and the only USCG-licensed guide between Little River and Georgetown. He pilots a 1997 118-foot DuraCraft backwater flats boat equipped with state-of-the-art electronics and fishing tackle. His specialty is shallow-water fishing in Murrells Inlet, Winyah Bay, and the Sampit and Waccamaw rivers. According to the season, you will be in search of flounder, winter trout, Spanish or king mackerel, black drum, bluefish, spots, sharks, spot tail bass, freshwater bass or catfish. Trips of approximately five hours cost $155 for one person and $185 for two. If, however, you fancy simply a scenic or photo-op trip, Captain Jim will accommodate up to four people at the cost of $30 per hour.

South Carolina

In the Air

Parasailing

Parasail Express, ☎ 843-357-777, Murrells Inlet, has an early-bird flight at 6 for $35 per person; at other times throughout the day the price is $45 per person. Special sunset cruises, departing at 8 pm, cost $20 per person. The minimum weight requirement is 80 lbs and the maximum 300 lbs.

Eco/Cultural Adventures

Gardens & Art

You should definitely set some time aside to visit the absolutely amazing **Brookgreen Gardens**, ☎ 843-237-4218, fax 237-1014, e-mail info@brookgreen.org, PO Box 3368, Pawleys Island, SC 29585.

Brookgreen Gardens owes its existence to the intellectual and philanthropist Archer Huntington (1870-1955) – heir of late 19th-century transportation multi-millionaire Collis P. Huntington and his wife, Anna Hyatt Huntington (1876-1973). Prior to their marriage in 1923 and afterwards, she was a sculptress of no little renown. In 1930, for the sake of Anna's health, they traveled to the South Carolina Low Country in search of a suitable property. In fact, they found four, which together comprised 9,000 acres between the Waccamaw River and the Atlantic Ocean. Brookgreen, Laurel Hill, Springfield and the Oaks had been thriving rice plantations up until the time of the Civil War, but had since fallen into disrepair.

Envisioning a quiet retreat from life's hectic pace, they set about fashioning a sanctuary where monumental works of art could be displayed within a sculpture garden that would be etched out of this natural wonderland. They used a magnificent allée of 200-year-old live oaks as the centerpiece for a butterfly-shaped plan of informal connecting gardens, thus creating a 300-acre natural gallery, the first public sculpture garden in the United States.

Brookgreen's theme became American figurative sculpture, including human and animal forms, in a naturalistic style. Not surprisingly, the works of Anna Hyatt Huntington, then recognized as one of the premier women sculptors in the world, are the most numerous, but from the gallery's inception the Huntingtons acquired works by their artistic friends and other leading artists of the period, with the concentration being on works from about 1880 forward. Since the

Huntingtons' deaths, the collection has been steadily increased, always keeping to the figurative tradition. In fact, some of the earlier works now on display are the more recent acquisitions. Today, there are even several pieces from the Neoclassical style, a school in the earliest traditions of American sculpture, which had its beginnings around 1825. Interestingly, American Neoclassicists, in pursuit of their art left, the United States to live in Italy. There they studied the great collections, were able to obtain beautiful white marble from local quarries, and found models willing to pose in the nude, all of which were unavailable in their homeland.

Brookgreen's collection now exceeds 700 sculptures, created by nearly 250 of the most influential American figurative artists of the last 130 years. The plant collection, worthy of attention in its own right, includes approximately 2,000 species and subspecies of plants, both native and adapted to the Southeastern United States. In sum, no matter your tastes, there will be plenty to please.

Brookgreen Gardens is also a wildlife sanctuary protected by the laws of South Carolina. As it is situated along the Atlantic Flyway, the variety of feathered visitors is especially wide during the spring and fall migrations. As many as 194 species of birds have been spotted here. It also contains a Wildlife Park where, within the 50 acres open to the public, are the Cypress Aviary, inhabited by snowy egrets, night herons, white ibis and other species, the Raptor Aviary, with birds of prey, an Otter Pond, an Alligator Swamp, a Fox and Raccoon Glade and a White-Tailed Deer Savannah.

Brookgreen Gardens, on the National Register of Historic Places and since 1992 designated a National Historic Landmark, offers a number of educational, informative and enjoyable programs throughout the year, many of which are free. If you schedule your trip here for a Sunday, you can take a 50-minute tour on *The Springfield*, a 48-foot pontoon boat. This excursion explores the freshwater creeks and abandoned rice fields at Brookgreen and introduces visitors to the rich animal environment of the Waccamaw River, including reptiles, amphibians, birds, mammals and insects. Maybe you will also catch a glimpse of the very unusual star-shaped chimney of the old Laurel Hill Rice Mill that soars 100 feet above the banks of the Waccamaw.

If you decide to visit on a weekend between Thanksgiving and January 1st, or on any day during Christmas Week, you are in for a treat. At those times, seated in a romantic horse drawn carriage, you will be regaled with a guide's tales of daily plantation life and holiday traditions. The rides conclude at the Old Kitchen, where a glowing fire and a glass of warm cider await you.

South Carolina

The gardens are open daily, with the exception of Christmas Day, between 9:30 and 4:45, with special summer hours, from mid-June to early September, of 9:30 to 4:45 on Sunday and Monday and 9:30 to dark, Tuesday through Saturday.

Kayaking

If you want to get a better perspective of the ecological system here in the Tidelands of Georgetown, then contact **Black River Expeditions**, ☎ 843-546-4840, at 21 Garden Avenue, Georgetown, just three miles north of town on Highway 701. They operate a naturalist-guided half-day tour, taking four hours and costing $40 per person, in an easily manageable, stable river kayak. You will travel through the cypress-tupelo swamps, old hand-dug canals and more open waterways, passing a variety of wildlife, including ducks, owls, alligators and numerous birds. You may catch sight of bald eagles, wood storks, the elusive swamp canary or a few sea turtles. If you have a shorter tour in mind, then from mid-April to Labor Day look for the Evening Tour, which lasts just 1½ hours and costs $15 per person.

State Park

Close to Murrells Inlet, and open seven days a week, is **Huntington Beach State Park**, ☎ 843-237-4440, www.prt.state.sc.us/sc, a hidden paradise in its own right. Among its many attractions is a 500-foot-long, handicapped-accessible boardwalk, which serves equally well as a platform for crabbing or wildlife observation. If you are a bird fancier, this is definitely the place to be; over 280 species having been recorded in the park. Swimmers will enjoy one of the state's best beaches, where shells, including the official state shell known as the Lettered Olive, and sharks' teeth can often be found. But stay out of the water when you venture near the freshwater lagoon unless you want a face-to-face meeting with one of the resident alligators. A series of programs and activities will bring the natural phenomena and Low Country history to life. These are held daily, with some scheduled for the evening hours, but we suggest you contact the park before you set out, to see if there is one that suits your tastes. Don't forget historic Atalaya, where Anna Hyatt Huntington created many of her famous works, most of which are to be found in Brookgreen Gardens, just across Route 17 from the park.

Where to Stay

Georgetown

 Alexandra's Inn, ☎ 843-527-0233, 888-557-0233, fax 520-0718, www.alexandrasinn.com, 620 Prince Street, is situated in the heart of Georgetown within a property that dates from the 1880s. A comprehensive renovation has restored the home to the style of that era, with pine floors, 11-foot ceilings and a fireplace in each room. The hosts, Sandy (Alexandra) and Rob Kempe, see their home as resembling "Tara," the home of Scarlett in the movie *Gone with the Wind* and have named each of the five guest rooms after a character in that story and decorated them likewise. Rates range from $95 to $195.

The **Mansfield Plantation Bed & Breakfast Country Inn, ☎** 843-546-6961, 800-355-3223, fax 546-6961, www.mansfieldplantation. com, Route 8, Box 590, Highway 701 North, just five miles from the center of Georgetown, offers an intriguing combination of accommodations and activities. Situated on the Black River and surrounded by a naturalist's paradise of 900 private acres, the stage is aptly set as guests approach this 275-year-old plantation house via an avenue of Spanish moss-draped live oaks flanked by slave cabins. Inside, in true antebellum style, visitors can experience the charms of a bygone era. The accommodations themselves are housed in three separate and historic guesthouses. Each of the eight rooms features private entrance, classical décor, fireplace and full private bath. They rent for between $95 and $115 a night.

The **King's Inn at Georgetown, ☎** and fax 843-527-6937, 800-251-8805, e-mail kingsinres@aol.com, www.bbonline.com/sc/kingsinn, is located at 230 Broad Street. Benjamin King, the prominent owner of Georgetown Rice Mill, erected this four-square Federal-style house in 1825, and it served as his residence until he died in 1854. It 1857, the property was deeded by King's trustee to Samuel T. Atkinson, a politically prominent citizen who would become a delegate to the secession convention. It was he who commissioned the distinctive double piazzas across the front of the house and adorned the interior with elaborate plaster moldings and ceiling medallions. Such grandeur is not easily overlooked, especially by one's enemies. As one of the largest and most modern in Georgetown, the home was sequestered by the Union forces' commander who used it as home and headquarters during the Civil War. Subsequent to that conflict, it was the Elks' home, then a boarding house prior to its purchase in 1926 by Mrs. Lyde Whitton, who enclosed the back porches for apartments. The Prince

George Episcopal Church procured the property in 1962 for use as offices and Sunday school rooms, selling it to a private owner 26 years later. The present owners, Marilyn and Jerry Burkhardt, envisioned the old home as a magnificent bed & breakfast and acquired it for that purpose in October of 1993. Rates are $89 to $139 per night.

Pawleys Island

The **Litchfield Plantation – A Country Inn Resort**, ☎ 843-237-9121, 800-869-1410, fax 237-1041, www.litchfieldplantation.com, PO Box 290, Pawleys Island, is a member of the Small Luxury Hotels of the World group. In fact, according to a recent Zagat survey, the Litchfield Plantation was given the highest rating of "excellent," qualifying it to be included in the "Top 50 US Inns and B&Bs" list. On 600 acres of a 1750s South Carolina coastal rice plantation, this extraordinary retreat offers every facility possible for the most delightful stay. There is much more to recommend the Litchfield Plantation than its guestrooms, however. The Carriage House Club presents distinctive gourmet Low Country and continental cuisine prepared by an award-winning chef, and an equally impressive wine list. The large freeform heated pool complex features a cabana that provides comfortable changing facilities; and two tennis courts are adjacent to the Carriage House Club. In addition there is a private freshwater marina, linked to the Intracoastal Waterway, which is home to the plantation's 56-foot yacht, *Arbitrage II*. Just a short distance away from the mansion and on the oceanfront is the Beach Club House. A three-story contemporary structure of glass and bleached cypress with dressing areas and showers on the ground floor, it has a second floor breezeway with kitchen facilities for enjoying a casual bring-your-own lunch or dinner, and a classier third floor that may be reserved for special occasions. Rates range from $150 to $450 a night.

Pawleys Pier Village, ☎ 843-237-4220 or fax 237-9874, Pawleys Island, has a most delightful location on the oceanfront surrounded by the 18th-century ambiance of the oldest beach resort on the East Coast. It has 54 two- and three-bedroom condominiums furnished in an elegantly modern style and each equipped with kitchen, washer/dryer, and private balcony overlooking a large pool and the Atlantic Ocean. During most of the year rentals are by the week only. If, however, you are planning a trip in the off-season – and that can sometimes be as attractive as the summer – give Pawleys Pier Village a call, inquire about vacancies, and ask for a rate.

Camping

Huntington Beach State Park is also one of South Carolina's premier camping parks. Facilities include 127 campsites, all with water and electric hookups, as well as picnic tables, and access to modern comfort stations with hot showers and restrooms. There are four small picnic shelters with tables and grills, a playground for the kids, lots of space on the beach for swimming, sunbathing, relaxing and fishing, nature trails and a boardwalk, plus a park store where you can buy at least some of the essentials. But the nearest town is only three miles away, so restocking is not a problem. The rate per night is $15. ☎ 843-237-4440.

Where to Eat

Georgetown

The Rice Paddy, ☎ 843-546-2021 or fax 546-0211, 819 Front Street, has a new location on Georgetown's waterfront and a reputation as one of the area's finest restaurants. The Rice Paddy is open for lunch Monday to Saturday from 1:30 to 2:30 and dinner on the same days between 6 and 10 pm. Reservations are suggested.

The River Room Restaurant, ☎ 843-527-4110, is at 801 Front Street on the Boardwalk. It has river views, a decidedly casual atmosphere and a reputation for serious seafood – particularly chargrilled fish. The River Room is open Monday through Saturday, with lunch served from 11 to 2:30 and dinner served from 5 to 10 pm.

Pawleys Island

Frank's Restaurant, ☎ 843-237-1581, on Highway 17 "at the red light," was once a grocery store but has graduated to prepared food. Expect dinner by candlelight in an intimate setting with a comfortable ambiance. Grilled dishes are prepared over oak on a wood-burning grill. The wine list is notably extensive. Frank's is open for dinner Monday through Saturday from 6 to 10 pm, with the bar opening two hours earlier.

Murrells Inlet

There are restaurants in abundance here – one on almost every block. And, as they are predominantly seafood specialists, the choice is yours to make. But we will recommend one establishment that is quite different from its cohorts.

Bovine's Wood Fired Specialties, ☎ 843-651-2888, 3979 Highway 17 Business, Murrells Inlet, with pretty water views, is different indeed. Only aged Angus beef and the freshest fish are used in the entrées. Cooked on the wood-fired grill using mesquite and charcoal for a truly unique flavoring, these range between $13.95 to $21.95. For a more casual meal, specialty pizzas emerge piping hot and temptingly aromatic from Bovine's famous custom-built wood burning brick oven, which burns oak and mesquite for flavoring. These Italian delights are reasonably priced at $6.95 to $8.95.

Garden City

The **Gulfstream Café,** ☎ 843-651-8808 or fax 357-2675, 1536 South Waccamaw Drive, uniquely among those on the Grand Strand, affords diners a view of the Atlantic Ocean on one side and of Murrell's Inlet on the other. This is a pleasant place to share cocktails and conversation – at the upstairs bar or on the deck while enjoying nightly live entertainment. Opening hours are 4 to 10 Tuesday through Thursday, with the closing hour extended a half-hour later on Friday and Saturday evenings.

Visitor Information

 Of course, there are numerous other places of interest in this fascinating historic district. The best way to learn about these, and many other things as well, is to pick up some brochures at the **Georgetown Chamber of Commerce,** ☎ 843-546-8436, 800-777-7705, www.myrtlebeachlive.com/tidelands, at Front and King Streets, open 9 to 5 daily.

Charleston

The name Charleston evokes visions of the grandeur and graciousness of bygone ages. Even today, few of the 20th century's more garish extremes have been allowed to distract from the beauty of this city, whose considerable history cloaks it in civility and charm.

■ History

The 17th Century

 Although it is known that Native Americans lived in the vicinity of present-day Charleston, the first English settlers did not arrive until 1670. The chain of events that led to its colonization were set in motion seven years earlier. On March 24, 1663, King Charles II, in repayment for political support in the battle against Oliver Cromwell to regain his throne, granted to eight eminent supporters a charter to a vast portion of land in the New World. This bestowed upon the Earl of Clarendon, the Duke of Albemarle, Lord Craven, Lord Berkeley, Sir William Berkeley, Lord Anthony Ashley Cooper, Sir George Carteret and Sir John Colleton (also known as the Lord Proprietors) the right to govern those lands and to exact a profit in any way they might wish, with only King Charles retaining ultimate control. In the King's honor the land was named Carolina – the Latin variation of Charles. In 1666, Captain Sanford took formal possession of the Carolinas on behalf of the Lords Proprietors. He named the two rivers, which flow around what was to become the city of Charleston, the **Ashley** and the **Cooper** – in tribute to Lord Cooper (later Lord Shaftsbury), the most influential of the lords. The names Albemarle and Carteret also feature prominently on modern-day maps of the eastern United States.

It was Lord Cooper's secretary, the philosopher John Locke, who made provisional plans for a new town and authored *The Fundamental Constitution of Carolina*, which was approved by the Lords Proprietors in 1669. The Constitution's edict specifying the guarantee of religious freedom would have a deep and lasting impact on Charleston's social development, attracting the immigration of diverse religious groups.

In that same year, 1669, the first Carolina colonists sailed from London in three vessels, the *Albemarle*, the *Port Royal* and the *Carolina*. Upon reaching Barbados, hurricane winds destroyed the first and damaged the other two. Finally, in the spring of 1670, the *Carolina* arrived in the Ashley River, and the first settlement, aptly named Charles Towne, was founded at Albemarle Point (now known as Charles Towne Landing). Beginning in 1680 and increasing dramatically upon Louis XIV's 1685 revocation of the Edict of Nantes, which had guaranteed the safety of the Huguenots in France, large numbers of French Huguenots came to settle in Charles Towne. By 1690 the population of the city was estimated at 1,200, making it the fifth largest in North America. It was at that time also that the city was officially moved to its present location and fortified with a wall, whose design included six bastions and a draw-bridged gate. Charleston, thus, was further distinguished as one of only a handful of walled cities to be built in North America.

The close of the 17th century brought great tribulation to Charles Towne, in the form of small pox and yellow fever epidemics, outbreaks of fire, an earthquake and a hurricane. Nevertheless, by the turn of the century, business generated by the plantations that lined the inland rivers had transformed Charles Towne into a major trading center. Its constitution, unlike those of most other Colonial cities, ensured religious diversity. During this period, French Huguenots, Anglicans, Presbyterians, Congregationalists and Jews flocked to the city, seeking both religious freedom and economic opportunities. The dozens of historic houses of worship that can be seen in Charleston today stand in reverent testimony to this era, earning it the sobriquet **"The Holy City."**

The 18th Century

In 1712, the territory of Carolina was subdivided into the colonies of North and South Carolina, with a governor being appointed for each. The following year, **The Powder Magazine** at 79 Cumberland Street, the oldest public building in the city and now a museum, began operation. In 1718, **Blackbeard the Pirate**, taking advantage of the removal of city fortifications to allow for expansion, carried out the boldest of his attacks upon Charles Towne itself. You can read in more detail about his exploits and capture in the Crystal Coast chapter. This and other aggressions left citizens feeling vulnerable and gave rise to a hail of protests directed against the Lords Proprietors for their failure to protect the land. In 1719, a **Revolutionary Assembly** convened, requesting the intervention of the King. Two years later, in 1721, South Carolina was declared a Royal Colony and placed under the governorship of **General Sir Francis Nicholson**. The change of ownership became official on July 25th, 1729, at which time King George bought out the interest of the Lords Proprietors.

By 1742 Charles Towne boasted a population of 6,800 and ranked fourth in size among all North American cities. Its ever-increasing wealth was based on trade in **rice** and the permanent blue dye, **indigo**. Such prosperity gave rise to a sophisticated and lavish lifestyle that was renowned around the world. Elegant architecture became one of the city's trademarks, and many of the more impressive homes and public buildings date from this period leading up to the Revolutionary War. As its fortunes increased, Charles Towne became increasingly dependent upon the contribution of thousands of **slaves**. West Coast African slaves were the most in demand, particularly for their knowledge of the cultivation of rice. Slaves made all of the bricks; most of the tradesmen, also, were highly skilled slaves. It is estimated that about 80% of the surviving 17th- and 18th-century buildings, and their accompanying furniture, were constructed by African-American craftsmen. Interestingly, after the day's work was completed, the slaves were free to hire themselves out, even being allowed to keep a percentage of their wages. Some, indeed, saved enough money to purchase their freedom and, as such, learned to read, owned property, paid taxes (of course) and enjoyed limited legal rights. In 1860, Charles Towne's population of 40,000 included 3,237 free persons of color, 30% of whom even owned their own slaves!

Ten years before Patrick Henry made it famous, **Christopher Gadsden**, protesting against the **Stamp Act** in 1765, incited resistance by using the Latin phrase "Aut mors aut Libertas," which translates as "Liberty or Death." In 1774 five prominent Charlestonians – Christopher Gadden, John and Edward Rutledge, Thomas Lynch and Henry Middleton – were named as delegates to the First Continental Congress, with the latter being chosen its president later that year. The Declaration of Independence came to Charles Towne in 1776, and was read out under the Liberty Tree close to what, today, is 80 Alexander Street. In late March of 1780 British forces laid siege to the city, which surrendered on May 12th after 40 days, thus beginning a 2½-year occupation.

In 1783, at the end of the Revolutionary War, Charles Towne was incorporated and had its name changed to Charleston. The conflict left commerce and trade devastated, however, primarily due to the loss of one of its staple crops, indigo. Production of this permanent blue dye had been subsidized by the British since 1742, and collapsed when the subsidy was withdrawn subsequent to the war. Three years later, on March 22nd, 1786, the General Assembly, bowing to political pressure from the more numerous settlers in the Upcountry, agreed to move the capital to Columbia, a brand-new planned town halfway between Low Country and Up Country, South Carolina. In early 1791, the Assembly moved into the stunning new capitol building there. In was in that year, too, that President George Washington spent a week in Charleston, as part of his grand tour of the Southern States.

South Carolina

The 19th Century

The development of the cotton gin and the planting of short-staple cotton brought a new cash crop and an increase in use of slave labor to the region. Industrial expansion, encouraged by the 1800 opening of the Santee Canal connecting the Santee and Cooper rivers, also boosted the economy. By this time, too, Charleston, with a population of 20,500, although small by northern standards, has risen to a position of some prominence as the most important urban center in the South. Edgar Allen Poe, then a young army recruit, was stationed at Fort Moultrie on nearby Sullivan's Island in 1828-29. During this period he collected ideas for a number of his works, including the The Gold Bug, a story including Carolina pirate tales.

In 1828, in disagreements between the states, South Carolina took the lead in registering its opposition to a new agricultural tariff by declaring the rights of states to nullify federal laws. In a foretaste of things to come, the state threatened secession from the Union in 1833, although Congress avoided such retaliation by the passage of a compromise tariff act. Nevertheless, problem after problem fueled the fires of militancy until, in November 1860, federal officials in the city resigned upon receiving the news of Lincoln's election. Shortly thereafter, on December 20th, the "Convention of the People of South Carolina" ratified an Ordinance of Secession, declaring the state an **Independent Commonwealth**. A few months later, on April 12, 1861, action replaced words as the first shots of the **Civil War** resounded with the shelling by Confederate forces of Fort Sumter. Devastation came quickly to Charleston, in the form of an 18-month siege by Federal forces that began in August 1863 and ended with the advance of General Sherman's troops on the city.

Following the war, fortunes improved little as the once profitable rice crop failed to rebound. Despair was compounded when, in 1886, an earthquake estimated at 7.5 on the Richter scale, caused $6 million worth of damage in the Low Country. What could not be foreseen at that time was that the very poor state of the economy would prove a blessing in disguise for Charleston. Much too poor to demolish and rebuild, the citizens salvaged whatever they could, inadvertently saving through that process two centuries of architectural treasures. A brief respite from hardship came in the latter part of the 19th century as the **cotton industry** brought some measure of prosperity to the region. Sadly, the boom was short-lived, as an infestation of the boll weevil consigned that chapter of Charleston's economic expansion to history.

The 20th Century

At the beginning of the 20th century the Naval Yard was completed, and it brought economic growth in its wake during World Wars I and II. Not long after that, Charleston's amazing kaleidoscopic array of architectural jewels began to attract the serious attention of tourists, and the influx of visitors that flocked to experience the history of the city gave birth to a brand-new business. The implications of this phenomenon were not lost on the more astute of Charlestonians and, in 1920, Susan Pringle Frost and others formed the **Society for the Preservation of Old Dwellings**, later to become the Preservation Society of Charleston. This marked the formal beginning of organized historic preservation, with the policy of urban conservation becoming, then, no longer a necessity but a choice.

 *In 1931 the city adopted the nation's 1st **Historical Zoning Ordinance**, protecting and thus preserving for posterity some 400 residential properties in a 23-block area south of Broad Street.*

Charleston's **Historic District** encompasses more than 2,000 buildings, 73 of which predate the American Revolution. Every type and style of architecture can be seen here: Colonial, from 1690-1740; Georgian, 1700-1790; Federal, 1790-1820; Classical Greek Revival, 1820-1875; Gothic Revival, 1850-1885; Italianate, 1830-1900; Victorian, 1860-1915; and Art Deco, 1920-1940. And you can't fail to notice the double house and the single house. The double house has a front door at the center with a room on either side; far more common, however, is the single house – only one room wide with its gable end turned toward the street. The front door opens into a porch, called a piazza. It is thought that the design was the result of property taxes once levied according to how many feet of street-frontage a house occupied.

Artists, writers, musicians and others with cultural tastes were drawn to this rather unusual ambiance; many went on to achieve national, and even international, acclaim. In the 1920s, Charleston became a household word as a dance craze bearing the city's name spread like wildfire across the nation. In 1935, on a more serious note, the Charleston Symphony Orchestra was founded. George Gershwin spent much time in Charleston researching the first American opera *Porgy and Bess*. Reflected in his story is the unusual cultural mix of the era and the area. A minority white elite co-existed, but very rarely mixed with, a colorful and numerically superior community of African descent.

Charleston Firsts

Given its long and illustrious history, it is not surprising that Charleston and vicinity have seen many firsts in the United States. Among these are:

■ The opening in 1700 of what is believed to be the first library.

■ The start of Henrietta Johnson's career as America's first recognized woman artist, in 1707.

■ The first public presentation of an opera in 1735.

■ the organization of the first fire insurance company.

■ The establishment of one of the nation's first theaters, The Dock Street, in 1736.

■ The planning and construction of America's oldest formal landscaped gardens at Middleton Place, circa 1741.

■ The formation, in 1749, of Congregation Beth Elohim, the oldest synagogue in continuous use.

■ The opening of the nation's oldest museum in 1773.

■ the formation of the first chamber of commerce in 1775.

■ The design by Robert Mills, the first native-born architect, of the first fireproof building in 1822.

■ In 1830, the inaugural run, on tracks stretching from Charleston to Hamburg, SC, of *The Best Friend*, the first steam locomotive to pull passengers in regular service.

■ In 1864, the first sinking of a vessel during a war by a submarine (the Confederate *CSS H. L. Hunley*).

Charleston Today

Throughout three centuries of history, Charleston, survivor of numerous wars, has also suffered a host of natural disasters – massive fires in 1698, 1740 and 1861; the earthquake of 1886; a succession of hurricanes in 1752, 1885, 1893, 1911; and, in 1989, Hurricane Hugo. Yet Charlestonians have never failed to bounce back, restoring and reinventing their hallowed city. Today visitors from around the world reap the benefits of their resiliency and determination.

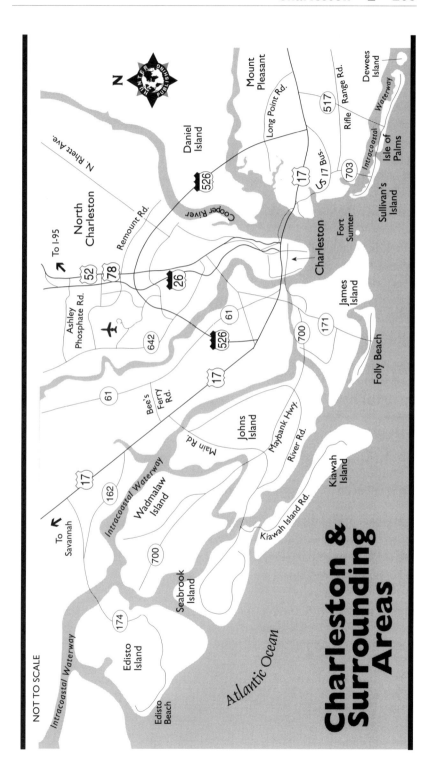

South Carolina

Charleston &
Surrounding
Areas

NOT TO SCALE

■ Getting Here

By Air

 Charleston International Airport is 12 miles west of the city on I-26 and is served by most of the major carriers, including American, Continental, Delta, United and USAir.

By Road

From the north or south, **Highway 17** is the main approach. The highway cuts through the heart of Charleston via the bridges over the Cooper and Ashley Rivers, and it provides easy access to all parts of the city.

From the west, **I-26** is the main route into the city. It terminates at its junction with Highway 17 in the center of Charleston. I-26 also provides access to several other major routes, including **I-95**, the alternate route north and south just west of the city.

By Rail

The **Amtrak** Station is at 4565 Gaynor Ave. in North Charleston. ☎ 800-872-7245.

■ Getting Around

By Car

 Getting around by car in Charleston can be a trial. Many of the downtown streets are narrow and one-way, and traffic is heavy, especially during rush hours, when it's best to stay off the streets. Parking can also a problem.

Taxis

Taxis are perhaps the most convenient way to get quickly from one place to another. Unfortunately, they're also the most expensive.

Public Transportation

The **Downtown Area Shuttle**, or DASH, is the most convenient mode of transport inside the downtown area. It has pickup points throughout the downtown and Historic Districts.

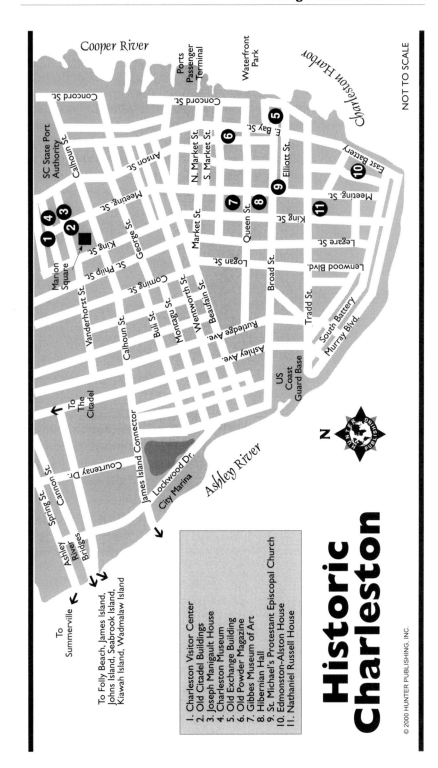

NOT TO SCALE

South Carolina

Cooper River

Ports Passenger Terminal

Waterfront Park

Charleston Harbor

Concord St.

Concord St.

SC State Port Authority

Calhoun St.

Anson St.

Meeting St.

N. Market St.

S. Market St.

E. Bay St.

Elliott St.

East Battery

Market St.

Queen St.

King St.

Meeting St.

George St.

Coming St.

St. Philip St.

King St.

Vanderhorst St.

Marion Square

Wentworth St.

Montagu St.

Bull St.

Beaufain St.

Logan St.

Broad St.

Legare St.

Lenwood Blvd.

Rutledge Ave.

Ashley Ave.

Calhoun St.

Tradd St.

South Battery

Murray Blvd.

US Coast Guard Base

To The Citadel

James Island Connector

Courtenay Dr.

Spring St.

Cannon St.

Lockwood Dr.

City Marina

Ashley River

Ashley River Bridges

To Summerville

To Folly Beach, James Island,
Johns Island, Seabrook Island,
Kiawah Island, Wadmalaw Island

N

1. Charleston Visitor Center
2. Old Citadel Buildings
3. Joseph Manigault House
4. Charleston Museum
5. Old Exchange Building
6. Old Powder Magazine
7. Gibbes Museum of Art
8. Hibernian Hall
9. St. Michael's Protestant Episcopal Church
10. Edmonston-Alston House
11. Nathaniel Russell House

Historic
Charleston

© 2000 HUNTER PUBLISHING, INC.

■ Sightseeing

Churches

St. Michael's Episcopal Church, ☎ 843-723-0603, is at the corner of Broad and Meeting Streets. Construction began in 1751 of a design that closely followed that of St. Martin's-in-the-Fields in London. It was the second Episcopal church in Charleston, and features a Palladian Doric portico and a storied steeple that rises 186 feet above the city. The clock was installed in 1764 and has kept time ever since. The interior is rich and extensively decorated; the pulpit is original. If you like to visit old churches, this one is a must. Open Monday, Tuesday, Thursday and Friday 9 to 5 and Saturday, 9 to noon. Admission by donation.

Historic Houses

In 1920, as detailed in Charleston's *History* section, Susan Pringle Frost and others formed the Society for the Preservation of Old Dwellings, which in 1947 became the Preservation Society of Charleston, ☎ 843-723-1623, 40 East Bay Street. Among the first of their purchases was the **Nathaniel Russell House**, at 51 Meeting Street, acclaimed as one of the nation's best examples of the neoclassical style of architecture. Nathaniel Russell, a native Rhode Islander, founder and first president of Charleston's influential New England Society, arrived in the city in 1765 and made his fortune soon after. Money, as we know, attracts money, and sometimes love as well, and in 1788 he married Sarah Hopton, the daughter of another prominent Charleston businessman who had also made his fortune in rice and indigo. In 1808 the couple finished construction of this magnificent mansion-house, noted for elaborate plasterwork ornamentation, geometrically designed rooms and an absolutely stunning free-flying curved staircase. Furnished with period antiques and works of art, many of which originate from Charleston, the house allows guests to see just how gracious life was for the city's elite; and to glimpse, on the flip side, the conditions under which the Russell's African-American slaves lived and worked.

Another mansion of this era is the **Aiken-Rhett House**, built by a merchant in 1818, but much expanded and redecorated by Governor William Aiken Jr. and his wife in the 1830s and 1850s. It has remained virtually unaltered since 1858. In fact, it remained in the family until 1975. It was purchased by the foundation in 1995 and is now open to visitors. Grand in style, especially the imposing entrance hall with a double staircase and protective cast iron railings, it is furnished with many treasures that the Governor, one of South Carolina's wealthiest citizens, and his wife accumulated on their travels in Europe. In contrast, as with the Nathaniel Russell House, you will be able to see what is considered to be America's best preserved urban slave quarters, more or less unaltered since the 1850s.

The **Powder Magazine**, at 79 Cumberland Street, is the only public building in either North or South Carolina remaining from the period of the Lords Proprietors. It is also owned by the Historic Charleston Foundation. The structure has served various other functions throughout its lengthy history, but has recently been restored to its mid-19th-century condition and opened as an historic site.

The two houses are open to the public throughout the year – with the exception of Thanksgiving Day, Christmas Eve and Christmas Day – Monday to Saturday from 10 to 5 and on Sunday 2 to 5 pm. The Powder Magazine, on the other hand, opens only between March and October. Tickets may be purchased at any of these locations, either on an individual or collective basis. The Charleston Heritage Federation offers the Charleston Heritage Passport, which gives a 20% discount off admission fees for the Gibbes Museum of Art, the Nathaniel Russell House, the Edmonston-Alston House, Drayton Hall and Middleton Place. So, if you plan to visit all of these, pick up your passport at the first place you visit.

The foundation also spends much time and effort preserving the architectural and cultural heritage of Charleston, which includes architectural rehabilitation and craft training. Visitors impressed with what they have seen will want to wander over to 105 Broad Street, home to the **Historic Charleston Reproductions Shop**, ☎ 843-723-8292 or fax 722-7129. Here, from 10 to 5, Monday through Saturday, you will find home furnishings, accessories and other giftware, including an array of jewelry adapted from ironwork motifs in Charleston. Each of these is authorized by the foundation and carries a product card detailing its historical significance.

But the Historic Charleston Foundation doesn't have a monopoly on historic buildings. The **Charleston Museum**, ☎ 843-722-2996 or fax 722-1784, 360 Meeting Street, founded in 1773, is the first and oldest such establishment in the United States. It boasts two National Historic Landmark houses of its own. The museum proper, dedicated to preserving and interpreting the social and natural history of Charleston and South Carolina, houses many interesting displays. Not least of these is the Charleston Silver Exhibit that includes inter-

South Carolina

nationally recognized works by local artists and pieces dating from Colonial times up to the late 19th century.

The first of the museum's two houses, the **Heyward-Washington House**, was built in 1772 by Daniel Heyward, a rice planter and father to one of the South Carolinian signers of the Declaration of Independence, Thomas Heyward Jr. It earned the second half of its name in 1791, when it was rented for the use of President George Washington, a guest of the city. Today, the home is filled with traditional Charleston-made furniture dating from the 18th century and including the priceless Holmes bookcase – considered one of the finest pieces of its kind in the Nation. The Heyward-Washington House also has the distinction of being the only 18th-century house open to visitors and retains its original kitchen buildings and carriage house.

The museum's other such property, the **Joseph Manigault House**, circa 1803, is a particularly graceful example of the Adams style of architecture. Designed by wealthy Low Country rice planter Gabriel Manigault for his brother Joseph, it features a very unusual curving central staircase and an impressive collection of Charleston, American, English and French furniture from the era.

The museum is open daily, Monday through Saturday from 9 to 5 and on Sunday from 1 to 5. The houses open Monday through Saturday from 10 to 5 and on Sunday from 1 to 5.

While still contemplating life in the early 19th century, set your course for the lower waterfront at 21 East Battery Street, where you will find the three-story **Edmonston-Alston House**, ☎ 843-722-7171, www.middletonplace.org, which has been featured in the TV series *America's Castles*. When the highly successful Charleston merchant Charles Edmonston built this splendid late Federal-style house in 1825, it was one of the first in what is now a prestigious area. The location was convenient for his business purposes, too. From the piazza he could monitor the comings and goings of vessels carrying his goods to and from the nearby wharves. The economic depression of 1837 left Edmondson in hard times, however, and he was forced to sell his house to Charles Alston, a member of a Low Country rice-planting dynasty. Alston made many structural changes, including adding a third-floor piazza with Corinthian columns and a second-floor iron balcony on the east, water-facing front. The home has its share of historical connections as well. It is said that General Beauregard and others watched the bombardment of Fort Sumter from here, and that Robert E. Lee once spent the night here after a fire threatened his hotel. The Alston family used the home as their city residence for more than 80 years. In fact, they still own it and live on the third floor to this day. Public tours of the first two floors are conducted by staff of the Middleton Place Foundation, Tuesday through Saturday from 10 to 4:30 and Sunday and Monday from 1:30 to 4:30.

Just over 50 years later yet another very impressive residence, the **Calhoun Mansion**, ☎ 843-722-8205, emerged at 16 Meeting Street. Built by George Walton Williams, a wealthy merchant and banker, this 24,000-square-foot house has 14-foot ceilings, a stairwell that ascends toward a 75-foot domed ceiling and a ballroom with a coved glass 45-foot-high skylight. This was described by important newspapers of the day as being the most complete home in the South. The home today boasts collections of Victorian furnishings, along with beautifully restored gardens, and has been featured in movies such as *Scarlet* and *North and South*. We wondered, as you might, how the property came by its name, and the answer is very simple: Williams' daughter married Patrick Calhoun, grandson of the famous John C. Calhoun.

Horse-Drawn Carriage Rides

Visitors to Charleston will soon ascertain that horse-drawn carriage tours are very popular here and, indeed, they offer a relaxed and romantic way of seeing this enchanting city. Select from either the **Old South Carriage Co.**, ☎ 843-723-9712, 14 Anson Street, whose guides can be easily identified by their red sash and Confederate uniforms, or the **Charleston Carriage Co.**, ☎ 843-723-TOUR or 577-0042, 14 Hayne Street. Both companies operate tours throughout the day that last around an hour and, if you are so inclined, you can visit their barns to get acquainted with the horses.

Private Home & Garden Tours

Visiting the houses that are open to the public is, indeed, interesting, but in Charleston there are many, many more beautiful and varied homes that remain in private hands. Curiosity, surely, makes one wonder about the elegance and history hidden from gaze beyond their walls. To get an insider's view, plan your trip to Charleston either in the spring or fall, when garden and holiday tours respectively allow a peak beyond normally closed doors.

In the spring, between mid-March and mid-April, when the flowers in the city are at their most colorful, the Historic Charleston Foundation offers the **Festival of Houses & Gardens**. The setting is the Historic District of Charleston, and the itinerary varies daily to allow an

South Carolina

experience of the architectural legacy of the distinctive historic houses, churches and other important public buildings. As tickets are limited, it is best to call ☎ 843-723-1623 well in advance for tickets and schedule information.

Alternatively, visit Charleston in the fall when the **Fall Candlelight Tours of Homes and Gardens** are presented by the Preservation Society of Charleston, ☎ 843-722-4630, 800-968-8175 or fax 723-4381, 147 King Street. The tours, held every Thursday, Friday and Saturday evening, showcase over 175 unique old homes and gardens in Charleston's world-famous historic district, with a different historic neighborhood being highlighted each night. This is a self-guided walking tour, with marshals along the route, where you can visit at your own pace eight to 10 properties, private houses, churches or other public buildings, all on the National Register of Historic Places. Tours usually take place between the middle of September and the middle of October; the recent ticket price was $30 per person. A recent innovation are two Sunday afternoon Garden & Tea Tours. Remember that high-heeled shoes are not allowed, that no smoking, eating or drinking is allowed in the homes, that neither photography nor video taping are permitted and that bathrooms are not readily available on the tours. Flashlights are useful during evening walks.

If you can't plan your trip at those times, then we suggest you contact the **House Tour**, ☎ 843-849-7660. Departing from the Mills House Hotel on Monday through Saturday at 9:30 am, this 2½-hour tour costs $25 per person and meanders through the historic part of Charleston, giving a glimpse of its spirit and past. You will also have the opportunity to visit the gracious interiors of two private homes and, afterwards, partake of refreshments in one of those seductive walled courtyard gardens.

Museums

The **Gibbes Museum of Art**, ☎ 843-722-2706, 135 Meeting Street, is the result of a $100,000 endowment given jointly to the Mayor of Charleston and the Carolina Art Association in 1888. It was the gift of James S. Gibbes, a wealthy Charleston merchant, to establish a permanent home for the Association. Its permanent collection features paintings, prints and drawings from the 18th, 19th, and 20th centuries by American artists. A series of portraits and landscapes provides a look at Charleston, South Carolina and many of their notable figures down through the years. Here you can see images of John C. Calhoun, Charles Manigault, Thomas Middleton, and others. The Elizabeth Wallace Exhibit includes tiny replicas of rooms from some of America's most historic buildings. Each has been painstakingly scaled down and reproduced by four craftsmen commissioned by Elizabeth Wallace. They range from a simple dining room in a Martha's Vineyard sea captain's home to the elaborate drawing room at Charleston's Nathaniel Russell House. The museum is also home to one of the world's finest collections of miniature paintings. The Charleston Renaissance Room features works by artists popular in Charleston during the 1920s and 1930s.

The **Old Exchange & Provost Dungeon**, ☎ 843-727-2165, 121 East Bay Street, completed in 1771, was an important 18th-century port, central to social, political, and economic life for the residents of early Charles Town. It was the place where town meetings were held and imprisoned pirates and Indians were kept. The election of South Carolina delegates to the First Continental Congress was held here in 1774 and, in March of 1776, the independent colony of South Carolina was declared from the Exchange steps. During the American Revolution, the building was converted to a British prison, the Provost, where signers of the Declaration of Independence were held. In 1778, the state convention to ratify the US Constitution met at the Exchange. Also, George Washington was entertained here several times during his southern tour in 1791. From 1818 until 1896 the Exchange was used as Charleston's post office, serving both Federal and Confederate governments. In 1917, the US Congress deeded the old building to the South Carolina Daughters of the American Revolution. Today, the Exchange is considered one of the most historically important buildings in the United States, and it is open for you to enjoy. The old British Provost Dungeon of 1780 on the lower level remains much as it was during the Revolution, with life-like representation of prisoners held below the elegant colonial halls of the Old Exchange; they offer a tiny peek into Charleston's somewhat turbulent past. Open daily from 9 to 5.

Walking Tours

As you might expect, there are numerous companies and individuals offering walking tours around Charleston. Most of these, though, are narrow in scope, concentrating on one subject or theme of their choice. That is not the case, however, with **The Original Charleston Walks**, ☎ 843-577-3800, 800-729-3420, fax 853-6899, e-mail info@ charlestonwalks.com, www.charlestonwalks.com, 334 East Bay Street, who advertise that they have "the Best Tours in Charleston's History." No matter your area of interest, whether it is exploring a particular time in Charleston's history, the Civil War, Slavery and

Freedom, Ghosts or even Murder and Mysteries, The Original Charleston Walks have a thematic tour for you. These depart from the Broad Street Gate entrance to Washington Park, located at 78 Broad Street beside the City Hall, and cost $12 per person. If you prefer a private tour, either at one of the scheduled times or at other times, that can be arranged at a fee of $60. Alternatively, if you want to customize a walk, the company will be happy to arrange that for you as well. Finally, if your interest is piqued by the Heyward-Washington House and the Edmonston-Alston House, you should opt for the Historic Homes Walk. Leaving on Tuesday through Saturday at 10 am, and costing $22 per person (which includes entrance fees), it meanders through the fascinating neighborhood south of Broad Street and visits these two mansions.

Patriot's Point

No visitor to Charleston can have missed the sight of the massive aircraft carrier *Yorktown*, World War II's famous "Fighting Lady," docked at Patriot's Point across the Cooper River from the city. What many might not know, however, is that the carrier is just one among many attractions at the **Patriot's Point Naval & Maritime Museum**, ☎ 843-884-2727, 40 Patriot's Point Road, the world's largest naval and maritime museum. The *USS Yorktown* (CV-10) is massively impressive, and she has a history of distinguished service. Following her commission on April 15, 1943, she took part in many World War II Pacific naval battles and patrolled the western Pacific during the Cold and Vietnam wars. A more peaceful mission was the recovery of the crew of Apollo 8, the first manned spacecraft to circle the moon. These days, at rest in Charleston, you can inspect many of the planes that once flew from her decks and, in the ship's theater, watch an Academy Award-winning film about the Yorktown.

Two additional surface vessels, the ***Destroyer Laffey*** (DD-724) and the ***Coast Guard Cutter Ingham***, may offer a lower silhouette, but they, in their own manner, are no less illustrious. The former, commissioned on February 8, 1944, took part in the D-Day landings a few months later, and was then transferred to the Pacific where, off Okinawa on April 16, 1945, she suffered a Japanese Kamikaze suicide attack. The *Laffey* also served in the Korean War, being decommissioned in 1975 after service in the Atlantic Fleet. The oldest of the vessels on display here, the *Ingham*, entered service in 1936 and, in a career that spanned over 50 years, earned 18 ribbons, thus becoming one of the most decorated vessels in US service. In 1942, on one of her 31 World War II convoys, she sank the German U-boat 626.

She served both in the Pacific theater and in Vietnam before, in more recent years, tracking illegal boat immigrants and drug runners.

The last of the vessels open to visitors is the submarine *Clamagore* (SS-343), which began her 30-year career in 1945, towards the end of World War II. Space here is cramped indeed and not very suitable for those who suffer from claustrophobia or have health problems.

Two other exhibits also deserve attention. The **Vietnam Naval Support Base** is a true-to-scale model showing the living conditions and operational areas utilized by Vietnam support base veterans. And the nation's most gallant fighting heroes are celebrated in the **National Congressional Medal of Honor Museum**, where medals and a variety of memorabilia relating to each award are on display.

During the summer months, between April 1st and September 30th, the museum is open from 9 to 6. It closes one hour earlier the rest of the year.

Out-Of-Town Attractions

Looking farther afield, the following places, different in character, are of much interest for excursions outside of Charleston.

Angel Oak, ☎ 843-559-3496, found just south of Charleston, at 3688 Angel Oak Road, Johns Island, is a live oak tree of the variety *Quercus Virginiana*, once highly favored for shipbuilding. Charleston is full of old oak trees, most of them Southern live oaks. But Angel Oak is special. The Point on which it stands once was part of a land grant made to Abraham Waight in 1717. Waight became a prosperous planter, owning several plantations. The great tree is named for the Angel family; Martha Waight married Justis Angel in 1810 and the Point continued under Angel ownership until it was sold to the Mutual Land and Development Corporation in 1959. Angel Oak itself was leased to the South Carolina Agricultural Society for $1 per year; they cared for it until it was purchased, along with the surrounding site, by S.E. Felkel in 1964. The Magnolia Garden Club cared for the tree and grounds until the late 1970s, when vandalism forced the owner to put a fence around the tree. That was when it became a tourist attraction. The City of Charleston acquired the tree in 1991; Angel Oak Park was opened to the public in September the same year. Live oaks are native to and found throughout the Low Country. They are particularly tall trees, with wide spreading canopies. On the oldest and largest of the species the lower limbs grow so big they rest upon the ground. So what's so special about this one? Although it's almost impossible to determine the exact age of Angel Oak, it's thought to be over 1,400 years old, and it's huge, standing some 65 feet high. The trunk has a circumference of 25 feet; its largest limb is 89 feet long and has a circumference of 11 feet; the canopy covers an area of 17,000 square feet. Open from 9 to 5 daily.

Boone Hall Plantation, ☎ 843-884-4371, America's most photographed plantation, is just six miles north of Charleston, on Highway 17. Major John Boone, a member of the First Fleet of Settlers who arrived in 1681, received this plantation, which once covered more than 17,000 acres – today the estate is a mere 738 acres – as a grant from the Lords Proprietors. The present mansion dates from 1935, although it was constructed along the lines of the original house, which was built around 1750. Of particular interest here is one of the few slave streets remaining intact in the United States. It is comprised of nine original brick cabins, built around 1743, which are all listed on the National Register of Historic Places. The main attraction here, though, is the world-famous half-mile Avenue of Oaks, draped by Spanish moss, which are themselves on the National Register of Historic Places. It is thought that the first oak was planted in 1743 by Captain Thomas Boone, and the oaks have been featured, as have the mansion and slave quarters, in numerous movies and TV shows – most notably, the ABC-TV mini-series *North and South*. These days, the Boone Hall Plantation is open for tours in the summer months, Monday through Saturday from 8:30 to 6:30 and on Sunday from 1 to 5, with slightly shorter hours during the rest of the year.

Cypress Gardens, ☎ 803-553-0515, some 24 miles north of Charleston off Highway 52, was originally part of Dean Hall, one of the Cooper River's most important rice plantations, a 3,000-acre antebellum estate that flourished from the 18th century until the Civil War. Today, all that's left of the once-great estate are the gardens created by Benjamin Kitteredge in the late 1920s around the cypress swamp that once provided irrigation for the plantation. Kitteredge, so the story goes, saw the reflection of a red maple in the black swamp water. From this inspiration he created the 160-acre garden. To see it in springtime is a rare experience; a profusion of azaleas, dogwoods, daffodils, and wisteria repeats itself in the reflections on the dark waters of the swamp. You can enjoy the spectacle either on foot or in the traditional way from a flat-bottom boat. There are more than three miles of footpaths that meander through the swamps, giving access not only to the gardens themselves, but to the abundance of wildlife that lives there: alligators, otters, pileated woodpeckers, ducks, barred owls and many others. Be sure to bring your camera. If you decide to see the gardens by boat, you can either relax and let one of the boatmen do the paddling, or you can paddle off the beaten trail on your own. Open daily from 9 to 5.

Drayton Hall, ☎ 803-766-0188, nine miles northwest of downtown Charleston on Ashley River Road (Highway 61), was built in 1738 by John Drayton, a young planter and member of the Privy Council of the royal governor. The plantation was established on land the young Drayton purchased next to that owned by his father, now known as Magnolia Gardens. The mansion was completed in 1742 after four years of construction. It's a grand and elegant structure, the oldest and finest example of Georgian Palladian architecture built before the American Revolution in America. The great two-story portico, with its Doric and Ionic columns built of Portland stone imported from England, was the first of its kind in America. Today, the old house, almost a palace, stands as a testament to wealth and opulence on a scale known only to a very few. The house remained under Drayton ownership through seven generations until 1974, when it was acquired by the National Trust for Historic Preservation. It's the only great house on the Ashley River to have survived the Civil War fully intact. It has come down the years almost unchanged from the day construction was finished: there's no running water, electricity, gaslights or central heating. The National Trust decided not to furnish the house, but to leave the interior open to interpretation. Unfortunately, no stretch of the imagination could ever reconstruct the elegance and opulence of Drayton Hall as it must have been during its heyday. Open daily from 10 to 4, March through October; 10 to 3 the rest of the year. Tours are conducted hourly.

Magnolia Plantation and Gardens, ☎ 843-571-1266, on Ashley River Road (Highway 61), 10 miles northwest of its downtown junction with Highway 17, is part of a 500-acre estate acquired by the Drayton family in 1676. The heirs still own it. The estate has been in the Drayton family for 10 generations and was opened to the public more than 100 years ago, making it the oldest man-made attraction in America. The gardens you see today were once the estate gardens; they have been described over the years by many an expert as the world's most beautiful, and perhaps they are. All through the year, but especially in springtime, the 50 acres of lawn and garden are a profusion of color, heavy with the scent of flowers. Set among swampland lakes and creeks and hundreds of live oaks, more than 250 varieties of azaleas, 900 varieties of camellias, and hundreds of other flowering plants provide an extensive season of color, with blooms for every month of the year. The Plantation House, successor to the one that would have been the oldest in the Carolinas, depicts life as it was on the rice plantation. Inside, you can see a display of works by local artists, and hundreds of Civil War artifacts and pieces of memorabilia. Outside, there's a petting zoo, complete with miniature horses (no more than 30 inches high), a wetland waterfowl refuge, biblical gardens, a wildlife observation tower, herb garden, maze, topiary garden, an original antebellum cabin and several walking and biking trails. Open daily from 8 to 5.

Middleton Place, ☎ 843-556-6020, is on Highway 61, 14 miles northwest of its downtown junction with Highway 17, on the banks of the Ashley River. It is an 18th-century plantation that survived both the American Revolution and the Civil War; it is also the location of the oldest landscaped garden in the United States. The original house was built in 1741 by Henry Middleton, a one-time president of the Continental Congress. Middleton Place House was built in 1755 as a gentlemen's guest wing and became the family home after the plantation was burned during the Civil War. The gardens are a reflection of the great English gardens of the 17th century. There are terraced lawns, lakes and surrounding gardens that bloom year-round with camellias, azaleas, magnolias, crape myrtle and roses. You can wander at will along the paths that meander through the gardens, from the reflecting pool, past the ancient Middleton Oak and the family tomb to the plantation stable yards and the house itself. A guided tour of the old family home will open a window to the family's past and its role in American history. You'll see collections of fine silver, portraits by Benjamin West and Thomas Sully, Charleston rice beds, and rare first editions by Catesby and Audubon. Open daily from 9 to 5.

■ Adventures

On Foot

Shopping

Visitors have plenty of choices in Charleston, but the following are some interesting suggestions:

If ever a name was indicative of an establishment's character, it is that of **The Silver Puffin**, ☎ 803-723-7900, at 278 King Street in the heart of historic Charleston. The owner deliberately chose the puffin, with its unique appearance and unusual habits, as the symbol for this extraordinary shop. Three types of puffin, nicknamed the sea parrot and clown of the sea, live in the coastal areas of the United States. The tufted puffin and the horned puffin are indigenous to the northern Alaskan coast. The Atlantic puffin makes its home from the northern tip of Maine up into the Canadian Atlantic Provinces, where it is the official bird of the Provinces of New-foundland and Labrador. With an estimated population of 20 million, the puffin is one of the more prevalent of the seabird species found within the Northern Hemisphere, possibly the only aspect in which in can be described as common. But, even in this, the puffin's methodology is uncommon. These birds mate for life, usually 20 to 25 years; and both parents share the task of incubating, for about 45 days and within a hole in the ground, the single egg laid by the female each year. Superb swimmers, but poor fliers, puffins will spend half the year out at sea, diving to great depths for food. To learn more about the puffin, and to find all manner of puffin models and paraphernalia, visit the Puffin Corner at the Silver Puffin. Also expect to find here many other items of distinction, imagination and charm. Among the kaleidoscopic array are Russian dolls, pieces of Chinese porcelain and Zimbabwean pottery, international and domestic hand-blown glass, items fashioned of cork, mirrors, jewelry, clocks and watches, a line of collectible soldiers, beautifully crafted decoys, irresistibly cuddly stuffed animals, and even an assortment of rather unusually decorated bowls for your pet. The Silver Puffin is open every day of the week from 10 to 6.

Charleston is certainly a town that takes its history seriously. Woven within the fabric of its identity is a wealth of traditions, some of which are immediately apparent, some more subtle. In the latter category are the quaintly attractive, yet durable and practical, **Battery Benches**. These are found throughout the city, most notably along the Battery, but also in such prestigious spots as the Courtyards at the Omni Charleston Place complex. From examining old photographs, it seems that the Battery Bench first appeared along Charleston's historic Battery during the mid-19th century. Now, as then, the side-pieces are made of heavy cast iron, poured into the original molds, which nearly a half-century ago were purchased, along with rights to produce the bench, by Geo. C. Birlant & Co. from the original manufacturer, the J. F. Riley Iron Works of Charleston. Look closely and you may find within the intricate foliate design of the castings some of the fauna indigenous to South Carolina during the 1800s – the inverted parrot or the fox and hound, for example. After they are carefully inspected, the sides are deep-dipped in the traditional "Charleston Dark Green" paint. Slats of durable South Carolina cypress are crafted to endure both wear and the weather. Particularly unusual is the double-length bench made at the request of the City of Charleston many years ago. To purchase one, make your way to **Geo. C. Birlant & Co., Antiques and Fine Gifts** at 191 King Street, where the helpful folks will take your order (in exchange for about

$230) and arrange to have a bench shipped to your home. There you can set the bench in your garden and relive the memories. ☎ 843-722-3842, 888-BIRLANT; fax 843-722-3846.

While you are at Geo. C. Birlant & Co., take a bit of time to browse through the collection of antiques. This is one of the largest and oldest antiques businesses in the Southeast. The highly respected antique dealer and auctioneer George C. Birlant founded it in 1929. Today, the legacy is carried on by his daughter and son-in-law, Marian and Phil Slotin, and their son Andrew, in the heart of Charleston's antique district. The business is housed in a very large three-story building constructed around 1840. The Slotins take several trips to England each year, selecting fine 18th- and 19th-century pieces – chests of drawers, Chippendale and Queen Anne dining chairs, sideboards, linen presses and secretary bookcases, as well as silver, china, crystal, chandeliers and lighting fixtures. .

Every now and again we find a store that is a little anachronistic in its approach – in other words, well worth a visit not only for a wide array of goods on display, but for its unique ambiance and personal service. **Luden's**, ☎ 843-723-7829, Charleston's oldest and largest marine purveyor, and a city tradition since 1867, falls into this category. When we visited it was located at Concord and Charlotte Streets, but due to construction works it will now be operating out of East Bay and Charlotte Streets. It was a curious mixture of a genuine chandlers (a ship's outfitter store with paint, hardware and rope), tiny museum, bookstore, men's outfitter, hunting store, authorized Orvis dealer and canoe dealer. Items of special interest for gifts (or to spoil yourself) are a full range of English Barbour waterproof jackets, Brazilian handmade hammocks, ornamental painted paddles that have cleverly been turned into horizontal hat stands, and a BBQ corner with everything you could possibly need. Also very much of interest is the most complete collection of Victorinox Swiss knives we have seen outside of Switzerland, including their Swiss Tool, and watches. Luden's is open Monday to Friday from 8 to 6 and on Saturday from 8:30 to 5.

Whether you are in the market to treat yourself or looking for a unique gift for someone back home, the **Washington Pen Company**, ☎ 843-723-7367, Majestic Square, 155 Market Street, merits a look. It is owned by brothers Keith and Andrew Twillman, who operate two similar stores in Washington DC, one on M Street and one at Union Station. Here you will find such quality manufacturers as Mont Blanc, Waterman, Cross and Pelikan, alongside wonderfully elegant examples by Jorg Hysek of Switzerland and Graf von Faber-

Castell. The check you stroke may not be small, however, with some special editions selling for up to $2,500! Much more affordable are the Havana Rollerball that comes in a cigar tube case (of course), and the Millenium Space Pen, supposed to write in any position. Swatch watches, too, are on show. If you have a child at home, a Winnie the Pooh or Mickey Mouse watch might be an appropriate gift. Also look for leather organizers, Crane stationery and other similar gifts.

Those of you who have a pooch or cat back home will want to stop by **Alpha Dog Omega Cat**, ☎ 843-723-1579, at 40 Archdale Street. And you needn't feel you are alone in spoiling your pooch with a special surprise. The three lady proprietors found, while planning the project, that nearly 80% of pet owners gave their dogs holiday or birthday presents. Here, amidst photos, newspaper clippings and cartoons of pets, are all the usual things you might expect of a pet shop and just about everything else in animal theme that you could want either for your pet or yourselves. The prices are equally varied, with some 19th-century signed British oil paintings running into many thousands of dollars.

The temptation of **Charleston Chocolates**, ☎ 843-577-4491, 800-633-8305, fax 577-2609 or e-mail rush@charlestonchocolates.com, 190 East Bay Street, will not be denied. You will find an incredible array of mouth-watering handmade gourmet delights. From in-house adaptations of European family recipes come sophisticated creations made of only the finest quality chocolate, fresh heavy cream, sweet AA butter, natural flavorings, fruits and nuts, with absolutely no additives, preservatives or sugar added. Such confections as Vanilla Butter Rum, Hazelnut Frangelico, Brandy Cherry, Raspberry Chambord, Grand Marnier, Champagne or Sarah Bernhardt Macaroon are just waiting to be savored. The store is open Monday to Saturday from 10 to 6 and, in season, on Sunday from noon to 5. Charleston Chocolates will also ship your favorites via Federal Express.

On Water

Cruises & Tours

It is nearly impossible to visit Charleston without being enticed to venture out onto the waters that surround it. As an added attraction, historic Fort Sumter is here in the harbor. **Fort Sumter Tours Inc.**, ☎ 843-722-1691, 205 King Street, has put together three tours designed to appeal to a range of tastes. They set to sea from the City Marina on Lockwood Boulevard.

The Fort Sumter Tour takes you across the bay to this National Monument and is the only tour that actually makes a stop there. At the fort, National Park Service Rangers are on hand to answer your questions as you explore the fort where the Civil War began and visit the museum.

The Story of Fort Sumter

Perhaps the most significant site in Charleston – certainly the best known – is this great fort in the middle of the harbor that commands the ocean gates to the city. It was here, against these huge ramparts, that the first shots of the Civil War were fired.

Major Robert Anderson, his hair already turning silver, was 56 when he became the first Union hero of the Civil War. He was a deeply religious man, cautious, reflective, but he was also a very courageous man, as his actions during the first few days of the war would demonstrate. Anderson, a southerner by birth and a graduate of West Point in 1825, 15th in his class, fought in the Black Hawk and Seminole Indian wars, served with General Winfield Scott in Mexico and, from November 1860, was the commander of the Federal garrison at Charleston Harbor. As he took up his command at Fort Moultrie, the political rift between North and South was rapidly approaching the point of no return, but he had little idea of the momentous events that were about to take place. Less than a month later on December 20, 1860 at a convention in Charleston, South Carolina became the first state to secede from the Union. Anderson was, in effect, now in command of three military installations located in the heart of a hostile foreign country. Fort Moultrie on Sullivan's Island, Castle Pinckney at the mouth of the Cooper River, and Fort Sumter – still under construction on a man-made island some miles from Charleston in the main ship channel. It's no wonder, then, that all eyes turned toward Charleston Harbor and Anderson's tiny command. So, on December 26th, under cover of darkness, he moved his men out of Fort Moultrie, across the harbor to Fort Sumter. Within days Confederate forces occupied Anderson's abandoned positions at Fort Moultrie, Castle Pinckney, Fort Johnson off Cummings Point and a floating battery off Sullivan's Island. Fort Sumter was completely surrounded by Confederate batteries.

As the New Year began, President Buchanan sent some 200 reinforcements and supplies to Anderson in an unarmed merchant ship, the *Star of the West*. On January 9, as the ship tried to pass around the point into Charleston Harbor, the Confederate batteries on Morris Island opened fire and turned it back. Anderson, with only 85 men and dwindling supplies, was left alone to face the enemy, now more than 5,000 strong. Tensions continued to mount as, during the following month, Mississippi, Florida, Alabama, Georgia, Louisiana, and Texas all seceded from the Union.

On February 28th,1861, representatives of the seven seceding states met in convention in Montgomery, Alabama, organized a government, and elected Jefferson Davis as the Confederacy's first president. The situation for Federal forces deployed in the Southern states now became exceedingly uncomfortable and so, with the exception of Fort Sumter, and Fort Pickens in Pensacola, all Union garrisons surrendered their positions to the new authorities and returned home.

By the time Lincoln was inaugurated on March 4th, it had become evident that the North would use force to subdue the rebellion and maintain the Union, and that Fort Sumter would be the focal point of the struggle. In late March, Jefferson Davis ordered Brigadier General P.G.T. Beauregard to Charleston to take command of the Confederate forces there. In the meantime, Anderson informed Washington that Confederate forces had heavily fortified Charleston and the Harbor, and that he lacked sufficient manpower, food and ammunition to meet the threat. Lincoln, although he was very much aware of the delicate situation, informed the governor of South Carolina that he intended to send a relief expedition to Fort Sumter to resupply the garrison with food and provisions. Once again, Lincoln, Anderson, and the world settled down to wait. They didn't have to wait long.

On April 1st, General Beauregard telegraphed a message to President Davis that he was ready to address the situation at Fort Sumter. On April 10th the governor of South Carolina informed President Davis of Lincoln's intention to resupply the fort. Later that day the Confederate Secretary of War Leroy P. Walker ordered Beauregard to demand of Major Anderson the immediate evacuation of the fort. If the demand was not met, then Beauregard was to "proceed in such a manner as you may determine, to reduce it." Pierre Gustave Toutant Beauregard, a vain and egotistical man, was considered a competent engineer and an able field commander; as a combat tactician, though, his abilities were somewhat limited. Beauregard was born in St. Bernard Parish, Louisiana, of wealthy Creole parents on May 28th, 1818. His upbringing was French, he spoke the French language better than he spoke English, and he was educated at a French military academy in New York. From there he entered West Point, where he was instructed by – you've guessed it – Robert Anderson, the erstwhile defender of Fort Sumter. Beauregard graduated from West Point in 1838, second in a class of 45. He was commissioned a second lieutenant in the Corps of Engineers and sent to Newport, Rhode Island. During the Mexican War he served as an engineer under General Winfield Scott, was wounded twice, and received two brevets for bravery. In January he was appointed superintendent of West Point, a position he held only a matter of days before being removed for his outspoken Southern sympathies. On February 20th, Beauregard resigned his commission in the Federal army and on March 1 accepted a commission as brigadier general in the Confederate States Army. By the end of March he was in Charleston, South Carolina, at the end of a long journey that had once again brought him face-to-face with his one-time instructor, Major Robert Anderson.

On April 11th, 1861, a three-man delegation arrived at the fort carrying Beauregard's ultimatum. The message read as follows: "I am ordered by the Government of the Confederate States to demand the evacuation of Fort Sumter. My aides, Colonel Chestnut and Captain Lee, are authorized to make such a demand of you. All proper facilities will be afforded for the removal of yourself and command, together with company arms and property, and all private property, to any post in the United States which you may select. The flag which you have upheld for so long and with so much fortitude may be saluted by you on taking it down." Anderson refused to surrender the fort, but communicated that if he did not receive supplies he wouldn't be able to hold out for more than a few days. The Confederate delegation reported this to Beauregard, who immediately wired Secretary Walker for instructions. Walker gave Beauregard leave to hold his fire until he received a commitment from Anderson as to when he would leave the fort. The delegation returned to Fort Sumter a little after midnight on the morning of April 12th and offered Major Anderson the following new conditions: "In consequence of the verbal observation made by you to my aides, Messrs. Chestnut and Lee, in relation to the condition of your supplies and that you would in a few days be starved out if our guns did not batter you to pieces, or words to that effect, and desiring no useless effusion of blood, I communicated both the verbal and your written answer to my communications to my Government. If you will state the time at which you will evacuate the Fort Sumter, and agree that in the meantime you will not use your guns against us unless ours shall be employed against Fort Sumter, we will abstain from opening fire upon you. Colonel Chestnut and Captain Lee are authorized by me to enter into such an arrangement with you. You are, therefore, requested to communicate to them an open answer."

Anderson conferred with his officers and sent word to General Beauregard that, unless he was fired upon, received new supplies or orders from Washington, he would evacuate the fort on April 15. The answer was deemed unacceptable and Colonel James Chestnut told

Anderson that, "Sir: By the authority of Brigadier General Beauregard, commanding the provisional forces of the Confederate State, we have the honor to notify you that he will open fire of his batteries on Fort Sumter in one hour from this time." The Civil War was about to begin.

Civil War Begins

True to his word, exactly one hour later at 4:30 on April 12th, 1861, Beauregard ordered his batteries to open fire. Lieutenant Henry S. Farley fired the first shell from Fort Johnson on James Island. For more than two hours the shelling continued, without the Federal garrison returning fire. Then Captain Abner Doubleday, more famous for his invention of the game of baseball, fired a 32-pounder at the Confederate battery on Cummings Point. He had this to say of his action: "In aiming the first gun at the Rebellion I had no feeling of self-reproach, for I fully believed that the contest had been inevitable. My first shot bounded off from the sloping roof of the battery opposite without producing any apparent effect. It seemed useless to attempt to silence the guns there, for our metal was not heavy enough to batter the work down. Our firing became regular, and was answered by the Rebel guns which encircled us on four sides of the pentagon upon which the fort was built. The other side faced the open sea. Showers of balls and shells poured into the fort in one incessant stream. When the immense mortar shells, after sailing high in the air, came down in a vertical direction and buried themselves in the parade ground, their explosions shook the fort like an earthquake."

At the time when Major Anderson moved his 85 men from Fort Moultrie, Fort Sumter, a pentagonal structure with walls 40 feet high and 12 feet thick, was still incomplete. Of the 140 seacoast cannon planned, only 40 had been installed, and only 21 of those were in a position where they could be used. That, compounded by a lack of powder and fuses for what few shells they did have, reduced the garrison to firing solid round-shot at the Confederate batteries. All that night and the rest of the day the Confederate batteries pounded the tiny Federal garrison, with little reply from the beleaguered fort. The following morning the bombardment resumed with increased vigor. Red-hot projectiles fell from the sky, setting the barracks and officers' quarters inside the fort ablaze, threatening the powder magazine, and choking the defenders with dense black smoke. All through the morning of the 13th Anderson's men huddled beneath the ramparts as shot and shell rained in upon them, firing a few hurried rounds at the enemy with each lull in the Confederate bombardment. A Federal Assistant Surgeon, Dr. Crawford, having no sick to attend to, volunteered to take command of one of the fort's batteries and later had this to say of the action: "All of the woodwork was in flames. The officers, seizing the axes that were available, exerted themselves in cutting away whatever woodwork was accessible. It soon became evident that the magazine with its 300 barrels of powder was in danger from the flames. And every man that could be spared was placed upon the duty of removing the powder, toward which fire was gradually progressing, now separated from the magazine by only one set of quarters. Not a third of the barrels could be removed. So thick was the cloud of smoke and burning cinders, that penetrated everywhere, that a cause of serious danger arose from the exposed condition of the powder taken from the magazine, and Major Anderson ordered that all but five barrels be thrown into the sea.

Late in the morning the Federal supply ships appeared at the mouth of Charleston Harbor but made no attempt to run the Confederate defenses. They stood off and watched as, slowly but surely, Fort Sumter was reduced to rubble around its defenders until, by early afternoon, with ammunition almost exhausted, Major Anderson decided to surrender the fort in order to spare his men from the relentless barrage.

On Sunday the 14th of April, 1861, with permission of General Beauregard, Major Anderson commenced a 100-gun salute to his flag before it was struck from above the fort. On the 50th firing the great gun exploded, killing one man and wounding several more; the only casualties of the engagement. The formal transfer of troops began at 4 and the Confederate and South Carolina palmetto flags were hoisted side-by-side over the battered fort. During the battle more than 3,400 rounds of cannon fire fell upon the fort, inflicting so much damage that it was never completely rebuilt.

The battle of April 12 and 13, 1861, was not the only action seen by Fort Sumter. On April 7th, 1863, Union Rear Admiral Samuel F. DuPont with a flotilla of seven monitors – the most formidable warships afloat – along with the ironclads *Keokuk* and *New Ironsides*, launched an attack on Charleston. Each ship carried a formidable array of weaponry, including one 11-inch and one 15-inch cannon. The fleet opened fire at noon on April 7th and was answered by 77 huge seacoast guns of the Confederate batteries located at strategic points around the harbor. The barrage from the monitors' huge guns further reduced the wreckage of Fort Sumter, but they too suffered heavy damage. Nothing could withstand the mighty projectiles from the shore-based batteries. Confederate gunners found their marks some 400 times. Decks were holed, armor plating ripped away, smokestacks torn from their mountings, and guns put out of commission. The *Keokuk* was shattered with more than 90 hits and sank during the night after the attack had been abandoned; the *Nehant* was hit 51 times, the *Weehawken* 53 times. All the monitors suffered extensive damage and Admiral DuPont lost his command as a result of his failure.

On the 14th of April, 1865, Robert Anderson, now a retired brigadier general, returned to Fort Sumter to raise again the flag he had hauled down four years to the day earlier.

Seeing Fort Sumter Today

The National Park Service took over the administration of the monument in 1948, and Fort Moultrie 14 years later. Work began on restoration until, by 1961, half of Fort Sumter had been excavated and a museum installed. Today, the damage Fort Sumter sustained is still very much in evidence. The battered walls, the embedded projectiles, and the great guns that once again stand silent guard over Charleston Harbor, all remain a symbol of the destruction of those dark, far-off days of the Civil War.

The Charleston Harbor Tour, on the other hand, offers a waterside view of Charleston. This gives a really different perspective of the city, and the narration is particularly informative. Our favorite, though, is the Dinner & Harbor Cruise. If you are blessed with a fine day, select a table on the outdoor deck of the 102-foot yacht and settle back for a three-hour cruise, which includes a four-course dinner. Add live music and dancing and the unparalleled backdrop of Historic Charleston to the equation and you have the recipe for an unforgettable experience.

Diving

Charleston Scuba, ☎ 843-763-3483, fax 571-5441, www. charlestonscuba.com, 335 Savannah Highway, Charleston, SC 29407, is a PADI Five-Star training center and provides a complete range of PADI-sanctioned courses ranging from entry level to instructor. The diveboat, *Trident*, is docked at Ripley Light Marina, just a half-mile from the store, and takes you on offshore charters to the numerous wrecks, ledges and gulches around the nearby coast. They also specialize in river dives in the Cooper and Edisto rivers and, although the visibility is as low as two to six feet, this one is for the artifact hunter (sharks' teeth are a special favorite). These dives are, by necessity, planned around the tides.

Sailing Ship Tours

The sight of a sailing ship, especially one with tall masts, will likely evoke fantasies of adventure and romance. While in Charleston, you can experience this for yourself on a two-hour afternoon or sunset cruise aboard the 84-foot, three-masted gaff topsail *Schooner Pride*, ☎ 843-571-2486, www.schoonerpride.com. This Class "C" Tall Ship, modeled to resemble the old coastal trading schooners, sets sail from the City Marina at Lockwood Drive every day between March 1st and the end of November. Either cruise (each one is different because she sails with the winds and tides) costs $17 per person. If you are so inclined, you may assist in raising and trimming the sails, or even take a turn at the wheel. Remember to take your camera, as these pictures will give you talking points for years to come.

Speedboat Tours

Some of you, doubtless, will prefer speed to the gracefulness of sail, and, if that is the case, we recommend you head across the Cooper River to Patriot's Point. There, between April 1st and the end of the summer season, you will find the 72-foot speedboat *Sea Thunder*, ☎ 843-881-3367, 22 Patriots Point Road, Mount Pleasant, which offers Charleston's most thrilling cruise. Skipping from wave top to wave top, with the power of the twin turbocharged V-12 diesel engines throbbing beneath you, the 90-minute tour takes you past naval warships and aircraft at Patriot's Point. Then alongside Charleston's waterside Battery, out past Fort Sumter, and then along the Intercoastal Waterway to the shoreline of Sullivan's Island and the Isle of Palms. Wear bathing suits if you like, or raincoats are available to protect you from the spray.

Fishing

To get in sync with the latest angling trends, inshore light tackle and fly fishing, get in touch with **Captain Richard Stuhr**, ☎ 843-881-3179547 Sanders Farm Lane, Charleston, SC 29492. As a native of the area and an Orvis-endorsed guide, he has life-long experience of the waters in and around the Low Country. Tours aboard his fully equipped action 18-foot boat are priced at $250 for a half-day, $300 for a three-quarter day or $350 for a full day. Prices quoted are for either one or two people, and include fuel, bait, ice and tackle. Depending upon the season you may come across a variety of species such as Spanish mackerel, bluefish, ladyfish, crevalle jacks, sea trout, red drum, sheepshead and flounder. Captain Stuhr will also give you, if you need it, casting instruction at $50 per hour.

If you haven't brought your own gear, or want to expand on what you have, head for **The Charleston Angler**, ☎ 843-571-3899, fax 571-4958, toll free 877 611-5374, www.charlestonangler.com. They are at 946 Orleans Road, A-5, in the West Ashley Shops, across from Citadel Mall. Owners Brad Harvey and Rick Hess specialize in fly fishing and light tackle and they carry a wide array of rods, reels, accessories, and attractive sports clothes. Don't neglect their friendly dog, the one that stars on the website.

In the Air

Operating out of an airport just 11 miles from the city center and reached by traveling I-26 west to Exit 211 A, **Flying High Over Charleston** can be reached at ☎ 843-569-6148.

Although they schedule many types of flights, we recommend the Historic Charleston and Sea Islands Tour, priced at $135 a couple. This gives a birds-eye view of historic downtown Charleston, Fort Sumter, Charleston Harbor, the aircraft carrier *USS Yorktown*, the Morris Island Lighthouse, three or four local plantations and over 40 miles of coastline.

Eco/Cultural Adventures

Spoleto Festival USA

In 1957, the Italian composer Giancarlo Menotti was invited to Charleston by Countess Paolozzi, and the city subsequently became home to the composer's "Festival of Two Worlds." In 1977, this festival evolved into the first Spoleto Festival USA, which, during its 22 subsequent seasons, has become America's premier arts festival, uniquely utilizing all aspects of the city as its stage. Over 100,000 people attend this festival, which lasts 17 days. Since the year of its inception, tourism to Charleston has increased threefold and more than $500 million has been invested in the revitalization of the historic central district. The festival takes place in late May and early June. For detailed information, visit them at www.spoletousa.org or write to Spoleto Festival USA, PO Box 704, Charleston, SC 29402.

Spas & Fitness Centers

The **earthling day spa**, ☎ 803-722-4737, 334 East Bay Street at Ansonborough Square, is an out-of-this-world facility dedicated to the creature comforts of mere mortals.

There, you can not only choose among numerous treatments and packages but, if you are feeling a little energetic, also take a session in the Pilates Exercise Studio. We expect most will want to partake of something more relaxing, however – perhaps a massage, either traditionally therapeutic, aromatherapy massage or neuromuscular therapy. Charges range between $60 and $75 for one hour, but you can choose either a 30- or 90-minute therapeutic for $40 or $90, respectively, or a 90-minute aromatherapy for $95. Or perhaps a Sea Salt Glow, a delightful exfoliating body scrub with sea salt and essential oils, at $40 for 30 minutes, will turn the tide. Or sweeten your disposition with a Milk & Honey richly conditioning exfoliation and total envelopment, at $79 for 75 minutes. Also check out the new Ayurvedic Body Treatments, well worth $95 for an ultra-relaxing experience: the Shirodhara uses herbal-infused oils, lasts 50 minutes and will cost you $85, while the Bindi Herbal Bliss is a detoxifying body-balancing exfoliation. If you want to go all out, book an All Day Retreat, which, for $295, gives five hours of total pampering and includes a healthy light lunch. If that's a bit beyond your means, consider a Perfect Morning, which costs $160, lasts three hours and includes sea salt glow, aromatherapy massage, and facial. Specially designed for gentlemen is a two-hour package, priced at $135, which includes a Biodroga basic facial, sea salt glow and half an hour of aromatherapy massage. Finally, before leaving, check out the full range of skin and body care products and the extensive selection of gifts, jewelry, books and tapes. Earthling day spa is open Monday to Friday from 9 am to 7 pm and Saturday from 9 am to 5pm. As the management likes to say, "a visit to the earthling day spa nourishes your body, mind and spirit."

The **Spa at Charleston Place** offers a selection of classic European beauty and therapeutic services. Expect to find a spectacular indoor/outdoor heated pool, a Jacuzzi set in the signature clock tower with a stellar view, a fully equipped fitness center, steam room and sauna, a lighted tennis court and an outdoor garden area for sunbathing. Treatments here – massage, skin care, body treatments, pedicure or manicure – can be booked on either an individual basis or as part of four Day Spa packages lasting between two and five hours. Even more enticing are three carefully created comprehensive Spa Packages, including accommodation. Package I (It's a Wrap) features a facial, pedicure, manicure, a wrap of choice, including an Energy Balancing Wrap, a Detoxifying Body Wrap or a Stimulating Circulating Wrap, and a healthy spa lunch. Package II (The Rejuvenation Express) is for those who opt to revitalize their tired skin and muscles. It includes a stimulating one-hour massage and a Personal Prescription Facial. Package III (The Invigorating Escape), the most pampering and enticing of the three packages, allows three treatments of your choice from the Spa's extensive menu.

Prices for the above three packages with Deluxe accommodations are $549, $395, and $529 respectively; with Club accommodations, $649, $540 and $629. Rates include double-occupancy, but only single treatments in The Spa. You can, though, for Packages I and II, share the services if there are two of you, and the one not taking a treatment can use the other facilities in the spa.

■ Where to Stay

The **Charleston Place**, ☎ 843-724-8410, fax 722-6952, www.charlestonplace.com, 130 Market Street, owned by Orient-Express Hotels, Inc., is considered the finest hotel in the city. It is the recipient of both the AAA Four-Diamond and Mobil Four-Star awards, and was ranked among the "Top 10 Hotels in North America" by *Condé Nast Traveler* in 1997.

Each of the hotel's 440 guestrooms, including the 42 suites, is sumptuously furnished with period pieces and Southern-style armoires. They also feature an opulent bath with Botticino marble and brass fixtures, separate workspace and seating areas, temperature control, ceiling fans, cable TV and direct dial telephone with voice messaging and data port capabilities. The most discerning will specifically request one of the 79 guestrooms on "The Club" floor. Rates recently were $360 for a Deluxe guestroom, $385 on the Executive Level and $395 for The Club. Suites ranged from $475 to $2,500.

The **Mills House Hotel**, ☎ 843-577-2400, 800-874-9600, fax 722-2112, www.millshouse.com, 115 Meeting Street, is Charleston's original antebellum hotel. It has a fascinating history. The AAA Four-Diamond and Mobil Four-Star facility has 214 luxurious guestrooms and 19 suites, each individually furnished with fine period pieces and demi-canopied beds. Rates range from $189 to $279 for a room or $249 to $650 for a suite, with a $40-$60 premium added for the Executive level.

The **Westin Francis Marion Hotel**, ☎ 843-722-0600, 800-433-3733 or fax 723-4633, 387 King Street, on the corner of King and Calhoun Streets by Marion Square, is the grande dame of Charleston's hotels. When it opened, in 1924, it was fashioned in the gracious European manner and, with 312 rooms, was the largest hotel in the Carolinas. By the end of the 1980s, as with many of its genre, it had fallen on hard times and sadly closed its doors. Thankfully, help was soon at hand. Six years later, in 1995, new owners began a $12 million restoration, retaining wherever possible the original fixtures and fittings, but adding all modern facilities. The result: a grand and gracious hotel, recalling an opulent lifestyle in a more genteel era. Guests today may choose from 226 well-appointed rooms, including 66 suites, offering a high degree of comfort. Rates depend on the season, but you can expect to pay between $119 and $199 a night.

The **Sheraton Charleston Hotel**, ☎ 843-723-3000, 800-968-3569, fax 720-0844, e-mail info@sheratonchs.com, www.sheratonchs.com, 170 Lockwood Drive, is a highrise hotel just a short distance from the historical center. The 333 well-appointed rooms and suites, many with floor-to-ceiling windows, offer majestic views over both the city and the Ashley River across the road. Expect to pay between $129 and $179 per night, depending on the season.

The **Charleston Vendue Inn**, ☎ 843-577-7970, 800-845-7900, fax 577-2913, www.charleston.net/com/vendueinn, 19 Vendue Range, prides itself on European-style service, and is certainly a place to go if you want to be pampered. It is also Historic Charleston's only waterview inn. Rates range from $125 to $235.

The **Fulton Lane Inn**, ☎ 843-720-2600, 800-720-2688 or fax 720-2940, 202 King Street, commissioned by the Confederate blockade-runner John Rugheimer, has a romantic and intimate ambiance. Surrounded by the comfort and grace of a bygone era, are a combination of deluxe, king, deluxe king and cathedral suites, many of which have a large whirlpool bath, luxurious canopied bed and wet bar. Some have a fireplace. Rates are $195 to $285.

The **Two Meeting Street Inn**, ☎ 843-723-7322, 2 Meeting Street at The Battery, Charleston's oldest and most elegant inn, has its very roots in romance. It was given as a wedding present by a bride's rather generous father in 1892. Established as an inn in 1931, it exudes a wonderfully traditional Charleston ambiance and is embellished with intricately carved oak paneling, family antiques, oriental rugs, heirlooms, and exquisite Tiffany stained-glass windows throughout. It has nine luxurious guestrooms, each with private bath and six designed as Grand Victorian rooms featuring 12-foot ceilings and canopy beds. Rates vary from $160 to $180 for the smaller rooms and from $230 to $270 for the Grand Victorian Rooms.

The **Market Street Inn**, ☎ 843-723-2177, fax 723-8847, e-mail info@marketinn.com, www.marketinn.com, 48 North Market Street, has a wonderful location overlooking the historic market, and is an inn with a difference. The ambiance is far from typically Charlestonian. While most B&Bs emphasize their historical connections, the innkeepers here, Michelle and Tom Loeber, have finished off the Market Street Inn in English Art Deco. There is a choice of five oversized guestrooms that are all eclectically decorated with pieces from both past and present; each has private bath, TV, telephone, ceiling fan and sitting area. Room rates vary from $89 to $185, depending upon the season.

Zero Water Street, ☎ 843-723-2841, fax 723-0433, www.0waterstreet.com, 31 East Battery, is the only bed and breakfast located on Charleston's Battery. Built in 1836, it has been owned by the present family since the early 1900s, opening as a B&B in 1995. There are just two suites here. Rates are $195 for the upper suite; the lower suite is $135 if you take one bedroom or $215 if both bedrooms are used.

The **Elliott House Inn**, ☎ 843-723-1855, 800-729-1855, www.elliotthouse.com, 78 Queen Street, built as a private residence in 1861, has always been restored with painstaking care to ensure its architectural and historical authenticity. There are 26 guestrooms, beautifully appointed with elegant period-style furniture, a king-sized or queen-sized canopied bed, Oriental rugs, freshly cut flowers and the expected modern amenities. King-sized bedrooms are $150 a night in the high season and $105 in the low season, and queen-sized bedrooms are $125 and $94, respectively.

■ Camping

Mount Pleasant

KOA Campgrounds, ☎ 843-849-5177 or fax 884-8855, is located north of Charleston. From the junction of I-526 and Highway 17 North go 4.9 miles north. It is open all year and has pull-through sites, a Kamping Kitchen, LP gas, movies, cable TV, firewood and a pool. A Kamping Cottage costs $89; tent site $17; RV campsite with water and electric $26, with a sewer $3 more and $2 more for air conditioning or electric heat. A Kamping Cabin is $39 for one room and $49 for two.

■ Where to Eat

The **Charleston Grill**, ☎ 843-577-4522, 224 King Street, is the premier restaurant in the Charleston Place Hotel. Under the guidance of Chef Bob Waggoner, it has garnered AAA Four-Diamond and DiRoNA awards and become the only restaurant in the state of South Carolina to earn Mobil Four-

Star recognition. The atmosphere is casually elegant. It is open for dinner, Sunday through Thursday from 6 to 10 and Friday and Saturday from 6 to 11, with the bar being open daily from 4 to midnight.

The **Barbados Room**, ☎ 843-577-2400 or fax 722-2112, is found in The Mills House Hotel. Its name is reminiscent of the lucrative trading relationship between Charleston and the West Indies during the 18th century. Here, in an especially warm and intimate ambiance, the specialty is Low Country cuisine.

The **Stono Café**, ☎ 843-762-4478, 1956 Maybank Highway, James Island, is about eight minutes from downtown Charleston. Chef Barry Waldrop's menu features Low Country cuisine, based on fresh seafood, pastas, vegetarian dishes and house specials cooked from an open kitchen. The waitstaff is attentive and the atmosphere is relaxed and casual. It is open for lunch, Tuesday through Saturday, from 11 to 2:30; for dinner, Monday through Thursday, from 5:30 to 10; and Friday-Saturday from 5:30 to 11. Sunday Bunch is served from 10 to 3.

Meritäge, ☎ 843-723-8181 or fax 723-8138, 235 East Bay Street, serves up a new, exciting and very lively concept in dining and entertainment. Building upon the Spanish tapas (small plate) theme, it has expanded it to include samplings with Continental American, Southern, Mediterranean, Caribbean, Thai and other Asian influences. The ambiance, too, has many influences. There is entertainment consists of a solo guitar act on Thursdays, live blues and jazz bands on the weekends and a solo act on the deck each Sunday. At other times, you may come across most anything – perhaps a belly dancer, magician or cartoonist. Meritäge, certainly unusual and different, is open from 5 to 1am, daily.

Slightly North of Broad, ☎ 843-723-3424 or fax 724-3811, 192 East Bay Street, is located in a 19th-century brick warehouse. Quite interestingly, the kitchen is in full view of the dining room through a brick arch that once served as the entrance to the warehouse from the bustling docks. Self-styled a "maverick Southern kitchen," the menu's emphasis is on regional seafood and vegetables, enhanced by a multicultural flavoring using a variety of herbs, spices and other ingredients. The décor, too, is unusual, and combines an assortment of chairs, a variety of brightly colored fabrics and walls painted to resemble aged stucco. A non-smoking restaurant, Slightly North of Broad is open for lunch, Monday to Friday, from 11:30 to 3 and for dinner nightly from 5:30 until late.

Slightly Up the Creek, ☎ 843-884-5005 or fax 856-9828, 130 Mill Street, Mount Pleasant, is located across the river and enjoys views of

Charleston Harbor and the shrimp boats in Shem Creek. This cousin of Slightly North of Broad has been renovated to resemble a Victorian seaside inn and offers the same maverick, contemporary, approach to cuisine. Also a non-smoking restaurant, Slightly Up the Creek is open for dinner nightly from 5:30 until late.

Captain Stacks, Seafood Grill & Steam Room, ☎ 843-853-8600, 205 East Bay Street, is a nifty place to go, either for lunch or dinner, any day of the week. It is very comfortable, relaxed and eminently affordable, with most entrées in the $12 to $16 range. Seafood dishes, obviously, dominate the menu, whether grilled, sautéed, broiled or fried, but keep an eye out for steamed specialties.

It is not difficult at all to find **Hyman's Seafood Company,** ☎ 843-723-6000, 215 Meeting Street; simply look for the crowds of people waiting to get in. Yes, it really is that popular, and not without reason. The choice, quality and value for money is unsurpassed. Seafood, the freshest of course, is the thing to order in this family-run restaurant, although there are a sprinkling of other dishes if fish isn't your thing. Hyman's is open daily, from 11 to 11 and, although no reservations are accepted, your name goes on a waiting list upon arrival, hence the crowds outside.

Magnolias Uptown/Down South, ☎ 843-577-7771, 185 East Bay Street, is on the site of Charleston's original Customs House. The circa-1739 warehouse was completely renovated and opened its doors as Magnolias in 1990, revealing an ambiance that combines old-world charm with modern décor. The latter is enhanced by the contemporary, vibrantly colorful, expressionistic oil paintings of the late Rod Goebel of Taos, New Mexico, which are displayed throughout the restaurant and were commissioned especially for Magnolias. It didn't take very long for the restaurant to establish itself as one of the city's favorites. In 1993 it was awarded the prestigious DiRoNA (Distinguished Restaurants of North America) Award of Excellence. The culinary style here deliberately reflects the name. Traditional Down South fare with a contemporary Uptown presentation is seen throughout the menu. It opens at 11:30 daily, with service ending at 10 on Sunday through Thursday, and 11 on Friday and Saturday.

Carolina's, ☎ 843-724-3800 or 888-486-7673, 10 Exchange Street, just off East Bay Street towards the Cooper River, is considered by many critics to be among the best in Charleston. Casually elegant and contemporary in style, it prides itself on its eclectic regional cuisine. Carolina's opens for dinner each evening at 5:30, and reservations are recommended.

South Carolina

The Sonoma Café and Winebar, ☎ 843-853-3222, 304 King Street, is housed in a beautifully restored Victorian theater and features a prominent outdoor dining area which allows a view of Charleston's shopping district. Sophisticated, yet still casual, the décor is a blend of Victorian splendor and 1990s elegance. The cuisine is eclectic, featuring modern American with Latin, Asian and Caribbean influences. It opens for dinner on Sunday through Thursday from 5 to 10, opening an hour later on Friday and Saturday.

Southend Brewery & Smokehouse, ☎ 843-853-HOPS (4677), 161 East Bay Street, is a typical microbrewery – light, airy and informal – serving a selection of permanent ales and a smattering of new brews. The back of the menu contains a schematic diagram describing the brewing process, explaining that beer is the oldest recipe known to man, dating back to 6000 BC. The cuisine is best described as regional American with Californian, Southwestern and Mediterranean influences. This is a great place for an inexpensive lunch or dinner, and, if you want a late brew, the bar is open until 1 nightly.

■ Visitor Information

i The **Charleston Visitor Reception and Transportation Center,** ☎ 843-724-7174, 375 Meeting Street, opens daily from 8:30 to 5:30 between April 1st and October 31st, closing a half-hour earlier the rest of the year. This is the most logical place to start your exploration of Charleston. There, you will find a well-trained and helpful staff and numerous brochures, maps and other guides that will help you find your way around. Strangely, although the Charleston Convention and Visitors Bureau has space here, it is not their headquarters. So, if you want information sent to you beforehand, you will need to call ☎ 800-868-8118 or check out their website at www.charlestoncvb.com.

Charleston's Barrier Islands

■ Kiawah Island

History

 The lovely island of Kiawah, located 21 miles south of Charleston, takes its name from the Native American tribe that once hunted, fished and lived here. The arrival of white men, however, with their deadly guns and diseases to which the Indians had no natural resistance, brought death to many and enslavement to those who survived.

In 1699, the Lords Proprietors, exhibiting questionable wisdom, granted title of the island to a certain George Raynor, who, documentary evidence suggests, was a pirate. Nevertheless, his family retained control of the island until 1719, after which a turbulent 50-year period saw ownership change numerous times. The Vanderhorst family then purchased it, retaining title for the next two centuries. During the epic events of those years, it was used as a place of rest and recreation for wounded junior officers in the Revolutionary War and, during the War of 1812, as a garrison for soldiers assigned to protect the city of Charleston. It was also in that city, on April 2, 1861, that the first shots of the Civil War were fired. During the hostilities, perhaps in answer to that initial insult, Union troops adorned the walls of the Vanderhorst mansion with their version of graffiti, and this can still be seen today.

Following that war, Arnoldous Vanderhorst IV returned home and, with the assistance of what slaves remained, resumed planting before 1880. He met an unfortunate end, however, falling victim to a hunting accident, and sightings of his ghost have been reported about the island on numerous occasions. His son, Arnoldous V, achieved very little success in his attempts to work the plantation and, from that time forward, members of the family rarely returned to Kiawah.

In 1951, in a very astute business move, C.C. Royal, a lumberman, purchased the island for the miserly sum of $125,000. The true depth of his discernment was verified 23 years later, when he sold it to a resort developer for $18.2 million! Since that date in 1974, this beautiful 10,000-acre island has been sculpted into the acclaimed, AAA Four-Diamond, **Kiawah Island Golf & Tennis Resort**.

Kiawah Island Today

The fact is that, once you pass through the security gates of the resort and into the privacy of this subtropical wonderland, there is no need to venture elsewhere. Everything you could possibly want, and more, is here awaiting your discovery – a classy 150-room inn, 530 villas and private homes for rent, five world-class championship golf courses, a pair of award-winning tennis complexes, the 21-acre Night Heron Park, an array of specialty stores, plus nine restaurants and lounges. The mixture of lush flora and fauna includes forests of tall pines, palmetto palms, magnolias and live oaks; among the natural inhabitants are 193 species of birds, 30 species of reptiles and amphibians, and 18 species of mammals.

Getting Here & Getting Around

From the north, approach the Charleston area on I-95 South and/or I-26 East to I-526 West. Take 17 South, travel about five miles, turn left onto Main Road and follow the signs to the Kiawah Island Resort.

From the south, follow I-95 North to 17 North (Charleston Exit 33). Clocking from the point where 17 turns into a four-lane highway, travel nine miles, turn right onto Main Road and follow the signs to the Kiawah Island Resort.

Bicycles can be rented from either the Heron Park Center office, located next to the basketball court, or at West Beach next to the Cougar Point Pro Shop, with both locations being open daily from 8:30 to 7 pm. You can also drive around the island in your own car.

Adventures

On Foot

Beaches

Plan to spend at least some time on the wonderfully pristine beach. With over 10 miles of beachfront, Kiawah Island has more than any other planned community of similar size in the United States. Running east to west, the beaches are so lengthy that points of reference are designated by mile markers in the dunes! Strolling here, it is easy to understand why *National Geographic Traveler* named Kiawah Island one of the two most romantic vacation spots on the East Coast. Whether searching for shells, sand dollars and conchs or watching the dolphins frolic in the surf, you will surely be fascinated again and again in this magical place. If you want company, then that can be arranged too. The Kiawah Island Resort hosts beach parties, with hayrides, bonfires and live musical entertainment. Umbrellas, chairs, sail boards, catamarans, kayaks and rafts can be rented at the beach. Call ☎ 843-768-6098.

Golf

Golf is the most conspicuous sport here. In fact, this resort is internationally famous in the golf world. Golfers can sample the modern golf course architecture of five different masters.

The most renowned course is, undoubtedly, Pete Dye's 7,300-yard **Ocean Course**, ☎ 843-768-2121, ext. 5300, which offers amazing views along 2½ miles of spectacular Atlantic Ocean scenery. Just months after its opening in 1991, the Ryder Cup matches of that year, which became known as the "War by the Shore," catapulted the course to legendary status. Millions of viewers watched entranced as Bernhard Langer's six-foot putt, the last shot on the last hole of the last match of the last day, narrowly missed the cup – resulting in a European defeat and the return of the Ryder Cup to America. In November of 1997 it hosted the 43rd World Cup and again commanded the golfing world's attention as the top two players from 32 countries were locked in a four-day battle for the championship. The rates to play here range from $114 to $149.

Other courses on the island are the 6,840-yard **Osprey Point**, ☎ 843-768-2121, ext. 4071, designed by Tom Fazio; Jack Nicklaus' legendary 6,899-yard **Turtle Point**, ☎ 843-768-2121, ext. 4050; and the newest, **Cougar Point**, ☎ 843-768-2121, ext. 1710, a 6,830-yard course designed by South African Gary Player. Rates for these last three courses vary from $87 to $114.

Alternatively, just off the island at Haulover Creek, is Clyde Johnston's Scottish-American-style **Oak Point**, ☎ 843-768-7431, at 6,759 yards and with green fees ranging from $46 to $80.

Tennis

Tennis fanatics, too, are in their element here. In fact, the superior facilities have earned accolades from *Tennis* magazine. They ranked Kiawah among the "Ten Greatest US Tennis Resorts." The **East Beach Tennis Club**, ☎ 843-768-2121, ext. 4010, located across from the Town Center, features 14 clay (composition) and two lighted Hartru courts. The **West Beach Tennis Club**, ☎ 843-768-2121, ext. 1720, close to the Inn at the resort, has nine clay (composition) courts, one of which is lighted, and three hard courts, also with one lighted. A neat invention here is a zoned practice court where the ball machine has an automated retrieval system. And you will love the price; guests of the Kiawah Island Resort are entitled to one-hour of complimentary court time, per day, at either of these clubs.

On Water

Boating

If you are interested in boating, a variety of small craft are available for hire through the resort. If, however, you want to venture a bit farther afield, we refer you to the Seabrook Island chapter of this guide (pages 304-305), where you will find information on **Bohicket Marina**. That is home to Bohicket Boat Adventure & Tour Co. and Bohicket Yacht Charters, both of which specialize in a variety of boating adventures.

Canoeing/Kayaking

Canoeing and kayaking are enjoying a resurgence in popularity, so you may wish to try the resort's 2½-hour Back River Excursion or the two-hour Marsh Creek Canoeing, $18 and $16 per person respectively. Kayaking options are 2½ hours of Marsh Kayaking at $30 per person or Ocean Kayaking at $35 per person.

Fishing

Aspiring fishermen, or women, among you will want to hook up with the Basics of Fly Fishing, a catch and release program, at $10 per person or the Salt-Water Fly-Fishing Field Trip at $45 per person. The latter, however, requires some familiarity with navigating a canoe.

Swimming

Swimming, in any one of three pools at the resort, is another popular pastime at the Kiawah Island Resort. The largest is 25-meter **Junior Olympic Night Heron Park Pool**, ☎ ext. 4070, which is open Sunday to Friday from 9 to 10 and Saturday 9 to 8. The 60-foot **Turtle Point Pool**, ☎ ext. 4056, is open similar hours; and the **Inn Pool Complex**, ☎ ext. 2066, on the ocean, is open daily from 9 to 11 pm.

Eco/Cultural Adventures

The Kiawah Island Resort, of course, recognizes that many guests will want to become more familiar with the island's natural wildlife and topography. To assist in this, a staff of naturalists operates an acclaimed nature program that will sensitize you to intricacies of the fascinating barrier island environment.

Begin in the Nature Room at Heron Park Center, ☎ 843-768-6001 (or ext. 6001 if calling from your room), open Monday through Friday from 8:30 am to 11 pm and on Saturday and Sunday from 8:30 am to 9 pm. On view are local snakes, lizards, turtles, a young alligator and other creatures of the salt marsh, as well as a ghoulish collection of bones and skulls.

The decision that comes next may be very difficult. Which of the many varied and interesting tours and workshops do you sign up for? Walking tours include the two-hour Birds of Kiawah and Beginning Birding; the 1½-hour Gators-N-Y'all, which explores the life of the largest reptiles in the United States, and Night Walks, discussing nocturnal creatures, constellations and the wonders of bioluminescence. Individually, these tours are priced at $3 per person. The two-hour Island Sampler, at $7 per person, delves into the secrets of the maritime forest, allows time for shelling along the beach, and gives an introduction to all manner of island creatures. A pair of biking tours is also offered: Biking into History and Wildlife in the Wetlands, each of which is self-explanatory, lasts two hours, and costs $7 per person ($11 with a bike rental).

Of interest also are a number of Presentations and Workshops. The Loggerhead Crawl, at $5 per person, gives an opportunity for participation in loggerhead turtle nest relocation and provides information on what can be done to protect this endangered species. The innovative one-hour Ocean Seining fosters first-hand discovery of local marine life. Participants pull a 30-foot net through the surf, then examine their "catch" in a view tank before releasing. The cost is just $3 per person.

Spas & Fitness Centers

 Make an appointment with **Kiawah Therapeutic Massage**, ☎ 843-768-2030, at the Kiawah Island Inn, for a relaxing treatment of your choosing. A one-hour massage costs $65, and an extra half-hour may be added for a very reasonable $25. Facial massages, using the new Belavi technique, cost $90 a session, and a combined 30-minute massage therapy is priced at $120.

South Carolina

Where to Stay

All of the choices below are part of the **Kiawah Island Resort**, ☎ 843-768-2121, 800-654-2924, fax 768-6054, www. kiawah-island.com, 12 Kiawah Beach Drive, Kiawah Island, SC 29455.

The **Kiawah Island Inn** consists of 150 guestrooms in four lodges – two overlooking the Atlantic Ocean and two overlooking scenic lagoons. Rooms are well appointed, modern in décor and each features private bathroom with bathrobes, alarm clock, television, telephone with data port, refrigerator and mini bar. The most recent off-season rates, between January 1 and March 3 and from November 14 to December 31, varied from $95 to $170 per night. High season, March 4 and November 13, commanded rates of $140 to $260. Outdoors, an oceanfront putting green allows golf enthusiasts to get a little practice and enjoy pretty views at the same time.

Kiawah Island Villas are located either near the Inn at the West Beach Village or at the East Beach Village, which is close to Night Heron Park. Option include the number of bedrooms (one to four), and the choice of view (scenic, ocean side and the more desirable ocean view). Villas are uniquely decorated, and each offers a spacious living room, full kitchen, dining room, bedroom and sun deck or screened porch. Our recommendation is a one-bedroom ocean view which, at West Beach Village, rents between $105 to $315 and, at East Beach Village, costs between $110 to $320. Discounted rates are available for those renting by the week.

The **Resort Homes of Kiawah Island** can be truly spectacular, though they are better suited to those planning a more extended stay. For those with the luxury of time, then, this is the way to go. Budget is more than a minor consideration here. For a week's stay, an oceanfront home rents for between $1,800 and $10,000.

Rates quoted for the inn, villas and resort homes are exclusive of tax and the daily service charge of $6 for an inn room or 6% if your choice is a villa. They do include, though, complimentary on-demand transportation around the island, one hour of free tennis, discounts of up to $45 off a round of golf, complimentary use of the resort's pools and exclusive use of the Kiawah Island Inn pool complex.

Where to Eat

As with other facilities at the Kiawah Island Golf & Tennis Resort, guests have plenty of choices when it comes to eateries – there are eight on the Island!

The newest and the most luxurious is the **Dining Room at Osprey Point** in the Osprey Point Clubhouse. Here, in an elegant ambiance enhanced by antiques, other exquisite furnishings and paintings, breakfast is available from 7 to 11 am, lunch is offered between 11:30 and 2:30, and dinner, à la carte or prix-fixe menu, is served from 6 to 8. Sunday brunch is a delight also, and is served between 11 and 2:30.

In the Kiawah Island Inn and overlooking the Atlantic, is the **Jasmine Porch**, where you will find the island's only daily full-service buffet breakfast between 6:30 and 11, and where lunch is served between 11:30 to 2:30, Monday to Saturday. The Champagne Buffet Brunch, on Sunday between midday and 2:30, is a bubbly affair.

The **Indigo House** serves up exciting interpretations of contemporary cuisine, with Mediterranean and Northern Italian influences in a casual atmosphere. It is open for dinner only, between 5:30 and 9:30, with the bar open between 5 and 11.

If you fancy breakfast, 7 to 11, or lunch, 11:30 to 3, then avail yourself also of the lovely ocean and golf course view at the suitably named the **Ocean Course Restaurant**. Our choice of seating is outside on the veranda. And if you are in the mood for a drink, visit the restaurant bar between 11 and 5.

The **Topsider Lounge** is the place to go for a bit of fun and relaxation between 5 pm and 1 am. They have a full range of sandwiches, delectable appetizers, a fine selection of imported cigars from the humidor and three 52-inch TVs showing sporting events.

The favorite for light fare is probably the oceanside open-air **Sundancer Grill**, with a tempting array of grilled burgers, nachos, fresh fruit plates and crudité platters. Time your visit for an early evening cocktail and request a seat on the upper deck, with stunning vistas of the sun setting over the Atlantic Ocean. Weather permitting, the Sundancer is open from 10:30 to sunset.

In the Straw Market you will come across the **Sweetgrass Café**, which is open for lunch, 11 to 5 pm, and for dinner, Thursday to Saturday, from 5 to 10.

South Carolina

The **Night Heron Grill** is found in the Night Heron Park Recreation Complex. It is open seasonally, weather permitting, from 10:30 to sunset.

If you would rather eat in your room, there are two options. The **Kiawah Pizzeria**, open 11 am to 9 pm, offers a choice of freshly baked pizzas, pasta dishes, hot Italian subs, salads, frozen yogurt and Italian desserts. Alternatively, from 7 am to 9 pm, in the Town Center at the island's only market, you can stock up with groceries, beer, wine, freshly baked bread and sweet treats, or freshly made sandwiches from the deli.

■ Seabrook Island

History

Seabrook Island, approximately 22 miles south of Charleston, is another of South Carolina's barrier islands. As with many of its kind, Seabrook was populated originally by Native Americans. During the Colonial period, English settlers, taking full advantage of the fertile environment, cultivated rice and indigo on what they called Jones Island. In 1753, the island was purchased by Ebenezer Simmons who, not so modestly, named it after himself. Several changes of proprietorship later in 1816, William Seabrook took ownership and thus the name as it is recorded today.

Seabrook Island Today

Today, the island is privately held and operated under the name of **Seabrook Island The Resort**. The owners personally guide the destiny of the island and fortunately place great emphasis on the protection and conservation of its natural resources and beauty. Access is controlled at the security gate, ensuring privacy for owners and guests alike, as they enjoy the 2,200 acres of grounds, bordered by 3½ miles of pristine beaches and the banks of the Edisto River. The scene is one of incredible natural beauty, teeming with wildlife and waterfowl. In addition, there are two championship golf courses, a tennis center, a fitness center, swimming pools, a 22-acre Equestrian Center, many restaurants, and a smattering of shops – all of which are for the exclusive use of owners and guests. And just outside the security gates, Bohicket Marina has a full array of boating and fishing adventures to offer, as well as a variety of restaurants and specialty stores.

It may not be as well known as its near neighbor, Kiawah Island, but that might be all the better if you are looking for a less commercial atmosphere.

Getting Here & Getting Around

From the north, approach the Charleston area on I-95 South and/or I-26 East to I-526 West. Take 17 South, travel about five miles, turn left onto Main Road and follow the road past the Kiawah Island Resort entrance. The Seabrook gate is just after the Bohicket Marina.

From the south, follow I-95 North to 17 North (Charleston Exit 33). Clocking from the point where 17 turns into a four-lane highway, travel nine miles, turn right onto Main Road and follow the road past the Kiawah Island Resort entrance. The Seabrook gate is just after the Bohicket Marina.

For a bit of easygoing fun, head over to Seabrook Island The Resort's **Recreation Pavilion**, open between 7 am and 8 pm in the summer, and closing an hour earlier during other seasons. For the young and the restless who want to expend some energy, either a bike or inline skate rentals are available at $6 per hour, $11 for a half-day, or $16 for a full day.

Adventures

On Foot

Golf

Back to the subject of golf, Seabrook Island's two championship golf courses offer sharply contrasting styles of play. **Ocean Winds**, at 6,761 yards and designed by Willard Byrd, presents formidable challenges, especially on the incoming nine holes. **Crooked Oaks**, created by Robert Trent Jones, Sr., is a more classically styled 6,746-yard course, winding through forests of huge, centuries-old oaks and pines. On either course, "birdies" are easily come by; just recently, the two courses were named South Carolina's first "Fully Certified Audubon Cooperative Sanctuary." Golf rates, for 18 holes, per person per day and including green fees and cart, range from $55 to $110, depending on the season. Of course, lessons and a full range of golf services are also available.

South Carolina

Tennis

Tennis lovers will find much to please them at the Resort as well. The **Racquet Club**, open between 8 am and dusk year-round, offers unlimited play for just $12 per person per day on 13 Har-tru courts. Lessons, private or in clinic, can be arranged, and racquets, balls and a ball machine can be rented at very reasonable rates. Be forewarned, though, that very conservative dress codes are in effect for both tennis and golf.

On Water

Boating

 Surely by now you will be of a mind to try out your sea (or river) legs. If so, the **Bohicket Boat Adventure & Tour Co.**, ☎ 843-768-7294 and fax 768-4962, at the Bohicket Marina, presents as wide an array of marine adventures as you are likely to find. If you want to master your own craft for the day, for a half-day, or for just an hour, then consider a boat rental. Some options, all radio-equipped, include a 15-foot, 60 hp Boston Whaler, a 23-foot, 200 hp Deckboat, a 16-foot, 25 hp skiff, or a 22-foot, 9 hp Catalina sailboat. Half-day rates begin at $100 and full-day rates go up to $390, with fuel costs not included. And if you don't happen to have your crabbing gear or rod and reel at hand, these can be rented with the boats at $4 or $5, respectively. Perhaps, though, you are not quite ready to go it alone. You may prefer to customize a tour on a 25-foot boat with a captain at $190 for two hours or $275 for three hours. The popular two-hour River Cruise explores the creeks, rivers and marshes for dolphins and other abundant wildlife. Or how about a tour in a two-person kayak?

Crabbing/Fishing

Crabbing equipment is available for $6 a day and fishing rods are rented out at $6 per hour, $11 for a half-day, or $20 for a full day, with the bait for both included in the fees.

If fishing is your sport **Bohicket Boat Adventure & Tour**, ☎ 843-768-7294 and fax 768-4962, at the Bohicket Marina, will arrange for flats fishing, where you will be hoping to land a redfish, trout or other local species. This trip lasts four hours and for two people (that would be you two) costs $250. A half-day or full-day in-shore trip angling for mackerel, blackfin, tuna, cobia and shark is another interesting option. According to the size of the boat, prices range from $340 to $1,000. Finally, if you really are serious about landing a big one, then you need to get right out into the Gulf Stream, home of the giant marlin, sailfish, tuna, dolphin and wahoo. The sheer distance necessitates that you plan for a full-day trip; and you will have to dig a little deeper in the pockets as well. These are priced between $600 and $1,350, dependent upon boat size. Vessels for either of these expeditions range from 25 feet to 55 feet, though each has a six-person capacity. The rates will seem a bit more manageable when you realize that everything is included, except your own food and drink.

Swimming

If you find yourself overheated you can cool off at the Resort's Beach Club pool complex. Open in the summer between 7 am and 10 pm, this features a junior Olympic-size lap pool, a family-size pool, heated from mid-March to December, and a wading pool. In addition, you will find numerous other pools in and around the accommodation areas.

Yachting

Call **Bohicket Yacht Charters**, ☎ 843-768-2647 or digital pager 571-8080, at 1880 Andell Bluff Road, Bohicket Marina Village. Agree on a date with Captain Jack McConnell, and prepare for an unforgettable experience aboard his 33-foot center-cockpit aft-cabin sloop. The rate is $290 for a three-hour sail, but give serious consideration to extending the adventure to five hours at $450. And if you want to try your hand at the helm, Captain Jack will let you sail the boat as much as you like. Full eight-hour cruises are available at $575. This allows you to combine the best of both maritime worlds: a frolic during the day on a secluded barrier island – the captain carries an inflatable dinghy to take you places the yacht itself can't reach – and an evening on board later.

On Horseback

Much more unusual, and unique to the Seabrook Island The Resort, is the **Equestrian Center**, home of the annual Charleston Summer Classic Horse Show. Horsemen and women, from experienced to wannabes, are thoughtfully accommodated. Beginner Trail Rides meander through the scenic woods, marshes and tidal creeks for $45 per person while an Advanced Trail Ride is offered at $55. More romantic and costing $65 is an exhilarating Beach Ride that tours the North Beach area. It is, however, limited to riders who have good control at walk, trot or canter. If you aren't quite at that level yet, private lessons, at $30 for a half-hour or $50 an hour, may be in order.

Spas & Fitness Centers

Serious exercise can be found at Seabrook Island The Resort's fully equipped **Fitness Center**, open from 6:30 am to 7 pm, with extended evening hours in the summer, at a daily fee of $15 per person.

Where to Stay

Seabrook Island The Resort, ☎ 843-768-1000, 800-845-2475, fax 768-3096, e-mail resort@charleston.net, www. seabrookresort.com, 1002 Landfall Way, Seabrook Island, SC 29455, offers not just a room, but one- , two- or three-bedroom villas. You can even rent a private home. Whichever you choose, you will find tasteful furnishings, a fully equipped kitchen, living room and dining room, TV and VCR, washer and dryer, and a supply of linens. Rates are determined by the view – Racquet Club/Scenic Area, Golf Area or the more preferable Ocean Area; by the season and by the type of accommodation (one- , two- or three-bedroom villa. By way of example, a one-bedroom villa in the Ocean Area costs between $135 and $250 per night.

Where to Eat

It is not necessary to leave Seabrook Island The Resort for dining, fine or casual. The **Island House Restaurant**, ☎ 843-768-2571, with scenic views over the Edisto Sound, is the choice for exquisite gourmet dining. Dinner is served from 6 to 9 pm, reservations are strongly recommended, and slacks and a collared shirt are required for gentlemen, with jackets preferred but not required. This restaurant is also open for breakfast from 7 to 10:30 and lunch from 11 to 3.

Less formal dining is on-site at the **Seaview Restaurant** or at **Bohicket's Lounge**, which stocks an excellent selection of domestic and imported beers and a range of vintages as listed on the regular and captain's wine lists. If you have a mind to eat lounging by the pool or out on the beach, then head to **Cap'n Sam's** for convenient take-out options. Rounding out the options are **The Half Shell**, a favorite open-air lounge and sports bar, and **The Pelican's Nest**, appropriately found nestling by the pools.

■ Pumpkin Island

Pumpkin Island is truly unique, and it is the smallest place in this guide – just one home upon one acre. Are you intrigued? That was our reaction when we came across a small ad in the *Boating News* that was captioned "Your Own Private Island – Charleston, SC." Having always had a Robinson Crusoe fantasy, we decided to investigate. What we found was fascinating!

There are numerous barrier islands up and down this section of the coast, many of which you will be familiar with and some of which are highlighted in this guide. It is doubtful, however, (unless you are an avid reader of the *Boating News*) that you have heard of Pumpkin Island, even though it is only 10 miles from the very popular Charleston. There is no ferry service; there is no hotel, B&B, or restaurant; and there are no stores. In fact, you will be the only people there; and that is the main attraction. Beachcomb or sun in total privacy (maybe European-style), explore miles of creeks and rivers, sail, swim, fish, go crabbing, gather oysters and clams, marvel at the antics of the many birds, keep a vigil for dolphins, or relax in the hammock – the choice is yours. There will be no one to distract you or to rush you. The time and the place are yours alone.

The accommodation, too, is delightful. In 1997, Hattie and Tom Bessent constructed on their lushly wooded island a small rustic cottage. And a more idyllic island hideaway couldn't be imagined. On the main floor, there are two bedrooms with a double bed in each, a kitchen and living area. Above is a sleeping loft with bunk beds and another double bed. There is also a large porch and deck for private frolics. Linens and towels are provided and, if you ask Hattie and Tom in advance, they will stock (at your expense) all of the food, drinks and other goodies you will need. The house systems work much like those on a cruise boat. When you first arrive, Tom and Hattie will accompany you to the island to acquaint you briefly with the area waters and to explain how the battery bank, recharged by a generator every two or three days, supplies electrical power for lights, appliances and water pressure. This does mean that there is no air conditioning, but there are fans and the house is constructed to take full advantage of the prevailing summer sea breezes. Gas heat will keep you cozy if you visit in winter.

Should you – and we can't imagine why – decide you want to venture out, the island village of Folly Beach is less than 15 minutes distance by boat. There you will find a beachfront park, ocean fishing pier, marinas, shops and waterside restaurants. Alternatively, the city of Charleston is near enough for a comfortable day or evening trip.

As you must have guessed by now, the only way to Pumpkin Island is by boat. If you haven't one of your own, though, don't fret. Hattie and Tom can make arrangements for you to rent one. Docking isn't a problem either. The island has a 25-foot floating dock accessible to smaller craft, and larger vessels can anchor in the deep, wide creek and take a dinghy in to land.

For more information, or to make a reservation ($120 to $150 per night; $800 to $1,000 per week), write **Tom and Hattie Bessent**, 684 Clearview Drive, Charleston, South Carolina 29412 or ☎ 843-795-6509. Then, plan to live out your very own Robinson Crusoe fantasy.

The Low Country

South Carolina's Low Country, south of Charleston, consists of four counties, one coastal and three inland. We are concerned here only with Beaufort County and the islands within its bounds. Beaufort County stretches southward from Edisto Beach and St. Helen Sound to Daufuskie Island, taking in Hunting Island, Tripp Island, Port Royal Sound, and Hilton Head Island. It's an area as famous for its history and scenic wonders as for its reputation as a world-class resort destination. The coastline here is a boater's paradise, with its intricate saltwater creeks and rivers that wind through the sea islands just offshore. Some of the islands are uninhabited, others have been transformed into exclusive luxury residential and resort communities; the largest of the sea islands is Hilton Head, known the world over for its fabulous golf courses. Here you can enjoy golf on a wide variety of courses or, if tennis is your game, you can tune up your volley under instruction from some of the world's best tennis pros. If you've come to the islands for sun, sand and sea, you won't be disappointed; mile after mile of soft white sand borders a clear blue ocean, cooled by the sea breezes that blow gently and constantly over the islands.

Then there's the shopping and fine dining. You'll find designer factory outlets and boutiques, and restaurants that range from the mom-and-pop seafood house to the best in fine and elegant dining. If you're a fisherman, these sea islands, saltwater creeks, rivers, and the ocean itself, offer opportunities that are second to none. Hikers and lovers of the great outdoors can wander the trails on the islands, follow the beaches, and watch for the loggerheads that come ashore to lay their eggs. These islands are home to more than 250 species of wild birds, at least as many species of rare plants, and a vast assortment of small animals. They are a mecca for nature and wildlife photographers. The scenery here is beautiful, often spectacular, and what photographer could resist a chance to do something different with Hilton Head lighthouse, one of the most photographed attractions in the United States?

■ Getting Here

 From the north and south, I-95 is the main route into the Low Country.

From the west, take I-26 from Columbia and head east toward Charleston. When you reach its junction with I-95, turn south and head on in.

An alternative route from Charleston and Savannah would be Highway 17; it, too, joins with I-95 just west of the islands, but it does provide a more scenic route for most of the drive.

■ Visitor Information

 Low Country and Resort Islands Tourism Commission, PO Box 366, Hampton SC 29924. ☎ 843-943-9180.

■ Sightseeing

The ACE Basin

This area – it takes its name from the first letters of three great rivers, the Ashepoo, Combahee and Edisto – is one of the largest undeveloped estuaries along the Atlantic coast, encompassing some 350,000 acres between the Combahee and Edisto Rivers. It teems with wildlife and harbors a variety of habitat types, including upland pine forest, bottomland hardwoods, freshwater wetlands and tidal salt marshes. More than 117,000 acres of saline, brackish and freshwater marshes provide a habitat for wintering waterfowl, as well as a permanent home for hundreds of species of wild birds, 17 of which are on the endangered list. Loggerhead turtles come ashore to lay their eggs on the beaches of Otter Island; bald eagles and osprey nest within the ACE; and for the first time in more than a century, wood storks have established rookeries there.

South Carolina

But what about us adventurers? The rivers provide excellent fishing for bass, trout, flounder and shad. The Edisto River is listed as a national canoe trail, and is the longest blackwater river in the United States. Finally, for those who like to get out and about sightseeing, there are old plantation homes, Civil War forts, historic graveyards and churches.

A Field Trip

Although most of the 350,000 acres of the ACE are in private hands or accessible only by boat, several roads probe the heart of the basin and offer glimpses of the area's various habitats. The following field trip – allow at least a half-day – follows those roads for some 60 miles and guarantees you will see lots of wild birds and animals in their natural settings, with stops along the way at public access points, boat docks, and other interesting sites. It involves some backtracking, but you won't find it boring, for the return trip presents a new viewpoint and fresh opportunities to enjoy the wildlife. Finally, this is a great way for the handicapped to enjoy the sights and sounds of one of America's last great wetland areas.

To begin the trip, from Jacksonboro go south on Highway 17 for seven miles to its junction with Highway 26 (Bennett's Point Road) and turn left. From there you'll drive east on 26 for 10.2 miles through mixed pines and hardwoods to the Brickyard Boat landing. It will be on the right, where you can park your vehicle and walk to the top of the bridge over the Ashepoo River. Here you can enjoy one of the few elevated views over the ACE Basin's tens of thousands of acres of managed wetlands and tidal marshes, most of which were created in the 1800s to grow rice. The great watery grass plain you see on both sides of the road is just part of the 12,000-acre **Bear Island Wildlife Management Area**, wildlife department-owned property managed primarily for wintering waterfowl. If you look at the sky above the wetlands, you might be lucky enough to see a soaring eagle, anhingas, woodstorks, even vultures. In wintertime these wetlands are home to flocks of widgeons, teals, pintails, mallards, and puddle ducks.

Drive on along Highway 26 for another 2.1 miles to the entrance for Bear Island Wildlife Management Area. Organized groups can arrange tours of the area, but unscheduled visitors can park at the gate, just beyond the houses, and view a variety of wildlife in the impoundments on either side. The gate area provides a good look at herons, egrets, cormorants, coots, willets, yellowlegs, wood storks, terns, gulls and many other birds, depending upon the season and water levels. At least 26 pairs of bald eagles nest in the ACE Basin, and you can often see them soaring overhead or perched in the trees on the far edge of the impoundment area to the right of the gate. Here, as in many of the basin's old rice fields, you should also be able to catch a glimpse of an occasional alligator sunning himself on the banks or floating almost submerged with only his eyes and nostrils showing above the water.

Return to the highway and drive on for another three miles to the end of the pavement, then take the dirt road to the right for another quarter-mile to Bennett's Point Landing, one of two most seaward points in the ACE Basin. The B & B Seafood Company next to the landing is typical of the many small, isolated seafood docks you can find along the coast of South Carolina. Just across Mosquito Creek, a tributary of the Ashepoo River, lies the **National Estuarine Research Reserve** and its many acres of salt marsh. From here you should be able to see brown pelicans and any number of species of gulls and terns; in fall and winter you might be able to catch a glimpse of a horned grebe, red-breasted merganser, or double-crested cormorant. You are now as far east as Highway 26 will take you, so you'll have to return the way you came all the way to Highway 17. Take your time and enjoy the drive, watching out for the wildlife along the way; you should be able to see deer, turkeys, gray and fox squirrels in the wooded areas. Highway 26 passes the gates to several large plantations, most of which were once a part of the rice industry but lately have become a part of the wintering waterfowl management program.

When you reach Highway 17 again, turn left and drive 3.7 miles, then turn left onto Secondary Highway 161, known locally as Dirt Wiggins Rd.; and that's what it is, a well-maintained dirt road. Drive on along Wiggins toward its junction with Highway 162, some six miles farther. The land along the road belongs to private owners. Do not trespass. Along the way, off to the left you'll be able to catch glimpses of the Donnelly Duck Marshes, you pass the gate to the **Donnelly Wildlife Management Area** as you drive to 161 along Highway 17. On the right is a Low Country world of scrub and shrubs, among which grows the devil's walking stick – you should be able to recognize it by its huge compound leaves – and the dwarf palmetto, a miniature relative of South Carolina's state tree.

Highway 162 (Paved Wiggins Rd.) joins 161 from the right, but you'll continue on along Dirt Wiggins for a few hundred yards more and then turn left along a short dirt road to Old Chehaw River Boat Landing, This is a lovely section of the drive. From here to the landing you'll pass through a shady maritime forest with old-growth live oaks and scrub pine. The Old Chehaw itself is a brackish tributary of the

Combahee and, like most of the creeks that meander through the ACE Basin, ebbs and flows with the tide, reversing itself four times a day. On the highland side, the Old Chehaw is bordered by small live oaks, on the marsh side by black needle rush. This is a land where the wildlife thrives and, if you stop for awhile, take your time and keep quiet, you should be able to spot all sorts of wild birds and small wetland animals.

Leave the landing, return to Dirt Wiggins Rd., and continue on to the left until you reach a small one-time railroad building that proclaims the town of Wiggins at the entrance to a private plantation. Turn right at the small green sign that reads "Public Boat Landing" and drive on along the narrow road for three miles through stands of mixed oaks and hickories – the home of deer, wild hogs and turkeys – until you come to its end at Field's Point Boat Landing. This is the other most seaward point in the ACE Basin. Here, on the banks of the mud-laden waters of the Combahee River, is a shady nether world of overhanging live oaks, beyond which lies St. Helena Sound and the Atlantic Ocean. The estuary here, which includes the five sea islands that are the core of the ACE Basin National Estuarine Research Reserve, produces millions of dollars worth of commercial seafood each year and provides some of the finest recreational fishing on the East Coast. At high tide, the waters rise to cover all but the tallest of spartina stalks, while at low tide the area is a great mud flat, where herons and snowy egrets poke around for whatever small fish may have been left stranded in the tidepools.

Having driven as far into the ACE Basin as you can go, it's time to return again to Highway 17. This time you can take Highway 162, rather than retracing the drive in along Dirt Wiggins Rd. It's a very pleasant drive and you want to take your time, perhaps stopping along the way to see some of the wildlife. Watch for white-breasted nuthatches, yellow-throated warblers, wood thrushes, indigo buntings, blue grosbeaks, painted buntings, red-breasted mergansers, yellow-breasted chats, and bluebirds. Highway 17 is seven miles from the junction of Highways 161 and 162.

If you'd like to see more of the ACE Basin, you can visit the **Grove Plantation** on the Edisto River south of Adams Run and Bonny Hall on the Combahee River, ☎ 843-846-9110. You can visit Westvaco's **Edisto Nature Trail** at Jacksonboro, and schedule a guided tour of Westvaco's new Bluff Trail, 13 miles south of Walterboro on Highway 17A, by calling Westvaco's Walterboro office at ☎ 843-538-8353. For information about visiting Bear Island and the Donnelly Wildlife

Management Area, ☎ 843-844-8957; for information about the National Estuarine Research Reserve, ☎ 843-795-6350.

Beaufort

■ History

Although it has been established that native Indians lived in this area perhaps as long ago as 4,000 years ago, it was as recently as the early 16th century that its written history began. In 1514, a Spaniard, Captain Pedro de Salazar, arrived to explore the Beaufort region. Thus, it gained the distinction of being the second landing site on the North American continent, after Ponce de León's arrival at St. Augustine, Florida. What Salazar found was one of the largest natural harbors on the Atlantic coast, an asset that did not go unnoticed. The Spanish named a short-lived settlement here Punta de Santa Elena – since anglicized to St. Helena – but later withdrew to concentrate their forces at St. Augustine. In 1562, Captain Jean Ribaut, a French Huguenot, established a small settlement almost within sight of present day Beaufort at Charlesfort, calling the area Port Royal. This, the first of the Protestant settlements in the United States, was ill-fated, however. Upon Ribaut's return to France to recruit reinforcements, the soldiers who remained revolted, built a ship, considered to be the first American built craft to cross the Atlantic Ocean, and returned to France.

English settlers did not arrive on the scene until over a century later. Then, in 1670 and under the auspices of the Lord's Proprietors, they founded Charles Towne, which would soon be known as Charleston. But it was not until 1711 that the first permanent settlement, a seaport, was laid out on this site and named in honor of Henry Somerset, Duke of Beaufort. St. Helena's parish Anglican Church was established here a year later, but Beaufort, the second oldest town in South Carolina, almost wasn't. It barely survived an attack by local Yemassee Indians in 1715. Soon, plantations growing rice and indigo flourished but, being labor intensive, their success was reliant upon large numbers of African slaves, so many that they formed the majority of the population.

Thomas Hayward of Beaufort, a local rice plantation owner, was among the influential men instrumental in bringing on the Revolutionary War by their signatures on Thomas Jefferson's Declaration of Independence. With the war came the occupation by British troops.

And in the heavy battles and skirmishes fought in South Carolina, the state lost more men to the conflict than any other colony. Lost, also, was the trade in indigo, as England had provided its main market.

Luckily, a replacement crop was soon found – Sea Island cotton. And with the brief exception of the War of 1812, the years leading up to the Civil War were ones of great prosperity and growth for Beaufort. The town's favorable location, on the water and with a southern exposure, meant cooler temperatures and fewer mosquitoes than inland on the rice and cotton plantations. Recognizing this, wealthy plantation owners of the period built fabulous mansions along the Beaufort River, designed in great part for entertaining.

The Civil War, however, was on the horizon and it brought an abrupt end to this elegant way of life and profound changes to Beaufort. By 1860, secessionist sentiment was rampant. That year, under the leadership of Southerners such as Beaufortonian Robert Barnwell Rhett, the Ordinance of Secession was penned in what is now known as Secession House, on Craven Street. Secession proved disastrous for South Carolina, and particularly for Beaufort. Union forces, recognizing the necessity of controlling a secure port on the southern Atlantic coast, sent an invasion force of 30,000 by sea in November 1861. Thus, Beaufort would remain occupied throughout the course of the war. In reaction to advance warning of the attack, the majority of white citizens fled the area, taking with them only what they could carry. Their glorious homes were left behind, virtually intact, along with over 10,000 slaves who had worked their plantations. It is, perhaps, ironic that this occupation, ruinous economically, actually saved the town from physical destruction as Union troops commandeered these homes for their purposes. The John Mark Verdier House on Bay Street, for example, served as the Union Army headquarters and the Episcopal and Baptist churches, among others, served as hospitals.

Cunningly, knowing that the owners were absent for the duration of the conflict, the US Government imposed a Federal real estate tax on both the homes and the land. When these were not paid, it quickly confiscated the property. The homes were auctioned to Union soldiers and civilians, while the plantations were subdivided into 40-acre tracts and sold for nominal amounts to the newly freed slaves. These newly independent farmers were taught trades at the Penn Normal School that opened in 1862 on St. Helena Island. In Beaufort, blacks outnumbered whites by more than seven to one during this period, and one of them, Robert Smalls, a former slave and Civil War hero, was among the first black representatives to the United States Congress.

In the 1890s thousands of acres of local land were sold to private hunt clubs, frequented primarily by wealthy Northerners. And these prestigious establishments added substantially to their land holdings when the Federal government released lands in 1931. A small US Naval station established on Parris Island was destined to evolve into a major Marine Corps Recruit Depot, which, along with a Naval Air Station, opened in 1941. This complex now forms the core of Beaufort's economic health. More recently, however, tourism has come to play a major role as well. Beginning in the 1970s, Beaufort gained favor as a location site for the film industry. Movie lovers will certainly recognize a familiar setting or two from *Forrest Gump* and *The War*.

These days, Beaufort is a quiet, picturesque little town, with an old-world antebellum style. It is a splendid place, well endowed with inns, B&Bs and restaurants.

■ Getting Here

From Charleston, take Route 17 south and then Route 21 to Beaufort.

From the west, on I-95, take Exit 33 to Route 17 North and then Route 21 southeast to Beaufort.

From Savannah, the more picturesque route is on Highways 17, 278 and then 170.

■ Getting Around

A good, quick way to become better acquainted with Beaufort is to join an organized tour. **Historic Beaufort Tours and Transportation**, ☎ 843-522-3576 or 888-747-8687, at 1002-B Bay Street, offers a one-hour professionally narrated horse-drawn carriage tour that passes more than 85 antebellum houses along its leisurely way. The cost is $14.50 per person. After that Beaufort is small enough to walk around, and you will only need your car for visiting out-of-town attractions.

■ Sightseeing

Aquarium

 The **North Street Public Aquarium**, ☎ 843-524-1559, 608 North Street, was the first public aquarium opened in South Carolina. It is open Thursday, Friday and Saturday from 10 to 6. But perhaps of more interest, the Aquarium offers a Riverwalk and Aquarium Tour, a 1½-hour guided tour of historic downtown Beaufort's riverfront. You will learn how a salt marsh estuarine river system functions, in layman's terms, and have an up-close view of the creatures that inhabit the local waters as you learn about their habits and life cycles. Walks are scheduled within a two-hour period on either side of low tide, and are available seven days a week, weather and tide permitting. It is wise to make reservations at least one day in advance. The cost is $15 per person, and the tour requires at least two participants.

Churches

St. Helena's Episcopal Church, ☎ 843-522-1712, 501 Church Street, dates from around 1724, but traces its beginnings to the founding of the parish in 1712. Thus, it is one of the oldest active churches in the United States. The architectural style is classically Colonial, and of special interest is the wooden altar carved by the crew of the *USS New Hampshire* while stationed here during the Reconstruction period following the Civil War. In the graveyard you can see tombstones that were used as operating tables during the Civil War, and a brick tomb built by a local doctor who suffered from an inordinate fear of being buried alive. He arranged to be laid to rest inside the tomb, which was stocked with food and an axe so that, if his worst fears were realized, he could escape. Needless to say, the axe was never used. St. Helena's is open Monday through Saturday from 10 to 4.

Historic Houses

If you are connected to the Internet, you may want to do a little virtual exploration at **www.beaufort-sc.com**, which has an on-line walking tour of Beaufort. Unfortunately, most of the historic houses, with the exception of those that now function as inns, B&Bs and museums, are in private hands, and not open to the public.

One that is open, though, is the **John Mark Verdier House**, ☎ 843-524-6334, 801 Bay Street, built by one of Beaufort's most successful merchants. The Marquis de Lafayette visited the home in 1825, and during the occupation of Beaufort in the Civil War it served as headquarters for the commanding Union general. Today, fully restored and furnished with antiques of the period, it stands as an excellent example of Federal-style architecture. Visit on Tuesday through Saturday between the hours of 11 and 4:30.

There are two occasions each year, one in spring and one in the fall, when some of the private houses do open. St. Helena's Episcopal Church has sponsored the Spring Tours for almost 45 years. These usually offer a Friday evening Candlelight Walking Tour of selected homes in Beaufort (for about $25 per person), and a Saturday Low Country Tour of local plantations. The latter includes a plantation lunch and entertainment for $35 per person. Both are operated by **E. C.W. Tours**, ☎ 843-524-0363, PO Box1043, Beaufort, SC 29901. Tickets are limited and non-refundable. Later, in the fall, the Historic Beaufort Foundation sponsors the **Fall Festival of Houses & History**, which will be celebrating its 16th anniversary in 2000. This lasts longer than one weekend, and we suggest you call ahead at ☎ 843-524-6334 for the exact dates and schedule.

Museums

The **Beaufort Arsenal Museum**, ☎ 843-525-7077, 713 Craven St., was originally built in 1798, rebuilt in 1852, and at one time housed the Beaufort Volunteer Artillery (BVA), the fifth oldest military unit in the United States. It was converted into a museum in 1939 and today houses an interesting collection of local Indian artifacts and art, relics of the American Revolutionary and Civil War, weapons, fossils and all sorts of plantation memorabilia. It is open on Monday, Tuesday, Thursday, Friday and Saturday from 10 to 5.

The **Parris Island Museum**, ☎ 843-525-2951, is in the War Memorial Building at the Marine Corps Recruiting Depot, 10 miles south of Beaufort. This museum is dedicated to the history and development of Parris Island and the Port Royal area, with an emphasis on Marine Corps recruit training and the history of the Marine Corps in the 20th century. There is quite a history to be told. A naval yard was constructed on Parris Island in 1883, and it grew to support a Marine barracks that was established not quite a decade later in 1891. Upon the closure of the Port Royal Navy Yard in 1911, the complex was used as a Navy brig (prison), before being handed over to the Marine Corps in 1915 for use as a recruit depot. Here, over 46,000 marines trained for World War I duty and 204,000 prepared for World War II. The island could accommodate as many as 20,000 servicemen at a given time. We were interested to learn that women, who have been an integral part of the Marine Corps since 1943, train only at Parris Island. In total, over 1,000,000 marines have graduated from this base and, these days, some 18,000 men and 1,500 women complete training here every year. The museum is open daily, except on Thanksgiving, Christmas, New Year's and Easter, from 10 to 4:30.

For those interested in seeing more of everyday life at Parris Island, the **Parris Island Visitor's Center**, ☎ 843-525-3650 or 525-3297, offers free narrated tours every Saturday through Wednesday at 1, although you must make a reservation at least one day in advance. Also open to the public is a **Friday Colors Ceremony** at 8 am, followed by **Recruit Graduation** at 9:15.

■ Adventures

On Foot

Golf

 With six golf clubs and a total of 162 holes, Beaufort is a great golfing destination. The scenery is often spectacular, and the crowds are far away. Here, you can take a week, play all six courses, and then go home satisfied with an experience you're not likely to duplicate.

The **Callawassie Island Club**, 15 minutes from Beaufort off Highway 170, offers 27 holes designed by Tom Fazio and set up as three separate nines that can be played in any combination to make four different 18-hole courses. It's a spectacular location, where you can play golf and tennis, swim and enjoy a little Low Country cuisine. Available to members and their guests only. ☎ 803-521-1533 or 800-221-8431.

Dataw Island, six miles east of Beaufort on Highway 21, offers two 18-hole and one nine-hole course designed by Tom Fazio and Arthur Hills. Again, the scenery is spectacular with lots of water and live oaks; the courses are challenging, but fun to play. Other amenities include tennis courts, a pool, dining room and a full service marina. ☎ 803-838-3838 or 800-848-3838.

The **Golf Professionals Club**, east of Beaufort on Rte 802 on Lady's Island, features two 18-hole courses, one with all the characteristics and blooms of Augusta National, the other noted for its moss-covered live oaks. ☎ 803-522-9700.

Fripp Island Ocean Point Golf Links, on Fripp Island, has a sea-side course that's almost breathtakingly beautiful. Bordered by ocean, woods and lakes and built to an authentic links design, the course brings water into play on 10 of its 18 holes. The private 3,000-acre resort and residential development also offers a 3½-mile beach, tennis courts, a marina and fine dining, Available to guests only. ☎ 803-838-2309 or 800-845-4100.

Country Club of Beaufort, at Pleasant Point Plantation, on Lady's Island, offers 18 holes of golf on a course where centuries-old live oaks, 100 acres of lakes, and vast stretches of salt marsh line the fair-ways and border the greens. Architect Russell Breedon made good use of the land's natural beauty. This one is too good to miss. ☎ 803-522-1605 or 800-869-1617.

Cat Island Golf Club, two miles east of Beaufort, is George Cobb's last creation and, so many say, his finest. Here you'll play 18 holes through the densely wooded interior and past scenic marshlands, with spectacular views over Port Royal Sound. This is golf at its best, one to talk about. ☎ 803-524-0300 or 800-221-9582.

On Water

Boat Trips/Cruises

 You haven't really seen Beaufort until you've seen it from the water. To do that, head to the marina where, at 2 every day for $17 per person, you can cruise the river aboard the *Islander*, ☎ 843-524-4000, fax 757-9304, www. islandercruises.com. The ship's design is reminiscent of the coastal steamers that carried passengers, freight and mail between Charleston and Savannah at the turn of the century. Throughout a very enjoyable 1¾-hour sail, the captain offers an entertaining and highly informative running (well, sailing) commentary, as you pass to the southern end of Parris Island, where you will have panoramic views of Hilton Head to the south and the Fripp Islands to north. Along the way, keep your eyes peeled for frolicking Atlantic bottle-nose dolphins, numerous wading birds, and a variety of other wildlife.

Deep-Sea Fishing

If you have a penchant for deep-sea or Gulf Stream fishing, we recom-mend Captain "Wally" Phinney, who has operated **Sea Wolf**

Charters, ☎ 843-525-1174, 5003 Luella Street, Beaufort, SC 29906, for 17 years. Captain Wally, US Army retired, has been acquainted with local waters since 1946. He received the highest national award for safety within the US Power Squadrons (Life Saving Award), in recognition of his rescue of three people from a sinking vessel 20 miles offshore in six-foot seas. He is also a Scuba Master Instructor and has a vast knowledge of local reefs and wrecks. He knows which fish prefer each place and when they are likely to frequent it. And he puts his knowledge to good working use. In fact, a 6 ft. 7 in., 104 lb wahoo, a mere five lbs below the state record, was caught on one of his charters. Captain Wally's speedy boat is powered by twin turbo-charged diesel engines of 250 hp. Departures are from Low Country Waters, Beaufort, and choices are a half-day trip at $330, a three-quarter-day trip at $430 or a full-day trip at $600. If you have your heart set on going all the way to the Gulf Stream, expect to pay $1,100 for a day's trip.

Fly-Fishing

The fishing opportunities are superb. If you are a serious angler, though, before heading for the water, head for the center of town. **Bay Street Outfitters**, ☎ 843-524-5250, fax 524-9002, e-mail Baystoutfr@aol.com, at 815 Bay Street, is the place to go for shallow-water fly-fishermen. Tony Royal, the owner, has gathered together the most qualified guides and instructors on the South Carolina coast to lead half-day ($250 per couple) or full-day ($400 per couple) charters. These scour the literally hundreds of miles of tide waters and grassy marshes, looking for reds, giant cobia, jacks, ladyfish or trout. You can be assured that there are plenty of fish out there year-round, but expect the approach and methods to change on a seasonal basis. No license is required on these charters, the price of which includes drinks on a half-day trip and drinks and a hearty lunch on the full-day trip. Come prepared, with deck or tennis shoes, hat, polarized sunglasses, seasonal clothing, sunscreen, rain gear and a camera. If, once you arrive, you find you have come up a little short in the way of preparation, don't despair. You can find what you will need, from incidentals to full fishing gear, at the Bay Street Outfitters Store. They carry a wide selection of rods, including the new TL-series, and a full range of tackle. They also provide rod repair service. Bay Street Outfitters also operates a One-Day Fishing School, segregated for men and women, and a Two-Day Redfish School, teaching advanced techniques, on certain days during the year. Call for more information if these interest you.

Kayaking

If you are feeling energetic and adventurous, we suggest that you contact **The Kayak Farm**, ☎ 843-838-2008, 1289 Sea Island Parkway, St. Helena Island, SC 29920. They invite you, following personal instruction in safety and in the proper use and selection of equipment, to take a half-day tour at $45 per person or a full-day tour at $65 per person. In this area, where the land meets the water, there are numerous possible excursions to choose from, with each nature tour including equipment, guides and expedition lunch or snack. Or, if you prefer, rent a kayak yourself, half-day for $30 or full day for $35, which includes a lightweight feathered paddle and a professional PFD. Necky, Current Designs or Heritage Kayaks make all of their kayaks, and first-time paddlers are both welcomed and encouraged.

Eco/Cultural Adventures

ACE Basin

 Nature lovers will certainly not want to overlook the largest pristine estuarine preserve on the East Coast, just to the northeast of Beaufort. There, the Ashepoo, Combahee and Edisto Rivers, combine in the St. Helena Sound to form what is known as the ACE Basin. The **ACE Basin National Estuarine Research Reserve** (NERR), ☎ 843-762-5437, PO Box 12559, Charleston, SC 29422-2559, was established in 1992 and includes over 140,000 acres of winding tidal creeks, brackish and salt marshes, barrier and marsh islands and other biologically rich areas. It is home to many endangered or threatened species and a mecca for both commercial and recreational fishermen. While the ACE Basin offers walking tours and workshops, we think the best way of getting to know this natural wonderland is to contact **ACE Basin Tours, Inc.**, ☎ 843-521-3099 or 888-814-3129, One Coosaw River Drive, Beaufort, SC 29902, and arrange for a tour. Then, at a predetermined time, USCG-certified and -licensed Captain Stan Lawson will welcome you aboard his *Dixie Lady*, a 38-foot covered pontoon boat, for a three-hour cruise among the tidal marshes and Sea Islands. You will be treated to history and nature lessons by Captain Stan, a lifelong resident of the area. As you glide past plantations and abandoned rice fields, you will likely see dolphins, alligators, eagles, ospreys, raccoons, minks, otters, deer, and more species of birds than you can possibly count. These tours are by reservation only, cost $25 per person, and depart from Coosaw Island, just nine miles northeast of Beaufort.

Festivals

At the riverside, Waterfront Park is home to three interesting events each year. The **Water Festival** runs for 10 days each July. In October, you can treat your taste buds to the **Shrimp Festival** and the **Beaufort By The Bay Winefest**. These are celebrating their 45th, sixth and 10th anniversaries, respectively, in 2000.

Hunting Island State Park

Another place well worth a visit, both for its beaches and its natural attributes, is the 5,000-acre **Hunting Island State Park**, ☎ 843-838-2011, www.state.sc.us. Found 16 miles east of Beaufort on Highway 21 at 1775 Sea Island Parkway, St. Helena, SC 29920, this park, with an ocean beach more than four miles long, is one of the most popular in the state. The name originates from its former use for hunting. In today's less threatening environment, it is home to as many as 125 species of birds, white-tailed deer and raccoons. Look also for specimens of South Carolina's state tree, the palmetto, otherwise known as the "cabbage palm." On the southern edge of the park, the Lagoon is a great place for surfcasting. Alternatively, privately owned Paradise Fishing Pier, ☎ 843-838-5455, extends 1,120 feet into Fripp Inlet. A visitor's center by the park's entrance features topical displays and the park naturalist conducts organized educational programs along the two nature trails or the marsh boardwalk. Undoubtedly, though, the highlight of your visit will be the historic 136-foot-high, 19th-century lighthouse, ☎ 843-838-2011, the only one of the seven South Carolina lighthouses open to the public. Between 10 am and 5 pm, you can climb to the top, if you have the necessary mental and physical disposition, for a magnificent view overlooking the island and coastline. Park hours are April to October, daily, from 6 am to 9 pm and 6 am to 6 pm the remainder of the year.

St. Helena Island

The second of our more unusual attractions is the **Penn Center**, ☎ 843-838-2432 or 838-2235, Martin Luther King Drive on St. Helena Island, a museum dedicated to the history of a unique and historically important school. Penn School, founded in 1862 by northern missionaries and named in honor of the first African-American to practice medicine on St. Helena Island, is the only public educational facility listed on the National Register of the Department of the Interior. The first school in the South dedicated to the education of Blacks, it taught the history and culture of the Gullah People and the West African connection. Today, it houses a very specialized museum, which displays artifacts and farm and blacksmith tools from throughout the school's history. It is open Monday through Friday from 11 to 4 and Saturday from 10 to 4.

The Gullahs

To grasp the significance of Penn School, it's helpful to know a bit about the Gullahs and their heritage. The climatic conditions of Africa's West Coast and the Sea Islands of South Carolina are similar, both being conducive to the cultivation of rice. Owners of rice plantations in the New World saw the value of acquiring slaves experienced in rice farming – namely the Gullah people of West Africa. And so, while most slave peoples were separated from one another to negate the chances of a rebellion, the Gullahs were, just as deliberately, kept together so as to capitalize upon their farming abilities. It was fortuitous for them, also, that the slave owners had an aversion to the hot and humid climate and a healthy fear of its accompanying scourge of malaria – to which the slaves had developed a resistance. Thus their owners more or less left the Gullahs to themselves, knowing that in any event living on the islands left them few opportunities for escape. In staying together, the Gullahs retained their traditional ways of life, and consequently still share many social similarities with people from the coast of West Africa, particularly those of Sierra Leone and Senegal. If you want to discover more about this fascinating African-American culture, contact **Gullah-n-Geechie Mahn Tours**, ☎ 843-838-7516 or 838-6312, on St. Helena Island. This group operates three two-hour tours a day, at a cost of $17 per person. There is also a Gullah Festival every May in Beaufort.

■ Where to Stay

The **Rhett House Inn**, 1009 Craven Street, is a most imposing mansion indeed. Originally built in 1820 and restored after the Civil War, it boasts a magnificent Greek Revival façade with a double wrap-around verandah, supported by elegant columns, and a curved staircase leading to the first floor. It has earned Mobil Four-Star and AAA Four-Diamond ratings, and has been featured as a location shoot for movies such as *Forrest Gump, Prince of Tides* and *G.I. Jane*. It has also hosted such stellar guests as Barbra Streisand, Demi Moore, Sharon Stone and Robert Redford. ☎ 843-524-9030, 888-480-9530, fax 524-1310, e-mail rhetthse@hargray.com, www.innbook.com/rhett.html. Rates range from $150 to $250 per night, and include a delicious breakfast, afternoon tea and evening hors d'oeuvres.

The **Beaufort Inn & Restaurant**, 809 Port Republic Street, was built in 1897 as a second home for a prominent Hampton attorney. It was sold in the 1930s, renovated, and, subsequently, opened as the Beaufort Inn, one of Beaufort's first boarding houses, and now holds an AAA Four-Diamond rating. ☎ 843-521-9000, fax 521-9500, e-mail bftinn@hargray.com, www.beaufortinn.com. Rates vary from $125 to $225 a night.

The **Cuthbert House Inn**, 1203 Bay Street, is the only one of the inns detailed here that directly overlooks the waterway. Built in 1790, the building is on the National Historic Register, and the inn holds a AAA Three-Diamond rating. ☎ 843-521-1315, 800-327-9275 (reservations only between 9 am and 9 pm), fax 521-1314, e-mail cuthbert@hargray.com, www.cuthbert-bb-beaufort.com. Rates range from $145 to $205.

■ **Where to Eat**

The **Beaufort Inn Grill Room & Wine Bar**, ☎ 843-521-9000, 809 Port Republic Street, occupying the first floor of the Beaufort Inn, has been awarded the AAA Four-Diamond award. It has among its offerings a rather unusual Chef's Game Selection, featuring seasonal game from around the world. Opening every day at 5 with no reservations needed, it also features many seafood dishes.

At **The Bank Waterfront Grill & Bar**, ☎ 843-522-8831, 926 Bay Street, you will find, at lunchtime or during the dinner hour, a wide variety of tasty meals. As you will see when you arrive, it really was, at one time, a bank. And it certainly makes a statement, with credit due to the management; and you won't have to overdraw your account to satisfy your appetite.

Ollies By The Bay, ☎ 843-524-2500, 822 Bay Street, shares a similar menu and a light-hearted ambiance with its counterpart, **Ollies Seafood Restaurant**, ☎ 843-525-6333, at 71 Sea Island Parkway on Lady's Island. Ollie, as the menu will tell you, is an oyster. The narration continues to explain that these tasty morsels were so numerous in surrounding waters that they were processed and packed in local factories, then shipped all over the country.

■ Visitor Information

The **Greater Beaufort Chamber of Commerce and Beaufort Visitors Center,** ☎ 843-524-3163, e-mail chamber@beaufortsc.org, www.beaufort.com, 1106 Carteret Street, is open daily between 9 and 5:30, and it has all manner of useful information and publications. Be sure to pick up a copy, or two, of the complimentary *Map of Historic Beaufort and Islands.* And if you are really intent on historical exploration, the "Historic Port Royal Walking Tour" pamphlet is available from the Historic Port Royal Foundation, ☎ 843-524-4333, 1004 11th Street, Port Royal, SC 29935.

Edisto Island

Edisto is one of South Carolina's barrier islands just to the northeast of Beaufort, across St. Helena Sound.

■ History

The Edisto Indians, hence the name, were the first inhabitants of the island. The first Europeans, Spanish explorers, arrived in the mid-1500s, established a mission, but didn't stay long. Then, in 1675, the Earl of Shaftsbury purchased the island from the Indians for a few beads. Indigo was the first crop on Edisto – you can still see traces of the old vats – but Sea Island cotton, grown here throughout the 19th century, was so highly prized it was often pre-sold before it was planted. Alas, the arrival of the boll weevil in the early years of the 20th century brought an end to this profitable product. Today, tourism is the main industry on the island, and the end to Edisto's unspoiled isolation seems inevitable.

■ Edisto Island Today

Getting here is easy; simply take Highway 17 and then Highway 174. Edisto Beach is an unspoiled stretch of white sand, bordered on one side by the Atlantic and on the other by lush saltwater marshes and meandering creeks and streams. Everywhere there are ancient, moss-covered live oaks.

South Carolina

Edisto Beach is for the family. Here you and the kids can play among the tide pools, go picnicking, swimming, sunbathing, shelling, crabbing and, of course, fishing. Nature puts on a full program of live entertainment: the seabirds are friendly, almost tame, crabs scurry busily about the sand, and the loggerheads come to the more remote sections of the beach to lay their eggs.

■ Camping

 Edisto Beach State Park, at 8377 State Cabin Rd. on Edisto Island, comprises more than 1,200 acres of beachfront campground with lots of facilities. There are 103 campsites, all with water and electric hookups, picnic tables and access to comfort stations with hot showers and restrooms. There are also five vacation cabins, all fully equipped with bed linens, and cooking and serving utensils. For recreation, there are five hiking trails and three nature trails, two small picnic shelters with tables and grills, as well as several miles of beach where you can go surf fishing. There's also a playground for the kids and lots of room to stretch out and relax in the sun. The rate is $15 per night; $52 for a cabin. Edisto is one of the few state-run facilities where you can make a reservation. ☎ 843-869-2156.

Hilton Head & Daufuskie Island

■ History

 It has been established that native Indians lived in the area for many millennia. The Indian Shell Ring in the Sea Pines Forest is on the National Register of Historic Places and dates back to 1450 BC. It was not until the early 16th century, however, that Spanish forces explored these coastal waterways. In 1562, Captain Jean Ribaut, a French Huguenot, established a small settlement at Charlesfort, almost within sight of present day Beaufort, naming the area Port Royal. This, the first Protestant settlement in the United States, was ill fated, however. Upon Ribaut's return to France for reinforcements, the soldiers who remained revolted and built a ship, considered to be the first vessel built in America to cross the Atlantic, and returned to France.

The English Arrive

A hundred years later, in August of 1663, an English captain, William Hilton, spotted the high bluffs of the island while exploring the Port Royal Sound. After visiting this 12-mile-long and five-mile-wide, foot-shaped Barrier Island, and modesty notwithstanding, he named it Hilton Head Island, with Head being the maritime word referring to headlands visible from the sea. In 1698 King Charles II granted several islands, and some of the mainland, to John Bayley. This area, with the exception of Hilton Head Island, was subsequently known as Bayley's Barony. The first white settlers did not arrive, however, until 1717, when the Lords Proprietors, in recognition of his actions in subduing the rioting Yemassee Indians, granted Colonel John Barnwell substantial acreage on the northwest corner of the island. By the time the Revolutionary War broke out, up to 25 families lived on the island, enduring frequent raids by the British, who burned plantations and captured slaves, which they later sold in the West Indies.

It was not until after the war that Hilton Head Island gained international recognition. Then, in 1790, William Elliott, an island planter, raised the first, and soon to be famous, long-staple Sea Island cotton. Working with his neighbor, William Seabrook, they discovered a new procedure for fertilization – alternating marsh mud and oyster shells annually – which produced record crops. Both cotton and rice crops, with the brief interlude caused by invasions during the War of 1812, brought prosperity in abundance, until by 1860 there were 24 area plantations in operation. This, though, this was not translated into the typical rise of mansions. In fact, the plantation owners, loathing the hot summers and fearful of the diseases caused by mosquitoes, spent little time on the island. They preferred, instead, to stay at their main residences, many of which can still be seen today in Beaufort or Charleston.

The Civil War & Its Aftermath

The Civil War, however, was as disastrous to Hilton Head's way of life as it was for the rest of the area. On November 7, 1861, in the Battle of Port Royal, the largest naval battle fought in American waters, Union forces won a decisive victory. As panicked plantation owners fled, 1,000 slaves or more were freed, and by the end of the war over 50,000 Union troops, support personnel and slaves were based on the island. An interesting aside: black males, on the island and in the immediate area, were forced into uniform, thus becoming the first blacks in the

Union forces. Later, these same slaves were able to purchase land with the money they had earned in their country's service. General Ormsby Mitchel, a Union commander who would die of malaria in 1862, had the foresight to establish, in the same year, the nation's first freedman's town, appropriately named Mitchelville. Home, at one time, to over 1,500 people, it slowly disappeared after the Federal troops departed. The island remained home, however, to small communities of former slaves. In fact, Special Field Order Number 15, issued by General William Tecumseh Sherman on January 15, 1865, granted the Sea Islands territories, from the Carolinas to northern Florida, to the now freed slaves and prohibited whites from settling there. The inhabitants survived on what they could raise from their small farms, and by hunting and fishing. And because they remained in a communal environment with little or no influence from American culture, these peoples, who have come to be called the Gullah, have retained to this day, in large part, the culture, traditions and language of their native West Africa. For a more detailed explanation of the Gullah and their link to West Africa, see page 342. This unique culture is celebrated each February when the month-long annual **Native Islander Gullah Celebration**, www.gullahcelebration.com, showcases the fascinating arts, crafts, history, music and food of these people. Year-round, **Gullah-n-Gechee Mahn Tours**, ☎ 843-838-7516 and **Gullah Heritage Trail Tours**, ☎ 843-681-7066, both offer you opportunities to experience this unusual culture.

In the 1890s thousands of acres of land in the surrounding areas were sold to private hunt clubs, which attracted primarily wealthy northerners. Much more land was acquired for this purpose when the Federal government released lands in 1931. By this time, over on the islands, the dreaded boll weevil pest had destroyed the cotton crop, and Hilton Head, with a population of around 300 blacks, was still accessible by water only.

The 20th Century & Today

In the 1950s, a group of entrepreneurs, including General Joseph Fraser, recognized that the tall pine trees, commonly known as Sea Pines and found throughout the island, were marketable for a number of uses. They set about buying up 19,000 of the island's 25,000 acres for their timber business. Modernization, though, was slow. It wasn't until 1951 that electric power finally came to Hilton Head Island and finally in 1956 a two-lane bridge replaced the ferry service as the main access to the island.

Around this same time, the General's son, Charles Fraser, had a grand vision for the future of Hilton Head Island and, in preparation for making it a reality, acquired a controlling interest in the family's holdings. The younger Fraser believed that if he offered a host of up-scale amenities such as golf courses and marinas first, then further development would follow. This, he conceived, would take the form of a series of communities masterfully planned to be of the highest value with the lowest environmental impact. These days, his legacy lives on in 11 major resort and residential communities that conform, in their own way, to the elegant "Hilton Head Look." According to 1997 research and profile studies, a population of 2,500 in 1970 has now dramatically increased to more than 35,000 permanent residents, with 2.38 million visitors arriving each year. Hilton Head Island, which attains and perhaps surpasses Fraser's high ideals, is now world renowned and plays host to such diverse events as the MCI Classic - The Heritage of Golf tournament, for the top PGA professionals, and the annual Renaissance Weekend, an intellectual informal think tank attended by a host of notables, traditionally including President Clinton.

Admittedly, our initial firsthand contact with Hilton Head Island was precipitated by research for this guide; and, while we had heard and read much about its attributes, we were not prepared to be quite so impressed. We found wonderful, unspoiled beaches, beautiful beachfront hotels/resorts, outdoor pools encompassed by impeccably manicured gardens, numerous marinas, hundreds of restaurants, and an abundance of shops and shopping centers. What is really amazing is that these wonderfully civilized and modern attractions reside in total harmony with and without distracting from the island's main attraction – its natural beauty. Attention has been given to even the smallest of details. It is as though, with painstaking care, these modern facilities have been sculpted out of the island.

■ Daufuskie Island

About a mile to the west of the southernmost point of Hilton Head Island, and separated from the mainland by the waters of the Calibogue Sound and Cooper and New Rivers, is Daufuskie Island.

History

 This island's earliest residents, native Americans, made their home here as much as 9,000 years ago. Many millennia later the plantation culture arrived with the planting of indigo and rice in the 1700s, reaching its peak during the 19th century when the Sea Island cotton crops brought much wealth. Indeed, at its zenith in the middle of that century, there were 10 plantations on Daufuskie Island alone, each competing with the other for grandeur and hospitality. In fact Melrose, constructed upon what is presently the site of the inn, which is a part of the Daufuskie Island Club & Resort , was considered to be one of the finest plantations in all of the Sea Islands. Its magnificent grand formal gardens were envied and the mansion was filled with furniture and artwork imported from England and France.

As with its neighbors, this grandeur came to an abrupt end as plantation owners fled Union forces upon the opening of hostilities in the Civil War. Following the war the island's only inhabitants were the former Gullah slaves, who, having purchased small plots of land, flourished economically by continuing the production of Sea Island cotton. This, too, came to an end, falling prey to the ravages of the boll weevil in the 1920s and of the economic depression of the next decade. The harvesting of oysters provided a temporary boom. Daufuskie oysters were hungrily sought by gourmets from around the world until pollution in the Savannah River closed the beds in the 1950s. The population of this island has always been small. In 1910 it was a mere 112 and, although this increased when the oyster trade was flourishing, it dropped again dramatically as those revenues subsided, reaching a low of 59 in 1980.

Around that time, resort developers woke up to the possibilities inherent on the sleepy island of Daufuskie. Not wishing to repeat what they believed to be mistakes made in developing neighboring coastal island resorts, they set out to create a simple, unspoiled retreat. To their minds, this meant no bridge to the mainland, no vehicular traffic, no motels, no malls and no theaters. It certainly did not mean, though, that luxury would be spared. The Daufuskie Island Club & Resort has carefully developed the island to include a private community at Bloody Point and a small oceanfront inn and beach cottages open to the public at Melrose. Prestigious golf courses, clubhouses, and a tennis center have been carefully blended into the environment as well. There is even an Equestrian Center, where novices or accomplished riders may take advantage of a wide array of programs. Add to these the natural charms of the island – pristine beaches, water sports, well-stocked freshwater lakes and the low key, very relaxed, atmosphere – and you have all the makings for an unforgettable escape.

Getting Here & Getting Around

From I-95, take the Hardeeville Exit and follow Route 46 East to its junction with Route 278, then follow that east to Hilton Head Island.

From Charleston, it is easier to take Route 17 to Route 21 to Route 170, then Route 278 south and east to Hilton Head Island.

Hilton Head Island is deceptively large, and the only realistic way of getting around is by car. On Daufuskie, there are horse tours, but otherwise an electric golf cart, a bicycle or your own two feet are the options.

Visitor Information

Hilton Head Island Chamber of Commerce, ☎ 843-785-3673, 800-523-3373, www.hiltonheadisland.org, PO Box 5647, Hilton Head Island, SC 29938.

Sightseeing

Amphibious Vehicle Tour

As you might expect on an island, you can choose from any number of boat trips, but, before we detail them for you, let us introduce you to a really unique way of getting around the Island, both on land and water. **Cool Stuff Tours**, ☎ 843-342-3000, 31 Hawkes Road, Box 1703, Bluffton, SC 29910, operates an amphibious vehicle that functions as both bus and boat and, for $29 per person, will take you on a 2¼-hour tour that does not repeat any scenery. Departing, rather incongruously, from the Sam's Club parking lot in the Port Royal Plaza (at mile 5 marker on Highway 278), it leaves at times that vary due to tires and tides. First, it drives you to the Intracoastal Waterway at Buckingham Landing, where it takes to the water and cruises south past Pickney Island, Jenkins Island, Spanish Wells, Bram's Point and Buck Island before traveling up Broad Creek, coming out of the water at the Old Oyster Factory, and driving back to Sam's Club. On this nifty narrated tour, you will both have fun and learn about dolphins, pirates, history, Indians, sailors and many other things.

Daufuskie Island

Just a mile away from Hilton Head Island, the quieter Daufuskie Island, accessible only by boat (or plane) as described above, offers many activities and a bit more peaceful environment. It is home to just one small, but particularly charming, inn that is open to the public and is detailed below. Daufuskie, indeed, is a perfect setting for lazing around the pool or strolling along the fantastic beaches, but those with energy to burn have options too. For sports lovers, there is golfing on either the Jack Nicklaus Signature or Tom Weiskopf/Jay Morrish-designed course, tennis, croquet, lawn bowling, water-skiing, parasailing, jet skiing, and any number of opportunities at The Equestrian Center. On the other hand, the island's history should not go unexplored. Beginning at 9 am and 4 pm daily, local Island historians lead 90-minute tours, during which you will hear the best of the local yarns; pass the historic and recently restored 1872 **Haig Point Lighthouse**; see the **Mary Fields Elementary School** where novelist Pat Conroy once taught; visit the **Mary Dunn Cemetery**, the lasting resting place of many prominent antebellum era families; the **First Union African Baptist Church**, used continuously for more than a century, and the **studios** of local artist Christina Bates and potter Bob Burns.

■ Adventures

On Foot

Beaches

The beaches of Hilton Head are truly spectacular, wide, hard-packed, ivory and white sands stretch for more than 12 miles along the coast of the island. Washed year-round by the warm waters of the Gulf Stream, and cooled through the summer by the ever-present sea breeze, these sands offer more opportunities to sunbathe, get wet, fish, romp and play than almost any other of the Sea Islands. Here you can rent a power boat, or a yacht, and go off for hours under a blazing sun. You can surf, water-ski, windsurf, parasail, jetski, even rent a kayak and take to the Intracoastal Waterway with paddle and picnic basket. If you're a fisherman, you can cast into the dark green waters off the beach, or take to the ocean in a fast-running charter fisherman in search of the great deep-water sport fish. Scuba divers and snorkelers will find more opportunities to plunge beneath the waves than they could handle in a month of Sundays.

Golf

Hilton Head is a golfer's paradise. With what must surely be the world's highest concentration of championship golf courses, you won't want for somewhere to play; deciding where is the problem. And these are not just ordinary courses. Each and every one has a distinctive character all its own; three are numbered among the nation's top 100 (Harbor Town, Long Cove and Colleton River). Many have the stamp of their architects all over them. Men like Pete Dye, Jack Nicklaus, Gary Player, Fuzzy Zoeller and Robert Trent Jones have created both monsters and princes among courses. Some skirt the ocean, others meander through the moss-covered live oaks, pine trees and magnolias of the island forests. Even beginners will find courses to match their abilities. With plenty of instruction available, you may well leave the island at least a couple of shots better than when you arrived.

If you just like to watch, and many of us do, there's plenty for you too. First, of course, there's the MCI Heritage Classic played each year at the Harbour Town Links; then there's the Merrill Lynch Shoot-Out, the Wendy's Three Tour Challenge, the Amoco I Centel Championship, and many lesser known but no less entertaining tournaments. There's always something going on.

Among the many courses are the following:

Arthur Hills, Palmetto Dunes, ☎ 843-785-1140, 18 holes, 6,651 yards, par 72, rated 71.4.

Arthur Hills, Palmetto Hall, ☎ 843-689-4100, 18 holes, 6,918 yards, par 72, rated 72.2.

Barony, Port Royal, ☎ 843-689-GOLF, 18 holes, 6,530 yards, par 72, rated 71.2.

Country Club of Hilton Head, Hilton Head Plantation, ☎ 843-681-GOLF, 18 holes, 6,543 yards, par 72, rated 71.7.

George Fazio, Palmetto Dunes, ☎ 843-785-1130, 18 holes, 6,873 yards, par 70, rated 74.2.

Harbour Town Links, Sea Pines Resort, ☎ 843-842-1892, 18 holes, 6,916 yards, par 72, rated 74.

Indigo Run Golf Club, Indigo Run, ☎ 843-689-2200, 18 holes, 7,014 yards, par 72, rated 73.7.

Island West, Highway 278 at Bluffton, ☎ 843-689-6660, 18 holes, 6,803 yards, par 72, rated 72.1.

Ocean Course, Sea Pines Resort, ☎ 843-842-1894, 18 holes, 6,933 yards, par 72, rated 70.

Old South Golf Links, Highway 278 at Bluffton, ☎ 843-785-5353, 18 holes, 6,772 yards, par 72, rated 72.4.

Oyster Reef, Hilton Head Plantation, ☎ 843-681-7717, 18 holes, 7,027 yards, par 72, rated 73.7.

Planter's Row, Port Royal, ☎ 843-689-GOLF, 18 holes, 6,520 yards, par 72, rated 72.1.

Robber's Row, Port Royal, ☎ 843-689-GOLF, 18 holes, 6,642 yards, par 72, rated 72.6.

Robert Cupp Golf Course, Palmetto Hall, ☎ 843-6894100, 18 holes, 6,522 yards, par 72, rated 70.1.4

Robert Trent Jones, Palmetto Dunes, ☎ 843-785-1136, 18 holes, 6,710 yards, par 72, rated 72.2.

Sea Marsh, Sea Pines Resort, ☎ 843-842-1894, 18 holes, 6,515 yards, par 72, rated 69.

Shipyard Golf Club, Shipyard, ☎ 843-689-GOLF, three sets of 9-holes. Choose which 18 you would like to play; 6,830 yards, par 72, rated 73.

Hiking

If you like to hike, you'll find there are endless miles of hard-packed sands for you to enjoy, even more miles of nature trails and pathways that lead to sparkling lagoons, tiny coves and inlets, and along the banks of slow-flowing creeks and the Intracoastal Waterway.

Shopping

If shopping means adventure, then Hilton Head Island offers the adventure of a lifetime. All across the island, you can explore offbeat locations, the harbor front, and the beaches in search of that something extra-special. There are nearly 300 stores and boutiques on the island, more than you could visit in a couple of months. Some offer all the excitement of big city shopping, others an out-of-the-way experience where you never know what is just around the corner. No matter what your taste, or budget, there's something on Hilton Head just for you: island-style fashions, Low Country arts and crafts, antiques, gifts, fine art, glassware, jewelry, off-brands and top-brands.

Colony Plaza, Coligny Circle, is on the beach, has more than 60 shops and restaurants, as well as a movie theater, grocery store, and the famous duck pond.

Low Country Factory Outlet, on Hwy 278 at Bluffton, is the place to go for bargain-priced name brands.

The **Mall at Shelter Grove**, in the middle of the island a half-mile north of the Sea Pines Resort, is Hilton Head's only enclosed mall. They're all here: JC Penney, Bell, The Gap, Banana Republic, Ann Taylor, Ralph Lauren, Polo, and many more; more than 50 shops, in fact. There's also a food court and several restaurants.

Nature, obviously, plays a very important role on Hilton Head Island, and there are two stores here that, by their very nature, will be of interest to visitors.

In the **Audubon Nature Store**, ☎ 843-785-4311, fax 785-6402, e-mail trunbt@aol.com, www.audubonnature.com, at the J2 Village at Wexford, proprietress Suzanne Trunk has assembled an array of enticing goods guaranteed to fascinate. Look for such things as brass and copper sculptures, wind chimes, frogs of all types, fluffy toys including life-sized dogs and cats, indoor fountains, CDs and tapes, jewelry, birdfeeders and seed, birdhouses, and houses for butterflies, ladybugs and bats. Those of you with kids at home will want to pay particular attention to the large and educational children's section. If you want to both amuse them and stretch their minds, then look for the science and nature activity kits, rocks, crystals and crystal growing kits, glow-in-the-dark items, games, puzzles, including the Triazzel, action toys, a dinosaur department, even CD ROMs and other multi media stuff.

Those of you who delight in watching and feeding the birds in your backyard will not want to overlook **Wild Birds Unlimited**, ☎ 843-681-4461, in the Festival Center at Indigo Park, 45 Pembroke Drive, Suite 130. These stores, as you may know, are franchised, but that does not limit the owner/proprietor from bringing a unique personality, through décor and selection of stock, to his/her particular store. Certainly, there will be bird feeders of every shape and size, birdhouses, feed and all kinds of accessories, but from that common ground, the items stocked can vary rather surprisingly. In this store, you can expect to find a wonderful selection of enamel and copper birds, pelicans, dolphins and fish; J. W. Stannard hand-tuned wind chimes; birdhouse jewelry; Andy Brinkley copper bird feeders; bat and woodpecker houses; small decoys; a squirrel station; a tortoise and frog corner; lamp stands, bell rings; decorative outdoor water faucets; clocks; binoculars and CDs and tapes. Two items that partic-

South Carolina

ularly caught our attention were the Windway Sounds of Nature Monitor – which includes a microphone to be placed beneath a birdfeeder and a receiver that mounts indoors for listening to the birds feeding; and unique mail boxes featuring a yacht and a duck.

Tennis

Hilton Head Island has over 300 courts, more than any other resort in the nation, and has earned the distinction of being America's top spot for tennis. In fact, in 1996 *Tennis Magazine* ranked four of its resorts among "the 50 greatest US tennis resorts."

The following is a list of Island tennis centers open to the public:

Hilton Head Island Beach & Tennis Resort, Folly Field Road, ☎ 843-785-6613, 10 hard courts, all floodlit.

Palmetto Dunes Tennis Center, Palmetto Dunes Resort, ☎ 843-785-1152, two hard courts, both floodlit, 23 clay courts with six floodlit.

Port Royal Tennis Club, Port Royal Resort, ☎ 843-681-3322, four hard courts, all floodlit, 10 clay courts with two floodlit and two grass courts.

Sea Pines Racquet Club, Sea Pines Resort, ☎ 843-363-4495 or 800-SEA PINE, 24 clay courts with five floodlit.

South Beach Racquet Club, Sea Pines Plantation, ☎ 843-671-2215, 13 clay court with two floodlit.

Van Der Meer Tennis Center, DeAllyon Road, ☎ 843-785-8388, 25 hard courts, three clay courts, with eight floodlit.

Van Der Meer Tennis University, Shipyard Plantation, ☎ 843-686-8804 or 800-438-0793, nine hard courts, 11 clay courts, with eight floodlit.

On Wheels

The **Hilton Head Bicycle Company**, ☎ 843-686-6888, 112 Arrow Road, rents bicycles for $12 per day, $15 for three days and $18 per week. They also offer free island-wide delivery and free accessories.

On Water

Catamaran

 If catamarans excite you, the person to contact is Jeanne Zailckas at **Advanced Sail, Inc.**, ☎ 843-686-2582 or 785-7131, www.hiltonheadisland.com/sailing. Based at the Palmetto Bay Marina, they operate the *Pau Hana*, loosely translated as "happy Hour," which, at 53 feet long and 26 feet wide, is Hilton Head's largest sailboat. With 49 comfortable seats, and ample deck area to move about beneath a hard Bimini top, it offers a choice of morning, afternoon or sunset cruises that last two hours and cost $20 per person. You are welcome to bring your own refreshments, and, of course, a camera to capture that memorable moment when you steer the boat. Advanced Sail, Inc. also operates the more intimate *Flying Circus*, which, at 27 feet long by 16 feet wide, is just perfect for a very romantic private charter. Jeanne will happily work with you to customize a trip and, if you wish, she will prepare a picnic basket, which can include champagne and oysters, among other goodies. The minimum cost is $150 for two hours, with each additional hour being an extra $60.

Cruise/Tour

Curiously quaint Daufuskie Island, just over the water from Hilton Head Island, is worth a visit; and the best way to go is via the **Daufuskie Island Adventure**, ☎ 843-842-4155, which begins with a 35-minute cruise departing from Harbour Town, the marina nearest to Daufuskie. Once aboard the *Vagabond,* your naturalist captain who will provide a running commentary on points of interest such as the historic Haig Point Lighthouse and ruins of antebellum slave quarters. After disembarking, a tour of the island includes admission to the 125-year-old African Baptist Church, takes in the remains of the Oyster Houses, and visits one of the finest unspoiled beaches in the Low Country. The total adventure, scheduled for 10:30 to 2:30, is offered year-round, although with a varying schedule, and costs just $29 per person.

Diving

Island Scuba Dive & Travel, Inc., ☎ 843-6893244, 888-689-DIVE, fax 681-9640, e-mail dive@islandscuba.com, www.islandscuba.com, 1B Mathews Court, Hilton Head Island, SC 29926, is a PADI 5-Star facility and a dive travel specialist. Besides offering Open Water

Diver Certification at various levels, it also offers Medic First Aid, Rescue Diver, Master Scuba Diver, Divemaster, Assistant Instructor and Instructor courses. Offshore diving is principally around the artificial **Hilton Head Reef**, which is just 13 miles from South Beach and is home to schools of spade fish, queen angelfish and sea turtles. In 50-60 feet of water, it is ideal for photography, for novice divers and for a relaxing dive. The **Eagles Nest**, 18 miles offshore, has two different diving sites, both in 70 feet of water and offering comfortable dives for both novice and advanced divers. The *Betsy Ross*, approximately 20 miles offshore is a 440-foot-long Liberty Ship resting in about 100 feet of water. Due to the depth, this is for advanced divers only.

Once the temperatures drop into the low 70s, river diving becomes more popular, and the visibility between October and may can reach 10 feet.

Fishing

Deep-Sea Fishing

Maybe you fancy a spot of sport fishing, with sharks, king mackerel, spanish, blues, redfish and cobia in mind. If so, contact Captain Chris Sanders of **Atlantic Reef Charters**, ☎ 843-689-3244, 888-689-DIVE (outside South Carolina), e-mail captcs@aol.com, www.islandscuba. com, 1B Mathews Court. He will take you out for a half-day's fishing offshore ($295) or for a half-day in the backwater ($225), with drinks and ice provided.

Fly Fishing

The popularity of saltwater fly fishing and light tackle fishing is on the rise and, if such strikes your fancy, Travers Davis, owner of **Lowcountry Outfitters Inc.**, ☎ 843-837-6100, 800-935-9666 or fax 837-6200, 1533 Fording Island Road, Suite 316, is the person who can meet your needs. Before continuing, however, let us explain that Lowcountry Outfitters Inc., is not on the island itself. It is in the Moss Creek Village Shopping Center, a short distance to the right after you cross the bridge from the island to the mainland. Upon request, Travers will arrange for you to go out with Captain Marty Pinkston, who has 20 years-plus of local experience, on his 18-foot Hewes Bonefisher vessel, the *Fly Boy*. Whether saltwater fly fishing, looking for redfish, Spanish mackerel, ladyfish, jacks or cobia, or light tackle fishing for king mackerel and tarpon, the rate will be $225 for a half-day (four hours) and $400 for a full day (eight hours).

Lowcountry Outfitters is not just about fishing, either. The wide range of rods, reels and lines share the space with an equally extensive array of stylish clothing suitable for casual wear, whether sporting or not. Look for lines from quality companies such as Ex Oficio, Columbia, Lewis Creek, Simms, C.C. Filson and Browning. Travers also carries a large selection of British waterproof/thornproof Barbour coats and, unusually, sweaters. There is also a substantial ladies section. There are well-stocked gun and hunting rooms as well. Lowcountry Outfitters also displays many special gift and souvenir items: decoys, binoculars, prints, books, knives, Victorinox Swiss tools, miniature ducks crafted of pewter by Jim Island Miniatures, and a walk-in humidor with a fine selection of cigars.

Kayaking

The environment around Hilton Head Island is ideal for kayaking, and there are several companies on the island offering such services. Of these, we recommend you contact **Outside Hilton Head**, ☎ 843-686-6996 or 800-686-6996, which operates stores at The Plaza at Shelter Cove and at South Beach Marina Village. They coordinate a wide variety of trips of varying length, which depart from one of three locations: Pinckey Island Wildlife Refuge from Schillings Boathouse, Broad Creek from the Old Oyster Factory, or Calibogue Sound from South Beach Marina. Among the shortest trips, lasting two hours and costing $35 per adult, combines an introduction to kayaking with a fun and educational nature tour. After a brief clinic covering the basics, your guide, also an experienced and interpretive naturalist, will lead you out to the marshlands for an upclose view of bird life and other indigenous creatures. You might also consider a Sunset, Full Moon, Morning Birding or Marsh Exploration tour, each of which costs $35 per adult and lasts two hours. Half-day, full-day and Overnight Retreat adventures are also available. If you are serious in wanting to learn fascinating facts and anecdotes about the marshes and their inhabitants, then pay special attention to the few days, on weekends, each year when the Author Tour is scheduled. This is led by the island's premier interpretative naturalist and author of *Tideland Treasure*, Todd Ballantine. The cost of $50 per adult includes a signed copy of that guide.

Even if you aren't into kayaks, a visit to an Outside Hilton Store can be an adventure in itself. Alongside Perception and Wilderness Systems kayaks and the accompanying paraphernalia is quite an array of other great stuff. Companies like Patagonia, Columbia, North Face and Birkenstock produce clothing that is as stylish as it is practical, and Outside Hilton Head stocks a full range of each, for both men and

South Carolina

women. Other sports are represented as well, with rollerblades and
in-line hockey gear in abundance. There are also displays of sports
watches, Victorinox knives, CDs featuring lively island-style music,
books and the really special Bollé sunglasses with interchangeable
lens.

Yacht Cruises

Vagabond Cruise, ☎ 843-842-4155 or 842-7179, Harbour Town, offers a variety of traditional sailings. If you have ever wondered what
it would be like to sail in a real America's Cup yacht, then this is your
chance. Currently in the Vagabond fleet is the 65-foot $4 million dol-
lar *Stars & Stripes*, a yacht skippered by Dennis Connor in the America's cup. These days, though, it is your turn to feel the excitement as
over 2,000 square feet of sails unfurl above you. The noon, 2 pm and
4 pm cruises cost $19 per person, while the 6 pm Sunset Cruise costs
$5 more. Their *Spirit of Harbour Town*, a 73-foot high-speed luxury
passenger yacht, offers novel transport to Savannah, but you may
prefer the Sunset Dinner Cruises. These are scheduled throughout
the year, although sailing times vary. Thursday and Saturday cruises
serve a prime rib meal, costing $45 per person, and the Friday cruises
feature a seafood buffet at an additional $4 each.

In the Air

AirStream Aviation, ☎ 843-785-7770, offers a 20-minute
Tour Hilton Head for $39.95 per person, or a Low Country
Tour that lasts 30 minutes and costs $49.95 per person.

On Horseback

Lawton Stables, ☎ 843-671-2586, at Sea Pines Plantation, offers a one-hour walking tour, with 10 minutes of pre-
instruction, through the 600-acre forest preserve for $35
per person.

Eco/Cultural Adventures

Hilton Head Island is not a place one comes to for serious
activities; people flock here seeking sun and fun. But this
island, the first eco-planned destination in the United
States, is a wildlife sanctuary as well. According to the Audubon Society, nearly 350 species of native American birds have been
spotted on Hilton Head Island over the past 10 years, with some 200

species making the lakes, marshes and shoreline of the island their home. On land there are deer, bobcats, otters and minks, while the surrounding waters are home to loggerhead turtles and bottlenose dolphins. The American alligator, too, is a famous resident of the island, with the massive male of the species reaching an average length of 12 feet and attaining a weight of 500 pounds. They are not as reclusive as one might imagine and visitors are likely to spot some during their stay on the island. If you want to learn more about these creatures, visit the **Coastal Discovery Museum**, ☎ 843-689-6767, fax 689-6769, e-mail hhimuseum@hargray.com, www.hhisland.com/hiltonhead/museum.html, PO Box 23497, 100 William Hilton Parkway, at the north end of Highway 278. It features two floors of interesting, some hands-on, exhibits, and offers 16 different tours and cruises around the island on six days a week.

Spas & Fitness Centers

We found a wonderful day spa on Hilton Head Island. The **European Spa**, ☎ 843-842-WELL (9355), fax 842-2456 or e-mail eurospa@hargray.com, 115 Executive Center, Corpus Christi, New Orleans Road, offers perhaps the widest array of aromatherapy treatments we have seen, for women, men or couples. Owner Elizabeth McGinnes, an Englishwoman, is the international representative to the National Association of Holistic Aromatherapy, and ensures that all of her staff are trained in clinical aromatherapy. Body wraps, for which you should allow 1¾ hours, come in the exfoliating spearmint, seaweed, and marine mud envelopment varieties, and cost $85 each. An aromatherapy body treatment, which takes two hours and costs $100, includes hydrotherapy tub, wrap, and body, face and scalp massage. Body rubs are also a popular item. The Stress Buster – a full body sea salt scrub followed by a hydrotherapy tub – and the Detox and Tone – a full body spearmint exfoliation scrub, underwater massage and a European toning treatment – each last one hour and cost $70. Patrons may choose from a number of different massages priced at $50 for 45 minutes, $65 for one hour, and $90 for an hour and a half. And to make sure you are covered from top to bottom, reflexology for feet, scalp and hands, and deluxe aromatherapy hand & foot care are also offered. For the ultimate in pampering, ladies will enjoy Elizabeth's Ultimate Spa package, described as a half-day treatment, but in reality taking nearly five hours. First, you will unwind and revitalize in a hydrotherapy tub with aromatic oils. An aromatherapy body wrap and full aromatherapy facial then precede a healthy snack and herbal tea. Hands and feet are attended to next and, for the finale, you will be treated to the benefits of an aromatherapy body massage. The cost is $205. Alternatively, The Royal Treatment, A Regal Spa Day, takes about 6½ hours, will set you back $285, and adds to the half-day package a sea salt scrub, body wrap of choice, deluxe paraffin wax hand and foot treatment, a choice of facial, lunch, light refreshments, and herbal tea.

Visitor Information

 For further information about Hilton Head Island, contact the **Visitor & Convention Bureau**, PO Box 5647, Hilton Head Island, SC, 29938, ☎ 843-785-3673, fax 785-7110, e-mail info@hiltonheadisland.org, www.hiltonheadisland. org. The friendly folks there will be happy to send you all the information you require, as well as an up-to-date listing of the upcoming events.

A WORD TO
THE WISE

Definitely keep an eye out for the annual **WineFest Weekend** *in March, when Hilton Head hosts the largest outdoor tented wine tasting on the East Coast. Over 100 wineries and more than 450 wines are represented. Admission at the last WineFest cost $25 per person, which included a souvenir tasting glass.*

■ Where to Stay

Hilton Head Island

 The **Crowne Plaza Resort**, ☎ 843-842-2400, 800-334-1881, fax 842-9975, is an 11-acre oceanfront resort with a nautical theme secluded in Shipyard Plantation, 130 Shipyard Drive, just off Highway 278. Their e-mail is info@crowneplazaresort.com. The website is www.crowneplazaresort.com. It has 340 elegantly appointed rooms, including nine suites, which each feature a balcony, with either a tropical, island or ocean view, coffee maker, in-room safe, voice-mail system, and dataports on the telephones. You'll also find three full-service restaurants, and the Dockers Poolside, a bar and grille with seating on a deck overlooking the pool and lagoon. Other communal amenities include: a full-service recreational facility with professional exercise equipment, indoor/outdoor whirlpools, indoor pool, outdoor activity pool and saunas, and 27 holes of golf, including a pro shop and clubhouse, in

Shipyard Plantation. Complimentary valet parking further empha-
sizes the importance that the Crowne Plaza places on service. Room
rates vary between $139 and $319 a night.

The **Westin Resort**, ☎ 843-681-4000, fax 681-1087, www.westin.
com, Two Grasslawn Avenue, opened in 1985 in the Port Royal Resort. It features classical architecture reminiscent of grand seaside
hotels at the turn of the century. It boasts an enviable 24-acre
oceanfront location on Port Royal Sound, the largest watershed in
South Carolina, formed by the confluence of seven slow moving navigable rivers: Beaufort, Pocotaligo, Tullifiny, Coosawhatchie, Broad,
Chechesee and Colleton. Among the 412 guestrooms, including 30
suites, is the magnificent Port Royal Suite, with over 2,046 square
feet of space and a private verandah and gazebo overlooking the Atlantic Ocean. You will also find an array of restaurants and bars,
ranging from the formal to very informal. Outside, admire the combination of waterfalls, reflecting pools, landscaped gardens, decks, terraces, and indoor and outdoor pools, bordered by a wide boardwalk
that takes you the few steps across the sandy dunes to the beaches of
the Atlantic Ocean. The sculptures of Walter Palmer will not escape
your attention, either; his human-sized pelicans, along with the two
real swans, are a whimsical diversion in the ponds. Recreation, too, in
many forms awaits your pleasure. The Port Royal Golf & Racquet
Club has three award-winning 18-hole championship courses; an
award-winning racquet club with 16 tennis courts finished in grass,
Har-tru and hard surfaces; a world-class croquet lawn and miles of bicycle and jogging paths. Within the hotel is a newly renovated, fully
equipped, fitness center with saunas, steam rooms, state-of-the-art
fitness equipment, and a qualified staff to assist you in fitness testing
and individualized programs. In 2000, there were two seasons, June
18 to August 31 (High Season) and March 12 to June 17 (Spring Season). The rates were, respectively, for an Island View $305 and $175,
Ocean View $365 and $205, Oceanfront $405 and $245, and the Royal
Beach Club $465 and $305. Suites ranged upwards from $400 during
high season and $345 during low season.

The **Hilton Oceanfront Resort**, ☎ 843-842-8000, fax 341-8033, e-
mail hiltonhh@hargray.com, www.hiltonheadhilton.com, located in
the 2,200-acre resort community of Palmetto Dunes, is a AAA Four-
Diamond beachfront paradise where accommodation is available in
any one of 324 rooms, including 32 suites. These, the management
rightfully claims, are the largest hotel rooms you will find on Hilton
Head Island. You are spoiled when it comes to activities. If you ever
tire of the three miles of private, pristine, white sandy beach, you
might try the Health Club, complimentary to guests, with its array of

South Carolina

Nautilus equipment, outdoor heated family pool, adult pool and two oceanfront whirlpools. Golfers will be in their element as they choose from either a Robert Trent Jones, George Fazio or Arthur Hills course, all of which are in Palmetto Dunes. Here, also, is the Palmetto Dunes Tennis Center, one of the top tennis resorts in the country, with grass, clay and Har Tru courts, six of which are floodlit for night play. Regular room rates vary, according to season, from $109 to $239.

Daufuskie Island

The **Daufuskie Island Club & Resort**, ☎ 843-842-2000, 800-648-6778, fax 681-3819, www.daufuskieresort.com, is in a central location on a 663-acre tract overlooking Calibogue Sound and the Atlantic Ocean. Reached by way of a 45-minute private ferry ride that departs from Salty Fare Village on Hilton Head Island, and accessed through 24-hour guarded privacy gates, the nostalgic antebellum-style building is at the end of an avenue of majestic moss-draped oaks. Accommodations are either in one of the inn's 52 spacious and well-appointed guestrooms or in a choice of 37 two- or four-bedroom cottages. Rates vary between high and low seasons and, in 2000, were $195 or $120 per night in the Inn, $440 or $300 for a two-bedroom ocean-view cottage, and slightly lower $410 or $260 for a two-bedroom cottage with a marsh view. Prices include the ferry ride and club transportation around the island.

■ Where to Eat

The **Tapas Restaurant**, ☎ 843-681-8925, fax 342-3366, e-mail thetapas@aol.com, www.tapasrestaurant.com, 11 Northridge Plaza (just to the right of the Cinema 10) is a small restaurant with a wonderfully bizarre décor and an equally attractive cuisine. Tapas, in this sense, don't equate to the original Spanish idea of small tidbits of food given free with your drink. Rather, it is the increasingly popular American version, wherein an extensive and highly varied menu offers what equate to slightly smaller than normal entrées – thus, allowing your palate to delight in a medley of different tastes. The wine list, although on the small side, is helpfully descriptive and complementary to the cuisine.

The **Spartina Grill**, ☎ 843-689-2433 or fax 689-3663, 70 Marshland Road, is refreshingly unusual. Named after the grass commonly found in the surrounding marshland, this upscale bistro, where you can eat inside or out, has a European décor and specializes in Mediterranean, seafood and California cuisine. The wine list isn't extensive, but is varied enough and nearly all are available by the glass. The Spartina Grill is open for lunch, Monday to Friday, from 11:30 to 2:30 and for dinner, Monday to Thursday, from 5:30 to 9 and Friday and Saturday from 5:30 to 10.

CQ's Restaurant, ☎ 843-671-2779, 140 Lighthouse Road, Sea Pines Plantation in Harbour Town, is in one of the oldest buildings on Hilton Head. Reminiscent of a Low Country rice barn, it was built by artist/sculptor Ralph Ballantyne in 1970, and features pine floors from an historic Jasper County church, ceiling beams from a Savannah warehouse and a staircase that supposedly came from a house of ill repute in the same city. The cuisine is inspired by the abundant varieties of fresh seafood, produce, fruits and vegetables available in the region, with signature dishes having French and Cajun influences. The wine list is extensive, with over 70 offered by the glass. There is also a wide range of martinis, small-batch bourbons and classic malts. CQ's is open year-round for dinner seven nights a week from 5 to 10 pm, with happy hour between 5 and 6.

Antonio's, ☎ 843-842-5505, G2 Wexford Village, is, as the name implies, an Italian restaurant, but with a spotlight on classic Italian seafood. A wall-sized wine rack demands your attention in the Tuscany Room – connected to the bar by a dual-sided brick fireplace, and romantic Italian music enhances the ambiance. Antonio's is open year-round, seven days a week, from 5 to 10 pm. Happy hour is from 5 to 7.

The **Old Fort Pub**, ☎ 843-681-2386, 65 Skull Creek Drive, Hilton Head Plantation, is adjacent to Fort Mitchel and has fantastic views over Skull Creek and the Intracoastal Waterway. The foyer is decorated with enlargements of historic photos of the Union troops that occupied the island, with accompanying narratives describing life during the Civil War. The glass-enclosed main dining room features a water view from each table, and is tastefully furnished with 20th-century antiques and reproductions. A really unusual feature of this restaurant is the rooftop "widow's walk," which you are encouraged to visit, glass in hand, via a spiral staircase from the Sunset Dining Room. And the view, especially at sunset, is worth the effort. The cuisine is best described as Southern-influenced American. The wine choice here is innovative. The Old Fort Pub offers three-ounce servings of three different wines, allowing you the opportunity to experience a variety of styles and tastes with your menu selections. Alternatively, you may choose three oz. or six oz. glasses or, of course, a bottle. The Old Fort Pub is open year-round. Lunch is served, Mon-

South Carolina

day to Saturday, from noon to 2:30; Sunday Brunch is served from 11 to 2:30; and dinner hour, every day, is from 5:30 to 10 in summer and 5 to 9 in winter.

The **Boathouse II Restaurant & Marker 13**, ☎ 843-681-3663, at 397 Squire Pope Road next to Schilling's Marina, overlooks Skull Creek, which is part of the Intracoastal Waterway. Creative variations on classic Low Country dishes and Southern favorites are served in a glass-enclosed dining room, allowing glorious views, featuring a massive fireplace, and decorated with trophy fish and marine life murals. In agreeable weather, you can dine alfresco on one of the extensive decks, where you will also find Marker 13, with a large covered bar. They offer appropriate fare from a separate menu, and live music six nights a week from May through October. Seafood dominates the dinner menu. The Boathouse II serves lunch from 11:30 to 3 seven days a week, Sunday Brunch from 11:30 to 3, and dinner from 5 to 10. The Happy Hour runs from 4 to 7 pm.

In **Juleps Restaurant**, ☎ 843-842-5857, 14 Greenwood Drive, in The Gallery of Shops, owners/operators Sam and Melissa Cochran, have created a warm and welcoming ambiance. Opened in 1991 it is one of only three restaurants on Hilton Head that belong to The Chaine des Rotisseurs, the oldest and largest gourmet organization in the world. Consequently, the menu is wide and varied. In addition to a wide selection of wines, Juleps has some great specialty drinks, including, of course, mint juleps.

Estill

Estill, located in the remote southeastern part of South Carolina near the Savannah River, is not a place that most people reading this guide will have heard of, let alone have gone to. That is, of course, unless they are seriously into hunting and wildlife.

■ Getting Here

From the north, Route 321 runs all the way to Estill from Columbia, SC.

From I-95, take the exit at Route 462, then follow that west to Route 278 north. When you reach the junction with Route 3, take 3 to Estill.

■ Adventures

On Foot

Hunting

Bostick Plantation, ☎ 800-542-6913, PO Box 728, Estill (about 10 miles from the town and 50 miles from Savannah), SC 29919, is run by the Bostick family, who are only one of 200 families that still maintain original royal tracts. Working with wildlife experts, they have spent the last 10 years enhancing the habitat and managing the growing population of trophy game. This has produced one of the finest commercial hunting facilities in the south. Not only that, they provide a hospitable ambiance for hunters in their rustic farmhouse lodge. Whether your tastes run to whitetail deer, quail, wild turkey or even Russian boar, this is the place for you.

A WORD TO
THE WISE

All hunters are required to have a valid South Carolina hunting license, and anyone born after 1979 must have a valid Hunters safety Course ID to hunt in South Carolina. Hunting licenses for out-of-state visitors are $105 for three days, $130 for 10 days and $155 annually.

Bow Hunting

Bostick Plantation has reserved 1,500 acres of land for bow hunting, with no guns or rifles being allowed in the area. The season is August 15th to January 1st for deer and year-round for boar, with the cost $195 per day or $495 for three days. The limit is two kills per day for a buck, doe or wild boar in any combination during season only.

Deer Hunting

The season is from the middle of August to January 1st, and the cost is $295 per day per person with two kills per day, buck or doe, limit. A three-day hunt is recommended if you want to bag a trophy buck.

Quail Hunting

Bostick Plantation offers the opportunity to hunt both wild and pen-raised birds, and the kennels are stocked with dogs that will adjust to almost any style of hunting.

The season runs from November 1st to March 15th and the cost is $345 per day per gun. There is a limit of 15 birds a day, with each additional one costing $6.50 each. Call for the special quail brochure.

Russian Boar Hunting

Bostick plantation has the best hog hunting in the South, with the boars, the offspring of Russian boars imported generations ago, flourishing in the ancient plantation swamps. Being smart, they have adapted well, and Bostick has one of the largest boar-to-acre ratios in the Southeast, with some weighing as much as 300 lbs. Hunting takes place year-round and costs $250 a day, minimum two days, with a limit of two boars per day. During the late spring/early summer last year they offered a three-day special for $495, with lodging included, with additional kills over two per day costing $200.

Russian Boar Hunting with Dogs

The season is January 1st to March 14th and May 1st to July 31st and with a guaranteed kill. The cost is $475 for a two-night stay. Additional kills $250.

Turkey Hunting

The season is March 15th to May 1st and it costs $345 per day, with a limit of one turkey in both the morning and afternoon.

Index